T0295656

Rethinking Markets in Modern India

To people operating in India's economy, actually existing markets are remarkably different from how planners and academics conceive them. From the outside, they appear as demarcated arenas of exchange bound by state-imposed rules. As historical and social realities, however, markets are dynamic, adaptive, and ambiguous spaces. This book delves into this intricate context, exploring Indian markets through the competition and collaboration of those who frame and participate in markets. Anchored in vivid case studies – from colonial property and advertising milieus to today's bazaar and criminal economies – this volume underlines the friction and interdependence between commerce, society, and state. Contributors from history, anthropology, political economy, and development studies synthesize existing scholarly approaches, add new perspectives on Indian capitalism's evolution, and reveal the transactional specificities that underlie the real-world functioning of markets.

AJAY GANDHI is an Assistant Professor at Leiden University in the Netherlands.

BARBARA HARRISS-WHITE is Emeritus Professor and Fellow at Wolfson College, Oxford University.

DOUGLAS E. HAYNES is Professor of History at Dartmouth College in Hanover.

SEBASTIAN SCHWECKE is an Associate Professor at the Indian Institute of Management in Calcutta.

Rethinking Markets in Modern India

Embedded Exchange and Contested Jurisdiction

Edited by

AJAY GANDHI
Leiden University
BARBARA HARRISS-WHITE
University of Oxford
DOUGLAS E. HAYNES
Dartmouth College, New Hampshire
SEBASTIAN SCHWECKE
Indian Institute of Management, Calcutta

CAMBRIDGE
UNIVERSITY PRESS

CAMBRIDGE
UNIVERSITY PRESS

University Printing House, Cambridge CB2 8BS, United Kingdom

One Liberty Plaza, 20th Floor, New York, NY 10006, USA

477 Williamstown Road, Port Melbourne, VIC 3207, Australia

314–321, 3rd Floor, Plot 3, Splendor Forum, Jasola District Centre, New Delhi – 110025, India

79 Anson Road, #06–04/06, Singapore 079906

Cambridge University Press is part of the University of Cambridge.

It furthers the University's mission by disseminating knowledge in the pursuit of education, learning, and research at the highest international levels of excellence.

www.cambridge.org
Information on this title: www.cambridge.org/9781108486781
DOI: 10.1017/9781108762533

© Cambridge University Press 2020

First published 2020

A catalogue record for this publication is available from the British Library.

ISBN 978-1-108-48678-1 Hardback

Contents

Figures

Tables

Contributors

Roger Begrich is a sociocultural anthropologist specializing in critical indigenous theory, in drug and alcohol studies, in global aging, and in the sociocultural study of the law and of the state. He is currently working on a book project on alcohol and indigeneity in the Indian state of Jharkhand, as well as collaborating with an illustrator on a graphic novel and website based on his research in Jharkhand. He is also beginning a new research project on global aging and polypharmacy. He has held postdoctoral positions at Harvard University, at the University of Basel, as well as at UC Berkeley, and taught at Bowdoin College, at the Johns Hopkins University (from where he also obtained his PhD), and at the University of Zürich.

Ajay Gandhi is an anthropologist and assistant professor in the Faculty of Governance and Global Affairs at Leiden University. From 2011 to 2017, he was a research scientist at the Max Planck Institute for the Study of Religious and Ethnic Diversity in Göttingen. He has conducted research primarily in urban India, and has published articles and book chapters on migration, materiality, space, the state, and transactional forms.

Barbara Harriss-White is Emeritus Professor of Development Studies and Fellow of Wolfson College, Oxford University. For fifty years, since driving from Cambridge to New Delhi, she has been fascinated by India's markets and has researched them through fieldwork, mostly in Tamil Nadu and West Bengal, primarily working on agricultural commodity markets. Currently, she is working on markets for waste and on criminal markets. Her most recent publication on Indian markets, *The Wild East? Criminal Political Economies across South Asia* (UCL Press), was published in open access form in 2019.

Douglas E. Haynes is a professor of history at Dartmouth College. He is the author of *Rhetoric and Ritual in Colonial India: The Shaping of a Public Culture in Surat City, 1852–1928* (University of California Press, 1991) and *Small-Town Capitalism in Western India: Artisans, Merchants and the Making of the Informal Economy, 1870–1960* (Cambridge University Press, 2012). He is currently finishing a monograph on advertising in western India during the interwar period. He also has coedited several books, including *Contesting Power: Resistance and Everyday Social Relations in South Asia* (with Gyan Prakash, Oxford University Press, 1992), *Toward a History of Consumption in South Asia* (with Haruka Yanagisawa, Tirthankar Roy, and Abigail McGowan, Oxford University Press, 2012), and *A Global History of Sexual Science* (with Veronika Fuechtner and Ryan P. Jones, University of California Press, 2017).

Matthew S. Hull is associate professor of anthropology at the University of Michigan. His research focuses on the nexus of representation, technology, and institutions. His book, *Government of Paper: The Materiality of Bureaucracy in Urban Pakistan* (University of California Press, 2012), winner of the 2019 J.I. Staley Prize from the School of Advanced Research, examines governance as a semiotic and material practice. He is currently working on the history and theory of the modern corporation, and police communication systems and lotteries in India.

J. Jeyaranjan is the founding director of the Institute of Development Alternatives, Chennai, India. He has been working on the political economy of change, in its various hues, in Tamil Nadu, India, for the past thirty years. He has authored nearly seventy-five research reports and published over fifty articles in leading journals and books. J. Jeyaranjan writes in Tamil regularly for various periodicals and newspapers.

Mekhala Krishnamurthy is an associate professor of sociology and anthropology at Ashoka University and a senior fellow at the Centre for Policy Research, New Delhi. She is an ethnographer of the state and market in contemporary India and has researched and published extensively on the political economy of India's agricultural markets and commodity systems – their regional diversity, institutional complexity, regulatory life, and social and political dynamics. Her other, related area of longstanding interest and research commitment, which she is pursuing in a number of field-based and writing projects, focuses on the institutional dynamics and everyday life of public systems and local bureaucracies, especially on the lived experiences of frontline functionaries of the Indian state.

Projit Bihari Mukharji is an associate professor at the University of Pennsylvania. He was educated in Calcutta, Delhi, and London and has taught in the UK, Canada, and the USA. Mukharji works on the histories of science and knowledge in modern South Asia. In addition to having written several articles, he is the author of *Nationalizing the Body: The Medical Market, Print and Daktari Medicine* (Cambridge University Press, 2009) and *Doctoring Traditions: Ayurveda, Small Technologies and Braided Sciences* (Chicago University Press, 2016).

Nikhil Rao is an associate professor of history at Wellesley College. His book titled *House, But No Garden. Apartment Living in Bombay's Suburbs, 1898–1964* was published by the University of Minnesota Press in 2013. He is also the coeditor, with Douglas E. Haynes, of a special issue of the journal South Asia titled *Beyond the Colonial City: Re-Evaluating the Urban History of India, ca. 1920–1970* (South Asia, 36, no. 3 (2013): 317–33, September 2013). His current work focuses on the enterprise of cooperative housing in post-Independence Bombay and the implications of this enterprise for notions of property and urban citizenship.

Andy Rotman is a professor of religion, Buddhism, and South Asian studies at Smith College. His publications include *Divine Stories: Translations from the Divyāvadāna, part 1* and *part 2* (Wisdom Publications, 2008, 2017), *Thus Have I Seen: Visualizing Faith in Early Indian Buddhism* (Oxford University Press, 2009), and a coauthored volume, *Amar Akbar Anthony: Bollywood, Brotherhood, and the Nation* (Harvard University Press, 2015). He has been engaged in textual and ethnographic work on life in South Asia for more than twenty-five years.

David West Rudner is a historical anthropologist of India based at the University of California, Los Angeles, with an interest in semiotics shaped by a background in analytic philosophy and linguistics. Most of his published work is based on research about the Nattukottai Chettiars, a merchant-banking caste that played a major role in south

India and southeast Asia. His monograph *Caste and Capitalism in Colonial India: The Nattukottai Chettiars* (University of California Press, 1994) has become one of the standard references in the study of colonial Indian markets.

Aditi Saraf is an assistant professor at the Department of Sociology and Anthropology, Ashoka University, Sonipat. Combining ethnographic and archival work, her research focuses on the relationship between commerce and sovereignty in Kashmir. More broadly, she works on questions of political economy, frontiers and mobility, militarization, material exchange, and place-making practices.

Sebastian Schwecke is an associate professor at the Indian Institute of Management Calcutta and research fellow at the Centre for Modern Indian Studies, Göttingen University. Having previously worked on Hindu nationalism, he currently works on the history and anthropology of extra-legal financial markets, published in several articles (including "A Tangled Jungle of Disorderly Transactions? The Production of a Monetary Outside in a North Indian Town," *Modern Asian Studies* 52, no. 4, 2018) and, in the near future, in the monograph *Debt, Trust, and Reputation. Extra-legal Finance in Northern India*.

1 | Markets in Modern India: Embedded, Contested, Pliable

SEBASTIAN SCHWECKE AND AJAY GANDHI [*]

Introduction

From the outside, the market in India is often seen as an exchange arena bound by state-imposed rules.[1] Those within – buyers and sellers, producers and consumers, brokers and advertisers, financiers and debtors, police and inspectors – understand it differently. Such parties collude and compete in myriad everyday activities. These include those of accumulation and circulation, of production and speculation, and of arbitrage and management.

Involved actors, in short, experience the Indian market dissimilarly from the ways in which many planners and policymakers comprehend it. This market is best understood as an ensemble of practices and institutions. It has active and reactive patterns of economic and socio-cultural practices, flexible adjustment and coping mechanisms,

[*] The editors offer gratitude to the participants, reviewers, and discussants, as well as institutions that nurtured this project. Peter van der Veer at the Max Planck Institute for the Study of Religious and Ethnic Diversity in Göttingen, as well as Ravi Ahuja and Patrick Eisenlohr at the Centre for Modern Indian Studies (CeMIS) at the University of Göttingen sponsored the workshop in December 2016 that was this collaboration's genesis. Leiden University's Asian Modernities and Traditions program offered a publication grant that facilitated an editorial meeting and copy-editing assistance. Beyond intellectual interlocutors, we give thanks to those who enabled this book to come to fruition: Shashi Chandok, Debjani Mazumdar, Michaela Dimmers, and, at Cambridge University Press, our editor, Phil Good.
[1] For an impressive argument on the treatment of markets and *the* market in economics, cf. Hodgson (2001). However, even approaches rooted in institutional economics, old and new, frequently highlight bureaucratic rule setting for markets, whether state-led or corporate, for instance Galbraith (1967). We do not contest the centrality of state or corporate planning for markets yet wish to point out how these are perceived by many Indian market actors as one among many elements shaping the structure of markets. This selective adherence and deliberate evasion thereby allows market participants to navigate framing rules in line with their different needs instead of merely adjusting to their seeming preeminence.

unforeseen contingencies and aberrations, and strategies of ambiguity and transgression. Transactional agents navigate gray areas and tacit understandings. They reproduce durable informal relations and customary practices. These dynamics only partially relate to state-led market-framing processes.

Today, India has an enormous, locally integrated and globally connected, and fast-moving economy. A corresponding interest in its commercial life has emerged with curious observers seeking empirical grounding and historical precision. Yet the sedimented streams of exchange on the subcontinent frequently remain elusive to academic inquiry. In spite of having spawned a large body of literature, Indian markets remain analytically opaque and underspecified.

Why is this so? For one, actually existing market histories and practices may misalign with conceptual categories. Writing on socio-economic processes in India has its own vocabularies. Privilege is, within mainstream economics, accorded to neoclassical conceptions cut and pasted to South Asia (Bhagwati & Panagariya 2013). In the broader social sciences, the cluster of keywords generated by this literature hints at reigning preoccupations. These include "informality," the "nation state," "capitalism," "modernity," "tradition," "rationality," "efficiency," "exploitation," "neoliberalism," and even varied meanings attributed to broad conceptions such as "embeddedness" (Chakrabarty 1989; Harriss-White & Jan 2012; Roy 2003; van Schendel & Abraham 2005). Assumptions of a unified, territorially bounded, and transparently readable market can render external or invisible – as historical facts and as everyday practices – the workings of finance and trade at the edges and interstices of this construct. These are commerce's hidden corners and blind spots, of which we simply do not know enough, and which unfold at different altitudes of transactional practice.

This book's collaborators see an opportunity here to offer new conceptualizations and analyses of markets that build on prior scholarship. Our approaches bridge a range of approaches in the social sciences and history. We analyze the knotty interdependence of legal, extra-legal, and outlawed markets. We emphasize the intersecting institutional, social, and moral dimensions that condition commercial life. We underline the braiding of community and capital, of socially embedded and legally enforced transactions. This focus accounts for complexity in how things are valued, advertised, circulated, and regulated. By doing so, this book shows that Indian markets – contemporary and historical alike – have depth and scale, and express character and specificity. While we can observe a deepening of capitalist orientation and commodification, and radical transformations even in recent times, other segments of market activity rely on modes of operation existing in parallel to or even in contravention of these processes. To get at this complexity, this book offers conceptual rubrics and unexpected entry points for the range of audiences below.

First, within the broader study of modern South Asia, this book aspires to theoretical ambition, disciplinary plurality, and timeliness. We draw inspiration from other domains where the convergence of historical and ethnographic perspectives has proved productive: public culture, the nation-state, everyday life, ethics, and cities (Bates & Mio 2015; Breckenridge 1995; Fuller & Benei 2001; Mines & Lamb 2010; Pandian & Ali 2010). Yet this plurality of approaches has been lacking in the study of markets. This is a surprising gap, for transactional life suffuses Indian society – from daily rituals to national elections – and one that we address.

Second, beyond regional specialists, this approach to exchange is relevant to the broader global south. India, like countries in Asia, Africa, and the Americas, was shaped by shared configurations of colonial regulation and overlapping sovereignty. The themes we take up in this volume – around commerce's competing orbits, cultural anchoring, and plastic accommodation – will resonate with observers of other postcolonial societies.

Third, this book seeks to rejuvenate the comparative analysis of markets and displace the dominance of Euro-American templates. Classical thinkers such as Karl Marx and Max Weber, for example, took seriously the counterpoising of Indian and European commerce as a way to understand the past and future of global capitalism (Anderson 2010; Weber 1958 [1916–1917]). Yet many commentators since presume a Euro-American vanguard to which non-Western countries such as India either imitate or deviate (Ferguson 2008). Such a modular and teleological approach is untenable. If anything, recent crises suggest that ideas of Western capitalism's seemingly foundational rationality and prosperity are misplaced (Piketty 2014).

Contributors to this volume thus perceive capitalism's unfolding from fresh angles that, in turn, may facilitate reevaluations of markets in Europe and North America. Ours is one moment in a wider conversation about the past, present, and future of global and local exchange (Graeber 2011; Parthasarathi 2011). This book seeks to reshape questions on markets that anthropologists, political scientists, historians, and heterodox economists will pose in future years. To detail this ambition, we now turn to the historical and social context of Indian markets, before describing thematic rubrics and individual chapters.

Background

India is a major world economy, in contemporary and historical terms. Well before the onset of European colonialism in the fifteenth century, the subcontinent was a key transregional hub for finance and trade in the Indian Ocean. The tentacles of Indian bankers and traders stretched to Central Asian bazaars, the East African littoral, and Southeast Asia's plantations (Amrith 2013; Gupta 2001; Machado 2014; Markovits 2000; Perlin 1993; Ray 1995; Rudner 1989). Through the colonial period, India remained a sophisticated entrepôt, dotted with nodes for collection and distribution (Bayly 1983; Chandavarkar 1994; Yang 1998). The subcontinent also endured as a manufacturing hub for commodities sent far afield, such as textiles, opium, and jute (Ali 2018; Dossal 1991; Farooqui 2006; Haynes 2012; Parthasarathi 2009).

This volume builds on earlier empirical work, using Indian markets as an entry point to broaden our general understanding of socioeconomic life. We flesh out the empirics of exchange and material aspects of commercial activity (Harriss-White 2003). Contributors provide historical texture to aspects of Indian law and regulation necessary to understand how markets unfolded in practice (Birla 2009; De 2018; Goswami 2004). They touch on moral, ritual, and cosmological notions that have been central to generating value and circulating things (Appadurai 1986; Bear 2015; Gell 2006 [1999]; Parry 1989; Raheja 1988). Finally, our writers delve into social concepts of trust, reputation, speculation, and reciprocity that underlie transactional life (Bayly 1983; Puri 2014).

We also seek coverage of newer aspects of commercial activity on the subcontinent, and links between historical and more recent changes. Since the 1990s and its integration with global capitalism, India's economy has radically transformed. Realms such as microfinance or commercial medicine have become markets unto themselves (Kar 2018; Pande 2014). The shopping mall and the free trade zone are now elevated aspirational symbols (Cross 2014). Property construction and urban redevelopment are a major theater for commercial competition and collusion (Bear 2015; Searle 2016). The emergence of the entrepreneurial subject and the monetization of cultural selves attend these processes (Besky 2014; Gooptu 2013). Public culture and mass media, in marketing brands and in producing content, bolster this commercialization (Mazzarella 2003; Nakassis 2016). Speculative jockeying, illicit flows, and criminal capture increasingly mark domains of exchange (Abraham & van Schendel 2005; Appadurai 2015; Harris-White & Michelutti 2019). Indian markets depend on (and promote) concrete infrastructure such as energy and transport and cultural intangibles such as value systems. They encompass newly commodified things and ideas as well as formerly unmonetized spaces (such as the domestic realm) and selves (such as aspirational consumption and labor discipline) (Harriss-White 2005; Huws 2003).

This volume is a comprehensive response to such established inquiries and emerging conditions. It offers historical depth, empirical texture, and political focus to the analysis of Indian markets, taking the conversation further. Our venture entails a broad conceptual approach, bringing various disciplinary backgrounds into one discussion in order to emphasize the complexity of the topic we are studying. We now specify how this conversation is organized, and the overarching concepts that scaffold individual chapters.

Thematic Orientation

This book celebrates a plurality of approaches to markets and exchange in India. We encompass and validate a range of historical and social science understandings. The usual ambition of a state-of-the-art venture is to take a combative posture: to exclude and renounce flawed or incomplete ideas.

We take a different tack: this volume acknowledges and builds on productive streams of previous inquiry in the social sciences and humanities. In so doing, we recognize the situation of scholarship in the twenty-first century. A wide spectrum of concepts and methods inform social, economic, and political processes, no less than in science. Some of these approaches are grooved into old disciplinary divides, some straddle them. The proliferation of newer keywords and subfields further fissions our conversation.

The authors in this volume offer robust frames for comprehension that promote an understanding of modern economic processes in India. Yet we do not subsume the book's constituent heterogeneity into a singular explanatory framework. Neither do we truncate the tension between overlapping labels and fluid readings. The reader engages with historians, anthropologists, geographers, and political economists on their own terms. Our contributors use concepts located or homed on their disciplinary planets and radiating across a shared scholarly galaxy.

In the following sections, we offer three thematic rubrics that organize this collective inquiry. The first is "embedded exchange"; the second, "contested jurisdiction"; and the third, "pliable markets." These should be understood as windows onto overlapping terrain rather than discrete molds of segregated content. Indeed, the friction between contributors' nomenclature and technique is deliberately left intact. In our view, theoretical discrepancy is not an obstacle to overcome. In the context of this book, it is a critical asset to cultivate. By doing so, we bring out the richness of discrete approaches to markets in India.

Embedded Exchange

The history of the social sciences offers us a vital arena of contest around the idea of embedding, beginning with modernity as an era and as an idea. Fields such as economics and sociology emerged with industrial capitalism, global colonization, mass migration, and the nation-state. In social science narrations, modernity was seen to have disrupted earlier certainties. Tradition was dissolved, custom was superseded, and culture was displaced.

This preoccupation in the social sciences with the extent to which socioeconomic processes are integrated and ingrained still reverberates. Twentieth- and twenty-first-century analyses revolve around it. Put simply, one of capitalism's effects is to extract value from production and surplus from labor. In so doing, it contrives to disembed the economy from society and politics. In Karl Polanyi's influential analysis, Victorian England's wage labor market manifests a rupture between capital and community (Polanyi 2001). In actual fact, capitalism has only partially succeeded in this effort to disembed markets from society in some cases, meeting with resistance from various sources in others. Examples abound from around the world in which Polanyi's rupture was far less pronounced.

There is a long line of scholarship on India influenced by these debates. For example, one focus has been how exchange is interwoven – or perhaps synonymous – with social relations and reciprocities (Laidlaw 1995; Parry 1989; Raheja 1988). This entwinement is visible in work on the *jajmani* system, entailing the customary circulation of gifts between elites and dependents (Wiser 1936). Beyond this, there are other codified social practices that inform economic traffic and behavior in the region. Among them are institutionalized forms anchored in precolonial institutions, such as debt bondage and caste and gender differentials in labor arrangements (Breman 2013). Land grants, such as *inam* or *waqf*, subject to religious jurisdiction and hereditary privilege, comprise another such expression. Analogously, one can examine semi-codified credit, insurance, and payment mechanisms, such as *hundi* or *hawala*, critical to transregional commerce (Martin 2009; Ray 1995). Such forms have exhibited a plasticity that was useful in Mughal-era commodity transfer, diaspora-led trade between the subcontinent and the Gulf, and in petty localized credit transactions. Customary payments and commission frameworks, such as *hafta*, *dasturi*, *dalali*, and *batta*, in evidence in the early colonial period, continue to inform brokerage activities and patron–client relationships. Reputational notions of trust and honesty, such as *abru*, *sakh*, and *vishwaas*, still condition commercial relations in Indian marketplaces (Bayly 1983; Rudner 1989).

Such a range of codified or semi-codified means and practices of organizing exchange – intersecting with regimes of agricultural and artisanal production – has been portrayed as central to the "bazaar economy." This notion connects market nodes across the Indian Ocean to the subcontinent. The "rise and demise" of this bazaar economy in its specific South Asian context – theorized by Rajat Kanta Ray (1995) in terms of its gradual subordination to global capitalism in the colonial era with reference to world-systems theory – forms a consistent backdrop to historical studies of Indian markets. It is equally applicable to Polanyian ideas of the "Great Transformation."

Observing practices of exchange in Indian markets, we can identify historical continuities in transactional grammars, as well as changes in their meaning and applications in the encounter with global capitalism. These overlaps and evolutions have not been captured by the argument on the bazaar economy's demise. Even the growing predominance of a capitalist world order reserves roles and creates uses for historically sedimented and socially embedded conceptions underlying exchange. These, in turn, affect the dominant principles of order in the economy.

These durable examples of how exchange has always been tethered to social practices and customary forms underline why this volume emphasizes markets, exchange, and transactions. Such a focus is in contrast to the emphasis on production and consumption that marks most inquiry into the Indian economy. In our collaboration, we use exchange to think about relationships and reciprocities. The term "transactions" enlarges the frame of action to refer to processes of exchange that can be durable but fast evolving, and have complexly entangled actors, even in the context of enduring relationships. The transactional is a realm that encompasses material exchanges, including ordinary market relations; and also denotes moral obligations and informational transfers.

It is helpful here to review how social scientists have approached embedded exchange in India. In the anthropology of South Asia, Fredrik Barth and McKim Marriott notably contributed to thinking about transactional culture. In his 1959 monograph, *Political Leadership among the Swat Pathans*, Barth saw the interactions between Pakhtun chiefs, followers, and saints, including gifting and hospitality, as conscious exchange activities. Chiefs recirculated harvest rents to others in public feasts, as prestations, and as credit. Barth's "transactionalism" was a response to then-fashionable theories such as structural-functionalism and Marxism. In another work, Barth underlined the importance of nonmonetary reciprocal exchange between different Pathan *qoum* or groups. The perpetual swaps of services among segmented occupational groups could, Barth maintained, be seen as analogous to the Hindu *jajmani* system (Barth 1981: 27).

For our purposes, two points continue to be useful here for exchange relations on markets that have undergone significant transformations since this time. First, a society saturated by transactions – public gifting in Barth's terms but also commodified market exchanges – means a social dimension that is incomplete and unfolding. Society does not exist without the perpetual labor of exchange. Second, the transactional here is not reducible to material expediency. The labor of the social yokes together the practical, the ethical, and the cosmological. The exchanges between leaders and others are entangled with expressions of generosity – a commitment to living with others and a publicized concern with their welfare – and with a past and future.

McKim Marriott is the other anthropologist of South Asia with a prominent focus on transactions as a fulcrum of social life. In the 1970s, he argued that South Asia "exhibits an elaborate transactional culture, characterized by explicit, institutionalized concern for givings and receivings of many kinds in kinship, work, and worship" (Marriott 1976: 109). For Marriott, matters of labor organization, status expression, public prestige, and political authority are not inscribed a priori but continually modified and refreshed through exchange. In other words, society does not exist as a passive externality or as a walled-off compartment but is constituted in and through exchange. An enduring and evolving set of relations is created and nurtured via transactions. This may include quotidian forms of communal exchange such as the sharing of food and drink. It also encompasses punctuated expectations and obligations: ritualized prestations, lifecycle gifts, and customary payments. The transactional realm's temporal horizons are elastic, bringing a tool to market analysis that can be used beyond Marriott's specifically South Asian emphasis (Appadurai 2015).

Other anthropologists have paid attention to this realm and have demonstrated how this rich universe of nonmarket exchange influences transactional grammars. In this literature, the back and forth of money, food, gifts, and substances is central to the dynamics of reproduction, boundary maintenance, and solidarity. Ethnographic studies of kinship and gender, for example, show how relations and relating are created through transactions. One repeated conception for articulating the import of both monetary as well as nonmonetary obligations on sociality is *lena-dena* (giving-and-taking). For example, Helen Lambert (2000) shows how relatedness, often seen as immutably fixed, can be actively modified by transactional means. Who is considered a relation may expand outside the boundaries of genealogy or blood via forms of reciprocal giving and taking.

This view is echoed in other ethnographies that describe customary forms of exchange. Gloria Raheja (1988: 222) shows that, in western India, the social idiom "to give from where one takes" rests on exchange both as a moral and material matter. Sylvia Vatuk (1972: 179) describes the incessant obligations of informal neighborly relations in North India through the prism of *lena-dena*. Claire Snell-Rood (2015: 47), discussing women slum-dwellers in Delhi, notes their emphasis on mutual support – *sahara dena/lena*. Attention (*dyaan dena*), affection, care, and sustenance provided by friends and relations, constitute critical resources in a precarious environment. Indeed, giving-and-taking is intriguing because it moves our attention outside of sociological silos. The prevalence of such exchange suggests entanglements across religion and caste.

How does our use of the concept of "embedded exchange" build on and differentiate itself from such works? We do not merely denote how economic exchange is inserted or immersed in society. There are four dimensions of our usage worth elaborating.

First, we define embeddedness beyond the sphere of community or culture. Our contributors show how modern market pursuits are shaped by but not confined within durable lineages of caste, ethnicity, gender, or religion. This is important to flag, for the social science and history of India underlines endogamous communities as the locus of analysis. In such analyses, paternalistic codes, caste hierarchies, community solidarities, and patriarchal authority are reworked to serve modern capitalism (Chari 2004; Haynes 1999, 2012). Such scholarship shows how the Euro-American decoupling of capital and community is untenable in India (Birla 2009; Harriss-White 2003; Roy 2018).[2]

Ethnic and religious affiliation, proximity to states, and control over markets privilege certain groups, consolidate authority, and maximize rents and profit. This is not to invite a reading of Indian markets as privileging the collective over the individual, compared to the West. We do not invent an Indian *homo collectivicus* to go along with homo hierarchicus. There is not a particularly "Indian" relationship between community and commerce. Community remains a locus of capital generation and accumulation on the subcontinent, although its importance is also coming under strain (Basile 2017).

At the same time, the individual must not be overlooked – and the rational, gain-maximizing and risk-minimizing individual of classical liberalism constitutes an example of a particular ideational structure of social embeddedness distinct in time and space. The social embeddings of markets in as well as beyond India do not

---

[2] For a review of recent scholarly endeavors to challenge this decoupling, cf. Virdee (2019).

simply rest on collective or community structures. Equally relevant are processes of communication, information flows and perceptions of equity in exchange, rationalities, prices, opportunity, obligation, propriety, reputation, trust, and risk. Many of these matters touch on community – and may be rooted in community. Others remain centered on the individual, underpinning complex webs of structuring exchange relations.

To encapsulate, much inquiry into exchange's immersion within sociality looks at bounded networks and community fealty at the heart of capitalism's unfolding. The contributors to this volume enlarge this focus in their stress on the cross-cutting understandings and grammars that allow for trade across collective lines. As Bayly argues, historically in India, forms of arbitration, brokerage, and "mercantile honour and credit" breached community demarcations, creating "wider solidarities on merchant people" (Bayly 2011: 117). Building on these durabilities, we demonstrate how exchange is embedded within relations that exceed one's social affiliation.

For example, Nikhil Rao shows how, in early colonial Bombay, a vibrant sphere of land use and transfer existed between native and migrant populations. Rather than a hermetic reproduction of community along exchange lines, his chapter suggests that crisscrossing customs allowed dissimilar actors to exchange and use land outside of state jurisdiction. Projit Mukharji's chapter discusses the use of printed texts in eastern Indian bazaars in the nineteenth century. These supernatural guides offered merchants, creditors, and investors recipes for bolstering commercial fortune. Mukharji demonstrates how this corpus of knowledge was borrowed promiscuously from Muslim and Hindu religiosity and was employed within a heterogeneous market ecology. Early twentieth-century advertising, as Douglas Haynes shows, constitutes another intermingling of individual and collective aspects of exchange. The proliferation of regional marketing for health tonics, for example, targeted the modern consumer as an individual, yet relied on collectively constructed notions of desirability and anxiety. Advertising partially disembedded exchange from existing social networks, but also reconstituted them in new configurations. In all these cases, embedded exchange constitutes a transactional realm that touches on, yet eventually transgresses, a specific community.

Second, we define embedded exchange as a transactional domain extant beyond locality as well as community. That is to say, a reader will not see exchange here tethered to a static and bounded realm of place. Embedded exchange in this way exceeds not just social but also spatial markers. Here, we build on works that underline how Indian market activity, stretching back before colonial modernity, was entangled with extra-local spheres (Amrith 2013; Machado 2014; Markovits 2000; Ray 1995; Rudner 1989). David Rudner's chapter illustrates, for instance, how embedded exchange has wide spatial latitude. He describes how Tamil financiers in the colonial period constructed a cross-oceanic banking empire between south India and Burma and Malaya. The Bay of Bengal proved an insufficient hindrance for close stitches between commercial investment in Southeast Asia and ritual reproduction in south India. Aditi Saraf's chapter, on how contemporary cross-border traffic in Kashmir self-consciously references traditional transregional ties, provides another thematic example. As she shows, in her ethnographic study of the dance between suppliers and regulators on the fraught national border, what is embedded is not lodged within putatively natural national borders but exceeds them.

Third, our use of embedded exchange has a temporal as well as a social and spatial dimension. It can be easy to overlook the durability of networks, processes, and idioms when studying transactional activity due to the latter's ephemeral appearance. Because exchange entails a prospective capacity to orient and navigate oneself, the endurance of anterior processes can be overlooked. Further increasing complexity are political and ideological ruptures, such as between colonial and postcolonial, or planned and laissez-faire economies. Such periodization obscures the contexts, continuities, and conditions that persistently inform exchange.

We emphasize embedded exchange in part to underscore how contemporary market forms, widely prevalent in India, have their own enduring lineages and entrenched temporalities. But rather than implying static continuity, these unfold from tactical adjustment and resourceful accommodation.

Illustrative examples are provided by Sebastian Schwecke and Andy Rotman's chapters on contemporary transactional culture in Banaras. Both show the surprising agility of traders and financiers as they use notions of reputation and trust to broadcast their social authority and boost their market position. These mercantile codes and trading pieties were not invented recently; but they endure to this day and have successfully adjusted to changing circumstances. A very different form of business acumen is described by Projit Mukharji, on the seemingly occult knowledge codified in Bengali bazaar guides, and their unproblematic intersection with business knowledge in alignment with colonial discourses on modernity. Sharing magical traditions from various communities and appealing to businesspeople across community divides, Mukharji discusses an alternative source of socially embedded norms and practices informing market decisions.

David Rudner shows how the Nattukottai Chettiar merchant caste nimbly adjusted their financial practices in response to colonial imperatives and opportunities. Modernity didn't displace and subsume earlier caste-based banking. Rather, it provided fertile grounds on which the Chettiars could expand and consolidate their wealth. Thus, Rudner's piece suggests that beyond the social location and spatial dispersal of exchange, a community–capital nexus evolved through distinct historical moments. Mekhala Krishnamurthy, instead, emphasizes how socially entrenched market activity can be through the associational structures of a single, spatially bounded locality: an agricultural *mandi* or wholesale market in central India. Her chapter analyzes the relational networks reaching out from the *mandi* to the state and vice versa, and their respective influences on the politics of the market as well as the political framing of the market. This interaction between the contextual specificities of local markets and regulatory intervention by the state resonates with Aditi Saraf's study of trade relations across the Line of Control between India- and Pakistan-controlled Jammu and Kashmir. Here, the political imperatives of intermittent conflict and arbitrary détente shape a market that nevertheless remains rooted in what the state defines as tradition. Douglas Haynes' chapter emphasizes how small-scale industrial entrepreneurs – in spite of their anchoring in local social structures – can act as agents of disembedding markets and reembed markets in new forms. It adds an important dimension to Polanyian discourses on markets that challenges the linearity of market trajectories in the unfolding of capitalism in India.

Fourth, and finally, our understanding of embedded exchange relates to moral aspects of market activity. A number of established studies emphasize the importance of ethical idioms and notions of distribution and reciprocity that are part and parcel of various South Asian cosmological systems (Besky 2014; Gregory 1997; Laidlaw 1995; Parry 1989). This strand of scholarship is in the background of our contributions here.

Andy Rotman, for example, describes the moral economy of the North Indian bazaar in Banaras. Such enduring exchange webs are sometimes seen as inevitably displaced by modern capitalism. Yet Rotman argues that urban merchants, hawkers, and consumers are immersed in a "matrix of affiliations" that serves to bind together the culture of piety and the culture of exchange. Here, exchange is emphatically embedded, in the signaling of divine fealty and social trust via pious performance. In Rotman's analysis, the bazaar could not exist in an abstracted form, yet exchange is not anchored in any one community. Rather, it is imbricated in neighborhood and urban affinities that have plural religious markers, similar to notions of trust depicted by Sebastian Schwecke.

Ajay Gandhi's chapter, on black money in India, also places importance on morality. Notions of injustice and unfairness turn those accused of having black money into synonyms for social subversion. Yet morality is not objectively absolute but about varied perspective; seen from the transactional horizon of usage, black money is sometimes more socially productive and relationally nurturing than its public vilification implies. Criminal markets, as depicted by Barbara Harriss-White and J. Jeyaranjan, necessarily rely on shared understandings of transactional moralities despite being marked as publicly debased. From a different perspective, Roger Begrich studies the transactional properties of alcohol in an Adivasi-dominated context in eastern India. In his fine-grained description of production and consumption's usages and meanings, Begrich suggests that discrete ethical understandings attend alcohol's commercial and customary intake.

The chapters that evoke embedded exchange demonstrate that we must be attentive to markets as social, spatial, genealogical, and moral bundles. Our contributors show that these interlaced webs of exchange and value are not separate from but constituted through gradations of community, geography, history, and ethics.

Contested Jurisdiction

Having described the necessity of anchoring exchange within a field of social reference points, we turn to the inescapability of power in structuring market activity. A second core premise of this volume is that multiple sovereignties, rather than a unitary state, frame transactional culture in India. These concurrent and sometimes contradictory authorities swaying commercial practice are encapsulated by our notion of "contested jurisdiction." There are two points here that are of particular importance. One regards the history of state regulation of market activity. The second concerns the issue of parallel and codependent authorities in exchange domains.

Despite the origins of regulatory intervention in India being traced to the second half of the nineteenth century, it was particularly with the late colonial state that robust interventions were enforced in market spheres (Goswami 2004; Tomlinson 2013). For example, the twentieth-century's world wars occasioned wide powers to ration, prohibit, and control the movement of commodities. The Second World War, specifically, allowed for newfound state powers to survey and sanction market actors. In certain instances, postcolonial state intervention into markets reincarnated and deepened this late colonial template (De 2018).

Nineteenth- and early twentieth-century legislation – setting up business structures, enforcing contract formats, frameworks for registration, regulation, and incentivizing compliance, and even the state's capacity to overrule market and property logics – was decisive for the proliferation of contemporary markets. This is perhaps more so than India's post-Independence flirtation with a command economy, and its flourishes such as bank nationalization or the "license-permit raj." Sudipta Sen's and Ritu Birla's interventions in the debate are particularly instructive. Sen provides an example of how exchange and authority were already intertwined during early colonial rule (Sen 1998). Birla's study of the legal history of these framing exercises gives a renewed impetus to study the effects of late nineteenth-century legal developments on contemporary markets (Birla 2009). The corollary to her concept of the definition of the "proper swindle" by colonial market framing policies – depicted through a study of bankruptcy litigation in the aftermath of the introduction of limited liability – is the continued existence and scale of business practices the Indian state perceives as "improper." This corollary depicts a realm of entrepreneurial techniques and market relations that evade or actively transgress the state's sway over the market.

From the mid-twentieth century the increased intervention in the market by the Indian state also had a counterintuitive impact. At one level, it tightly regulated a licit sphere – the fantasy of the planner's map corresponding to the actual city. But it also indirectly generated illicit domains where vibrant commercial activity unfolded (Harriss-White 2003). Thus, state regulation, in its baroque complexity, created the grounds for evasion, manifest in the vibrant transactional dances reductively glossed as "corruption" and "informality." The host of measures from the 1950s and 1970s, encapsulated in the phrase "license-permit raj," shows this. In one sense, then, regulation creates the conditions for illegality and extra-legality. In other cases, the state regulates by not regulating and therefore by choosing not to impose its imprint on market segments.

Contestation should not, however, imply open conflict or a zero-sum competition for supremacy. In actual fact, markets are remarkably accommodating domains. We can usefully borrow insights here from the history and anthropology of Indian politics. Studies suggest that in precolonial, colonial, and postcolonial terms, monolithic forms of authority were not the norm; rather, fragmentary and codependent ones prevailed (Hansen 2005). If layered influence and overlapping adjudication define Indian political life, commercial activity, too, is marked by such contested jurisdiction. Therefore, a term like market authority needs to be specified, and not automatically conflated with the state. For indeed, there are spheres of market activity, such as urban property, where authorization depends on ethnic institutions and religious leaders, not state actors.

Several chapters suggest that rather than open friction between competing centers of authority, there is selective collusion and, indeed, selective scrutiny by the state in its various manifestations. The colonial and postcolonial state in India has intermittently inquired into market practices, and sporadically (sometimes arbitrarily) imposed its directives. The state is only one of the authorities which, at different scales, is relevant to transactional life. This partial authority and intermittent scrutiny no doubt shapes the jurisdictions of exchange: but it is better understood as a collaborative dance than an annihilatory battle. Contested jurisdiction here may mean the diverging imperatives of states and municipalities vis-à-vis the central government; how precolonial and colonial forms chafe against modern reforms; the clashing and converging operations of associations and unions as well as agents of the shadow economy; and how community and corporate forms of reputation, trust, and obligation are in tension with state extraction.

Several contributors to this volume illuminate such contested jurisdiction. Avoiding the presentism under which what we describe may be analyzed as state dysfunction, cultural pathology, or customary patronage, our historical and contemporary examples show how Indian market life has a genealogical specificity and therefore a contemporary expression.

For example, Sebastian Schwecke suggests how North Indian financiers adapted to state banking reforms and money lending legislation during the twentieth century. His chapter suggests that informality is, at one level, the outcome of market framing processes. At another level, it is an ensemble of practices facilitating extra-legal business in contexts where the informal handling of business relations is comparatively more advantageous to entrepreneurs than adherence to the state's regulatory demands. David Rudner describes Chettiar merchant-banking activities stretching, in the nineteenth and early twentieth centuries, from south India to Southeast Asia. These were built on precolonial modes of organization capable of synchronizing with, as well as tactically circumventing, the colonial state's regulatory apparatus.

Nikhil Rao looks at the competing and contradictory imperatives of a nonmonolithic, multilayered early colonial state in Bombay. He describes the vitality of overlapping jurisdictions in constituting urban property as a market. Colonial land tenures did not displace but were imbricated with precolonial Maratha forms as well as pre-British Portuguese templates. Douglas Haynes' chapter, in turn, on early twentieth-century advertising, studies the struggle of authority from an entirely different angle. Here, various market participants contended to establish their authority over consumer product meanings. Producers that directly communicate a product's significance undercut their earlier reliance on the marketing services of merchants and traders. Haynes suggests how central the symbolic and discursive, as much as the regulatory and institutional, is to market life's contested jurisdiction.

Moving to the contemporary era, Andy Rotman's chapter, conversely, depicts the remarkable primacy of merchants and shop-keepers in the North Indian bazaar in controlling how their own reputations broadcast their products' meanings. Despite competition from global branding norms and glossy shopping malls, bazaar actors retain an enduring socioeconomic clout. Barbara Harriss-White and J. Jeyaranjan, in their study of the illegal sand market in Tamil Nadu, illustrate an aspect of what one could generalize as

capture and release. They show how unevenly formulated regulation and irregularly implemented policing condition the contours of
exchange. Criminal and shadow economies, no less than legal and
legitimate ones, ingeniously accommodate regulatory sway and its
abrupt vacuum. Matthew Hull examines, in contemporary Punjab,
an uneven set of regulatory practices producing a lottery market.
This is a sphere of tiered codependencies: the official Punjab lottery,
those of other states, and illegal operators running competing numbers games. Regulation inadvertently creates the grounds for commercial activity outside the fold of legality: legal enforcement is
parasitically used by less endowed actors to generate subsidiary
market activity. The "overlapping orbits" between the Punjab
state and other states, and between states and the central government, in regulatory and infrastructural terms, evolve into a lottery
market defined both by mutual reliance and ongoing feuds.

Roger Begrich outlines the parallel and symbiotically intertwined
networks of legal and illicit alcohol production among tribal communities in Jharkhand. These networks depend not only on their toleration by state authorities – in contrast to their less flexible demarcation
in law – but on notions of custom-based solidarity between Adivasi
bureaucrats and populations. As with the other chapters on contemporary markets, a seemingly clear cat-and-mouse game between state
regulators and market actors shades into the gray of complicity and
dissimulation. Finally, Mekhala Krishnamurthy analyzes how agricultural wholesale markets in Madhya Pradesh are state-authorized
and framed yet have disparate authorities and imperatives that have
significantly changed over time. New authorities and new roles
emerge to realign state-society-market relations in postcolonial
history.

The general point drawn from this thematic rubric of contested
jurisdiction concerns the ways in which commercial competitors, in
regulatory, infrastructural, symbolic, legal, and organizational
terms, both converge and collaborate, and compete and combat.
Far from being impeded by regulatory uniformity or consistency,
market actors deftly accommodate what is capricious and plural.
Historical and contemporary players in Indian markets, we suggest,
are not impaired by or waiting for modernization or implementation;
they move with the multiplicity of monarchs who exercise sway over
commercial life.

Pliable Markets

Something that is pliable has both an elastic suppleness and bears influence from its surroundings. These meanings bear on this volume's notion of "pliable markets." We draw attention to the malleability of exchange activity as it unfolds in India; we further note how yielding and amenable market actors and spaces are.

The first meaning of pliability concerns the flexibility of markets as they expand and contract, bend and reconstitute, and develop new technologies that persist alongside old ones. Indian markets have adapted through colonial underdevelopment, enduring forms of social segmentation, and selective state interventions. We survey some of these, noting that the state itself creates markets within its operational orbit. Apart from well-elaborated markets in many goods and services, there are illicit ones such as those for exams, jobs, and basic services, and standardized and institutionalized quasi-markets. Then there are markets – for straightforwardly illegal goods as well as for lotteries, urban property, gold, alcohol, weapons, and cash itself – in which state regulation, sometimes inadvertently but also symbiotically, brings exchange activity into being. Finally, there are illegal markets in illegal commodities, among them drugs, body parts, trafficked women, and antiquities (Harriss-White & Michelutti 2019). This volume pinpoints such interdependent, co-constitutive, and fluid aspects of exchange in India.

The second level at which we suggest the value of the concept of pliable markets concerns the susceptibility of exchange to social, political, and moral influences. Pliability is manifested when exchange is capable of adjusting to, evading from, and coping with, government and community forms and practices. Markets can be seen as ensembles of factors or forces that oscillate, balance, or neutralize one another. Further, exchange at its elemental is about giving and receiving, a back and forth that has narrative and symbolic elements. Markets are crucial sites for meaning-making creatures because transactions are always politically shaped, socially influenced, and ethically attuned. Their pliability is partially an outcome of the need to operate under a range of allegedly noneconomic factors that suffuse their functioning, one that cannot, for instance, ignore the enduring relationship of market spheres to religious institutions and community authorities (Osella & Rudnyckyj 2017).

This volume looks at markets of various types. Its novelty is not just a focus on tangible commodities but also on immaterial value. Contributors identify vibrant spheres of exchange: in alcohol production and distribution, in sand mining and circulation, in lottery numbers and speculation, in money siphoning and redistribution, and in vernacular advertising and publication. They also describe domains of desire, anxiety, danger, transgression, and immorality in markets of advertising, moneylending, branding, and cash.

Thus, we have markets of stuff and markets of substanceless stuff.[3] Markets here are considered material and immaterial forms that may be commodified, regulated, and circulated. Such markets are subject to informal or formal authority and framing. Abstracted and more embedded forms and transactions coexist and intersect. Within this ambit, this volume explores sand, alcohol, advertising, finance, brands, property, money and lotteries as markets. This focus helps us to underline that economic processes are absolutely central to Indian cultural, political, and moral matters.

The idea of distinct ruptures – say between colonial or postcolonial – is not as interesting as attention to how contemporary forms (*waqf* property), financial mechanisms (*hundi*) and commission frameworks (*dalali*) have their own lineages and continuities. Even the practice of the Indian state curtailing or impeding certain market operations and commodity circulations – from textiles, electronics and gold in the twentieth century, to lotteries, grain, alcohol and high-denomination banknotes in the twenty-first century – has a historicity. This is drawn out when contextualizing market framing and recognition. In this volume's conversation with the wider literature on global capitalism and markets, we argue for attention to the genealogies of markets, not assuming a shared unfolding or operational universality.

Our contributors explore the workings of pliable markets in different ways. Both Ajay Gandhi and David Rudner's chapters concern how monetary liquidity flows along relational ties. In Gandhi's case, black money can be seen, despite the ideological demagoguery attending it, as buttressing community ties. Black money is pliability itself: a market of value that is not just bendable but, in nationalist discourse, spectral.

---

[3] While markets for substanceless stuff encompass a much wider range of exchanges, one particularly evocative treatment of these markets can be seen in the market for spectrum (Bhatia 2019).

Gandhi argues that this seemingly obscure and immoral transactional market in black money is from a different perspective embodied in social investments and ties, and thus possibly productive. In Rudner's case, merchant-caste banking hinges on social relationships: financial transactions cannot be disaggregated from kinship considerations. In Sebastian Schwecke's chapter, financial transactions in North India depend on knowing and connecting. Trust and reputation emerge, in Schwecke's analysis, as distinct arenas of exchange when the Indian state starts to enforce procedural forms for financial transactions.

Nikhil Rao discusses how Bombay's peripheral land was transmuted, via legal rulings and municipal regulation, into parceled, commodified, and speculative property. Rao observes the scale of the city expanding as a market constitutes around land, an elastic commerce and culture eventually hardening into today's Mumbai. Douglas Haynes describes how early twentieth-century vernacular advertising enabled commodities to acquire novel meanings in provincial settings. Well-being and domestic happiness become, for Indian producers, the grounds for expanding local markets in vernacular tonics and remedies. Aditi Saraf outlines how cross-border trade in militarized Kashmir expands and contracts with the vicissitudes of state authorities. There are officially approved regimes of nonmonetary barter and social imperatives toward risk and profit. Market actors at militarized crossings must adjust athletically to policy fluctuations affecting them. Matthew Hull depicts the fluidity of Punjab's segmented lottery market in the face of regulatory realities and shifts. Various state lotteries joust with illegal lottery operators, each exploiting the particularities of legislation and bans, to fill a vacuum or take up more space. The chapter on illegal sand mining by Barbara Harriss-White and J. Jeyaranjan demonstrates the ways in which the structure of these markets shifts in line with changes in political power. Finally, Roger Begrich describes how Jharkhand alcohol producers attend to the different predicaments and expectations in selling the liquid. Production and circulation are highly contextual, meaning the market disappears and reconstitutes, with shifting regulative forces and community requirements.

These chapters show how Indian markets have an adaptive quality. Here a solid binary of informal and formal can no longer be tenable with such gradations and entanglements of (in-)formality. These expressions of the pliable market – in alcohol, lotteries, sand, money, goods, and land – reiterate how markets, far from being static and sociologically bounded, exhibit a remarkable plasticity. They are enmeshed with and will accommodate to new geographies and diverse constituencies, bending to what is unpredictable and emergent.

Conclusion

Indian markets are not distinct entities removed from society and ought to be understood via their intricate links with state and society. Exchange can be more capaciously understood by accounting for its social embedding, its contested and concurrent authorities, and its malleable capacity. Celebrating the kaleidoscope of scholars inquiring into various Indian markets, our chapters address widely different domains, yet, reading them together, connections between embedded exchange, contested jurisdiction, and pliable markets proliferate.

This volume contains writing by anthropologists, historians, and political economists. With this diversity of disciplinary backgrounds, and the existing thematic rubrics, we simplify matters for the reader by ordering chapters historically. Starting with contributions broadly on early and late colonial era history, the contents shift towards the twentieth century, and onward into the contemporary period.

Over time – throughout this time – markets in India have changed significantly, although clearly not in a linear fashion. Instead, as we argue, the meaning of markets has constantly been renegotiated by a multitude of participants engaged in multifaceted forms of exchange. The contributors to this volume have not only striven to portray new angles and entry points for rethinking markets in line with the fascinating diversity of scholarly inquiry into this topic. At a more fundamental level, they have observed and celebrated the propensity and aptitude of market participants to rethink what markets mean to them.

References

Abraham, I & van Schendel, W (eds.) 2005, *Illicit Flows and Criminal Things: States, Borders, and the Other Side of Globalization*, Indiana University Press, Bloomington,

Ali, TO 2018, *A Local History of Global Capital: Jute and Peasant Life in the Bengal Delta*, Princeton University Press, Princeton.

Amrith, S 2013, *Crossing the Bay of Bengal: The Furies of Nature and the Fortunes of Migration*, Harvard University Press, Cambridge.

Anderson, K 2010, *Marx at the Margins: On Nationalism, Ethnicity, and Non-Western Societies*, University of Chicago Press, Chicago.

Appadurai, A 1986, "Introduction: Commodities and the Politics of Value," in A Appadurai (ed.) *The Social Life of Things*, Cambridge University Press, Cambridge, pp. 3–64.

Appadurai, A 1996, *Modernity at Large: Cultural Dimensions of Globalization*, University of Minnesota Press, Minneapolis.

Appadurai, A 2015, *Banking on Words: The Failure of Language in the Age of Derivative Finance*, University of Chicago Press, Chicago.

Barth, F 1981, "The System of Social Stratification in Swat, North Pakistan," in F Barth (ed.) *Features of Person and Society in Swat: Collected Essays on Pathans*, Routledge & Kegan Paul, London, pp. 16–54.

Basile, E 2017, "Civil Society and Small Town Capitalism: The Case of Arni," *Decision*, 44, 2: 133–45.

Bates, C & Mio M (eds.) 2015, *Cities in South Asia*, Routledge, New York.

Bayly, CA 1996, *Empire and Information: Intelligence Gathering and Social Communication in India, 1780–1870*, Cambridge University Press, Cambridge.

Bayly, CA 1998 [1983], *Rulers, Townsmen and Bazaars: North Indian Society in the Age of British Expansion 1770–1870*, Oxford University Press, New Delhi.

Bayly, CA 2011, "Merchant Castes: Identities and Solidarities," in MM Kudaisya (ed.) *The Oxford India Anthropology of Business History*, Oxford University Press, New Delhi, pp. 99–121.

Bear, L 2015, *Navigating Austerity: Currents of Debt Along a South Asian River*, Stanford University Press, Palo Alto.

Besky, S 2014, *The Darjeeling Distinction: Labor and Justice on Fair-Trade Tea Plantations in India*, University of California Press, Berkeley.

Bhagwati, J & Panagariya, A 2013, *Why Growth Matters: How Economic Growth in India Reduced Poverty and the Lessons for Other Developing Countries*, Public Affairs, New York.

Bhatia, J 2019, "Crime in the Air. Spectrum Markets and the Telecommunications Sector in India," in B Harriss-White & L Michelutti (eds.) *The Wild East? Criminal Political Economies Across South Asia*, UCL Press, London.

Birla, R 2009, *Stages of Capital: Law, Culture, and Market Governance in Late Colonial India*, Duke University Press, Durham.

Bohannan, P & Dalton, G (eds.) 1962, *Markets in Africa*, Northwestern University Press, Evanston.

Breckenridge, C (ed.) 1995, *Consuming Modernity: Public Culture in a South Asian World*, University of Minnesota Press, Minneapolis.

Breman, J 2013, *At Work in the Informal Economy of India. A Perspective from the Bottom Up*, Oxford University Press, New Delhi.

Chakrabarty, D 1989, *Rethinking Working-Class History: Bengal 1890–1940*, Princeton University Press, Princeton.

Chakrabarty, D 2002, *Habitations of Modernity: Essays in the Wake of Subaltern Studies*, Permanent Black, New Delhi.

Chandavarkar, R 1994, *The Origins of Industrial Capitalism in India: Business Strategies and the Working Classes in Bombay, 1900–1940*, Cambridge University Press, Cambridge.

Chandavarkar, R 1998, *Imperial Power and Popular Politics: Class Resistance and the State in India, c. 1850–1950*, Cambridge University Press, Cambridge.

Chandavarkar, R 2009, *History, Culture and the Indian City*, Cambridge University Press, Cambridge.

Chari, S 2004, *Fraternal Capital: Peasant-Workers, Self-Made Men, and Globalization in Provincial India*, Stanford University Press, Palo Alto.

Chibber, V 2003, *Locked in Place: State Building and Late Industrialization in India*, Princeton University Press, Princeton.

Cohn, B 1996, *Colonialism and Its Forms of Knowledge*, Princeton University Press, Princeton.

Cross, J 2014, *Dream Zones: Anticipating Capitalism and Development in India*, Pluto, London.

De, R 2018, *A People's Constitution: Law and Everyday Life in the Indian Republic*, Princeton University Press, Princeton.

Dodd, N 2014, *The Social Life of Money*, Princeton University Press, Princeton.

Dossal, M 1991, *Imperial Designs and Indian Realities: The Planning of Bombay City, 1845–1875*, Oxford University Press, New Delhi.

Farooqui, A 2006, *Opium City: The Making of Early Victorian Bombay*, Three Essays Collective, New Delhi.

Ferguson, N 2008, *The Ascent of Money: A Financial History of the World*, Penguin, New York.

Fuller, C & Benei, V (eds.) 2001, *The Everyday State and Society in Modern India*, Hurst, London.

Galbraith, JK 1967, *The New Industrial State*, Mifflin, Boston.

Gell, A 2006 [1999], "The Market Wheel: Symbolic Aspects of an Indian Tribal Market," in *The Art of Anthropology: Essays and Diagrams*, Berg, Oxford, pp. 107–36.

Gooptu, N (ed.) 2013, *Enterprise Culture in Neoliberal India: Studies in Youth, Class, Work and Media*, Abingdon, Routledge.

Goswami, M 2004, *Producing India: From Colonial Economy to National Space*, University of Chicago Press, Chicago.

Graeber, D 2011, *Debt: The First 5000 Years*, Melville House, New York.

Gregory, CA 1997, *Savage Money: The Anthropology and Politics of Commodity Exchange*, Harwood, Amsterdam.

Gupta, AD 2001, *The World of the Indian Ocean Merchant 1500–1800: Collected Essays of Ashin Das Gupta*, Oxford University Press, New Delhi.

Gupta, CD 2016, *State and Capital in Independent India: Institutions and Accumulation*, Cambridge University Press, Cambridge.

Guyer, J 2004, *Marginal Gains: Monetary Transactions in Atlantic Africa*, University of Chicago Press, Chicago.

Hansen, TB 2005, "Sovereigns Beyond the State: On Legality and Authority in Urban India," in TB Hansen & F Stepputat (eds.) *Sovereign Bodies: Citizens, Migrants, and States in the Postcolonial World*, Princeton University Press, Princeton.

Hardiman, D 1996, *Feeding the Baniya: Peasants and Usurers in Western India*, Oxford University Press, New Delhi.

Harriss-White, B 2003, *India Working: Essays on Society and Economy*, Cambridge University Press, Cambridge.

Harriss-White, B 2005, "Commercialisation, Commodification and Gender Relations in Post-Harvest Systems for Rice in South Asia," *Economic and Political Weekly*, 40, 25: 2530–42.

Harriss-White, B (ed.) 2015, *Middle India and Urban-Rural Development: Four Decades of Change*, Springer, New Delhi.

Harriss-White, B & Jan, MA 2012, "The Three Roles of Agricultural Markets. A Review of Ideas About Agricultural Commodity Markets in India," *Economic and Political Weekly*, 47, 52: 39–52.

Harriss-White, B & Michelutti L (eds.) 2019, *The Wild East? Criminal Political Economies Across South Asia*, UCL Press, London.

Haynes, DE 1999, "Just Like a Family? Recalling the Relations of Production in the Textile Industries of Surat and Bhiwandi, 1940–60," *Contributions to Indian Sociology*, 33, 1–2: 141–69.

Haynes, DE 2012, *Small Town Capitalism in Western India: Artisans, Merchants and the Making of the Informal Economy, 1870–1960*, Cambridge University Press, Cambridge.

Hodgson, GM 2001, *How Economics Forgot History. The Problem of Historical Specificity in Social Science*, Routledge, London and New York.

Huws, U 2003, *The Making of a Cybertariat. Virtual Work in a Real World*, Merlin Press, London.

Jain, K 2007, *The Economies of Indian Calendar Art*, Duke University Press, Durham.

Kar, S 2018, *Financializing Poverty: Labor and Risk in Indian Microfinance*, Stanford University Press, Palo Alto, CA.

Kudaisya, MM (ed.) 2011, *The Oxford India Anthropology of Business History*, Oxford University Press, New Delhi.

Kumar, A 2002, *The Black Economy in India*, Penguin, New Delhi.

Laidlaw, J 1995, *Riches and Renunciation: Religion, Economy, and Society Among the Jains*, Clarendon Press, Oxford.

Lambert, H 2000, "Village Bodies: Constitution, Locality and Affection in Rajasthani Kinship," in M Böck and A Rao (eds.) *Culture, Creation, and Procreation: Concepts of Kinship in South Asian Practice*, Berghahn, New York, pp. 81–100.

Ludden, D 2004, "The Formation of Modern Agrarian Economies in South India," in BB Chaudhuri (ed.) *The History of Indian Science, Philosophy and Culture: Vol: VII, Economic History of India, 18th–20th Centuries*, Oxford University Press, New Delhi, pp. 1–40.

Machado, P 2014, *Ocean of Trade: South Asian Merchants, Africa and the Indian Ocean, C. 1750–1850*, Cambridge University Press, Cambridge.

Markovits, C 2000, *The Global World of Indian Merchants, 1750–1947: Traders of Sind from Bukhara to Panama*, Cambridge University Press, Cambridge.

Markovits, C 2008, *Merchants, Traders, Entrepreneurs: Indian Business in the Colonial Era*, Permanent Black, Ranikhet.

Marriott, M 1976, "Hindu Transactions: Diversity Without Dualism," in B Kapferer (ed.) *Transaction and Meaning: Directions in the Anthropology of Exchange and Symbolic Behavior*, Institute for the Study of Human Issues, Philadelphia, 109–42.

Martin, M 2009, "Hundi/Hawala: The Problem of Definition," *Modern Asian Studies*, 43, 4: 909–37.

Mazzarella, W 2003, *Shoveling Smoke: Advertising and Globalization in Contemporary India*, Duke University Press, Durham.

Mines, D & Lamb, S (eds.) 2010, *Everyday Life in South Asia*, 2nd edn, Indiana University Press, Bloomington.

Mines, M 1996, *Public Faces, Private Voices: Community and Individuality in South India*, Oxford University Press, New Delhi.

Nakassis, C 2016, *Doing Style: Youth and Mass Mediation in South India*, University of Chicago Press, Chicago.

Osella, F & Rudnyckyj D (eds.) 2017, *Religion and the Morality of the Market: Anthropological Perspectives*, Cambridge University Press, Cambridge.

Pande, A 2014, *Wombs in Labor: Transnational Commercial Surrogacy in India*, Columbia University Press, New York.

Pandian, A & Ali, D 2010, *Ethical Life in South Asia*, Indiana University Press, Bloomington.

Parry, J 1989, "On the Moral Perils of Exchange," in J Parry & M Bloch (eds.) *Money and the Morality of Exchange*, Cambridge University Press, Cambridge, 64–93.

Parry, J & Bloch, M 1989, "Introduction: Commodities and the Politics of Value", in J Parry & M Bloch (eds.) *Money and the Morality of Exchange*, Cambridge University Press, Cambridge.

Parthasarathi, P 2009, *The Spinning World: A Global History of Cotton Textiles, 1200–1850*, Oxford University Press, Oxford.

Parthasarathi, P 2011, *Why Europe Grew Rich and Asia Did Not: Global Economic Divergence, 1650–1850*, Cambridge University Press, Cambridge.

Perlin, F 1993, *The Invisible City: Monetary, Administrative and Popular Infrastructures in Asia and Europe, 1500–1900*, Variorum, Aldershot.

Piketty, T 2014, *Capital in the Twenty-first Century*, Belknap Press of Harvard University Press, Cambridge, MA.

Polanyi, K 2001 [1944], *The Great Transformation: The Political and Economic Origins of Our Times*, Beacon, Boston.

Puri, SS 2014, *Speculation in Fixed Futures: An Ethnography of Betting in Between Legal and Illegal Economies at the Delhi Racecourse*, University of Copenhagen Press, Copenhagen.

Raheja, GG 1988, *The Poison in the Gift: Ritual, Prestation, and the Dominant Caste in a North Indian Village*, University of Chicago Press, Chicago.

Ray, RK 1995, "Asian Capital in the Age of European Domination: The Rise of the Bazaar, 1800–1914," *Modern Asian Studies*, 29, 3: 449–554.

Roy, A 2003, *City Requiem, Calcutta: Gender and the Politics of Poverty*, University of Minnesota Press, Minneapolis.

Roy, T 2018, *A Business History of India: Enterprise and the Emergence of Capitalism from 1700*, Cambridge University Press, Cambridge.

Rudner, D 1989, "Banker's Trust and the Culture of Banking Among the Nattukottai Chettiars of Colonial South India," *Modern Asian Studies*, 23, 3: 417–58.

van Schendel, W & Abraham, I 2005, *Illicit Flows and Criminal Things: States, Borders, and the Other Side of Globalization*, Indiana University Press, Bloomington.

Searle, L 2016, *Landscapes of Accumulation: Real Estate and the Neoliberal Imagination in Contemporary India*, University of Chicago Press, Chicago.

Sen, S 1998, *Empire of Free Trade. The East India Company and the Making of the Colonial Marketplace*, University of Pennsylvania Press, Philadelphia.

Srivastava, S 2007, *Passionate Modernity: Sexuality, Class, and Consumption in India*, Routledge, New Delhi.

Tomlinson, BR 1979, *The Political Economy of the Raj 1914–1947*, Macmillan, London.

Tomlinson, BR 2013, *The Economy of Modern India From 1860 to the Twenty-First Century*, Cambridge University Press, Cambridge.

Vatuk, S 1972, *Kinship and Urbanization: White Collar Migrants in North India*, University of California Press, Berkeley.

Virdee, S 2019, "Racialized Capitalism. An Account of its Contested Origins and Consolidation," *Sociological Review*, 67, 1, 3–27.

Weber, M 1958 [1916–1917], *The Religion of India: The Sociology of Hinduism and Buddhism*, Free Press, Glencoe.

Wiser, W 1936, *The Hindu Jajmani System: A Socio-Economic System Interrelating Members of a Hindu Village Community in Services*, Lucknow Publishing House, Lucknow.

Yang, A 1998, *Bazaar India: Markets, Society, and the Colonial State in Bihar*, University of California Press, Berkeley.

2 | *Banking in the Bazaar: The Nattukottai Chettiars*

DAVID RUDNER

South Asian Markets and "the Bazaar"

South Asian history is marked by an overall trend in which expanding kingdoms conquered other kingdoms and extended their control ever more deeply into tribal territories in their own hinterlands. The expansion was not just a military one. Royal dynasties invested in the infrastructure of their domains, supporting an expansion of irrigation works, construction of temples and monasteries,[1] and an explosion of new towns and cities that served as nodal points for trade and revenue networks both within and between kingdoms.[2] Varieties of these urban settlements formed nodes in central place market networks. Some places specialized as market towns; others set aside special market precincts to which trade was variably segregated on a constant or periodic basis. In almost all cases, Western observers have been struck by what they saw as a noisy, chaotic, and confusing situation and a lack of apparent government regulation over these markets. Yet, in spite of a broad geographic distribution that extends beyond South Asia and arguably throughout the world, these markets are often viewed

---

[1] Temples and monasteries may not be viewed as "infrastructure" by readers who assume that only formal economic institutions in Western economies perform economic functions and who exclude religious institutions from doing so by fiat. That is not the position taken here. For detailed analysis of economic functions performed by "noneconomic," religious institutions only alluded to in this chapter, see Rudner (1994).

[2] There is no escape from controversy in academia and major debates continue to swirl around complex issues about the nature and degree of centralized power exerted by different states over their growing domains, the nature and degree of political autonomy of tribe-dominated or caste-dominated territories at least nominally under control of a king or emperor, and the economic isolation and autonomy of "peasant" villages within these territories.

less as a widespread, commercial institution than as the defining hallmark of Middle Eastern society: the bazaar.

The Middle Eastern Bazaar?

Clifford Geertz is, perhaps, the clearest and most influential proponent of this kind of Weberian anthropology in which Middle Eastern bazaars are singled out and contrasted with analogous hallmarks for other societies: the *kula* in the Trobriand Islands, caste in India, bureaucracy in China, and so on (Geertz 1963, 1978, 1979).[3] Yet, it is rather peculiar that bazaars are viewed as exemplary of Middle Eastern society since bazaars satisfying every definition that I have come across are found throughout the world. Similarly, anti-comparative sentiments that surface from time to time in the social sciences notwithstanding, castes or caste-like formations are not exclusive to South Asia.[4] On the contrary, it is clear that wherever we find bazaars, we also find a variety of informal merchant castes or caste-like social formations – from *nisbas* in Morocco to *jatis* in India – that exist in linkage with other kinds of institution, including various kinds of governmental body and an even wider variety of craftsman and commodity producer.

Moreover, these caste-like social formations – and certainly the artisanal and merchant castes of South Asia – only function because

---

[3] For discussion of this kind of Weberian essentialism in the Indian context, see Arjun Appadurai (1986).

[4] "Caste" is a multivalent term even within the South Asian context in which it is typically used, let alone the more general use to designate "caste-like" social formations adopted in the present chapter. Accordingly, I note that my use of the term in this context refers to what South Asian specialists distinguish as *jati* rather than *varna*, that is, as referring to endogamous kinship groups, typically segmented into component clans and lineages in various structural arrangements, and typically reflecting an adaptation to an occupational specialization. Geertz's objection to viewing Moroccan *nisbas* as "caste-like" seems to reference characteristics of the ideological classification of *varnas* rather than a sociological analysis of *jatis*. The situation is further complicated by cultural values surrounding the formation of marriage alliances between lineage groups in Dravidian kinship systems found in southern India. Finally, both *varna* and *jati* should be distinguished from "castes" in the sense of ethnicized or racialized social formations in colonial and independent India. See David Washbrook (1973, 1975). For a recent treatment of caste-as-*jati* consistent with mine and written from both an historical and a comparative perspective, see Sumit Guha (2013).

of the presence of bazaars. Indeed, prominent south Asian historians such as Rajat Ray and Sugata Bose suggest that we understand much of commerce around the Indian Ocean rim by conceiving the South Asian trading world as one in which merchants made "informal" use of caste membership, not just to win profits as individual businessmen but to construct merchant castes as institutions for trade and banking that could operate across permeable national boundaries between local producers and artisans and the global market (Bose 2006; Ray 1988, 1994, 1995).

In doing so, however, they alter Geertz's use of the term "bazaar" to designate not a noisy marketplace of mutually transacting clients depending on negotiated personal relationships but, rather, an institutionalized system for financial intermediation between government authorities and localized commodity producers, artisans, and petty shopkeepers:

> The nineteenth-century Indian economy may be said ... to have consisted of three distinct social agglomerations: (a) a Westernized enclave of banks, factories, mines, plantations, corporations, managing agencies, and import-export firms with weak linkages to the rest of the economy; (b) the *bazaar*, a wellintegrated complex of *shroffs* [merchant-bankers], *arhatiyas* [commission agents] and wholesale merchants, operating in inland trade through negotiable instruments of credit (*hundi*); (c) the subsistence economy of the peasants, artisans, and petty dealers who had no access to either bank or hundi credit, and who were therefore compelled to rely on usurious loans from moneylenders .... These social agglomerations ... were separated from each other by the fact that credit did not move from one complex to the next in a sufficiently large volume. (Ray 1994: 12)

The present chapter adopts the framework laid out by historians such as Ray and Bose to suggest that a hands-off government, a corresponding unregulated and information-poor marketplace of petty producers and shopkeepers, or the presence of commercially "informal," castes or caste-like social formations playing a market-regulatory function in the absence of government regulation constitutes the bazaar. Rather, all three "agglomerations" constitute variables that distinguish bazaar economies from other economies. This chapter takes up the question of the articulation of these agglomerations in colonial India as seen through the lens of a specific caste of merchant-bankers who provided credit and financial intermediation throughout the multiple markets of South Asia and the Indian Ocean rim.

The Nattukottai Chettiars or Nakarattars[5]

Merchant-bankers operating in and across different kinds of market in
South Asia face the fundamental challenges of any businessman, but
the commercial institutions they deployed have undergone substantial
changes over time. In particular, the arrival of European trading companies in the sixteenth century defined the emergence of a new, historically specific system of linkages between commercially specialized
castes, local markets, and a Euro-centered mercantile and industrial
complex (Abu-Lughod 1989; Dale 1994; Levi 2002; Markovits 2000;
Rudner 2011). Within this context, bankers operated outside the law.
This is not to say that they and their actions were considered criminal.[6]
Rather, the law was simply blind to many caste-based techniques for
trade and banking;[7] a situation that led government banking committees in the early decades of the twentieth century to declare that some
things that merchants did were impossible – such as forming contracts
or using *hundis* (bills of exchange) as currency (Madras Provincial
Banking Enquiry Committee (MPBEC) 1930; Rudner 1994). Despite
such pronouncements, merchants continued to operate, much as do
honey bees, informed by physicists that they cannot fly. They did so not
by operating within formal market institutions that were organized by
state-based institutions of contract law, commodities markets, stock
markets, and central banking systems, instead they constructed commercial relationships and institutions built around ideas and values
concerning caste, kinship, and temple membership, all of which operated informally to organize and facilitate commerce.[8]

---

[5] The following discussion excerpts and severely abridges chapters 1, 4, 5, and 6 of
Rudner (1994).
[6] In contemporary parlance, such merchant activities and institutions are classified
as "informal," a term that encompasses both informal "gray" market activities
and criminalized, black market activities (cf. Hart 1973, 1985, 2014).
[7] Blind to many of these techniques, the apparatus of government, especially its
procedures for defining legal rights through case law and legislation not only
were *not* blind to other techniques, it was actively engaged in creating and
formalizing new legal rights under colonial law. For case law, see WS Weersooria
(1973). For legislation, see Ritu Birla (2009).
[8] This is not to say that Indian bankers failed to take advantage of opportunities to
service, invest, or participate in business ventures structured or regulated by
Western-style principles but, at least in the case of the Nakarattars, until roughly
the 1920s and 1930s, they did so with support from their caste-based banking
system.

The Nakarattars[9] (or Nattukottai Chettiars, as they are generally known outside their caste) were the chief merchant-banking caste of colonial south India and Southeast Asia. They do not appear in the Western historical record until the beginning of the nineteenth century. But Nakarattar oral tradition and indigenous documents maintained in the temples of Tamil Nadu extend our knowledge about their past back to the seventeenth century (Rudner 1987), when they were primarily small-scale, itinerant salt traders in the interior of present-day Tamil Nadu. By the eighteenth century, some individuals had extended their business operations of pearl, rice, cloth and arrack as far as Ceylon in the south, while others were trading rice and wheat as far as Calcutta in the northeast. They were also involved in money lending and other credit-extending operations. By the nineteenth and early twentieth centuries, especially after the opening of the Suez Canal, Chettiars had become the chief merchant-banking caste of south India. They were the major sources of finance for myriad agrarian transactions between Burma, Ceylon, Malaya, and the Madras Presidency. They played a major role in government finance. They dominated the role of mercantile intermediary between British rulers and local populations by monopolizing important components of the credit, banking, and agrarian systems of Southeast Asia, and they remitted huge amounts of capital from Southeast Asia back to their south Indian homeland for industrial investment and large-scale philanthropy.

Four historical trends coincided and opened up new commercial opportunities, ideally suited for Nakarattar banking operations during the colonial period that concern us in the present chapter:

1 The British completed their conquest of Burma and Malaya in the 1850s and 1860s, opening up the interiors of these countries for colonial development and exploitation.
2 With the opening of the Suez Canal in 1869, the volume of trade between Asia and Europe increased and the possibility for large-scale export of agricultural and other bulky commodities presented itself for the first time.
3 British exchange banks established themselves firmly throughout South and Southeast Asia, foreclosing old Nakarattar investments in moneylending and exchange banking for European firms, but at

---

[9] Often transcribed as "Nagarathars."

the same time offering Nakarattars a new source of venture capital
to carry out alternative investments.
4 Finally, unlike the situation in post-1850s Madras, the provincial
   governments of Southeast Asia adopted policies that encouraged,
   rather than restricted, Nakarattar investments in indigenous agricultural industries.

Nakarattars responded to all of these changes in their commercial
environment by expanding their business far beyond south India to
invest with agriculturalists, plantation owners, and mine operators
throughout Southeast Asia. In this capacity, they made a unique and
central contribution to the growth of the plantation economy in
Ceylon, the emergence of the Burmese rice market, and the development of Malaya's rubber and tin industries.

In the twentieth century, Nakarattar commerce contracted. Starting in
the 1920s and increasingly through the first half of the twentieth century, the business environment of British India was altered in crucial
ways by the development of nationalistic movements in Southeast Asian
countries, the general growth of legislation restricting indigenous forms
of banking, and increased industrial opportunities within India for non-
British businessmen. The consequences were significant for the
Nakarattars. Their caste organization began to unravel in the face of
multigovernmental interference with traditional banking practice. Elite
members of the Nakarattar caste began a gradual transfer and freezing
of investment capital by shifting from mercantile to industrial ventures.
Nonelite Nakarattars – perhaps 80–90 percent of the caste – were forced
to scramble for new employment opportunities and they began working
in government and business offices, although many of these were owned
or managed by elite Nakarattars. The present chapter, however, limits
its attention to the organization of the Nakarattar banking system, at its
peak, during the colonial period from 1870 to 1930.

Being a Nakarattar in Colonial India

To be a Nakarattar in colonial India was to belong to one of the great
"country fort" houses (*nattukottai*) of Chettinad and to worship one's
family's deity (*kula teyvam*) in one of the seventy-six villages of Chettinad.
As young Nakarattar boys grew up (I have very little information about
young girls), their families trained them for business and, when they were

old enough, apprenticed them to family firms with agency houses located in far-flung business stations throughout South and Southeast Asia. After a three-year tour of duty, the boys would return to Chettinad, to their families, to their neighbors, and to their temples. They would rest briefly there, perhaps no more than the three-month summer during which most Nakarattar marriages and temple ceremonies occur. They would then return to work in the outside world as young men. On their second tour of duty, they might return to the employ of the same firm for which they had worked before, perhaps now working as the principle agent (*mudali*) in the agency house. Alternatively, they might take over as resident proprietor or partner in an agency house for their own firm. Eventually, a Nakarattar businessman would retire to Chettinad where he would direct the activities of agents for his own family firm and join the round of ceremonies with the women, children, and other retirees who resided permanently in Chettinad.

Long before this, when family and financial circumstances permitted, a young man's joint family (*kutumbam, valavu*) would take advantage of his periodic return to Chettinad and arrange a marriage with an auspicious bride from another family. The ceremony initiated an elaborate pattern of gift-giving and potential business cooperation within kindred formed by patrilineal relatives (*pankali*) of the husband and wife. This pattern of gifting and cooperation continued until all children born to the couple were established in alliance-forming marriages of their own. Alternatively, it might be continued beyond the marriage of offspring if two joint families of (what anthropologists call) "cross relatives" within the kindred chose to renew the alliance begun with the original marriage. In either case, candidate families for marriage alliance were chosen from within the same territorial division (*pirivu, vattakai*) of Chettinad. Both families would register the marriage at their respective clan temples (*Nakara-k-kovil*).

It bears emphasizing that, in contrast to many standard models of Dravidian kinship systems (of which the Nakarattar system is one), marriage alliances between these segmentary descent groups were *not* determined by systems of kinship classification and associated prescriptive rules for marrying cross-cousins.[10] Instead it was exactly the opposite. Nakarattars lived in a social universe with hundreds or

[10] Arguments about Dravidian kinship terminology are extensive, elaborate, and highly specialized. For my position, see Rudner (1990, 1997).

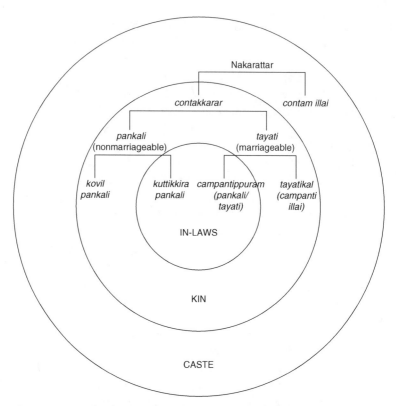

Figure 2.1 Levels of social distance in Nakarattar kin relationships

even thousands of potential marriage alliances to make. They forged *actual* alliances, however, with only a very small selection of families, which, moreover, could be adjusted from generation to generation. The effect at any given time, however, was to define social distance (see Figure 2.1) between groups of relatives that reflected not only "distance" in terms of blood and marriageability but also in terms financial cooperation (detailed examples of investment in marriage alliances and lineage and clan temples are provided in Rudner (1994, chaps. 8, 9)).

Overview of Nakarattar Banking

Many Nakarattars loaned money to agriculturalists and artisans within the Madras Presidency, especially within their Chettinad homeland and within the rice-growing regions and coastal ports of Tirunelveli and Thanjavur. But business in the Presidency was risky and paid a poor return on investment. As a consequence, the majority of Nakarattar business dealings in the late nineteenth century took place overseas in Southeast Asia. Supported by the British colonial administration, they supplied credit to anyone who required it at interest rates that were exorbitant by today's standards, but generally far lower (in some cases, by an order of magnitude!) than that supplied by their competitors.

A major reason for their success is that – especially after adapting and expanding their preexisting merchant-banking system to meet the needs of the English East India Company – they incurred relatively low costs in acquiring loanable funds from each other (through elite members of the caste – *adathis*), from the British banks, or from the Imperial Bank of India; low costs, that is, relative to the cost of credit faced by competing money-lenders from other castes who lacked access to the caste-specific credit facilities of the Nakarattars. Consequently, Nakarattars could charge lower rates of interest than their competitors and still make a healthy profit. No figures are available for the entire colonial India (including provinces in Southeast Asia as well as in the Indian subcontinent). However, figures from Burma are available for the years at the end of the colonial period and provide a good indication of interest rates from various sources of credit (Table 2.1). Although there may have been fluctuations in rate averages in the preceding period, there is no reason to believe that the overall structure of the credit market would have altered.

The relatively low interest rates charged by Nakarattars were rarely undertaken as acts of selfless charity, although Nakarattars did occasionally suggest a rather lofty motivation (just as bankers do today) in hearings by the colonial government. Certainly their clients were under no such misapprehension (Adas 1974). Under the colonial government, Southeast Asian agriculturalists lacked legal rights and the local organization made moneylending in Madras very risky. And, in an economic environment in which agricultural return on borrowed money was marginal, they often lost the land that they had improved as much by the labor of their hands as by inputs of Nakarattar capital. Nevertheless, it was Nakarattar bankers who provided the financial wherewithal for many Southeast Asians to make a living and who ultimately made possible the development of tea and coffee plantations in Ceylon, the rich rice frontier of lower Burma, and the tin and rubber industries of Malaya.

Table 2.1 *Interest rates on Burmese credit market, 1935–1942*

Loan source	Rate (% per annum)
Sources offering restricted or no services to agriculturalists	
Exchange banks and leading commercial banks	4–6
Coop societies and government loans	12
Dawson's Bank	9–21
West Coast Burmese bankers and moneylenders	6–18
Sources offering loans to agriculturalists	
Burmese moneylenders	12–35
Chinese and other moneylenders offering *sapabe, sekywe, sa-pe*, and similar loans	200+
Nakarattar bankers	9–34

Source: Tun Wai (1962: 136)

The major source of Nakarattar pride and honor, however, was their families, their business acumen, and their devotion to their gods: three indissociable components of Nakarattar life. In their Tamil homeland, Nakarattars gave generously to Siva temples in their *urs* (residential village) and in their *Nakara-k-kovils* (clan temple). They contributed to temples for Siva, Aiyyanar, and the goddess for villages in their leased land. And they made contributions for the construction of Murugan temples with the other Nakarattar bankers in their *nakaravitutis* (Nakarattar "rest houses" or choultries) wherever they did business. As recently as 1980 when I first began to explore Nakarattar history, a wealthy Nakarattar textile mill owner expressed that he proposed to give 1,00,000 rupees to each of the twenty-three major Saivaite temples in India. He fully expected God to bless his family and his business to make this possible. Even today, local Nakarattar castes associations around the world continue to their tradition of massive religious offering and secular philanthropy (Rudner 2011).

Nakarattar Deposit Banking

Particularly during the colonial period, banking was the core of Nakarattar business. In conducting their business, they relied not only on the developing legal apparatus of the colonial government to enforce legal contracts (Weersooria 1973) but also, and of particular significance for this chapter, on their own communal institutions for monitoring and sanctioning acceptable behavior. In doing so, they took two primary considerations into account: (1) the nature of the social relationship established by the transaction and (2) the conditions under which the principal amount of the transaction needed to be returned to the creditor. On this dual basis, Nakarattar bankers distinguished four basic kinds of deposit and many kinds of loan. The present chapter deals only with deposits, particularly those with discrete interest rates and terms of maturity that both reveal and constitute variable relations of trust between different Nakarattar caste and religious institutions.

Nakarattar bankers accepted two kinds of current deposit or *kadai kanakku* ("shop" accounts). These comprised demand deposits and a unique Nakarattar transaction called a *nadappu* or "walking" deposit. Nakarattars also accepted fixed-term (two-, three-, or six-month) deposits from fellow Nakarattars called *thavanai kanakku* ("resting" accounts), and fixed-term deposits from non-Nakarattars called *vayan vatti kanakku* ("fixed-interest" accounts). The interest rate for *nadappu* deposits served as a benchmark for rates paid on other deposits and, in this respect, was similar to the prime lending rate set by the central bank of a modern nation-state. In this case, however, the *nadappu* rate represented the interest that Nakarattars paid one another for deposits made to their *kadai kanakku* accounts. The rate was established on the sixteenth day of every month at meetings of Nakarattar bankers in major business centers, notably, Devakottai, Madras, Colombo, Penang, and Rangoon. *Kadai kanakku* deposits paid simple interest at the *nadappu* rate calculated for the period during which a deposit was maintained. By contrast, *thavanai* deposits paid compound interest, adding the appropriate increment to the principal at intervals of two, three, or six months depending on the terms of the deposit. *Vayan vatti* deposits paid interest at a rate calculated by the addition of a few *annas* per month over the *nadappu* rate (1 anna = 1/16 rupee). But like *kadai kanakku* deposits, they paid only simple interest.

These Nakarattar interest-setting practices established a staggered system of interest rates with two consequences. First, it allowed bankers to attract relatively cheap *nadappu* deposits from fellow Nakarattars for use in current accounts, subject to unpredictable demand. Second, it also allowed them to attract more expensive but more predictable fixed-term *thavanai* deposits from fellow Nakarattars with no immediate cash flow crisis. In both cases, however, Nakarattars assured themselves of access to deposit capital at a cost that was cheaper than the *vayan vatti* rate paid to non-Nakarattars, and far cheaper than the interest charges incurred by borrowing money in secured or unsecured loans.

One aspect of Nakarattar techniques for establishing and standardizing interest rates deserves comment in the present context. The procedure is described in the Burmese Provincial Banking Enquiry Commission (BPBEC) Report:

[The nadappu rate] is fixed in the evening of the 16th of every Tamil month at a meeting held at 9 p.m. in the Nakarattar temple at Rangoon, and it holds good for all the current Nakarattar month including the sixteen days already passed .... The meeting discusses the general financial situation, and fixes the current [nadappu] rate for the current month with this, taking into account the current pitch and tendency of the *thavanai* rate, the rates current amongst the Marwaris, Multanis, and Gujaratis [other Indian banking castes] and the rates for advances by the joint-stock banks to Nakarattars. As every firm has both income and expenses determined largely by this rate, great care is taken to fix the rate according to the needs of the situation. But for the first sixteen days of the month before the rate is fixed, there is a general consensus of opinion as to the rate that will be fixed, the weekly adjustment of *thavanai* rate and the discussions incidental to that adjustment being sufficient guide. (BPBEC Report 1930: 225)

According to this description, the relationship between *nadappu* and *thavanai* rates gave mathematical priority to the former in that the simple *nadappu* rate was taken as the basis for calculating compound interest payments on *thavanai* deposits. In practice, however, *nadappu* rates were fit to the fluctuating interest paid on *thavanai* rates; that is, they were fit to interest rates that Nakarattars were willing to pay in order to maintain a predictable reserve of capital in the form of *thavanai* deposits. Prior to the 1920s, determining the *thavanai* rate had, apparently, been a relatively informal affair, subject to competition among Nakarattars for deposits. But by 1920, the *thavanai* rate was:

[F]ixed in a systematic way every Sunday morning at 9 o'clock by a meeting in Rangoon temple, subject to modification during the week in case that [was] generally desired by the community .... It [was] not fixed according to the current [nadappu] rate; in fact the relationship [was] the other way about, the course of the thavanai rate being a consideration when fixing the current rate. (BPBEC Report 1930: 227)

The significance of this procedure in the present context is the light it casts on the Nakarattar understanding of banking. For Nakarattars, the primary consideration in setting interest rates was to attract fixed-term *thavanai* deposits and thereby maintain a predictable reserve of capital to underwrite the full range of their credit-extending activities. Without this ability, each individual banker would have had to depend on his own personal capital to finance money lending and commodities trading. But, by working together in a reliable and systematic way, by setting interest rates, and by ensuring inexpensive access to deposit capital to one another, Nakarattars were able to draw on the collective assets of the entire caste.

This is not to say that each Nakarattar attracted deposits from all Nakarattars. The system as a whole was divided into local segments, based on residential and kinship groupings (see Figure 2.1) and the location of agency houses. Membership in these different segments was not exclusive and Nakarattars maintained cross-cutting ties in various differently constituted segments. But segmentation did not eliminate the flow of deposit capital. Rather, by defining social and financial distances between bankers, it created the channels through which capital flowed. Finally, the largest Nakarattar bankers, called *adathis* or parent bankers, functioned as lynch pins for the entire system by acting as clearing houses for the transfer of financial instruments from firms that might have no dealing with one another but that shared a common relationship with an *adathi*.

Hundi Transactions and Other Transfers of Credit Between Nakarattars

The major Nakarattar financial instrument for all transactions was the *hundi*, a kind of bill of exchange or written order for payment that its drawers used much in the way that Americans use checks drawn on their checking accounts. To draw a *hundi*, a client had to open up an account and maintain a correspondence relationship with a banker. *Hundi*s were sometimes used just to transfer funds from one location to another (a facility employed primarily by Nakarattars among themselves) but they were more typically employed in financing trade transactions by

Nakarattars and non-Nakarattars, alike. Tun Wai (1962: 50), a Burmese banking authority, estimates that in Burma, before 1930, perhaps 75 percent of Nakarattar *hundi*s were trade *hundi*s. In such cases, a paddy merchant, for example, bought a shipment of paddy at a local market in Burma with cash that he transferred to the seller by drawing a *hundi* on his account in a local Nakarattar banking office. The Nakarattar banker encashed the *hundi*, receiving a discounting fee of 1–3 percent, and took custody of the railroad receipt for the paddy shipment, even though the transaction was not a loan and did not incur rates of interest charged on loans. The banker sent the *hundi* and the receipt to his firm's main office in Rangoon along with instructions to debit the merchant's account. If the banker had no office in Rangoon, he sent the *hundi* and receipt to another banker (perhaps, but not necessarily, an *adathi*) with whom he maintained an account. The first banker could thus rediscount the *hundi* with the second banker who normally extended the service without charging a further discounting fee. In order to regain the railway receipt and take possession of his paddy from either banker, the merchant had to maintain a deposit account with the Rangoon banker in a satisfactory manner.

Chettiars made use of four basic *hundi*s:

1 *Dharshan hundi*s or demand drafts (literally, "sight" *hundi*s) were payable against a *kadai kanakku* account within a three-day grace period of presentation to a person and at a place specified in the *hundi*.

2 *Nadappu hundi*s (literally, "walking" *hundi*s), were also payable against a *kadai kanakku* account. *Nadappu hundi*s were instruments unique to Chettiars and were neither demand drafts nor fixed-period term drafts but, instead, were discounted at the convenience of the drawee, whose only obligation was to pay interest at the *nadappu* rate until he chose to encash them.

3 *Thavanai hundi*s (literally, "resting" *hundi*s) were payable against *thavanai* accounts and operated like short-term certificates of deposit. The banks (the drawees) need not pay on demand until after the specified date, usually sixty to ninety days after the bill was drawn. Their term to maturity was called a *thavanai*, a "period of rest."

4 *Pay order hundi*s were used as receipts given in lieu of dowry payments made during a marriage ceremony. They were drawn against special compound interest bearing *thavanai* accounts known as an *accimar panam* accounts.

Available information about these *hundi*s, however, is generally confusing and inconsistent, especially for *dharshan* and *nadappu hundi*s. For example, although most authorities suggest that all Nakarattar demand drafts paid interest at the *nadappu* rate, examination of sample *hundi*s reproduced in the Report of the Madras Provincial Banking Enquiry Committee reveals a subset of *dharshan hundi*s that paid no interest.

In fact, this inconsistency is less problematic than the suggestion that both *dharshan* and *nadappu hundi*s paid same interest at the *nadappu* rate. If it was the case that no *dharshan hundi* paid interest, people would have paid the *dharshan* discount fee only if they wanted to transfer capital and guarantee encashment at their convenience rather than that of their bankers. They would have drawn *nadappu hundi*s if they had no expectation of any cash flow crisis, if they viewed their *nadappu* deposits as safe interest-bearing deposits, and if they had no worries about their banker's ultimate ability and willingness to cash the *hundi*. The fact is, however, that some *dharshan hundi*s did pay interest. Their availability creates a puzzle because the liquidity of *dharshan hundi*s would have eliminated any incentive to draw *nadappu hundi*s with an identical yield but with uncertain conditions of encashment. One possible solution is that Nakarattar bankers may have had sufficient control over mechanisms for transferring funds to withhold *dharshan hundi*s from clients and, instead, offered *nadappu hundi*s as the only available option. Another and even more likely solution is that the drawing of *hundi*s was quite a flexible matter and hinged on the specific situation of the drawer and the drawee. This would account for inconsistency on the part of analysts attempting to construct a uniform model of Nakarattar *hundi*s.

The kind of flexibility that seems to be suggested by the evidence of *hundi*s themselves raises another problem, however, because Nakarattar bankers also offered clients facilities for drawing sixty to ninety-day *thavanai* deposits. It is not clear why anyone should wish to deposit their money at the lower *nadappu* rate of interest unless they were assured of definite repayment more quickly than the terms to maturity offered by *thavanai hundi*s. We can only assume that the actual performance of Nakarattar bankers confirmed their financial trustworthiness and ability to meet demands for repayment without causing unacceptable cost or delay.

*Hundi*s were not regulated under colonial laws concerning negotiable instruments and were distinguished from "true" bills of exchange on the ground that their terms of encashment were not unconditionally specified. In general, they specified two conditions of payment: (1) they indicated the particular fund which the drawer was to reimburse or a particular account that was to be debited with the amount and (2) they included a statement of the transaction that gave rise to the bill. In addition, *nadappu hundi*s specified no obligatory conditions for encashment, whatsoever. Because of the former stipulations and the absence of stipulations about payment in the case of *nadappu hundi*s, all Nakarattar *hundi*s fell outside the scope of the Negotiable Instruments Act, and hence they were legally unenforceable (BPBER 1930: 150; Krishnan 1959: 53; MPBEC 1930 I: 51–2).

In spite of this, it is important not to invest the legal view of *hundi*s as nonnegotiable with more significance than it deserves, especially if that view coincides with an unclear understanding about the sanctions and procedures under which *hundi*s were actually drawn. Although Nakarattar *hundi*s had no standing in a court of law, Nakarattar bankers made collective decisions about interest rates that standardized the cost of credit. In addition, their own communal tribunals (*pan-chayat*s) and their practice of maintaining custody of railway and shipping receipts on trade *hundi*s kept a check on dishonest practices. In other words, together with careful accounting procedures and a practice of systematic correspondence among cooperating bankers, the various collective, Nakarattar institutions effectively regulated transactions and minimized the risk of default to a remarkable extent. Indeed, one banking expert whose personal knowledge of the system allowed him to keep the law in perspective notes:

In the case of 136 firms doing business in Chettinad to the extent of 11 crores of rupees [Rs. 110,000,000] the bad debts come to only Rs. 4.3 lakhs [Rs. 430,000] which works out to 1/2% on the total volume of business. (Krishnan 1959: 41)

Nakarattar Accounting

The scale of Nakarattar banking was enormous and various banking inquiry committees devoted considerable effort to estimating just how much money Nakarattars collectively owned and controlled (Rudner 1994: 69–73). While the resulting estimates vary wildly, even the most generous estimates miss the true financial power of Nakarattar banking by failing to carry out a dynamic analysis of the velocity of Nakarattar credit transfers or the creation of money by making carefully timed loans on marginal reserves. While it is not possible to carry out such an analysis here, a close look at Nakarattar accounting techniques offers a glimpse into the powerful resources of the Nakarattar banking system. The following discussion is based on analysis of account books maintained by a large Burmese agency for the years 1912–1915 and 1918–1921. I refer to these books primarily to describe Nakarattar accounting categories and the sources of capital available to a Nakarattar agency. I do not use them to characterize the specific financial role of this firm (let alone of Nakarattars taken collectively) in the context of Burmese and Nakarattar commercial history.

Nakarattar account books were designed to accomplish many functions. One book, called *peredu*, recorded all payments and receipts. An informant claimed that the book utilized a general ledger and that it employed double-entry bookkeeping. I am not prepared to grant the accuracy of these English glosses of a technical Tamil accounting vocabulary, as they do not, in fact, appear to comply with the principles of double-entry bookkeeping. This *peredu* seemed to consist of a number of subsidiary ledgers, describing various transactions and listing the associated payments or receipts in two separate columns: one for credit entries (*adhaya*) and the other for debit entries (*varavu*). Unlike a double-entry bookkeeping system, however, each transaction was recorded as a single entry. There was no additional, simultaneous entry crediting or debiting the agency's cash account in the same amount. Instead, the two columns of figures describing each account seem to provide a way of correlating the expenses incurred by the account with the income it generated. In some cases, this gives the appearance of a standard, Western-style double-entry (i.e., where credits equal debits). But this is purely accidental or else it reflects some real-world understanding that existed between the banker and the client rather than a bookkeeping procedure.

Since this is a point about which there is some confusion, it is worth emphasizing that a *peredu*'s debit and credit entries seem to represent clearly separate transactions and frequently showed a net difference between credits and debits. Nevertheless, its correlation of income and expenses incurred by an account may be what my informant meant by double-entry bookkeeping. It is also the case that each column of figures recorded in the *peredu* maintained a running total and provided a final net balance for each year. But I could locate no general ledger summarizing all of the various transactions, or any overall balance sheet. In other words, the *peredu* lacked the defining characteristics of a Western-style general ledger.

In general, the function of Nakarattar account books was to provide a picture of an agency's relationship with each of its clients, with separate listings of expenses and revenues. This function served the interests of both the agent and his client. Entries were carefully made on the occasion of any financial transaction, rather like a passbook in an American savings bank. In some cases, they were even initialed by the client. In any case, the information these ledgers contained could, in principle, have been pulled together into a general ledger and a balance sheet. But they were not. Rather, they seem to consist of different kinds of subsidiary ledger (Table 2.2) apparently contained in the *peredu* of a Burmese agency house.[11]

Proprietor's Capital and Deposit Capital from Other Nakarattars

Before I present my analysis of Nakarattar accounting categories, it is important to emphasize a crucial distinction between *governmental* classifications of total Nakarattar assets and Nakarattar accounting categories employed as part of individual business operations. This distinction is important because most analyses of Nakarattar capital are concerned with the former and base their classifications on testimony and interviews with members of the Madras, Rangoon, or Colombo Nattukottai Nakarattar Associations, presented to various Provincial Banking Enquiry Committees around 1930. In general, these documents estimate that the ratio of Nakarattar "borrowed capital" to "own capital" ranged between 15 and 35 percent (Rudner 1994). Burmese banking authority, Tun Wai (1962: 42), however, suggests that Nakarattar liabilities in pre-Depression and post-Depression Burma actually represented 60 percent of all their capital in 1929 and 84 percent in 1935. The point I wish to emphasize here, however, is that Tun Wai's (along with the various banking inquiry committees)

---

[11] For my own provisional general ledger and balance sheet based on the agency's account books, see Rudner (1994). In addition to their *peredu* accounts, Nakarattars maintained additional sets of books used for other purposes. Again, see Rudner (1994).

Table 2.2 *Summary statements for subsidiary ledgers in a* peredu *account book of a Nakarattar agency in Rangoon, 1915–1919*

Subsidiary ledger	Credit	Debit
1 Auspicious credits in the name of various deities (expense: cash paid to deities' accounts)	23	23
2 Capital remitted from overseas headquarters	21,000	21,000
3 *Adhaya-Varavu* (profit and loss account; a net receipt after deducting interest payments due by the business on deposits kept, primarily interest receipts)	74,649	74,649
4 No entry (salary summaries)	–	–
5 Capital remitted to overseas headquarters	20,877	20,877
6 Interest payments and miscellaneous expenses	51,515	51,515
7 Long-term deposits of Nakarattars (thirty-four clients)	75,262	75,262
8 Fixed assets purchased during the year	57	57
9 Charitable expenses	216	216
10 Firm's business expenses in Cambodia	3,656	3,656
11 Short-term (two-month) deposits (156 clients)	–	–
12 Firm's business in Maniyuva branch	70,377	69,077
13 Local Nakara Dandayuthapani Temple accounts and deposits by other Nakarattar firms on behalf of various temples	6,545	6,545
14 Deposits kept by Nemam Temple	77,300	77,300
15 Deposits from Burmese and Chinese "VIPs" and from Indian friends (many of these bear no interest)	–	–
16 Other current accounts (demand deposits)	–	–

was focused primarily on the overall role of the Nakarattars in Burma. He was not concerned with the kinds of distinction that Nakarattars made in accounting categories used by individual businessmen. This is because Tun Wai was not describing the capital structure of an individual agency or firm, but the aggregate capital of the entire caste's operations in Burma.

By contrast, as Tun Wai notes, Nakarattar businessmen do need to maintain accounts of individual transactions and they are careful to distinguish between the proprietors' own capital (*mudal panam*) and deposits by close relatives (*sontha thavanai panam*). Indeed, it is clear from information contained in Nakarattar account books and from interviews with surviving Nakarattar bankers that there are major differences between aggregate classifications of Nakarattar assets provided to banking enquiry committees and the nonaggregated classification of liabilities that Nakarattars employed in their own account books. One of the most significant differences reflects precisely the importance of different kinds of reserve deposit with different terms to maturity, just among Nakarattars themselves. The Nakarattar system of interfirm depositing in effect created a single corporate bank with branch offices wherever Nakarattars did business.

All my informants confirm Tun Wai's interpretation of *mudal panam* as confined in its application just to proprietor's capital and *sontha thavanai panam* as an umbrella term for deposits from any kinsman (*contakkarar*). In addition, however, bankers whom I consulted used the term *mempanam* ("surplus funds") as an even more embracing umbrella category to refer to any deposit besides the proprietor's own *mudal panam*. This included deposits by relatives such as *accimar panam* (dowry deposits from in-laws) and dowry deposits from any other Nakarattar outside the joint family (*valavu*) that owned the firm. In addition, *mempanam* also included subcategories of deposits from non-kin Nakarattars and from non-Nakarattars, including the following:[12]

1 Principal's personal funds (*mutal panam*).
2 All other funds (*mempanam*):
   (a) *accimar panam*: literally, deposits from Nakarattar women usually dowry monies of wife and daughters-in-law of the proprietor, that is, from his affinal relatives (*tayati*)
   (b) *tanatu murai panam*: deposits from other Nakarattars including agnatic relatives from the proprietor's lineage (*kuttikkira pankali*) and clan (*kovil*), nonkin from his own and neighboring villages, etc.
   (c) *kovil panankal* or *dharma panankal*: deposits from Nakarattar controlled or influenced temples, etc.
   (d) *atathi katai panam*: loans from Nakarattar "parent banks" (*atathis*)
   (e) deposits from Burmese or Chinese clients
   (f) *vellaikkaran panam*: loans from European banks; available to only 3 to 4 percent of Nakarattar bankers, that is, the largest *atathi*s or parent banks.

---

[12] Source: Somalay Interview, March 25, 1981.

If we isolate entries for the *mempanam* deposits in the *peredu* available to me (corresponding to its items 1, 7, 13, and 14 in Table 2.2) and compare them with entries credited to the proprietor's headquarters' account (item 2), the lesson is startling. In this agency, at least, *mutal panam* – the proprietor's own capital – did not constitute 65–85 percent of its sources of funds, as it would have if there was a direct correspondence between, on one hand, the proportion of aggregate Nakarattar-owned funds to all Nakarattar working capital in Burma and, on the other hand, the proportion of an individual proprietor's own capital contribution to the working capital of his agency house. Instead, the proprietor's funds in this specific agency were barely 12.5 percent the amount of funds deposited by his relatives.

In other words, based on the evidence for this particular banking firm, Nakarattar proprietors generally contributed 10–20 percent of the working capital of their agency offices in the form of long-term *thavanai* deposits. These were frequently repaid to the proprietor during the course of his agent's three-year contract in a sequence of regular remittances. Conventions for financial transactions between a banking agency and its other clients also depended on maintenance of deposit accounts with the agency. According to KV Krishnan (1959: 125), and here we are speaking of deposits made to individual banking agencies, non-Nakarattar deposits made up, at most, another 20 percent of an agency's working capital. In other words, considering the proprietor's own deposits (*mutal panam*) and various kinds of non-Nakarattar deposits, it is possible to estimate the proportion of working capital contributed by deposit from other Nakarattar firms as between 60 and 80 percent of all deposits. Again, this is supported by books from the Burmese agency analyzed above.

One final feature of Nakarattar financial transactions should also be noted in connection with the distinction between Nakarattar and non-Nakarattar clients. In the case of their non-Nakarattar clients, transactions were always recorded on a cash basis; that is, only actual cash receipts and disbursements were entered in a firm's ledger. By contrast, transactions between Nakarattars (including the proprietor and his agency) were recorded on a mercantile or accrual basis; that is, they credited one another with the appropriate amount of interest due and exchanged *vatti chitti* sheets (memoranda of interest calculations). The accounts they held with one another were normally reconciled only at

three-year intervals, coinciding with the termination of a Nakarattar
agent's tenure as head of a banking agency.

Caste-Based Banking in the Bazaar

Organized banking underwent massive changes in India and around
the world over the course of the twentieth century. Some of the largest
Nakarattar firms reinvented themselves as modern, Western-style, joint
stock companies or assumed their Western trappings while nevertheless
retaining control. But, by and large, the Nakarattar deposit banking
system had all but disappeared from South and certainly Southeast
Asian credit markets by the time the Reserve Bank of India was established in 1935. As a consequence, and indeed, even before then, the
majority of Nakarattar businessmen had already begun to lose easy
access to the collective resources of their own caste. Research remains
to be done that would measure the degree to which, over the course of
the twentieth century, elite Nakarattars effectively alienated what had
been a vast, liquid pool of communal capital by investing it in proprietary, fixed-capital industrial ventures from textiles mills to steel rolling
plants to cinema studios and movies. But regardless of the caste's
business trajectory subsequently, it is undeniable that Nakarattars
played a significant role in South and Southeast Asian banking and
commerce, prior to the rise of state-regulated banking in 1935.

They did so by organizing themselves into a complex, segmentary
network of interdependent family business firms. Each firm dealt
individually in commodities trading, moneylending, domestic and
overseas banking operations, or industrial investment. But beyond
this – making possible every other commercial venture in which it
engaged – each family firm operated as a commercial bank: taking
money on deposit and drafting *hundi*s and other financial instruments for use in the transfer of loanable capital to branch offices
and to other banks. As a result, every Nakarattar firm was tied
together with all of the others to form a unified banking system,
playing a major role in the credit markets of South Asia and the
Indian Ocean rim.

Unlike modern Western banking systems that rely on government-
controlled, central banks, Nakarattars constructed kinship-cum-
commercial relationships based on reputation, record of financial decisions, and maintenance of reserve deposits by family firms linked

according to caste-defined social relationships based on business territory, residential location, descent, marriage, and common cult membership. As a consequence, individual Nakarattars operated as representatives of the caste as a whole and not as isolated businessmen limited to the resources of a single-family firm. In other words, the Nakarattar banking system was a caste-based banking system. Individual Nakarattars organized their lives around the participation and management of various communal institutions adapted to the task of accumulating and distributing reserves of capital. The financial transactions in which they engaged created an ensemble of social relations that constituted the Nakarattars as a particular kind of community: a financial community that functioned as both a caste and a bank within the wider Indian society.

References

Abu-Lughod, J 1989, *Before European Hegemony: The World System A.D. 1250–1350*, Oxford University Press, Oxford.

Adas, M 1974, *The Burma Delta: Economic Development and Social Change on an Asian Rice Frontier 1812–1941*, University of Wisconsin, Madison.

Appadurai, A 1986, "Is Homo Hierarchicus?," *American Ethnologist*, 13, 4, 745–61.

Birla R 2009, *Stages of Capital: Law, Culture, and Market Governance in Late Colonial India*, Duke University Press, Durham.

Bose, S 2006, *A Hundred Horizons: The Indian Ocean in the Age of Global Empire*, Harvard University Press, Cambridge.

Burmese Provincial Banking Enquiry Committee (BPBEC) 1930 *Report. Volume I, Banking and Credit in Burma, Volume II, Written and Oral Evidence*, Rangoon.

Dale, SF 1994, *Indian Merchants and Eurasian Trade, 1600–1750*, Cambridge University Press, Cambridge and New York.

Geertz, C 1963, *Peddlers and Princes: Social Development and Economic Change in Two Indonesian Towns*, University of Chicago Press, Chicago.

Geertz, C 1978, "The Bazaar Economy: Information and Search in Peasant Marketing," *American Economic Review*, 68, 2, 28–32.

Geertz, C 1979, "Suq: The Bazaar Economy in Sefrou," in C Geertz, H Geertz, & L Rosen (eds.) *Meaning and Order in Moroccan Society. Three Essays in Cultural Analysis*, Cambridge University Press, Cambridge.

Guha, S 2013, *Beyond Caste: Identity and Power in South Asia, Past and Present*, Brill, Leiden.

Hart, K 1973, "Informal Income Opportunities and Urban Employment in Ghana," *Journal of Modern African Studies*, 11, 3, 61–89.

Hart, K 1985, "The Informal Economy," *Cambridge Journal of Anthropology*, 10, 2, 54–8.

Hart, K 2014, "Informality: Problem or Solution?," Presentation at the World Bank PSD Forum 2006, Washington DC, 4–6 April, The Memory Bank. A New Commonwealth – Ver 5.0.

Krishnan, V 1959, *Indigenous Banking in South India*. Bombay State Cooperative Union, Bombay.

Levi, SC 2002, *The Indian Diaspora in Central Asia and Its Trade, 1550–1900*, Brill, Leiden.

Madras Provincial Banking Enquiry Committee (MPBEC) 1930, *Volume I, Report, Volumes II–IV, Written and Oral Evidence*, Madras.

Markovits, C 2000, *The Global World of Indian Merchants, 1750–1947: Traders of Sind from Bukhara to Panama*, Cambridge University Press, Cambridge and New York.

Pillai, AS 1930, "Monograph on Nattukkottai Chettis Banking Business," *MBPEC*, I: 1170–217.

Ray, R 1988, "The Bazaar: Changing Structural Characteristics of the Indigenous Section of the Indian Economy before and after the Great Depression," *Indian Economic Social History Review*, 25: 263.

Ray, R 1994, "Introduction," *Entrepreneurship and Industry in India, 1800–1947*, Oxford University Press, Delhi, 1–69.

Ray, R 1995, "Asian Capital in the Age of European Domination: the Rise of the Bazaar, 1800–1914," *Modern Asian Studies*, 29, 3, 449–554.

Rudner, D 1987, "Religious Gifting and Inland Commerce in Pre-Colonial South India," *Journal of Asian Studies*, 46, 2, 361–79.

Rudner, D 1989, "Banker's Trust and the Culture of Banking Among the Nattukottai Chettiars of Colonial South India," *Modern Asian Studies*, 23, 3, 417–58.

Rudner, D 1990, "Inquest on Dravidian Kinship: Louis Dumont and the Essence of Marriage Alliance," *Contributions to Indian Sociology*, 24, 2, 153–74.

Rudner, D 1994, *Caste and Capitalism in Colonial India. The Nattukottai Chettiars*, University of California Press, Berkeley.

Rudner, D 1997, "Re-exhuming Dravidian Kinship: A Response to Parkin," *Contributions to Indian Sociology*, 31, 2, 299–311.

Rudner, D 2011, "Merchant Castes," *Oxford University Online Dictionary of Hinduism*.

Somalay, 1981, Interview by author, Chennai, March 25.

Tun Wai, U 1962, *Burma's Currency and Credit*, Department of Economics, University of Rangoon, Rangoon.

Washbrook, D 1973, "Country Politics: Madras, 1880–1930," in J Gallagher, G Johnson, & A Seal (eds.) *Locality, Province and Nation: Essays on Indian Politics, 1870–1940*, Cambridge University Press, Cambridge.

Washbrook, D 1975, "The Development of Caste Organization in South India, 1880–1925," in CJ Baker & DA Washbrook (eds.) *South India: Political Institutions and Political Change, 1880–1940*, Macmillan Company of India Ltd, New Delhi.

Weersooria, WS 1973, *The Nattukkottai Chettiars: Merchant Bankers in Ceylon*, Tisara Prakasakayo, Dehiwala.

3 | Space in Motion: An Uneven Narrative of Urban Private Property in Bombay

NIKHIL RAO[1]

> Any analogy drawn from the historical land tenures of India proper would be unsafe, and the land tenures of Bombay must be treated on a separate footing.[2]

Introduction

In an article written in 1995, shortly after liberalization reforms were announced in India, *The Economist* characterized Bombay (present-day Mumbai) as "the most expensive slum in the world."[3] The slummy character of the city was attributed to the failure of the city's property market to function efficiently. Still more specifically, the magazine attributed the failure of the property market to a set of "absurd" regulations that "profited the very few and hurt the very many." These included an all-India land ceiling regulation dating from 1976 that capped the area of land that any individual could hold in any particular city at 500 square meters; a rent control law dating from 1947 that froze rents on existing buildings at 1940 levels and that restricted rent increases on new constructions to a modest "standard rent"; and a set of labor laws that made it difficult for employers in struggling industries to lay off workers, shut down the factories, and sell off the land, which could then be used for other purposes such as housing.

---

[1] I'm grateful to the editors of this volume for their comments on draft versions of this chapter. I'm also grateful to Shree Chandrashekhar Chore, then AMC-Estates, for permission to consult records in the reading room of the Estates Department, Municipal Corporation of Greater Mumbai.
[2] From the judgement of Justice Scott, in the case of *Shapurji Jivanji vs the Collector of Bombay*, (1885) ILR 9 BOM 483, para. 9.
[3] The most expensive slum in the world, *The Economist*, 335, 7913 (May 6, 1995): 35–6.

In *The Economist*'s view, such regulations infringed on the logic of property markets, hampering the workings of supply and demand, and the policy corrective would be to disembed the market from these obfuscating regulations.[4] And indeed, the state in India – and specifically in Bombay – has gone a long way toward embracing precisely these steps. The Land Ceiling Act was repealed in the 2000s, rent restriction laws were weakened in 1999, and labor laws were weakened or subverted to permit land use conversion. Further, the state has explicitly turned to the market to address the problem of slums and housing more generally, relabeling itself as a "facilitator" – rather than a "provider" – of housing.

Despite these measures, the problems of high prices compounded by inadequate services and infrastructure identified by *The Economist* in 1995 appear, if anything, to have gotten worse. The predicament of growing inequality in increasingly unlivable cities has generated a large body of scholarship seeking to understand the present-day city.[5] Such scholarship, too, accords tremendous explanatory power to the forces of "the market," and more generally to "neoliberalism" and the sweeping changes brought about by this arrangement of politics and economics. A shared feature of such scholarship is the assertion that neoliberalism – specifically the turn away from the state and to "the market" – unleashes depredatory forces that unyoke the economic sphere from broader cultural and social contexts, many of the latter of which were formed during the decades of the planned and centralized economy of independent India.[6] In different ways, thus, supporters of liberal market reforms, state bureaucrats, and critics of the neoliberal agenda all rely on understandings of "the market," and

[4] I am using "disembedding" in a slightly modified sense from the way it is used by Chris Hann, who in turn draws on the work of Karl Polanyi to characterize the liberal fantasy of the self-regulating market. In Polanyi's account, liberalism's endeavor in the nineteenth century was to disembed the market from social and cultural contexts (Hann 1998: 1–47, 2007: 287–318). In the accounts provided by Hann and other anthropologist scholars, especially those of the former Eastern Bloc, the work of neoliberalism amounts to a new disembedding process, this time from the strictures of the command economy.

[5] Weinstein (2014) is one example of a large body of scholarship that seeks to understand the present-day city from the perspective of housing.

[6] For an account that challenges the conventional view that the 1991 reforms in India were "pro-market," see Kohli (2006). Kohli argues that these reforms were, rather, pro-business, and should be understood as having begun in 1980 rather than in 1991.

specifically the property market, in their analyses of the present urban predicament.

At the same time, some scholars argue that property ownership is the implicit condition of citizenship in Indian cities under neoliberalism.[7] Even slum redevelopment schemes have as their desired outcome the transformation of "squatters" into "owners" of property, rather than renters.[8] "Property" and "market" are thus two terms that enjoy extraordinary significance in contemporary discussions of the urban predicament. Yet both these terms have lengthy, problematic, and interconnected histories in South Asia, especially in the case of colonial port cities such as Bombay, Calcutta (present-day Kolkata), and Madras (present-day Chennai), which, as bridgeheads of British presence in the subcontinent, had long histories dating from well before British hegemony was established.

If neoliberal state policies currently attempt to disembed the property market, this would not be the first time such a thing has been attempted. Indeed, a great project of the colonial state in the nineteenth and early twentieth centuries was to create a market in landed property. Much of the efforts of the state were directed towards agrarian lands; historical scholarship, therefore, has been less attentive to the question of the colonial state's attitudes and endeavors in the arena of urban lands and property. As Anish Vanaik has noted, even though it is widely acknowledged that property ownership was a crucial factor in the emergence of Indian claims to representation and self-determination in the urban realm in Bombay, and that landlords played a dominant role in the municipal realm of the early twentieth century, the basis of landlords' power – landed property and the property market – has not been much analyzed.[9]

[7] See the Introduction to a special issue of the *Journal of South Asian Development* on urban property in India (de Neve and Donner 2015: 255–66, esp. 255).
[8] Vinit Mukhija's work gives a detailed account of how this process is supposed to work in Mumbai (Mukhija 2003, 2016: 125–39). Ursula Rao's work explicitly explores slum redevelopment, the desired goal of property ownership, and implications for urban citizenship for the city's non-elites (U Rao 2010, 402–24, 2013: 760–79). For an analysis that shows how the meaning of private property rights are contested and transformed in such slum redevelopment programs, see Raman (2015: 369–95).
[9] Anish Vanaik, "Introduction," *Possessing the City: Property and Politics in Delhi, 1911–47* (book manuscript, no page numbers). I am grateful to the author for sharing his book manuscript, forthcoming from Oxford University Press in late 2019.

This chapter explores the emergence of landed property in Bombay as a site of value and exchange. It considers the long history of land and revenue in Bombay, beginning with the accession of Bombay to British rule in the late seventeenth century. My aim is not to survey this long history but rather to identify key moments and transitions in the emergence of property as a commodity. Mariam Dossal's work is the most significant book to trace the colonial state's efforts to create a capitalist land market in Bombay (Dossal 2010). She has identified the problems posed for this project by the "maze of tenures" (Dossal 2010: 11) to be found in Bombay: the complicated landholding arrangements that conferred different kinds of rights onto occupants and that confounded the East India Company's efforts to establish exactly what rights *it* had, even though Bombay was supposedly its possession. (And which prompted Justice Scott to make the extraordinary pronouncement in his judgement, which forms the epigraph to this chapter.) In Dossal's account, these tenures were obstacles to be negotiated by the colonial state in relentless pursuit of a land market.

This chapter extends Dossal's argument and argues that the colonial state had a shifting and occasionally even ambivalent position on private property. While undoubtedly there was an effort to create a land market based on the idea of private property, this imperative contended with and occasionally was trumped by another factor: the legacy of the colonial state's efforts to establish its hegemony in the late seventeenth and eighteenth centuries precisely by arguing that *all* of Bombay was the property of the Company, and that all landholders were occupying their lands at the pleasure of the Company. This tension within the idea of property endured and shaped the most decisive phase of the colonial state's effort to create a property market in the city: the Bombay Improvement Trust's effort to acquire vast swathes of land and impose a planned vision. Central to this vision was the desire to reorganize land into a grid of plots: with its sharp, clearly defined edges, and its temporal horizons determined by a strictly defined lease, the plot was the spatial and temporal realization of the effort to disembed land from social and cultural contexts and render it a free-floating, unencumbered commodity.

The plot as commodity represented an effort by the Improvement Trust to flatten out the history of land and to create a sort of Year Zero. The leaseholds under which these plots were alienated were designed to offer the security of private property, and thus were supposed to facilitate the functioning of a robust market for lands. Rather than see the Improvement Trust's efforts as the culmination of a teleological account of the colonial state's efforts to create private property, this chapter underscores the uneven and often contradictory nature of the state's and other actors' views on private property. Above all, this chapter draws attention to the ways in which the changing character of lands at the urban edge in relation to the growing city led the state and other actors to strategically assume positions either embracing the modern property form or rejecting it in favor of a longstanding customary tenure. Put differently, at various times, specific proprietary rights appeared to have greater significance than others in such a way as to suggest that the notion of private property was – and remains – highly context specific. For instance, in some contexts the privilege of being secured from reassessment by the state was paramount, while, in other settings, the ability to alienate land proved more significant. In a very fundamental sense, this chapter argues that understanding property requires renewed attentiveness to the temporal dimension, to the fact that cities expand and evolve over time to encompass agrarian lands at the edge, and that the urbanization process should therefore be understood as *space in motion*.

Land Before Private Property

The origins of colonial rule – and the emerging understanding of the English East India Company of itself as a sovereign – were bound up with clarifying the nature of property. A brief survey of the early history of Bombay indicates as much since the preeminent question on the minds of British officers was determining and establishing what rights they had over their new possession.[10] When Bombay was handed over to the British by the Portuguese in 1661, early British efforts to claim possession of the territory were rebuffed by the Portuguese under various pretexts. Even after the British finally did gain possession in 1665, it remained to be established what exactly "possession" meant, because the Portuguese Viceroy in Goa had imposed stringent terms

[10] My account of the early tenures of Bombay in this section draws upon the pioneering revenue history written by D R Vaidya for its temporal framework (Vaidya 1948 [1914]: i–xlvi).

determining who may or may not be taxed, who may reside in the territory, and so on (Dossal 2010: 9–10; Vaidya 1948 [1914]: 4).

The terms of the Charter by which the English East India Company took control of Bombay from the Crown mandated that the Company held the territory in a fashion "as of the manor of East Greenwich," which also meant that no sale of any part of the territory was permitted (Warden 1814: para. 14). The burden of truly asserting Company sovereignty continued to rest on the latter's questionable ability to tax the occupants of Bombay, the landholders among whom held land under a Portuguese tenure called "Pension and Tax." An early effort to investigate the titles of various landholders – and thereby establish the Company's rights to reassess the tax due – provoked such distress and discontent that the city's Indian and Portuguese inhabitants offered to pay an annual supplement to the old quit rent that had been paid to the Portuguese, on condition that their titles not be further investigated (Warden 1814: paras. 28–9). Terms of occupancy were finally settled via the agreement of 1672 known as Aungier's Convention, which essentially regularized the existing landholdings and recognized landholders' right to pay customary dues "notwithstanding any defect of Title."[11] By the terms of the Convention, the Pension and Tax landholders, a certain class of whom were also known as "Fazendars," were recognized as secure from reassessment.

While the Fazendari landholders from the Portuguese period thus exercised great influence over certain parts of the Bombay territory, the British reserved for themselves the area that subsequently became the Fort, as well as proprietary rights over the foreshore lands and over waste and uncultivated lands. Over the course of the eighteenth century, the Company, seeking to increase revenues from the islands, invited various communities to settle in Bombay. Parsi merchants from Surat settled within the Fort, while weavers from Bassein, goldsmiths and blacksmiths from Surat, and other artisans settled in the areas just outside the Fort, which became the native town. These were often settled on a form of tenure known as quit rent. Meanwhile, cultivating communities such as Kunbis and Bhandaris were invited

---

[11] From the twelve articles proposed by *Fazendars* (landholders) of Bombay and accepted by the British as part of Aungier's Convention in 1672, cited in Dossal (2010: 23).

to settle the uncultivated lands – many of which were claimed from the sea through the building of breaches to keep sea tides out. Such tenures were named after the kind of produce that the land yielded: for instance, the land reclaimed from the sea as a result of closing the "Great Breach" on the west of the islands yielded a certain coarse rice termed "salt batty," and hence was named "salt batty" land or *Foras* tenure. (The Portuguese term *Foras* originally referred to the dues paid by holders of Portuguese-era tenures but appears to have changed in meaning by the nineteenth century to refer specifically to such "salt batty" lands.) The assessment on these lands was initially waived entirely, and then set at a very low rate for most of the eighteenth century. Lands in the north of the island yielded a superior type of rice known as "sweet batty" and were referred to as *Toka* lands after the term for the customary rent on such rice, payable in kind. Additionally, three large grants of land – *Inam*s – were made at various points in the eighteenth and nineteenth centuries to various members of the Wadia family in recognition of services rendered by them. Such *inami* lands were free of assessment. Still other lands were granted by the English East India Company in the 1820s and 1830s as *sanad*s – revocable and reassessable – to facilitate settlement and expansion of the city outside the Fort walls. These last two tenures were instances where the Company issued new tenures in Bombay city that were based on older Maratha forms of holding.[12] Various incentives were offered to attract settlement, including protection from aggressors, freedom of religion, and, importantly, lax building regulations (Dossal 2010: 34–6). The agrarian origins of such lands would prove to have significance as urban settlement expanded into these areas over the course of the late nineteenth and twentieth centuries, and these substantial swathes of land were converted into urban property.

Throughout the eighteenth century, thus, the British in Bombay were subject to a pair of contradictory imperatives that would go on to have significant implications for emerging ideas of property. On the one hand, the British were anxious to establish their sovereignty. Securing their ability to reassess lands and even to resume lands as needed constituted a defining feature of what it meant to be sovereign. On

[12] Vaidya (1948 [1914]) offers a brief account of the specific nature of each tenure, from which my account is drawn. Dossal 2010: 34–6 provides an account of the Company's efforts to attract various settlers.

the other hand, the British were also motivated to attract settlement and promote economic activity, an imperative that compelled them to recognize older privileges of Portuguese tenure holders, extend new privileges on favorable terms, and, in general, refrain from asserting their sovereignty in too assertive fashion.

The contradictory compulsions of the two imperatives described above were underscored in a pair of pronouncements in the early nineteenth century, when the East Indian Company, now in a significantly stronger position than a century earlier, sought to assert its hold over Bombay as the city emerged as command center for the Company's empire in western India. The first comprehensive survey of the city was underway, and an important objective of this was to establish the Company's right to reassess and resume lands held under the various tenures to be found in Bombay. Captain Thomas Dickinson, the officer in charge of the survey, submitted his report on the tenures to be found in the Fort area in 1813, and argued that the Company as sovereign retained the right to reassess and resume quit rent lands and to reassess Pension and Tax lands to be found in the Fort. When this report was passed on to government for remarks, the occasion led Francis Warden, Chief Secretary to Government, to issue a detailed set of observations on the tenures. Warden disagreed with Dickinson and argued that although these lands had been Crown lands, nonetheless the "custom of the manor" had "converted public into private property" (Warden 1814: para. 69). In other words, Warden argued that the land had transformed from a feudal tenure into private property. He went on to establish this by showing that initially the holders of land had been obliged to provide military services to the sovereign when called on; beginning in 1718, however, this obligation to provide military service was replaced by a cash payment called a "quit rent," intended to reimburse the Company for expenses incurred in construction of fortifications and other defensive measures. Further, the fact that government had invited people to settle there had signaled to landholders, argued Warden, that the lands could be held in perpetuity.

In general, Warden upheld the rights of improving occupants over the rights of the sovereign, partly on pragmatic grounds and partly on principle.[13] He was especially critical of the Company's announcements

---

[13] Basing his conclusion on a seventeenth-century description of cultivated lands in Bombay by John Fryer, Warden went so far as to argue that much more of the

of intent to reassess and resume land over the course of the eighteenth century, which remained threats and were not actually executed. Such empty threats had the effect, he argued, "instead of operating the effect intended of recovering the Company's rights, [instead to] have produced a result directly opposite of weakening their claims, and of legalizing those of individuals" (Warden 1814: para. 86). Proceeding from principle, Warden argued that an increase in revenue to be gained by reassessments on land would be more than offset by the dampening effect such reassessment would have on economic activity (Warden 1814: para. 236). For Warden, the state's revenues could be better enhanced by keeping ground rents low, and thus encouraging economic activity.

Meanwhile, at around the same time, Hugh Munro, the collector of land revenue, was seeking to assert the interests of the Company over the landholders of the *Foras* lands being cultivated by Kunbi cultivators. According to Munro, these cultivators had been taking liberties over the decades that were not permitted to them. Many had constructed buildings and other structures, and some of these lands were now being used for purposes other than cultivation. Many had also proceeded to alienate and mortgage the lands, which they were not supposedly allowed to do. Still more confusingly, multiple occupants of a single holding, usually family members, each felt authorized to engage in mortgaging or alienating land, with the result that the same piece of land might have been mortgaged or alienated to more than one party.[14] Munro proposed to reassess these lands to reflect the changing land use, and to resume lands if holders refused to pay the revised rents, or if it was determined that lands had been alienated without authorization. These proposals were submitted to the Advocate General HG Macklin for opinion. Macklin's opinion paralleled that of Warden. He maintained that the Company's invitations to Kunbis and other cultivators contained an implicit, if not explicit, understanding that the lands were to be handed over in perpetuity. Furthermore, the fact that government had been aware of land transactions by cultivators,

land of Bombay than was acknowledged in Aungier's Convention was probably "private property" of individuals. Cultivating the land was thus, for Warden, a crucial step in making it one's own (Warden 1814: para. 64).

[14] See Advocate General AS LeMessurier's account of the *Foras* land settlement for an outraged description of the liberties the Kunbi cultivators had been taking with lands on which they only had, according to him, the right to cultivate (LeMessurier 1854: 3–4).

but had yet not intervened, signaled an implicit acknowledgement that these landholders were authorized to transfer property (Vaidya 1948 [1914]: 27).

By the early nineteenth century, thus, the state's perspective on land and real property was ambivalent, if not contradictory. On the one hand, the state embraced an accommodating policy of permitting existing forms of occupancy to continue without much interference. Such an attitude was driven partly by compulsion – the imperative, especially in the seventeenth and eighteenth centuries – to attract settlement in the territory – but was also couched in a physiocratic endorsement of the sanctity of improving occupancy as the basis for a robust economy and society. On the other hand, the state perceived its ability to assert its rights as sovereign over land as an indicator of its hegemony, and therefore repeatedly sought to test its right to reassess and resume lands. Such motivation was compounded by the imperative to address problems of urban planning as the city grew in size in the late eighteenth and early nineteenth centuries.

The state's position vis-à-vis lands in Bombay (and presumably also in Calcutta and Madras) was thus, I argue, different from the generally accepted argument regarding the colonial state and property. This well-known argument maintains that the colonial state sought to establish a "rule of property," seeking to set up a class of property owners with itself as sovereign. This argument draws on the actions of the colonial state with respect to agrarian lands following the conquest of Bengal and Madras in the later part of the eighteenth century.[15] Beginning with the *zamindari* settlement in Bengal in 1793 and the *ryotwari* settlement in Madras in the early nineteenth century, and moving to the various settlements in Bombay, UP, Punjab, and so on, historiographical common sense assumes an unruffled surface to the state's attitudes with respect to private property.

[15] Two classic works that established this argument are Ranajit Guha's *A Rule of Property for Bengal: An Essay on the Idea of Permanent Settlement* (Guha 1996 [1963]) and Burton Stein's *Thomas Munro: The Origins of the Colonial State and His Vision of Empire* (Stein 1990). Both Guha and Stein were attentive to the manner in which their protagonists faced significant resistance from their compatriots in their efforts to impose their respective settlements. Yet these complexities have been abstracted away and the historiographical common sense now maintains that the colonial state always, from the beginning, sought to create private property.

This argument has also been extended to characterize the colonial state in Bombay: as an enterprise seeking to create a capitalist property market.[16] Yet the colonial state's position in the early port cities in the seventeenth and for much of the eighteenth centuries was quite different than it was in 1793, and its attitudes towards its land in these territories was thus also quite different. Less concerned with any overarching project of transcending feudal relations and establishing private property, the English East India Company in Bombay was more concerned in the late seventeenth and eighteenth centuries with successfully replacing the Portuguese as lord of the manor and establishing its seigneurial rights over its tenants. In the urban realm, it was only in the early nineteenth century that a strong position advocating for private property could be seen, as in the position of Warden discussed above. And it would only be in the second half of the nineteenth century, as described in the following section, that urban private property – with attendant rights and obligations – was generally promoted by the colonial state as the preferred form of occupancy. By the late nineteenth century, however, as will be seen below, the state's advocacy of private property contended with the growing needs of the state to resume lands to manage the process of urban growth.

Both "property" and "market" were evolving under the circumstances outlined above. The urban state in Bombay was never monolithic or uniform in character. Different organs and officers of the state espoused priorities that were often at odds with one another, as indicated above. While one aspect of the state repeatedly sought to assert itself as sovereign and lord of the manor, within whom all land vested, in fact various categories of landholders were de facto acknowledged to be property owners by another aspect of that very state. Such "contested jurisdictions," an idea elaborated in the Introduction to this volume, would only get accentuated over the course of the nineteenth century as the need for municipal governance increased in urgency, and as the municipal state thus emerged as a realm with priorities and imperatives often diverging from those of the provincial/regional state.

Neither did the state ever exercise complete conceptual control over what "property" meant, or how it was traded. The de facto property owners mentioned above were participating in a robust "market" for

---

[16] This is one significant argument of Dossal's *Theatre of Conflict* (Dossal 2010). It is well-developed in Shekhar Krishnan's review of her book (Krishnan 2010).

property, mortgaging, alienating, and acquiring lands in ways that were not entirely enframed by the state's rules for such exchanges, and often lay entirely outside such rules. Yet clearly such exchanges subscribed to norms and rules established by community and custom, what the editors in the Introduction to this volume refer to as "embedded exchange." Parsis, Kunbis, Kolis, Khojas, Bhatias, and other communities engaged in exchanges of land did so almost always without transacting in titles or other documents that signaled the state's control and oversight over the market. Even more intriguingly, transactions appear to have been done between members of different communities, suggesting that the norms of exchange were also shared across communities.

The Acknowledgment of Private Property

By the second half of the nineteenth century, land held under certain tenures were grudgingly acknowledged by the colonial state to be property. At the same time, as the city burgeoned and grew, the old imperative of tolerating various forms of occupancy to attract and retain settlement yielded to a new imperative of being able to resume lands in order to control development and tax it accordingly. This change reflected a profound transformation in the perception of the connections between land, wealth, and revenue. In early colonial India, agrarian land had been seen as the primary source of wealth; by the second half of the nineteenth century, urban lands too were coming to be seen as a potential source of wealth, and the colonial state sought to partake of this wealth by seeking to tax lands – and especially transfers of land – accordingly.[17] The colonial state began viewing the lands of Bombay as on the path to becoming urban property and sought to devise new ways of extracting value from this distinctive

---

[17] Dossal (2010), esp. 105–24. This point has also been made more recently by Debjani Bhattacharyya (2016: 468). Such a change in colonial revenue administration mirrored changes in the metropole, notes Bhattacharyya, as reflected by the passage in 1860 in Britain of a legislation to tax urban property. Meanwhile, Anish Vanaik notes that urban property was never more than a "practical problem" for colonial officials and had never really served as an important source of revenue (Vanaik, "Introduction," *Possessing the City: Property and Politics in Delhi, 1911–1947* (book manuscript)). Vanaik's work focuses on Delhi; in Bombay, I suggest, by the second half of the nineteenth century urban property was coming to be seen as a source of wealth.

asset. Successfully assessing the status and value of lands was now a potential source of enhanced income, rather than a test of the colonial state's sovereignty, as it had been in the eighteenth and early nineteenth centuries.

In Bombay, such a change in perception was reflected in a series of settlements of the older tenures. Already by the early nineteenth century, land held under Pension and Tax and also quit rent arrangements were beginning to be seen as private property, in the sense that they were exempt from reassessment and could be transferred. Through government resolutions in the second half of the nineteenth century, the Pension and Tax and smaller quit rent and *Foras* holdings – those paying less than Rs. 10 each year – came to enjoy a status resembling freehold property: on payment of thirty years of assessment, the annual cess was "redeemed" and these landholders then did not have to pay annual dues.[18] Private property thus emerged in a curious, backdoor sort of way: not explicitly and in a positive sense, since no formal record of rights could be established, but rather in a negative way, through the recognition of the rights of these holders to retain their lands in perpetuity, free of arbitrary assessment.[19] This pattern was repeated in the 1851 *Foras* Settlement Act, which effectively extinguished the freehold rights of government over certain *Foras* lands in favor of the landholders there, thus rendering those holders into property owners.

The 1860s and 1870s were marked by economic growth, land speculation, and expansion in Bombay. It became clear that the areas of cultivated and wastelands in the north of the city were changing in character as the city expanded northward and northeastward. Seeking to secure its share from the property exchanges that appeared to be taking place, the colonial state embarked on a second major survey from 1865 to 1872 of what was now, as a result of reclamations, the island city of Bombay. As scholars have noted, although launched with the goal of serving as a record of rights, this survey ended up only

[18] G. R. no. 88, dated January 9, 1874, extended the option to holders of Pension and Tax land to redeem their lands of future assessment upon payment of thirty years' worth of rent. As recorded in statement showing lands wholly or partially exempt from assessment, provided by FF Arbuthnot, Collector of Bombay, to Secretary, Revenue Department, GoB. MSA/RD/Vol. 4/ 1876, 187.

[19] Although it is not explicitly formulated in these terms, this is also one of the central arguments of Shekhar Krishnan's dissertation (Krishnan 2013, esp. chapter 5).

partially successful in this regard on account of the resistance posed by landholders to any sustained investigations into their titles (Krishnan 2013: 159). Even identifying the exact borders of holdings, let alone verifying titles, proved very difficult on account of the resistance the surveyors encountered from the occupants (Vaidya 1948 [1914]: 171–2). Still, based on this survey, the provincial government passed the Bombay City Land Revenue Act in 1876, a legislation that sought to stabilize the relationship between the state and various classes of landholders, seeking on the one hand to provide assurances of security to landholders while on the other hand setting out universal principles that would establish the state's ability to reassess and resume land. The survey and the legislation based on it were also clearly efforts to encompass the trade in land within the formal structures of the market.

Reflecting the survey's recognition that there existed a robust exchange of lands despite landholders not having much way of title, the Bombay City Land Revenue Act established the category of the "superior holder," or "the person having the highest title" to any piece of land.[20] The previous revenue law (Regulation XIX of 1827) had used the terms "owner" and "occupant," suggesting an understanding of landholders as consisting of two groups: those who had clear title and were therefore owners, and others who were merely tenants.[21] The 1876 Act's usage of "superior holder" reflected an acknowledgment of what the first great survey of 1811–1827 had already suggested and what the Laughton survey in 1872 had underscored: that practically no one had clear title to the lands they occupied, and that occupancy consisted of a dense force field of interlocking claims. The "superior holder" was the person who emerged at the strongest position within this force field. Still, despite this, there was a trade in land, suggesting that those alienating and those acquiring lands shared a set of conventions governing exchange.

While lands held under Pension and Tax, *Foras*, quit, and *Inami* tenures were acknowledged as private property, the state sought to exercise its rights over remaining lands – the bulk of which were under the *Toka* tenure – now with the imperative of simultaneously controlling and profiting from urban growth. Immediately following the

---

[20] Bombay City Land Revenue Act, Section 3, para. 4 (p. 152). Also noted by Krishnan (2013: 169).

[21] Editor's annotation to Section 3, para. 4, Bombay City Land Revenue Act, 154.

passage of the 1876 Bombay City Land Revenue Act, the Collector, FF
Arbuthnot sought to raise the assessment on *Toka* lands. He noted that
these lands were now being used for a variety of purposes: "The
produce of these lands is various. On some of it rice only is grown,
other parts of it give good garden land, some is built upon, some is
worked as stone quarries, from some of it earth is taken for reclamation
purposes and some is kept waste for grass and grazing."[22] Arbuthnot
consequently proposed a revised assessment on *Toka* lands, but his
proposal met with resistance from within the Revenue department,
with the Revenue Secretary EW Ravenscroft noting in a handwritten
scribble that in his view, "the proposal of the Collector if sanctioned
will lead to endless litigation and will cause infinitely more trouble and
annoyance to the present holders of land than the increase is worth."[23]
For Ravenscroft, the prospect of raising the assessment, especially
without clear grounds, appeared to disturb the bedrock of guarantees
on which the property regime was seeking to establish itself.

In 1879, the government proposed what it considered a compromise
solution: it sought to steeply revise the assessment due on *Toka* lands
upward; but it also extended a guarantee that these lands would remain
free of further upward revisions for a period of fifty years, until 1929.

But Ravenscroft's warning, mentioned above, proved prescient as
a significant challenge arose when the state attempted to put this
reassessment of the *Toka* lands into effect, leading to a landmark
judgment by the Bombay High Court.[24] The area in question lay just
to the north of the limits of settlement at the time, but clearly lay in the
path of the expanding city. The case of Shapurji Jivanji vs Collector of
Bombay, on which the Bombay High Court passed judgment on
April 27, 1885, basically tested the question of whether the defendant
(the Collector) could reassess the rents on the land based on the compromise arrangement vis-à-vis *Toka* lands, described above.[25] The
plaintiff (Shapurji Jivanji), among whose legal team was the legendary
Phirozeshah Mehta, contended that he was only obliged to pay the

---

[22] FF Arbuthnot to Chief Secretary, RD, GoB, no. 583 of 1876. MSA/RD/Vol. 84/
1876, 5.

[23] Handwritten note of EW Ravenscroft, Secretary, RD, May 15, 1876, in ibid.,
44.

[24] Vaidya notes that this decision represented a precedent-setting test case of the
state's rights over lands in the aftermath of the arrangements arrived at in 1876
Land Revenue Act (Vaidya 1948 [1914]: xliii).

[25] (1885) ILR 9 BOM 483.

customary rent. There are several aspects of this case that relate to the discussion so far. First, Justice Scott noted that the plaintiff landholder only had rent bills going back a few years, even though he had occupied the land for a much longer period of about fifty years. In the rent rolls generated from the Dickinson survey in the early twentieth century, the land was described as *Foras* land. In the earliest rent bills that Jivanji could produce, which dated from 1868, the land was, however, reclassified as *Foras Toka*.[26] Notably, this reclassification meant that Jivanji was unable to benefit from the victory won by the *Forasadars* in the 1851 *Foras* Settlement Act, by which certain *Foras* lands were declared free of reassessment. In the 1879 rent bill, the land was once again reclassified as *Toka* land. Extraordinarily, for unspecified reasons, even the nature of the agrarian tenure under which the land was held appears to have changed in time. This might have been a result of a conscious decision by officials at certain points to reclassify the lands; more likely, this reclassification came about because of the lack of exact and consistent correspondence between revenue documents such as rent rolls and rent bills, on the one hand, and the actual tracts of land, on the other hand.

Justice Scott's decision upheld the Collector's right to reassess the land and began by pointing out that Jivanji's lands, now reclassified as *Toka* lands, did not belong among those lands that had successfully campaigned against reassessment. More importantly, Scott argued that the character of the land had changed entirely. It was no longer merely agrarian land that was entitled to pay customary rent. Rather, it was space in motion: land that stood to profit from changing circumstances of industrialization, urbanization, and increase in prosperity. And so, went on Scott: "[I]t is not only legal, but politic and just, to increase assessment in accordance with the increased value of the land, so far as that increase is caused, not by the increased exertion of the holders, or the improvements made by them, but by the growth of general prosperity under the influence of good administration."[27] Scott here is arguing that the character of the land has changed as a result of growth, industrialization, and urbanization, all of which are not the direct result of the landholders' own labor. Continuing to pay a low,

---

[26] This was a tenure that characterized the pasturage land that was attached to *Toka* lands.

[27] Justice Scott, *Indian Law Reports*, vol. 9, 1885, Bombay Series, 486.

customary agrarian assessment would amount to receiving rent, which was not aligned with liberal principles. Rather, the land should be viewed and assessed as urban property.

Jivanji's argument, meanwhile, was based on a claim that he was entitled to pay a customary rent, and that his land was held under one of the protected tenures. In a peculiar way, in order to maximally assert his proprietary interest in his land and thereby secure his protection from reassessment, Jivanji tried to assert the non-market nature of the land. Scott, meanwhile, argued precisely that the land was urban property and should be assessed as such, not derive rent from its customary designation. "Property" and "market" did not necessarily always go together; in this instance, Jivanji sought precisely to assert the customary nature of his holding, rather than argue that his holding was private property.

The ambivalence of the state towards property in the lands on the urban edge has to do, I suggest, with the ambivalent status of such lands themselves. The state had a clear-cut policy with respect to agrarian land: it sought to establish private property relations – yet falling short of absolute, fee-simple freeholds – with the incentive of enhancing agricultural output and thus land revenue. With respect to urban lands, the state was much more reluctant to alienate lands and allow private property. This had to do with the desire of urban governments to be able to control building, resume land for public purposes, and, of course, to profit from the much more rapid enhancements of value of urban land over agrarian land. Lands on the urban edge, which were under cultivation but which appeared to lie in the path of the expanding city, posed a challenge since they straddled these two positions. They were thus "edge-lands" in two senses: first, they were neither entirely agrarian nor quite yet rural; second, in terms of occupancy they fell on a spectrum between private property and outright tenancy. Some of these lands had over the course of the nineteenth century come to be seen as private property, but could occasionally seek to assert their customary nature, as Shapurji Jivanji sought to do.

From Landholding to Plot

By the last decade of the nineteenth century, the challenges thrown up by rapid urbanization compelled the colonial state to more aggressively regulate growth. Thus, while seeking to further develop the urban property market with all the attendant protections from state intervention that private property would bring, the colonial state also simultaneously sought to increase its powers to resume lands for public purpose. In pursuing these dual – occasionally contradictory – ends, the colonial state relied on the longstanding ambiguities in the meaning of property that have been elaborated in the preceding sections.

An outbreak of plague in Bombay in 1896 occasioned the formation of the Bombay Improvement Trust, a planning body charged with cleaning up the congested areas of the older parts of the city, constructing broad new boulevards to better "ventilate" these crowded areas, and to develop the northern parts of the island for residential settlement. Elsewhere, I have argued that one of the BIT's most significant achievements was to acquire large swathes of land held under various tenures, to clear them of existing settlements, and to alienate them on the basis of standardized leaseholds. Taken in combination with the networks of roads that connected the older parts of the city in the south with the newer areas in the north, these measures went a long way in creating the idea of the city as unified market for lands (N Rao 2013: 23–24). Here I want to explore more closely the process of land acquisition and the replacement of the "landholding" with the "plot" and elaborate what that meant for the property market.

Land acquisition on the scale embarked on by the Improvement Trust brought into sharp focus the meaning of "property": under what circumstances could the state compulsorily acquire land? Also, the issue of what compensation was to be paid in turn threw into relief the "market," since compensation was presumably to bear some relationship to the "market value" of the lands to be acquired.[28]

From the outset, the procedure of land acquisition by the state made it apparent that "the State" was not a unitary entity, and that different organs of the state had different interests in the land. When the Improvement Trust sought to acquire land in Sion for the Sion-Matunga scheme, for instance, it butted up against the Salt Commissioner, who controlled and occupied much of this area being used as salt pans. The latter office fought the BIT's efforts to acquire its land for the Trust's suburban scheme and argued that salt was an Imperial concern and thus

---

[28] For a brief account of some of the challenges faced by the BIT in establishing "market value" in the context of land acquisition, see N Rao (2013: 32–6). For a more extensive effort to capture the monumental and byzantine processes of land valuation, see Krishnan (2013: 109–49).

served a much broader constituency that transcended the local context, whereas the BIT's "improvements" were primarily for a selective group of ratepayers. At issue here was the operative notion of "public" in the definition of "public interest" used in the eminent domain acquisition being pursued by the BIT.[29]

But such instances of contested jurisdiction came up in most striking fashion when the Improvement Trust sought to acquire lands held on *Toka* tenure in the 1900s, most of which were in the north and northeast areas of the island, where the BIT was pursuing its suburban schemes. As noted above, the *Toka* tenure had yet to be recognized as private property; when the BIT went ahead and acquired *Toka* lands and awarded compensation to the *Toka* landholders, the Collector's office stepped forward as representative of the provincial government (and therefore as representative of the sovereign) and claimed a share of the compensation as a party with an interest in the land.[30] Initially, the Trust's Special Collector divided the award between the landholder and the state government, which meant that the landholder received well below what such lands would otherwise have fetched in the "market." Landholders challenged the Special Collector's awards and took their case to the Tribunal of Appeal. The latter body ruled that in terms of the Land Acquisition Act, which was the legislation authorizing the BIT's acquisitions, the government could not be construed as an "interested person" when it itself was acquiring land, and only "interested persons" were entitled to compensation by this Act.

This was a landmark ruling that shook the confidence of the state, judging by the furious correspondence this ruling generated. The Tribunal had effectively ruled that the BIT and the Collector, as representative of the provincial government, were both basically "the government"; the latter could not step forward and compensate itself. The only way for the Collector's office to claim any compensation would be if the Trust correspondingly increased the size of the award to include the portion that would become due to the Collector. Here was an instance where one organ of the state (the Tribunal of Appeal) ruled against the acquisitive ambition of another organ of state (the BIT) and

---

[29] MSA/RD/Vol. 219/1908, Comp. 1188, 167–98.
[30] I have briefly alluded to this problem in Rao, *House, But No Garden*, pp. 39–40. The following discussion is based on new material, to be found in MSA/RD/vol. 226/1908 and develops my earlier preliminary observations.

the customary right of the Sovereign (the Collector in this instance) in favor of the *Toka* landholder.

Land acquisition was a laborious process involving, first, visits to the holding in question (the borders or even location of which might not correspond to those recorded on the survey sheets). The superior holder had then to be established, and various other claimants and mortgagees to be determined. Finally, the land had to be assigned a value, which was complicated by the fact that such lands were often used for multiple purposes, both agrarian as well as quasi-urban: for instance, land might be used for rice cultivation for a part of the year, and also used for brick manufacture for another part of the year to service the needs of the adjacent city.

Lands that had multiple claimants, used for various purposes, and whose borders were inexact had to be acquired and then repackaged and realienated as a plot. This entailed the fixing of temporal horizons and spatial boundaries. Even before the BIT was formed in 1898, city authorities were investigating the optimal relationship between the state, landholders, and land. Reluctant to alienate land on a permanent basis, they sought a form of occupancy that offered occupants a certain measure of security while also allowing the state the opportunity to reassess land as its situation changed: in other words, keeping in mind that urban land was space in motion, and thus did not remain constant in its usage and therefore in value. The modern leasehold, variable in term depending on the nature and location of the land, appeared to offer the answer. Although leases had been issued by the English East India Company in Bombay from as early as the early eighteenth century, Warden had already noted in the early nineteenth century that these efforts to lease land – and thereby stipulate the terms and duration of occupancy as well as form of use – were utterly useless (Warden 1814: paras. 76–7).

With the growing demand for land and the state's growing sense that it should profit from this boom, colonial officers in the late 1880s initiated a discussion of standardizing the form of leases such that government stood to profit from any increases in value. In 1889, while looking to lease out plots of land in Dharavi, Parel, and Mahim, the Acting Collector of Bombay proposed a modification and standardization of the method of leasing. Previously, the method consisted of alienating the land by auction, with an initial payment and then a nominal annual rent for the duration of the lease. The problem with this system, noted the Acting Collector, was that: "Government does not gain anything more than the fixed annual rent till after the expiry of the lease, though the value of the land may enormously increase during the currency of the lease."[31] Instead, the Collector proposed a system whereby the land would be leased out for fifty years on a relatively large annual rent, which would, in turn, increase periodically, first after ten years and then again after twenty years from the commencement of the lease. In this way, government stood to benefit from what was presumed to be a more or less steady increase in value of lands, even for locations on the urban periphery such as in Dharavi, Mahim, and Parel. Here then was the attempt to institutionalize the perception of urban land as space in motion, to somehow capture the dynamic and changing character of the urbanization process.

This form of leasing did not gain sufficiently in popularity among prospective Indian acquirers of land. Initially colonial officials thought that it was the prospect of progressive increase in lease rents that had led to unpopularity; but an insightful note by the Collector in 1890 argued that it was not so much the fact of progressively increasing rents as that the term of fifty years was felt by potential lessees to be too short that had rendered the current system of leasing unpopular; given that the land was now urbanizing and therefore going to be built on with (expensive) structures for dwelling, rather than used for cultivation or, at most, for housing less-elaborate structures such as cattle sheds, longer leases were called for.[32]

A committee appointed to study existing practices of letting out land and make recommendations for a formal system of leasing appears to have accepted the above argument.[33] The leasing structure suggested by this committee laid out the guidelines by which land would subsequently be parceled out by the state to landholders. As older leases or tenancies-at-will elapsed, they would be replaced by the new lease

---

[31] Memorandum from Collector of Land Revenue, Customs and Opium, Bombay, No. L.R. 807, 25 March 1889, in MSA/RD/Vol. 125/1890, Comp. 144, 341.

[32] Letter from AM Monteath, Collector of Bombay to Chief Secretary, Revenue Department, No. 2241 of November 19, 1890, MSA/RD/Vol. 241/1891, 252. Monteath wrote: "People will not build substantial houses and cannot therefore utilize the land to the maximum advantage unless they have security of tenure for a longer period." Ibid., p. 253.

[33] Letter from JM Campbell, TD Little, and AV Frere to Secretary, Revenue Department, February 29, 1892, MSA/RD/vol. 309/1893, Comp. 918.

form, now usually of ninety-nine- or even 999-year term for residential and commercial buildings. The members of the committee could not have imagined, when they issued their report in 1892, that the lease structure they proposed would so quickly be put into such extensive effect: after the plague outbreak in 1896 and the formation of the Bombay Improvement Trust, vast areas of the city – both in older slum districts as well as in arable areas on the urban fringe – were acquired in the years between 1898 and 1925, and older forms of occupancy were replaced with the leasehold.

The proliferation of leaseholds represented an important step in the creation of the property market in that they represented a standardization of time horizons, creating a predictability that facilitated exchanges of landholdings. Yet it should be evident that while the colonial state sought to represent leaseholds as "property" in that leaseholds were guaranteed to be free of reassessment during their term, at the same time the state was reserving for itself the right to revisit the leasehold and its conditions on expiry of the term, or on violation of the conditions of the leasehold. In this way, while appearing to sanction private property by issuing lease-holds, the colonial state was also attenuating the inviolability of private property.

Parallel to such temporal fixing, the Bombay Improvement Trust was also obsessed with the spatial fixing of land into parcels with sharp edges. At around the same time that city authorities had concerned themselves with the temporal horizons of land in the late 1880s, they also concerned themselves with what they termed "encroachments": the fact that many landholders were actually occupying lands that exceeded the boundaries of the parcels that they officially held, and for which they were taxed.[34] Once again, the sense of emergency generated by the plague allowed the Improvement Trust to address this issue with a vigor that would not have previously been possible. After acquiring huge areas of land in the northwestern, northern, and northeastern parts of the city, much of which would have been held on Pension and Tax, *Foras*, and *Toka* tenures, the Trust proceeded to lay out these areas with street patterns and residential lots. These lots were

---

[34] This issue generated an extensive and fascinating correspondence. See, for instance, MSA/RD/Vol. 265/1890, Comp. 969. The main issue here was whether the encroachments could be taxed by the Collector's office at its own discretion, or whether they were bound to tax the encroachments per the conditions of the tenure of the official landholding.

then alienated by auction along with an extremely stringent set of conditions. Some of these conditions entailed time limits within which building needed to commence. A whole other set of conditions detailed the obligations incumbent on the lessee to clearly and visibly demarcate the edges of the lot by constructing a wall, which, in turn, had to be of a specified height, built using specific materials, painted a certain color, and so on.[35] Further, the land had to be completely evacuated of previous occupants and material before "vacant possession" could be handed over to the winner of the auction and the plot came into existence. It was only after vacant possession was granted, and subsequently that construction was completed, that the lease was issued, and the plot assumed its complete temporal and spatial form.

Such a process, with all the rigor in controlling temporal and spatial surfeit, was directed at purging the land of previous associations and rendering it into neat parcels that could be traded in frictionless fashion. Yet, as might be imagined, such an effort to flatten time and sharpen the physical edges often posed challenges. Consider the following example, far from uncommon in the records, of an instance when things did not go smoothly. This was a parcel that eventually ended up becoming Plot No. 384 of the Dadar-Matunga estate of the Improvement Trust.[36] This piece of land was originally agreed to be leased, following auction in November 1917, to a pair named Dhirajlal Vrindavandas and Jagmohundas Vrindavandas. Issues arose immediately, as the latter neglected to pay the deposit that accompanied the agreement to lease. After the deposit was finally paid in May 1918, it took the BIT until April 1920 to be able to evacuate the land of persons and material and offer "vacant possession."[37] These delays were caused because the land might still have been in the process of being cleared, leveled, and laid out in a street pattern, and laborers and their materials might have been on site. By March 1923, the BIT was once again hounding the Vrindavandas brothers for arrears in lease rents.[38] In response, the lessees' solicitors responded requesting more time to

[35] Some of these specifications are detailed in Rao (2013: 166).
[36] All details taken from Plot File, Plot 384, Dadar-Matunga Estate, MCGM Estates Dept.
[37] Letter from Estate Agent, BIT, to Vrindavandas and Vrindavandas, April 17, 1920. Plot File for Plot 384, Dadar-Matunga Estate, MCGM Estates Dept.
[38] Letter of Estate Agent, BIT to Vrindavandas and Vrindavandas, March 15, 1923, in ibid.

pay the arrears, as well as requesting an extension on the usual stipulations that building be completed shortly after signing the agreement to lease. They argued that "our clients have suffered heavily during the last monetary crisis and have no moneys to build," and therefore requested time "during which they hope that their affairs will be readjusted and they would be able to build."[39]

The extension was granted by the BIT, not so much out of any spirit of generosity as the fact that the depressed land market meant that the Trust had to compromise on its own standards and make exceptions of this sort.[40] Still, by 1924 the Vrindavandas brothers had fallen in arrears with their lease payments. On being urged by the BIT to persuade their clients to pay up the arrears or else face the prospect of termination of the lease, the Vrindavandas' solicitors wrote back to say that they themselves had not been able to get in touch with their clients, and to the best of their knowledge these men had "left Bombay about three years ago and [had] gone back to Vishanagara native place in Baroda state as [they were] involved in pecuniary circumstances [sic]."[41] In other words, financial distress had led them to flee. A further effort by the Trust to follow up with Chunilal Sanghani, the broker who had represented the Vrindavandas brothers when they first approached the BIT and a man very involved in brokering land transactions in this area in this period, yielded no success.[42] Finally, almost eight years after the plot was agreed to be leased in 1917, the Trust concluded that there was no point in pursuing the deal any further and formally withdrew from and cancelled the transaction, electing to retain the Vrindavandas' deposits against the arrears in rent that were due to them.[43]

In this case, the Vrindavandas brothers literally fled to the hills to exit a deal that was proving adverse to their evolving interests and situation.

---

[39] Letter of Shamrao, Minocheher, and Hiralal, Solicitors, to Estate Agent, BIT, March 27, 1923, in ibid. The "monetary crisis" referred to is the collapse of the 1916–1922 boom, which had led to a burst of speculation in the market for lands.

[40] BIT Trustees' Resolution No. 231 of April 10, 1923, Extract from Proceedings of the Bombay Improvement Trust, April 10, 1923, in ibid.

[41] Letter of Shamrao, Minocheher, and Hiralal to Estate Agent, BIT, April 7, 1924, in ibid.

[42] Letter of Estate Agent, BIT, to Chunilal Sanghani of July 28, 1924, and latter's response of July 31, 1924, in ibid.

[43] BIT Trustees' Resolution 62 of February 17, 1925, Extract from Proceedings of the Bombay Improvement Trust, February 17, 1925, in ibid.

The Trust's efforts to create and regulate the land market were repre-sented by the lease, which sought to compress time and create a Year Zero, at which point land transformed from mere space into an urban plot with a suitable building on it that could subsequently be traded in rational fashion. Yet, such efforts to create a land market were some-times undone, in a perverse way, by the broader, shifting context of supply and demand itself: in this case, the changing circumstances of the land market between 1917 – when the deal was struck at the beginning of a speculative bubble – and about 1923, when the land market had just tanked and the Vrindavandas brothers were beginning once again to default on their rent payments and proving unable to begin construction. It was not until 1935 that things seem to have picked up and the plot was leased out again. This meant that the land lay fallow between first being put up for auction in 1917 and September 1935, when a new agreement to lease was signed with one Vishram Velji.[44]

When plots lay fallow in this fashion, they were subject to encroachment, sometimes by laborers working to clear other, nearby plots, and sometimes by others looking for a place to put up their shelter. Indeed, the records are replete with instances of the BIT (and its successor, the Estates Department of the BMC) seeking to plug metaphoric holes in the neat, impervious walls it was seeking to build between plots of land. Consider another case in the Sewri–Wadala scheme of the BIT, close to the Dadar-Matunga scheme discussed above. Here too the effort to successfully lease out Plot 38 was long drawn out, lasting from 1940 to 1952, and involved many prospective lessees. During the course of the negotiations, one sticking point had to do with the BMC's efforts to grant vacant possession of the plot to one Ramniklal Shah, who was being represented by the same Chunilal Sanghani, featured in the case discussed above. Sanghani, writing on behalf of his client, noted testily that the plot, which was described as vacant, was not actually vacant and had never been so because "the said plot has been occupied by the contractor Mr Nanji Bhavar since last many months and it has never been vacant since it has been occupied by him since he started the building work of the adjoining

---

[44] Resolution 261 of Improvements Committee, BMC, September 17, 1935, Extract from Improvements Committee Proceedings of September 17, 1935, in ibid. The subsequent course of the plot file reveals that this agreement to lease proved more successful, and that a building did arise on this plot.

plot."[45] Just as the effort to compress time discussed previously was sometimes compromised by the course of events, similarly the effort to carve out neatly hermetic plots was occasionally unsuccessful in sealing off the spillover of people and material.

The temporal and physical definition of the plot described above went in conjunction with other measures taken by the state to capture the trade in lands and encompass them within a formal market. The passage of the Indian Stamp Act (1899) sought to charge duty on instruments used to effect transactions, while the Indian Registration Act (1908) sought to compel actors to register transactions involving real property. In the 1910s, new surveys of urban lands were launched in Bombay, Calcutta, and Delhi, which once again sought to serve not just as topographical surveys, but rather also to establish records of rights. Once again, these efforts to establish title were quashed, but differently in Bombay than in Delhi. Shekhar Krishnan has shown the way in which furious resistance put up by Bombay's landholders – or property owners – derailed the effort to formally establish them as such (Krishnan 2013: 187–96). In Delhi, Anish Vanaik notes that Wilson's survey map of Delhi, drawn in the 1910s, was proposed by the Delhi Municipal Corporation (DMC) to also serve as a register of property; however, Department of Revenue and Agriculture vociferously argued that "'a record of rights' is a sort of insurance against litigation and is no concern of a semi-private body such as a municipality, but is a matter for the state" (Vanaik 2015: 318–9). In different ways, for different reasons, the effort to officially and formally encompass property rights using the instruments of representation available to the state were thwarted in both cities.

Conclusion

In 1969, the Maharashtra government finally succeeded in passing the Bombay City (*Inami* and Special Tenures) Abolition and Maharashtra Land Revenue (Amendment) Act. This legislation sought to finally do away with the *Inami*, Pension and Tax, *Fazendari*, quit and ground rent, *Foras*, and *Sanadi* tenures, extinguishing the right some of these holders had to collect revenue, the protection from reassessment these

---

[45] Letter No. 677 of Chunilal Sanghani to the Estate Agent and Land Manager, BMC, August 3, 1949. Plot File of Plot 38, MCGM Estates Dept.

tenure holders had also enjoyed, as well as the freedom from assessment entirely enjoyed by those who had "redeemed" their assessment by paying up thirty years of rent. Instead, holders of lands on these tenures were now to be assessed on the basis of the "market value" of their holdings. Market value, in turn, would be determined by the sale history of unbuilt plots in the vicinity of each holding.[46] In other words, this legislation took a further step towards viewing these lands as private property and taxing them as such.

Although efforts had previously been made to abolish these tenures, they had proved unsuccessful due to the resistance offered by landholders.[47] It was only the political will generated in the Nehruvian state – and specifically the imperative to enact land reforms beginning with the "abolition of intermediaries" – that permitted the Maharashtra government to enact this legislation. (And that too, only twelve years after it was first proposed in the Legislative Assembly in 1957, on account of furious resistance.)[48] Holders of these various tenures wanted to retain them because of the protections they enjoyed; curiously, but unsurprisingly, they therefore rejected the reclassification of their land as urban property, which is what the new proposed leaseholds would have rendered them into. Rather, they preferred to hold on to their customary tenures. In a move similar to that made by Shapurji Jivanji in the case discussed above, they sought to maximize their proprietary rights – protection from reassessment – by asserting the customary, not-private-property nature of their holding.

The 1969 legislation abolishing "special tenures" might appear to signal a final blow to the peculiar nature of landholding in Bombay, and the decisive arrival of private property and a property market. Taken in conjunction with the neoliberal reforms beginning in the 1980s, the abolition of special tenures might also appear to signal the arrival of a consensus between the state and different categories of

[46] Bombay City (Inami and Special Tenures) Abolition and Maharashtra Land Revenue Code (Amendment) Act, 1969, paras. 2–4, 8.

[47] Landholders on these tenures argued that since the bulk of these lands housed residences and factories, the increased revenue burden would partially be passed on to the people living and working in these premises, thus creating hardship for a wide swathe of the population. See "Inami tenure abolition: Bill will do harm," *Times of India*, September 10, 1963, p. 8.

[48] For an account of the broader context of the attack on intermediaries in the Bombay province, which captures the fervor of Nehruvian land reform rhetoric, see Patel (1950).

landholders that "private property" was the optimal desired form of landholding.

Yet, it would appear not to be the case. A recent presentation by the Property Owners' Association of Bombay, a longstanding interest group lobbying since 1924, includes a demand of government for various reforms to rationalize the property market in the city. Titled "Making Mumbai a World Class City," the presentation includes expected calls for a further deregulation of legislations enforcing rent control and building heights. An important aspect of the Property Owners' Association's platform includes a demand that the "all tenure of lands should be converted to free-hold tenures" on payment by the landholder of 0.5 percent of the value of the land (Bhattad 2015). Apparently, the 1969 abolition of special tenures legislation had not quite brought about the conversion to freehold that it was designed to effect through its effort to tax lands on market basis, rather than by custom.

Why would property owners now want their lands to be converted to freehold, when in the 1960s they had fought the state's efforts to transform the customary nature of their tenures into market-based property? And why would the state be reluctant to assent to property holders' wishes, when it had passed a law in 1969 seeking exactly this outcome? One possible reason has to do with the incentives for redevelopment that have been offered by the state government since the 1990s. As many scholars of the present-day city have documented, redevelopment is the panacea through which the state government seeks to address all manner of issues in the housing system: slums and dilapidated buildings, both privately owned and owned by an assortment of state entities, and which, taken together, constitute a substantial portion of the city's housing stock, are to be transformed into structures appropriate to a world-class city through the efforts of private enterprise. To attract private enterprise to the project of redevelopment, the state offers incentives in the form of extra building rights that [re]developers can sell off at market prices. At the current (extremely high) value of land and housing in Mumbai, landholders stand to make windfall profits through these incentives, either by redeveloping their land and buildings themselves, or by selling off their land to a developer.

But in order to avail of these windfall profits, landholders must now establish that they are actually owners of the lands on which their

buildings stand. If they are only landholders on this or that customary
tenure, then they will be entitled only to a portion of the potential
profits, as the state has been moving aggressively to lay claim to lands of
which it remains the manorial lord, and from whose windfall arising
from redevelopment it seeks to profit. (Much as the Collector, as
sovereign over the *Toka* tenures, demanded a share of the compensation awarded by the BIT to the landholder in the early 1900s, discussed
above.) The potential for redevelopment and subsequent realization of
windfall profits has once again shifted the terms of the equation: where
in the 1960s, landholders saw it to be in their interest to assert the
customary nature of their holdings to lessen property tax, now these
same landholders seek to get their holdings declared as private property, so that they can maximally benefit from redevelopment.

Brenda Bhandar has recently argued that in colonial settler contexts,
property titling has "effectively diminished ways of relating to the land
that do not conform to capitalist property norms" (Bhandar 2018: 78).
Meanwhile, South Asian urban historiography has also tended to
characterize the colonial city as marked by the gradual yet inexorable
emergence of a property market. Scholars have shown how the colonial
state sought to create a property market, on the one hand, while also
arguing that the privileges associated with urban citizenship were dis-
proportionately directed towards property owners (Hazareesingh
2000: 800), on the other. What this meant in the Indian setting, however, was not always quite in alignment with the liberal notion of
property. Indeed, this chapter has sought to show that one particularity
of Indian modernity lay in the fact that "property" had shifting meanings in the Bombay context, sometimes at variance with the liberal
understanding. The chapter's recapitulation of the tenurial history of
the city has shown how, at various points, the state and the city's
occupants took varying – often contradictory – positions on property
depending on the broader context of the ends being pursued.

The notion of the property market presumes that "property" pre-
cedes "the market." Yet this chapter has sought to show that notions of
"property" remain fluid and flexible, and that various actors avail of
these flexibilities to adapt the meaning of occupancy to further their
particular ends. It is the prospect of "market" – that is, fluctuations in
the broader contexts of supply and demand – that occasions a certain
urgency to fix the meaning of "property." Thus, the privileges associated with property were sometimes most effectively asserted not by

claiming ownership, but rather by emphasizing the customary character of landholding. The state, meanwhile, sought to assert its sovereignty precisely by emphasizing the urban property-character of lands in Bombay, deemphasizing the customary character of tenures such as the *Toka* tenure. Conceptualizing the urbanization process as space in motion, as this chapter has sought to do, offers a framework within which to understand the shifting meanings of property, and the strategic uses to which these various meanings were put by various state and nonstate actors in Bombay.

References

Bhandar, B 2018, *Colonial Lives of Property: Law, Land, and Racial Regimes of Ownership*, Duke University Press, Durham.

Bhattacharyya, D 2016, "Interwar Housing and Rent Profiteering in Calcutta," *Comparative Studies of South Asia, Africa, and the Middle East*, 36, 3: 465–82.

Bhattad, BR, Making Mumbai a World Class City, for Property Owners Association 2015 presentation delivered on February 9, 2015, viewed on May 29, 2019 (www.poamumbai.org/).

Dossal, M 2010, *Theatre of Conflict, City of Hope: Bombay/Mumbai, 1660 to Present Times*, Oxford University Press, Oxford.

Guha, R 1996 [1963], *A Rule of Property for Bengal: An Essay on the Idea of Permanent Settlement*, Duke University Press, Durham and London.

Hann, CM 1998, "Introduction: The Embeddedness of Property," in CM Hann (ed.) *Property Relations: Renewing the Anthropological Tradition*, Cambridge University Press, Cambridge, pp. 1–47.

Hann, CM 2007, "A New Double Movement? Anthropological Perspectives on Property in the Age of Neoliberalism," *Socio-Economic Review*, 5: 287–318.

Hazareesingh, S 2000, "The Quest for Urban Citizenship: Civil Rights, Public Opinion, and Colonial Resistance in Early Twentieth Century Bombay," *Modern Asian Studies*, 34, 4: 797–829.

Kohli, A 2006, "Politics of Economic Growth in India, 1980–2005," *Economic and Political Weekly*, Part 1 (April 1): 1251–9; and Part 2 (April 8): 1361–70.

Krishnan, S 2010, "Micro-History of Mumbai," *Economic and Political Weekly*, XLV, 36.

Krishnan, S 2013, Empire's Metropolis: Money, Time and Space in Colonial Bombay: 1870–1930, unpublished PhD thesis, Massachusetts Institute of Technology.

LeMessurier, AS 1854, "Report on the Foras lands," in Papers Connected with the Settlement, under Act No. VI of 1851 of the Foras Lands in Bombay. Selections from the Records of the Bombay Government, No. III (New Series), Bombay Education Society's Press, Bombay, pp. 3–4.

Mukhija, V 2003, *Squatters as Developers? Slum Redevelopment in Mumbai*, Routledge, London.

Mukhija V 2016, "Rehousing Mumbai: Formalizing Slum Land Markets through Redevelopment," in EL Birch, S Chattaraj, & SM Wachter (eds.) *Slums: How Informal Real Estate Markets Work*, University of Pennsylvania Press, Philadelphia, pp. 125–39.

de Neve, G & Donner, H 2015, "Introduction: Revisiting Urban Property in India," *Journal of South Asian Development*, 10, 3, 255–66.

Patel, GD 1950, Agrarian Reforms in Bombay (The Legal and Economic Consequences of the Abolition of Land Tenures), published by the author, Bombay.

Raman, B 2015, "The Politics of Property in Land: New Planning Instruments, Law, and Popular Groups in Delhi," *Journal of South Asian Development*, 10, 3: 369–95.

Rao, N 2013, *House, But No Garden. Apartment Living in Bombay's Suburbs, 1898–1964*, University of Minnesota Press, Minneapolis.

Rao, U 2010, "Making the Global City: Urban Citizenship at the Margins of Delhi," *Ethnos*, 75, 4: 402–24.

Rao, U 2013, "Tolerated Encroachment: Resettlement Policies and the Negotiation of the Licit/Illicit Divide in an Indian Metropolis," *Cultural Anthropology*, 28, 4: 760–79.

Stein, B 1990, *Thomas Munro: The Origins of the Colonial State and His Vision of Empire*, Cambridge University Press, Cambridge.

Vaidya DR, 1948 [1914], "Introduction," *The Bombay City Land Revenue Act, No. II of 1876*, Bombay Central Press, Bombay, p. 4.

Vanaik, A 2015, "Representing Commodified Space: Maps, Leases, Auctions, and 'Narrations' of Property in Delhi, c. 1900–1947," *Historical Research*, 88, 240: 318–319.

Warden, F 1814, "Report on the Landed Tenures of Bombay," *Selections from the Records of the Bombay Government No. LXIV (New Series)*, Education Society's Press, Bombay.

4 | Magic of Business: Occult Forces in the Bazaar Economy

PROJIT BIHARI MUKHARJI

This article is about occult forces in the "bazaar economy," which, since Clifford Geertz coined the term (Geertz 1978: 28–32), has been studied fairly extensively in South Asia and elsewhere (Ray 1995: 449–554; see also Bayly 1988; Birla 2009; Jain 2007; Yang 1998). Geertz had argued against the tendency to see the bazaar as either a "penny capitalist" real-world analogue of the purely competitive market of neoclassical economics or an institution so embedded in its unique sociocultural context that it defied economic analysis altogether. Instead, Geertz felt that a productive blending of anthropology and economics could render the bazaar amenable to universal economic frameworks, while simultaneously making those frameworks more inclusive. In the universalizing vein, Geertz argued that the fundamental maxim that sellers seek to maximize profits, buyers desire maximum utility, and that price is determined by relating supply and demand was as true in the bazaar as anywhere else. Hence "capital, skill, and industriousness play," he argued, "along with luck and privilege, as important a role in the bazaar as they do in any economic system" (Geertz 1978: 29). Where the bazaar *was* distinctive, however, was in the way these seemingly universal economic processes actually operated. Geertz zeroed in on information scarcity as the distinctive feature of the bazaar. He formulated it into a dictum: "[I]n the bazaar information is poor, scarce, maldistributed, inefficiently communicated, and intensely valued" (Geertz 1978: 29). To overcome this information poverty and pursue the universal aims of profit or utility maximization, *bazaaris* developed a range of special strategies including ethnicization, spatial localization, clientization, etc. (Geertz 1978: 31). In stark contrast to this ahistorical, structural image of the Geertzian bazaar is Rajat Kanta Ray's figure of it. Ray categorically rejected the Geertzian image by stating that "nothing could be further from the sense in which the bazaar in understood in those parts of Asia where the term is used extensively" (Ray 1995: 452).

85

The term bazaar, Ray pointed out, was used in one of two senses. First, it referred to urban centers of wholesale commerce, especially in contradistinction to rural marts known as shandies or *haats*. It was the latter that seemed to partially resemble Geertz's bazaars. Second, it referred to the indigenous money market that financed wholesale and long-distance forward trading with the aid of a range of financial instruments such as promissory notes, different types of bills of exchange, etc. (Ray 1995: 452). Ray was interested in how these historical senses of the bazaar were related to the rise of modern, capitalist economies. For Ray, "the bazaar was a sector defined by the imposition of European domination. The bazaar was a new forma-tion in the Afro-Asian economy, its rise intimately associated with the coming of the global capitalist economy of Europe. These were related but distinct phenomena, one no less important than the other in shap-ing the economic and social life of the tropics" (Ray 1995: 455).

Clearly distinct as these two pioneering and influential formulations of the bazaar economy are, they share one thing in common: both figures of the bazaar are utterly disenchanted. Perhaps in reaction to the hoary and now disreputable tradition of writing of the bazaar as a space of chaos and irrationality, most recent scholarly accounts have been at pains to reframe the bazaar as a space of rationality. Whether such rationality was embedded in the structural strategies for dealing with information scarcity or the historically developed economic net-works of Asian finance, there was no account here of the role of the occult, the supernatural, or the divine. Later scholars who have been relatively more attentive to the seemingly "extra-economic" actions of bazaar operatives have persisted in this disenchanting vein. When CA Bayly encountered archival evidence of Banarsi merchants in the late eighteenth and early nineteenth centuries engaging in a number of expensive religious activities – such as worshipping account books or caring for cows – he rationalized it in terms of merchants' need to build up commercial credit:. "Men honoured the gods and the sacred ani-mals," he declared, "but a reputation for piety no doubt redounded to their commercial credit" (Bayly 1988: 378–9). What such commercial functionalism has done is allowed for a complete historiographic neglect of the complex knowledge of and about the role of occult forces that motivate many merchants, traders, and customers in South Asia.

While I lean more closely to the accounts of Ray and Bayly in historicizing the space of the bazaar, I also want to break with their disenchanted image. Instead, I see the bazaar as a historical space that has also developed its own rich body of complex epistemologies and ontologies of exchange. The logic of these epistemologies does not fit into our binary models of rational/irrational action. The basic concept of why and how the relationships and practices involved in buying and selling operate frequently did not assume a disenchanted world of social action. Merchants, shopkeepers, customers, and many others frequently understood fundamental actions such as why one shopkeeper turns a profit and another a loss, why customers flock to one shop and not another, or why a business partner cheats her cosharer, etc. while another does not, not in terms economic or social rationalities, but rather within a complex matrix of occult forces. A secret incantation might have drawn customers away from a neighboring store to one's own, a spell cast by a competitor might have sown discord between the cosharers of a business, an amulet worn by the shopkeeper might be the secret of her higher profits.

Most forms of rationality that derive from the European Enlightenment of the seventeenth century are premised on a notion of "facts" that could be established by "observations." These observed facts in turn evidence regularities that are engendered in, rather than outside, Nature (Schaffer 1987: 55–85). Both the abstract reasoning of the formal economists and the social rationality of anthropologists and historians partake of this post-Enlightenment view of "reason." Kajri Jain calls this inability of such reason to comprehend what it cannot accommodate into a regime of factuality and observability, the "limits of secular reason." She points out that: "[T]he refusal to subscribe to a regime of provable truth and falsity is tantamount to blindness, an inability to see at all" (Jain 2007: 9). Here "observability" per se is, in fact, subordinated to a very specific type of observing: what Steven Shapin and Simon Schaffer have called the production of "experimental facts" through well-calibrated and structured "technologies of witnessing." At the core of such observation is the claim of repeatability (Shapin and Schaffer 1989). Consequently, the status of facticity is denied tout court to any phenomenon that is "unobservable" or unrepeatable and located *outside*, rather than *inside* Nature (Mukharji 2018: 31–40).

In the context of South Asian economic history, it is only recently that some historians have begun to challenge the prism of facticity through which commerce and trade were seen. Sudipta Sen's work on precolonial marketplaces for instance, has demonstrated how the meanings, practices, and activities attached to eighteenth-century Bengali marketplaces resisted any easy reduction to spaces of pure economic transactions. The religious, political, and social aspects of these bazaars were not simply operating to maximize profits (Sen 1998). Histories that seek to reconstruct workable models of distinct indigenous or precolonial styles of commerce often overlook this irreducibility. Along a slightly different track, Ritu Birla has historicized the way a new notion of "the economy" as an object of knowledge and governance was itself constituted within colonial administrative and legal discourses. These discourses had to then find ways of translating novel subcontinental forms of mercantile activity into its own framework (Birla 2009). What Sen and Birla's work shows us is that we need to be a lot more circumspect about identifying a "real economy" and thereby naturalizing an abstraction ("the economy") that is of a relatively recent and colonial vintage. In the rampant use of spells, incantations, power objects, and so forth by shopkeepers and others, we notice the existence of a parallel way of conceptualizing commerce that is not organized according to the same principles of natural/unnatural, observability/repeatability, etc.

These parallel conceptions and the amulets, incantations, or spells that sustained them were not simply randomly produced or used. They and complex knowledges about them were developed over time, by specific actors and within particular traditions of knowledge. Studying this knowledge then illuminates a very different epistemic space of commercial activity on the subcontinent. This is what I will call the occult bazaar.

The occult bazaar is neither a single, geographically specific bazaar, nor the kind of ahistorical, structural figure of Geertzian anthropology. It is rather a specific epistemic space in which commercial transactions are seen to be influenced by occult forces that are considered to be real and have concrete, real effects. The way these occult forces are mobilized by those involved in buying and selling is by the use of occult technologies, that is, spells, incantations, amulets, magic diagrams, secret rituals, etc. I deliberately avoid speculating both on whether these occult technologies work at all and/or whether they might have unstated social functionalist goals. I want to trenchantly resist the notion that there is some kind of an "actual economy" that is more real than the epistemic understandings I am calling the "occult bazaar." Hence, I do not want to translate the use of and belief in occult technologies back into the registers of social action or subjective psychology.

The epistemic space of the occult bazaar is anchored in the world of small shopkeepers and tradesmen. Contrary to Ray's contention that the word "bazaar" is used exclusively for urban wholesale markets, according to Gyanendramohan Das' early twentieth-century Bengali dictionary that refers to *bajar* as any space for buying and selling. The verb *bajar kora* ("to do bazaar") entails going to a bazaar and buying commodities (Das 1916: 1083). It is almost never used in the context of wholesale trade, but rather retail buying by individuals. Furthermore, the latter usage is also imprecise about the space of the bazaar as being fixed. Retail buying at small neighborhood stores might also be referred to as *bajar kora*. Following this usage, I will argue that the physical space in which the occult bazaar is most palpably present is in the context of small retail trades. This is not to suggest that other types of firm and merchant are entirely alien to the occult bazaar. Indeed, it is most likely that larger firms and businesses also employ occult technologies. But as we shall see later in this article, going by the kinds of occult technology I have discussed in my archive, I will suggest that small retail trade is where the occult bazaar is most fully materialized.

The chronology of the occult bazaar is difficult to determine. There is clear but circumstantial evidence that a variety of occult forces and technologies were at play in bazaars throughout the subcontinent since at least the nineteenth century. The densest textual traces of the occult bazaar in eastern and northern South Asia, however, date mostly from the 1980s. I will discuss these chronologies in greater depth in later sections, but I will concentrate largely on the Bengali-speaking areas of India and Bangladesh in my analysis.

Here I should also clarify my choice of the word "occult" in preference to the word "religious" that scholars before me have so often used. My choice is informed by two considerations. First, following Talal Asad and others, I find "religion" as a category inadequate to realities it claims to connote in South Asia. Its Protestant origins overemphasize doctrine and belief that risk obscuring ways of acting and being that do not always conform to the doctrinal codes. Second, this emphasis on doctrine and belief also leads, in the South Asian context, to the production of clearly demarcated demographic silos such as

Hindus, Muslims, Jains, etc. Any evidence of practical blurring of these
demarcations then can only be read as "syncretism," "hybridity,"
"eclecticism," etc, thereby further naturalizing the original demarcations by framing the blurred reality as mere moments or episodes when
the lines are crossed. None of this is reflected in the practices of the
occult bazaar.

My approach also determines the archive through which I access the
bazaar. My archive is neither oral lore nor government reports on what
is observed. Neither indeed are they ethnographic observations. It is
rather a body of printed texts produced by occult specialists.
Textualization and publication evidence a degree of formalization
and reflexivity about the practices that are lacking in both oral and
governmental reports, not to mention the utter "exteriority" of ethnography. The texts I use are in Bengali and Hindi, published from
Calcutta, Dhaka, Delhi, and Kamrup (Assam). Most of the texts,
however, lack publication dates. Moreover, such texts have never
been systematically collected by any major public or academic library.
As a result, they are incredibly difficult to date. Based on a fairly large
collection of these texts that I have built up over the years and judging
from their typographic styles, I would suggest that the majority of them
date from the 1980s and later. There are, however, antecedents to these
texts that go all the way back to the mid-nineteenth century, and
perhaps even earlier if we consider manuscripts.

The occult bazaar that is instantiated in these texts is not unrelated
to the hegemonic abstraction designated as "the economy." At many
points the occult bazaar and the economy are interpolated into one
another. For instance, there are several spells and amulets in the
Bengali and Hindi texts that I am using designed to win court cases.
Litigation, of course, arises from the violation of either contractual
obligations or of state regulations. Both of these violations relate to the
economy. Yet, the occult bazaar impinges on it at the point when
someone chooses to use a spell, an amulet, or some other occult
technology, *in order to* determine the outcome of the litigation.
These interactions, however, do not militate against the relative autonomy of these two domains of abstraction. The abstract rules and
regulations of the economic bazaar do not directly shape the rules
and regulations of the occult bazaar.

In what follows, I will outline the occult bazaar as a discursive object
and outline the rationality that animates it. I shall divide the article into

four sections. I will begin by drawing together a number of disparate references to various kinds of occult belief, practice, and technology scattered in a variety of extant works. My intention in assembling these temporally and geographically dispersed references from across the subcontinent together is to lay out a very broad background against which to consider the evidence for the occult bazaar. While my own archive was produced largely in post-1980s eastern, and to a lesser extent northern, South Asia, I want to emphasize its connections to practices and beliefs beyond this discrete chronological and geographic context. Second, I will describe the body of printed books that are my main archives. Here, I will outline the nature and contents of the books and give as comprehensive a history of these poorly archived books as I can. I will also, in that section, distinguish the knowledge in these books from the category usually designated as "religion." The third section will analyze, from the internal evidence of the texts, the kinds of practice and practitioner who use this knowledge. The fourth section will address the occult bazaar itself and lay out its contours. It will do so by outlining the kinds of relationship and exchange that are discussed in my archive. Finally, a brief conclusion will pull the various strands of the discussion together and offer a general summary of the argument.

The Occult Bazaar in History: Introduction and Interpretation

A number of authors, both old and new, have caught glimpses of the occult bazaar. The older, usually colonial, authors, tended to report on occult beliefs and practices as instances of native credulity and categorized them as either "superstition" or "popular religion." Their contemporary nationalist writers, however, have sought to assimilate these practices into a largely homogenous religious tradition. Recent authors, in sharp contrast, have tended to see these practices and beliefs as part of the culturally specific forms of commercial rationality. They in turn have categorized these occult practices as forms of "religious" practice. The very different politics, categories and overall frameworks of the old and new authors notwithstanding, they have produced a fairly rich archive documenting the occult bazaar.

Colonial bureaucrat-ethnographers who produced some of the earliest reports of the occult bazaar tended to see it within the framework of superstitions. Edgar Thurston, for instance, listed a number of such

"superstitions" among the shopkeepers of south Indian bazaars. He
reported that many shopkeepers refused to sell items considered connected to bad luck or poverty after sundown. Thus, clothsellers would
not sell black cloth after lamps were lit. Hardware stores refused to sell
nails or needles after sunset. And, paintshop owners would not sell
white paint in the evening. Likewise, most shopkeepers would never
keep their measuring tools upside down. This, in fact, became a major
problem when the colonial state asked arrack sellers to keep their
measures inverted to help dry them out. Thurston describes the dogged-
ness with which the shopkeepers resisted this demand (Thurston 1912:
31–2).

Three aspects of these practices are worth underlining. First, the
relatively pervasive ideas about misfortune or bad luck that operated
in south Indian bazaars of the time. Second, the fact that shopkeepers
believed that particular actions on their part could influence future
prosperity. Finally, that there was nothing obvious in the way future
prosperity was connected to particular types of commodity. The connections between white paint, black cloth, and nails are hardly obvious.
The recursion of these specific items to prosperity, good fortune, or
success was something that had obviously developed in a specific context. Thurston did not give us clues as to who developed these ideas and
when, although the example of the arrack sellers clearly shows that new
objects (such as the new types of measuring tool) were modifying and
expanding existing practices. We see the outlines of a dynamic
epistemic space that is operated by accepting the reality of occult forces.

Unlike Thurston's description of "superstitions" of south Indian
bazaars, William Crooke, another intrepid colonial bureaucrat-
ethnographer writing mainly about North India, chose to categorize
comparable practices as forms of "popular religion." He wrote of how
the North Indian bazaars were replete with charms against the Evil Eye:
"The number of these charms is legion," he exclaimed. A merchant in
the bazaar, he reported, "writes the words Ram! Ram! several times
near his door, or he makes a representation of the sun and moon, or
a rude image of Ganesa, the godling of good luck, or draws the mystical
Swastika." The merchant's home too was replete with such "charms."
Crooke reported visiting a merchant at home in Kankhal, Haridwar,
and seeing the outside of his house adorned by the images of a large
number of deities and seers, ranging from Shiva, Parvati, and Yamaraj
to Uddalak, Narada, and Bhagiratha (Crooke 1896: 160–161). Several

colonial authors, including Crooke, also reported the worship of Ganesha, whom the latter dismissively dubbed the "godling" of luck (Martin 1914: 191; Rodrigues 1842: 11–12).

Crooke's category of "popular religion," although problematic in many ways, inadvertently revealed the limits of the seemingly more respectable category "religion." For one, "popular religion" became a sort of horizontally integrated, fuzzy category where the better known "religions" such as Hinduism, Islam, Jainism, etc., tended to blur into one another. It also expressed the redundancy of high theological dogma of these faiths and the practice on the ground. Indeed, for Crooke "popular religion" functioned as a kind of debased domain where theology had become desiccated by ignorance.

Unfortunately, it is difficult to contrast these colonial voices with South Asian ones because most South Asian authors tended to ignore the practices of the occult bazaar. One notable exception, however, was the Bengali practice of *hal-khata*, where a number of rituals were performed around the inauguration of new account books. Kalipada Mitra, writing in 1938, described how old accounts were settled, new account books started, and old retainers had their contracts verbally renewed (Mitra 1938: 115). Eight years later, Jogeshchandra Ray, a well-known botanist, astrologer, and man of letters, gave another brief account of *hal-khata* (Ray 1946: 209). Both Mitra and Ray however, slotted the practice into an age-old Sanskritic religious tradition. More recently, historian Sufia Uddin points out that in Bengal, *hal-khata* is widely celebrated in mercantile communities (Uddin 2006: 135).

Recent scholars have excavated the colonial archive to describe a far wider set of practices connected to the occult bazaar. As I have already mentioned, Bayly documented many of these practices common in the Banaras region in the late eighteenth and early nineteenth centuries. He recorded for instance, the expenses incurred by merchants in order to bathe in the Ganga, in gifting Brahmins, etc. Bayly wrote that: "[G]ods were considered to be integral, living members of the family, so that elaborate provisions were made to see that they were clothed, fed and fanned during the hot weather." Besides these family deities, he also noted that most merchants paid for the worship of the goddess Lakshmi, especially during the special occasions of Diwali and Holi (Bayly 1988). He conceptualized these actions as building up the social credit of merchants. Piety allowed the merchant to build up his and his family's creditworthiness and achieve the twinned familial goals of wealth and honor.

Dipesh Chakrabarty, writing about modern Bengal, documented comparable practices, although he conceptualized them very differently. He saw the worship of deities such as Lakshmi and Ganesh as creating a sense of community in the bazaar. He also argued that rituals were used to spatially distinguish the shopfloor from the outside and thereby recreate a kind of quasi-domestic space within the shop. He drew particular attention to the ways in which shopkeepers accentuated the threshold that marked the shop's interior off from the external space. Most conspicuous among the practices discussed by him, however, was the widespread practice of established merchants in a bazaar jointly sponsoring a single bazaar temple (Chakrabarty 2002: 74).

The issue of merchants building or sponsoring places of worship in the bazaars of western India have been discussed in greater detail by Douglas Haynes. He described how a number of artisanal communities built temples, shrines, and mosques in the nineteenth century in Surat. The Surti Khatris built a temple for their *Kuladevi*, the Padmasalis built a temple to their community deity, Markandeya, and Momin merchants built mosques in Malegaon and Bhiwandi. Haynes argues that the building of these places of worship "certainly contributed as well to the development of group coherence" (Haynes 2012: 85). Elsewhere, Haynes also points out that the existence of institutions of communal worship provided an arena for social patronage that allowed the richer merchants to exercise forms of indirect power over their laborers and employees (Haynes 2012: 156).

Valuable as these insights are, each of these modern scholarly descriptions translates the practices into a social functionalist register. Bayly interprets them as functions that enhance commercial credit. Chakrabarty reads them as cues to the structural organization of space. Haynes interprets them in terms of group coherence and social power within the mercantile communities. None of these interpretations is inaccurate, but neither do they engage with the ways in which the *bazaari*s themselves thought of these actions. The imposition of a social functionalist logic on these actions obviates any need to explore how the practices themselves developed, who fostered them, and exactly what those who performed them thought of them. There is also the easy assimilation of these actions into the category of "religion" without much actual reflection on whether and why we should call these practices "religious." Some of the spells that I have found in my archive, for instance, even threatened the "deities" and "spirits" being addressed. Rather than forms of religious worship, these activities are better conceptualized as occult technologies.

Occult technologies, I will insist, bear only a superficial resemblance to religious rituals. They are, in fact, tools for a much more instrumental manipulation of occult forces and agencies than would usually be expected in the context of religious rituals. These occult technologies do not invoke theology or demand belief or faith. Like any other technology, they merely emphasize the mechanical application of a set of rules properly, without the least expectation of devotion, faith, etc. A few examples will help clarify both the nature of what I am calling occult technology and why it is distinct from forms of religious worship.

One such occult technology, included in an undated Bengali text dating possibly from the 1980s, involves the following: "Hanging a picture of a person standing in front of cows and playing a flute in a room, shop or place of business and respectfully offering the picture joss-sticks and incense every day, ensures that one is not burdened by debt and the chances of incurring losses are reduced" (Shastri n.d.: 163).

In another instance from the same text, an incantation is recommended for obtaining a job or for increasing one's income. The author of the manual that offers this particular occult technology mentioned that "this is an Islamic verse (*Musalmani ayat*) and Muslim brothers (*Muslim bhaira*) tend to use this more often" (Shastri n.d.: 146).

A third occult technology given in the same manual recommended is as follows: "To remove obstacles and impediments in your business first make four rag dolls. Then recite the *mantra* given below 108 times and blow on the dolls. After that bury the dolls in the four corners of your shop or place of business. Thereafter continue to recite the *mantra* 108 times every day" (Shastri n.d.: 153).

It would be clear to anyone familiar with South Asian bazaar iconography that the first occult technology that I cited might well be taken to refer to prints or posters showing the Hindu god, Krishna. Yet, what is remarkable is that nowhere in the text is the figure described as a Hindu god. Thus, we might well envisage a situation where a non-Hindu hangs such an image in his shop and offers joss-sticks (*dhup-dhuna*) to it. To an external observer this might simply appear to be the worship of Krishna. Yet, as is clear from the instructions, the image is neither imagined as Krishna nor are acts such as the offering of joss-sticks conceptualized as worshipping Krishna. Similar examples can be found of the use of the images of Ganesh and Lakshmi in ways that clearly displace their specifically "Hindu" identities and render them simply instruments whose manipulations lead to success in business.

The second technology that I have cited explicitly clarifies this breach between the source of these occult forces and technologies within religious cosmologies and their operation outside the register of "religion." It is admittedly of Islamic origin and yet the statement that "Muslim brothers tend to use it more often" plainly suggests that there is no essential link between the Islamic faith and the use of this occult technology. The greater use of the specific technology by Muslims is merely incidental. There is no essential or necessary connection between being a Muslim and using this particularly, seemingly Islamicate, occult technology.

Finally, the third example demonstrates that not all occult technologies are conspicuous or socially visible. Unlike the images hung on walls, the recitation of incantations and the burying of potentiated rag dolls are usually not conspicuous social acts. They, like much else in this realm of activities, are performed in isolation and in secret. While the diehard social functionalist might still argue that the reason for hanging up the Krishna-like picture is a way of conveying piety or sociomoral credit to potential customers or fellow *bazaaris*, it would be impossible to make such claims about actions whose performance emphasizes secrecy and inconspicuousness.

Whether we agree in calling these occult technologies "religious" or not therefore, this much at least is clear that they confound categories such as "worship" as well as the trenchant framework of social functionalism that scholars have tended to turn to whenever confronted by evidence of the occult bazaar. To locate the ways in which these occult technologies operate, we need to get beyond social functionalism.

Bazaar Grimoires

The printed books that form my primary archive for delving into the contours of the occult bazaar might be described as bazaar grimoires. Owen Davies defines grimoires as "books of conjuration and charms, providing instructions on how to make magical objects such as protective objects and talismans. They are repertoires of knowledge that arm people against evil spirits and witches, heal their illnesses, fulfill their sexual desires, divine and alter their destiny and much else" (Davies 2010: 1). As is clear from Davies' phrase "and much else," these books are exceedingly eclectic and hence difficult to comprehensively define. Yet, they have been well-known across several ancient, medieval, and modern cultures.

Unfortunately, little detailed information exists on South Asian grimoires. Their history, in any case difficult to access owing to secrecy and poor archiving, has been almost entirely neglected. Yet, one can frequently buy these books at roadside stalls, railway stations, and bus depots throughout much of South Asia. I have seen and bought such books in Calcutta, Dhaka, and Delhi and have no doubt that they could be procured at many other locations in the region. The contemporary publications range in price from between 50 and 600 rupees. They come with striking dustjackets and are sometimes nearly 1,000 pages in length. Also, remarkable is the fact that many of them are printed entirely in red ink.

I call these books bazaar grimoires to signal both their affinity to and distance from the European grimoires. Besides the obvious linguistic differences between the two, the former are also located within a textual economy that is, in spite of their relatively high prices, considered fairly lowbrow. Both their circulation and content have long implicated them in the world of the South Asian bazaars.

The major libraries usually did not systematically collect these books and hence their historical evolution is difficult to study. Moreover, many of the books, despite being published works and going into several editions, are undated. This might either be a result of copyright issues, because much material is often reproduced in texts of this genre, or because the books often uniformly claim that the knowledge contained in them is of ancient provenance. However, it may be the lack of dates that makes a historian's task all the more challenging. This makes the books in general and their overall evolution difficult to date. Based on the texts that I have been able to find, however, I will suggest a relatively loose chronology for the evolution of these texts, while also noting that the aura of timelessness that accrues to the books owing to the difficulties in dating them firmly is very much a part of the social authority they carry.

The earliest Bengali grimoire I have been able to find is a slim volume known as the *Bangiya Biswasya Mantrabali* (Trusted Bengali Mantras) held at the British Library. The anonymously published text dating from 1863 is a mere twelve pages in length and mostly concerned with medical topics such as exorcisms and the treatment of snake bites (Anon (Gupta Pracharak) 1863). The incantations included in the collection invoked a range of sources of occult power including both Hindu deities such as Mahadev and Sri Ram, as well as Islamic figures such as Ghazi Pir, the Prophet, etc.

Books such as the *Bangiya Biswasya Mantrabali* appealed to both Hindus and Muslims. As a result, in 1910 Oyajuddin Muhammad published a book titled the *Echhlamiya Mantra* (Islamic Mantras) in which he tried to convince Muslims not to use the spells of the nonbelievers (*kufri mantra*). Ironically, his own collection of mantras, too, however, invoked several non-Islamic sources of occult power.

These early printed texts might have evolved out of earlier manuscript collections of spells and incantations. Panchanan Mandal's collection of early-modern Bengali manuscripts at Santiniketan contains some manuscript examples of spellbooks (Mandal 1963: 365). Both the manuscripts and the early printed works from the nineteenth century were dominated by healing spells and love magic. Occult technologies for shopkeepers did not seem to feature in them.

It was in the interwar years that we begin to see the printed Bengali grimoires containing occult technologies that might have been used in bazaars. Two types of such technologies are worth mentioning. First is a suite of occult technologies aimed at getting rich. These were not directly offered to shopkeepers or businessmen but, of course, they might well have been used by them.

It was the second set of occult technologies that were more directly connected to the retail trades of the bazaar. These, however, were what might be called negative occult technologies or technologies of occult attack. They were aimed at destroying the wares of particular bazaar tradesmen. One such technology, for instance, was meant to destroy the clothes in possession of a washerman (*rajak*). Another was to destroy the fish of a fisherman (*dhibar*). A third was to destroy the spinach of a spinach farmer. A fourth was to destroy the betel leaf (*paan*) grown by a betel leaf farmer. Yet another was to destroy a milkman's milk and so forth (Dutta 1924: 113–15).

These interwar Bengali texts were relatively larger than the nineteenth century ones. They were usually just under 200 pages in length. Also, interestingly, around this time, many of these books began to be printed entirely in red ink. This might have been a mimicry of certain manuscript practices, but there is no clear discussion of why this change occurred.

As far as I can tell the basic format, size, and content of these bazaar grimoires remained largely unchanged from the interwar decades to the 1980s. Thereafter, there was a veritable explosion in both their size and contents. From the 1980s, the books kept growing fatter and fatter and often were over 1,000 pages in length. Their prices too shot up from a few rupees to a few hundred rupees. Moreover, new printing technologies have allowed more visually rich dustjackets to contribute toward this explicit religious coding of the books. The colorful pictures of deities and other communally marked symbols, especially on the dustjackets, clearly locate the contents of the books within this or that contemporary "religious" silo. Yet, they are ever more eclectic in the occult agencies and powers they invoke. Consider, for instance, these examples from another undated Bengali bazaar grimoire published in Calcutta:

Kuvera Mantra: Repeat a particular *mantra* invoking the god of wealth, Kuvera, 5,00,000 times. Thereafter recite another *mantra* to the same deity. While the latter *mantra* is being chanted, light nine lamps and pour milk into them. Thereafter repeat a third *mantra* 5,00,000 times while performing a fire offering (*homa*). (Bhattacharya n.d.: 188–9)

Magic Square: On the first Thursday of any *shuklapaksha* (brighter half of the lunar month) write out a particular "magic square" seven times using black ink. Thereafter recite the *Bismillah* followed by the *Durud sharif*. Follow this again with the *Bismillah* and repeat a particular *mantra* 101 times followed once more by the *Durud sharif*. (Bhattacharya n.d.: 773–4)

Both these occult technologies are aimed at expanding one's business and increasing profits. They appear in the same book alongside a number of other technologies. Yet, they draw clearly on religious traditions that are usually taken to be distinct. The "magic square" explicitly invokes Allah and does so broadly through formulas available in the Islamic tradition, whereas the Kuvera Mantra draws mainly from Hindu tradition. Yet, being placed side by side and being offered to the same reader/user they clearly disengage these actions and powers from the specific religious context that they are affiliated to.

Even more subversively, the contents of these books also force us to reconsider the category of "religion" itself. The occult technologies recommended in the books do not always conform to our received ideas of what "religious" practice is. Consider for instance, the following examples from the same source I have just cited:

Write out a particular "magic square" 700 times upon a birch leaf using an ink made by mixing saffron and Ganga-water and a pen made from the branch of the jasmine tree. Do it on a Friday. Once it is done, roll it into a number of small balls with wheat flour and feed it to the fishes. This will bring success to your business. (Bhattacharya n.d.: 188)

Likewise, we find the following in a book published in Kamrup, Assam, in 2000:

Write out a particular "magic square" on a piece of paper. Wrap it in a piece of green cloth. Insert it into an amulet and seal it with wax. Hang the amulet anywhere in the shop. This will increase the sales in the shop. (Bholanath 2000: 347)

A third instance of the manner occult forces are instrumentalized in nondenominationally stipulated ways can be seen in a text published in Dhaka in 2007:

Write out a particular verse from the Quran upon a small wooden tablet and hang it up on the wall of a shop to increase the sales. The verse is to be copied out in Arabic. (Hakim 2007: 162)

Neither of these examples invoked any theology or required any specific belief or faith. Given the range of different religious traditions they draw from, they did not even specifically require any specific creedal commitment. In fact, the books are fairly clear that occult technologies would work for whosoever employed them irrespective of that person's religious faith. This is particularly clearly seen in the third instance. While the books regularly transliterate into Bengali all Quranic verses or Sanskrit mantras that need to be recited aloud, it never explains or translates any of them. In the third example I have offered here, it does not even transliterate the verse, giving instead the Arabic script to be copied out. The user, it is clear, needs neither to comprehend the meaning of the verse nor even to have faith in it, as long as he or she copies it out and puts it on the wall of the shop. Consequently, the shopkeeper does not need to be a Muslim to be able to successfully use this technology. Therefore, while they clearly draw on religious traditions, they seem to conceptualize the occult forces they seek to manipulate as being operational beyond the bounds of theological boundaries.[1]

The kind of operations involving occult technologies that we notice in the bazaar grimoires do not necessitate devotion or belief and have little use of formal theologies. All that one needs to do to achieve the particular type of success in her business is to deploy a particular occult technology according to the prescribed rules of its usage. In that sense, the bazaar grimoires are like glorified users' manuals that accompany any technology. What is worth clarifying, however, is that for this body of knowledge, these user manuals are all there is. There is no other, more "theoretical" – or more appropriately "theological" – text that is available. All that exist are these manuals for manipulating a range of numinous powers for success in business.

Patterns of Practice

One partial drawback of the archive of bazaar grimoires is that they do not tell us anything about how these occult technologies were actually used. What they do tell us is how they are meant to be used. Given the extent to which past ethnographic observers were insensitive to the logic of these practices, those observations, too, are of limited value in reconstructing usage. While undertaking a more sensitive ethnography specifically targeted at learning how these technologies are used might help illuminate contemporary usage, they, too, are of limited use in reconstructing historical practice. Yet, on reading the bazaar grimoires carefully, we are able to reconstruct at least some idealized patterns of practice. In fact, it is precisely this idealization of practice that I want to highlight to substantiate my point that the occult bazaar constitutes an independent, albeit admittedly not entirely insulated, sphere of discursive abstraction, distinct from the discursive object called "the economy." Just as writers on economics, be they economists, sociologists, ethnographers, or state functionaries, create abstracted figures and patterns of practice, so, too, do the authors of bazaar grimoires.

---

[1] Talal Asad has argued that "religion" itself is a category produced by and through European colonialism. Asad also contends that the category is utterly inadequate for non-European or "non-Enlightenment" traditions (Asad 1993).

One of the most regular figures of practice that we encounter in these bazaar grimoires is the shopkeeper seeking to increase sales in her shop. A practice that is frequently recommended to such a shopkeeper is to place a particular material object at specific places in the shop. These objects can be both conspicuous and inconspicuous. Among the more conspicuous recommendations are instructions to hang particular illustrations or images in the shop. In one instance, an undated Bengali text published in Calcutta known as *Sarba Siddhidata Pustak* (Book that Gives off All Fulfillments), enjoins the shopkeeper to hang a picture of the goddess Lakshmi on a wall inside the shop. After opening the shop every morning, he is enjoined to offer joss-sticks and incense to the image and recite two specific incantations 108 times each. This, it is said, will augment his sales forthwith (Bhattacharya n.d.: 582). Likewise, in another instance, found in an immensely popular Bengali book published in Dhaka, which was already in its eleventh edition in 2007, the shopkeeper is told to hang a Quranic verse written out on a wooden plaque being hung up on a wall (Hakim 2007: 162). A third and slightly different recommendation, also found in the text from Dhaka, required the shopkeeper to write out a particular magic square written in Arabic and hang it anywhere in the shop (Hakim 2007: 236). Yet another similar occult technology, included in the *Sarba Siddhidata Pustak*, required the user to write out a specific magic square using red sandalwood paste on any wall in the shop on the day of Diwali. Subsequently, the user had to offer incense and joss-sticks to the magic square every day, in order for the business at the shop to thrive (Bhattacharya n.d.: 623). Interestingly, neither of these technologies required the plaque or the square to be placed in view of the customers or the shopkeepers. Like an occult magnet of sorts, it would be effective irrespective of where the shopkeeper hung it in the shop.

In some cases, the recommended practice or object had to necessarily be kept inconspicuous. Thus, in one case, *Sarba Siddhidata Pustak* instructed the shopkeeper to write out a magic square with red sandalwood paste, alongside the name of his firm, and simply keep the square inside his cashbox for profits to grow (Bhattacharya n.d.: 171). In another case found in the same source, the businesswoman was instructed to make a swastika sign with vermillion on either the cashbox or safe on the day of Diwali. Thereafter, she had to offer flowers to it while uttering an incantation to Kuvera (Bhattacharya n.d.: 198). A third technology, described in a Bengali book published in Mograhat in West Bengal, required the shopkeeper to write out and place a specific magic square in her shop before dawn on the "time of either Qamar, Shams, Mushtari, or Zohra" (these are, respectively, the ruling stars of Monday, Sunday, Thursday, and Friday) (Rummal 2010: 173). What is worth noting about these practices is that they are clearly not always visible either to the customer or to the competitor. While we might be able to imagine cashboxes placed in a way that they remain visible, clearly placing a magic square *inside* the cashbox or writing out a magic square before dawn (and placing it anywhere, however, inconspicuous), would render it invisible to anyone other than the person who had access to the cashbox. This, once again, testifies to the inadequacy of social functionalism to illuminate the occult bazaar.

Distinct from the above patterns of practice, but even more inconspicuous, are those practices that involve a shopkeeper performing the recommended actions away from the physical space of the shop. One such occult technology is recommended for shopkeepers who import foreign goods for sale in their shops.

Even less socially conspicuous are those practices that are clearly to be performed in isolation. One occult technology, mentioned in a book by one Girishchandra Bholanath published in Kamrup, Assam, targeting those engaged in importing goods for sale from foreign countries, instructed the businessman to write out a particular magic square using mustard oil on a birch leaf and then bury it in secret in a nearby forest (Bholanath 2000: 486). Likewise, another similar technology in the same text, intended to help those whose businesses were failing turn them around, involved filling up a clear bottle with mustard oil and then throwing the bottle into any lake, pond, or river (Bholanath 2000: 609). A slightly different but more interesting example of a figure of practice, described in the *Sarba Siddhidata Pustak*, and which was to be conducted in isolation, required the shopkeeper to begin by entrapping a crow on a Thursday afternoon. The crow was to then be kept in a cage and fed and given water regularly until Sunday. On Sunday, the crow was to be fed a special diet of yoghurt mixed with sugar. On Monday morning, when he shopkeeper opened his shop he was to step into it with his right foot first. That evening, after the shop was closed, the crow was to be set free (Bhattacharya n.d.: 123). Nowhere was the shopkeeper enjoined to bring the crow to the shop or perform any conspicuous action at the site of the business. Clearly, the whole set of actions could be, and was possibly expected to be performed at the shopkeeper's home and hence potentially outside the purview of both customers and competitors. Another occult technology, mentioned in Bholanath's book, involved the user chanting a particular mantra 108 times on a handful of black gram after taking a bath on a Sunday morning. Later, the potentiated black gram was to be scattered in the shop (Bholanath 2000: 242). Once again, the fact that mantra was to be chanted on a Sunday morning, and not necessarily at the shop, meant that there was little chance of its being observed by any significant social group.

What seems more important to the success of these occult technologies than social visibility are particular temporal rhythms. Specific days of the week, as we can see from the examples I have already offered, are particularly crucial to the performance of certain types of action connected to specific occult technologies. The fact, for instance, that a crow is to be trapped on a Thursday afternoon, fed the special diet on a Sunday, and released on the following Monday, or that the black gram has to be potentiated on a Sunday, all draw attention to the importance of particular days of the week for particular actions. The use of the reigning stars for the days of the week to refer to the days in one of the instances cited above underlines the way in which weekly temporality is conceptualized in dealing with occult technologies. Although, once again, the braiding of many different cosmological frameworks in the same text usually means that it is impossible to discern a single temporal grid that will work for all the occult technologies. Yet, the notion that each day has a distinctive occult value or charge is clearly shared across the whole family of practices.

Certain annual rhythms are also significant. A number of technologies, for example, require specific actions on the day of Diwali, which, of course, is an annual festival. In one case included in Bholanath's book for instance, a magic square had to be carved on a sheet of copper and then "enlivened" (*pran pratistha*) on Diwali before being placed inside the cashbox or safe (Bholanath 2000: 543). *Dol purnima* or Holi was another potent annual festival on which certain occult manipulations could be effected (Shastri n.d.: 155–6). This emphasis on specifically auspicious days also evinces a conception of each day as having a different occult potential.

Besides these annual and weekly rhythms, there are also a number of occult technologies that call for specific daily rhythms of performance. The swastika on the cashbox, for example, required the daily offering of incense to keep it active. Another interesting occult technology mentioned by Bholanath required the shopkeeper to daily write out a specific magic square, roll it into a wick with some cotton, and burn it in a lamp with either jasmine or sesame oil for a fixed number of days (Bholanath 2000: 339).

Like time, space too acquires a set of very specific and nuanced potencies in the occult bazaar. Dipesh Chakrabarty's observation about the importance of the threshold can be deepened further by looking at the particular potencies of specific locations within and without the shop. Consider, for instance, the surface and volume of the cashbox, which, as we have seen above, was the site for the operation of several occult technologies. Similarly, the shops' walls on occasion were mobilized for and by specific occult technologies. In one instance drawn from the *Sarba Siddhidata Pustak*, the shopkeeper was advised to recite a mantra 108 times into some water and then sprinkle the water on to the walls of the store (Bhattacharya n.d.: 145). These instances demonstrate that the whole space within the shop was not homogenous. Different parts of it, viz. walls or the cashbox, had a particular value that distinguished them from all other places in the shop. In certain cases, the goods themselves or the place where they were stored were distinguished from other places, such as the shopfront. In one case described in the text from Mograhat, West Bengal, for instance, the shopkeeper is advised to write out a specific *ayat* from the Quran and place it among the products he is selling (Rummal 2010: 79). In another instance in Bholanath's work, a magic square was to be written out and then washed with water with the washing water then being sprinkled on the unsold products in the shop (Bholanath 2000: 339).

This is not to suggest that the shop as a whole never acted as a single spatial unit. There were indeed instances where "shopkeepers will use their own rituals for marking the area of the shop as enclosed space" (Chakrabarty 2002: 74). The scattering of black gram anywhere in the shop or the lighting of lamps with specially potentiated wicks all suggested that the shop as a whole formed a single spatial unit. My point, however, is to demonstrate that these were not the only, or even the most numerous, spatial practices used by shopkeepers to manipulate occult forces.

The basic logic of practice that becomes visible in the bazaar grimoires therefore conveys three important insights. First, while some practices are certainly conspicuous and might have a secondary social function to signal piety, etc., not all the practices are equally conspicuous. Some are distinctly secretive. This suggests that the practices as a whole cannot be explained away in terms of their social functionalism. Second, time is not conceptualized as being homogenous or uniform when it comes to the operations of occult forces. Their successful manipulation requires the calibration of occult technologies to intricate temporal classifications as well as attending to certain routines rhythms of practice. Finally, the spatial grids within which the occult forces operate are also complex and differentiated. While the shop as a whole is sometimes mobilized as a single spatial unit, the space within it is not conceptualized as being uniform. Certain spaces, such as cashboxes or the surface of goods, are particularly pregnant sites for the operations of occult forces.

Aside from these structural aspects of the practices described in the bazaar grimoires, we also notice a reasonably complex set of abstract figures of agency. Thus, just as scholars pursuing social functionalist approaches described abstract figures of agency in the bazaar such as "clients," "patrons," etc., so too do the authors of bazaar grimoires describe a set of abstract agents such as the "shopkeeper seeking to increase profits," "shopkeeper incurring losses," "shopkeeper who stocks foreign goods," etc. The last figure is particularly redolent in the Bengal region where the creation of new international borders after 1947 has meant that a lot of small-scale bazaar trade actually operates across international boundaries and thus faces a different set of exigencies than those traders whose shops are further away from the border and its volatility.

The existence of such abstract agents and specific structures of temporal and spatial operation, I will argue, testify to the fact that the occult bazaar is a specific, coherent, and abstract discursive figure that is relatively independent of the economic space conceptualized by social functionalists. In fact, bazaar grimoires make absolutely no mention of the social functions of the occult technologies whatsoever. Instead, they premise the success of these occult technologies on their ability to change the fortune of the user by transforming the way other specific actors, such as employees, customers, business partners, regulators, and rivals, engage with the user. But this transformation is not understood in psychological terms. Rather, the occult technologies are seen to have a direct effect on all concerned parties unmediated by psychological factors.

Occulted Relationships

Historical and anthropological studies of the bazaar economy have tended to focus overwhelmingly on the modalities through which sellers and customers interact. Geertz has described the "clientization" that operates between sellers and buyers, reading it as functional adaptation in a context where economic transactions are conducted within under conditions of information paucity (Geertz 1978). Comparably, Chakrabarty has described the linguistic practices by which sellers establish a kind of pseudo-kinship with the customer in a bid to reduce the risks involved in transactions (Chakrabarty 2002: 75). Illuminating as these discussions are, they are also narrowly focused on only a single type of transactional relationship in the bazaar, namely that between buyers and sellers.

Close attention to the bazaar grimoires reveals a far more diverse set of relationships that constitute the bazaar. Buyers and sellers are only two figures within a much more complex sociology involving workers, owners, debtors, state functionaries, and so on. Occult technologies are used by much wider array of actors and agents, such as cosharers, employees, debtors, creditors, etc.

To understand and map these relationships, we must begin by first getting a general sense of the kind of bazaar trades that might use occult technologies. The bazaar grimoires make several explicit references to the many different types of trade that the occult technologies are targeted at. One such list, mentioned in Bholanath's *Asal Lajjatun Nechha*, lists all the trades on which the god Shani (Saturn) presides. These include a lengthy but motley set of occupations that can be parsed into two groups for clarity. First, there are the businesses that specialize in a single commodity, viz. iron, steel, coal, stones, glass, cement, plastic, leather, *kambal* (blankets), cattle, *pan* (betel leaf rolling), mustard oil, alcohol, spirit, black peppers, *kolai* (gram), and *surma* (lead sulfide). Second, there are certain professions such as machine operators, judges, clerks, painters, real-estate agents (*jami kena-becha*), *dalals* (go-betweens), drivers, rickshaw pullers, *dhopa* (washermen), peasants, diggers, and, perhaps most interestingly, those who sells magic, incantations, etc. (*jadu-mantra-tantra*)

(Bholanath 2000: 758). These, however, were only those métiers on which Shani exercised dominion. This document was far from being an exhaustive list of all the possible occupations in and of the bazaar. Other bazaar grimoires listed a number of other trades such as "shops that sell tea, *lassi*, and soda-water," potters, boatmen, betel cultivators, dairy farmers, etc. (Shastri n.d.: 472).

There are three aspects of these enumeration of trades amply clarifies. First, the intricate classification of trades points to a complex framework that does not lump all types of bazaar transactions together. The fact that the same occult forces that affect automobile drivers and rickshaw pullers for instance cannot affect boatmen, demonstrates a classificatory grid that is both nuanced and discriminating. At the same time, it also blurs our usual divisions between trades, occupations, and jobs by classifying the clerk, the rickshaw puller, and the *surma* seller in the same group. Clearly the familiar distinctions between salaried jobs and businesses or those desk jobs and small trades are redundant in the classifications of the bazaar grimoires. Second, the inclusion of peddlers of magic among the other occupations of the bazaar is significant. Clearly the bazaar grimoires thereby reflexively locate their own purveyors and practitioners among the trades of the bazaar itself, rather than as a component of some abstract domain of "religion." In this regard, it is also important to note that the priest is never mentioned among the occupations of the bazaar. Third, the inclusion of the judge – which clearly stands out – in the list demonstrates that the world of the bazaar is not entirely cut off from the more elite apparatus of the state. In fact, a fairly large number of occult technologies are putatively directed towards the judge or magistrate.

The world that emerges on perusing the list of trades and occupations listed in the bazaar grimoires is essentially one of small businesses, shops, and trades. At its higher end are wholesalers of iron, while at its lower end are the betel leaf rollers and *lassi* makers. This testifies to a certain degree of scalar integration. While we know from the works of Bayly, Haynes, and others that fairly large businesses also had recourse to occult forces, the bazaar grimoires we have been studying do not seem to directly reference such large, wealthy businesses. Instead, the target users of the occult technologies contained in the bazaar grimoires seem to be the medium to small businesses.

Aside from the nuanced grouping of different trades, the bazaar grimoires also describe a range of different relationships in the occult bazaar. To begin with there is, of course, the figure of the customer. The following is an example, found in a text published in Dhubri, Assam, of a technology that directly mentioned the customer:

If the sales in a shop are low, because of which profits are also low then the shopkeeper should do the following: write out this particular *ayat* [in Arabic] on a piece of paper either three hours after sunrise on a Monday or five hours after sunrise on a Friday or before sunrise on a Thursday on a piece of paper. Paste the paper on to a piece of piece-board and hang it up somewhere in the shop where the buyers (*khariddar*) will clearly notice it. (Fakir 1830: 251)

In addition to the customer, the bazaar grimoires also mention a number of other transactional relationships. Among these are the figures of the creditor, debtor, and defaulter. There are several occult technologies aimed at freeing oneself from a debtor or conversely those that are aimed at making a defaulter pay up. Consider, for instance, the following occult technology, described in a text from Dhaka: "If any person who is in debt, were to write out the following magic square (*naksha*) every morning and put it into balls of wheat flour and throw it into a river for seven consecutive days, then by Allah's mercy one or the other way of repaying the debt will become available" (Hakim 2007: 103). The reverse situation is invoked in the following occult technology, from the same text: "Whosoever recites the *surah al-mulk* 41 times will find some means of recovering the money he has given as a loan" (Hakim 2007: 103). In another case mentioned in an undated text from Calcutta, the occult technology was directed at delayed payments, rather than at unpaid loans per se. The *Tantra-Mantra-Yantra O Totka* described four different magic squares for such delayed payments. These were to be written out on a piece of paper and then consecrated by burning incense and joss-sticks. The whole process was then to be repeated. Thereafter, one of the two squares was to be kept in the cashbox, while the other was to be pasted on the first page of the "ledger" (the English word being used). This *yantra* will compel the buyers to pay up quickly and settle their accounts (Shastri n.d.: 166). Some of the occult technologies also distinguished between personal loans and business loans (Shastri n.d.: 167).

Taken together, these figures evidence a complex understanding of the types of agency exercised in the occult bazaar that go far beyond the simple dichotomies of buyer–seller or client–patron. The occult bazaar recognizes not only a range of different types of transaction and agent, but also distinguishes between the different temporalities that organize financial transactions. This complex schema further reinforces my contention that the bazaar grimoires constitute the occult bazaar as a distinct discursive space.

Although the bazaar grimoires eschew targeting large businesses, even medium and small businesses often employ others. The image of bazaar trading as being purely about individual proprietor-operators and customers is highly misleading. As a result, there are several occult technologies that address the employer–employee relationship. Consider for example the following occult technology, found in a book published in Calcutta:

If the employees of your firm get together and refuse to work, if you need to repeatedly find replacements or they simply keep leaving your firm, then do the following: On a Saturday quietly pick up any piece of iron that you find on the way to your factory or workplace. Once you arrive at your workplace wash the iron nail with buffalo's urine and then wash it with Ganga water. Thereafter hammer it into the wall in the room where your employee works. Be sure to hammer it in hard, so that you can hang things on the nail. Once this is done, so long as the nail remains steady your employee will also remain steady. (Shastri n.d.: 149–50)

A somewhat more sinister technology included in the text from Dhubri, Assam, was meant to make a runaway employee return. It enjoined the employer to write out a magic square, put it on a *charkha*, and turn it in reverse. As a result, the employee would return within two days (Fakir 1830: 193).

In contrast, there were a range of technologies available for employees to contest the power of the employer. Consider for instance, the following instructions in the text from Mograhat:

If any person is compelled to go to an oppressor (*jalim/zalim*) everyday, either for a law-suit or in the course of his regular job, then do the following. After the *fajr namaz* on a Thursday recite the following verse 40 times and blow into a mixture of fragrant oil and the essence of musk. Repeat this for a week. After that apply the mixture to your own body and go to the oppressor. God willing, that very day your wishes will be fulfilled. (Rummal 2010: 71–2)

It is interesting how this technology blurs the lines between the oppressive employer and the judge. The occult technologies available for use by the employee include those that will enable one to get a job, those that will make the employer more lenient, and ones that will help an unhappy employee leave the job.

Besides customers, debtors, and employees, a small number of occult technologies were also targeted at cosharers or business partners. One of the bazaar grimoires, undated work published in Calcutta, actually elaborated in some detail about the nature of the relationship. It wrote that: "[The practice of] accepting a partner (*anshidar*) into a business or a partnership business (*angshidari byabsha*) is very ancient (*pracheen*). This partnership can be between two people or several people. My intention in saying all this is that partnership businesses are like a pot broken in the middle of a market (*haate hanri bhenge jawar moto*). That is to say that partnership businesses are frequently unsuccessful. There are [also] some firms where this is not true. There all the partners work with love and dedication" (Shastri n.d.: 149). The author then went on to describe some occult technologies to run a partnership firm "smoothly and successfully."

Taken together the range of relationships towards which occult technologies are directed, testifies to the structural complexity of the occult bazaar. This is not a simple economic space in which buyers and sellers operate with unmediated immediacy. Transactions form part of a complex set of relationships and there are myriad negotiations that cannot be summed up in the binary relationship between the buyer and the seller. Unfortunately, most of the models of the bazaar economy that extant scholarship offers to some extent simplify the structural complexity of the bazaar and reduce the range of roles and relationships in it. But the bazaar grimoires, written as they are for practical ends, cannot ignore this complexity.

Accounting for this multiplicity of roles and relationships in the occult bazaar also reveals the multiple fault lines that *bazaari*s had to navigate. They had to simultaneously negotiate with employees, partners, debtors, and creditors, besides the customers per se. Each of these relationships was potentially troublesome but also necessary. In each of them, occult forces had a role to play and thus occult technologies could be used to control them. Moreover, these technologies were not exclusively available to any one side. The debtor might have used them against the creditor and vice versa, just as the employer and employee or the partners and cosharers might have used such technologies against one another.

The mutuality and orthogonal nature of occult technologies of the bazaar are nowhere more obvious than in dealing with rivals and competitors. Several technologies are available to both "attack" and "defend" one's shop or business. Consider, for instance, the following instructions in the text from Mograhat: "If anyone wants to stop the sales at someone's shop, he [should] write out the magic diagram (*naksha*) given below and bury it underneath the shop" (Rummal 2010: 154). In exact contrast to this, we find the following instructions in a text from Calcutta attached to a different occult technology: "If your business is not running smoothly and you face obstacles and impediments, or if some malicious person has tied your business or used some *tantric* instrument (*tantric prayog*) to destroy your business, if buyers have stopped coming to your store and your income has decreased, then use this instrument on the night of *Holi*, that is, *Dol purnima* [to free your business from the malign force]" (Shastri n.d.: 155). Rivals, therefore, are one of the most prominent kinds of actor in the occult bazaar and each bazaar must simultaneously use both defensive and offensive occult technologies to deal with them.

Conclusion

The bazaar is a space that is awash with occult forces. These forces have occasionally been glimpsed in passing in the extant scholarship but seldom been interrogated on their own terms. The tendency to argue for their rationality by finding a social function for them has, perhaps unwittingly, obscured the range and complexity of the framework within which they operate.

While this chapter is far from being a comprehensive survey, what I have shown is that there is a substantial body of formalized, textual knowledge pertaining to the ways in which occult forces operate in the bazaar and the ways in which they might be manipulated. It is not my objective to argue that these forces are "real" or to propose some social function that will explain why they are "efficacious" even if they are not "real." My humble ambition is to simply show that they are not only widely believed in but that there is a fairly extensive body of knowledge that has been developed around them that historians have mostly ignored.

In making this case, it is obviously important to also distinguish these forces and their manipulation from the register of "religion." As I have demonstrated above both the nature of the occult technologies and the eclecticism which is evinced in the texts that contain these technologies, militate against the putative implication of these technologies and forces onto the register of "religion." It is clear that irrespective of whether we think of religion-as-faith or religion-as-ideology, to use a useful distinction proposed by Ashis Nandy (1988: 177–94), it does not cover the species of actions that I have been calling occult technologies. They force us to rethink the monopoly we have allowed to the category of "religion" over the occult forces in the bazaar.

The body of knowledge about these forces has engendered a coherent and complex discursive object that I have designated as the occult bazaar. This occult bazaar as a discursive object is independent of, although not insulated from, the other major discursive object, viz. "the economy," which provides an abstract representation to explain the transactions of the bazaar. It is structured by a complex emic rationality that engenders its own specific temporal rhythms, spatial maps, and classification of forms of transactional financial agencies. In delineating occult bazaar and the contours of its emic rationality, I want to break with the hoary tradition of social functionalism that has informed most accounts of the "rationality of the bazaar" and bear witness to the fact that *bazaaris* have their own forms of complex forms of rationality that are organized around the formal knowledge of occult forces and their manipulation.

References

Anon. [Gupta Pracharak] 1863, *Bangiya Biswasya Mantrabali (Trusted Bengali Mantras)*, Prakrita Jantralaya, Calcutta.

Asad, T 1993, *Genealogies of Religion: Discipline and Reasons of Power in Christianity and Islam*, Johns Hopkins University Press, Baltimore.

Bayly, CA 1988, *Rulers, Townsmen and Bazaars: North Indian Society in the Age of British Expansion, 1770–1870*, Cambridge University Press, Cambridge.

Bhattacharya, S n.d., *Sarba Siddhidata Pustak*, Rajendra Library, Calcutta.

Bholanath, G 2000, in AS Tibra & G Chakrabarty (eds.) *Koka Panditer 200 Shata Bachhar Purber Asal Lajjatun Nechha*, Kamrup Kamakhya Tantra Mantra Publication, Kamrup.

Birla, R 2009, *Stages of Capital: Law, Culture, and Market Governance in Late Colonial India*, Duke University Press, Durham.

Chakrabarty, D 2002, *Habitations of Modernity: Essays in the Wake of Subaltern Studies*, University of Chicago Press, Chicago.

Crooke, W 1896, *The Popular Religion and Folklore of Northern India*, vol. I, Archibald Constable & Co., London.

Das, G 1916, *Bangla Bhashar Abhidhan* (Dictionary of the Bengali Language), Indian Press, Allahabad.

Davies, O 2010, *Grimoires: A History of Magic Books*, Oxford University Press, New York.

Dutta, D 1924, *Rakshasitantram*, 8th ed., Sankar Press, Calcutta.

Fakir, NU 1830, *Adi O Asal Lajjatunnechha Sarba Manaskamna Pustak*, Assam Library, Dhubri.

Geertz, C 1978, "The Bazaar Economy: Information and Search in Peasant Marketing," *American Economic Review*, 68, 2: 28–32.

Hakim, L 2007, in Dost M Bharati (ed.), *Adi O Asal Solemani Tabijer Kitab ba Elaje Lokmani*, trans. MH Khan, 11th ed., Solemani Book House, Dhaka.

Haynes, DE 2012, *Small Town Capitalism in Western India: Artisans, Merchants and the Making of the Informal Economy, 1870–1960*, Cambridge University Press, Cambridge.

Jain, K 2007, *Gods in the Bazaar: The Economies of Indian Calendar Art*, Duke University Press, Durham.

Mandal, P 1963, *Punthi Paricaya*, vol. 3, Vidya Bhavan, Santiniketan.

Martin, EO 1914, *The Gods of India. A Brief Description of Their History, Character & Worship. With 68 Illustrations and Map*, Dent, New York and London.

Mitra, K 1938, "The New Year Festivals," *Man in India*, 18, 2–3: 106–21.

Mukharji, PB 2018, "Occulted Materialities," *History and Technology*, 34, 1: 31–40 (2 January).

Nandy, A 1988, "The Politics of Secularism and the Recovery of Religious Tolerance," *Alternatives 8, The Politics of Secularism and the Recovery*, vol. 132, 177–194.

Ray, J 1946, "Pragjyotishapura," *Modern Review*, 79, 3.

Ray, RK 1995, "Asian Capital in the Age of European Domination: The Rise of the Bazaar, 1800–1914," *Modern Asian Studies*, 29, 3: 449–554.

Rodrigues, EA 1842, *The Complete Hindoo Pantheon, Comprising the Principal Deities Wrshipped by the Natives of British India Throughout Hindoostan: Being a Collection of the Bods and Goddesses Accompanied by a Succinct History and Descriptive of the Idols*, E.A. Rodrigues, Vepery, Madras.

Rummal, GH 2010, in MM Ahmed (ed.) *Kanjul Husayn – Tabijer Kitab*, trans. MA Qasemi, 3rd edn, Ahmed Publications, Mograhat.

Schaffer, S 1987, "Godly Men and Mechanical Philosophers: Souls and Spirits in Restoration Natural Philosophy," *Science in Context*, 1, 1: 55–85.

Sen, S 1998, *Empire of Free Trade : The East India Company and the Making of the Colonial Marketplace*, University of Pennsylvania Press, Philadelphia.

Shapin, S & Schaffer, S 1989, *Leviathan and the Air-Pump: Hobbes, Boyle and the Experimental Life*, Princeton University Press, Princeton.

Shastri, B n.d., *Tantra-Mantra-Yantra o Totka*, General Library and Press, Calcutta.

Thurston, E 1912, *Omens and Superstitions of Southern India*, T. Fisher Unwin, London.

Uddin, SM 2006, *Constructing Bangladesh: Religion, Ethnicity, and Language in an Islamic Nation*, University of North Carolina Press, Chapel Hill.

Yang, AA 1998, *Bazaar India: Markets, Society, and the Colonial State in Gangetic Bihar*, University of California Press, Berkeley.

5 | Vernacular Capitalism, Advertising, and the Bazaar in Early Twentieth-Century Western India

DOUGLAS E. HAYNES [*]

In David Davidar's novel *The House of Blue Mangoes* (2002: 160–68), set in early twentieth-century Tamil Nadu (c. 1910), the main character is an indigenous medical practitioner (*vaidyasalai*) named Daniel Dorai, who discovers a lotion that lightens skin color. Calling it "Dr. DORAI'S MOONWHITE THYLAM," he tries out the product on his family. Soon news spreads in his town about the cream's remarkable properties. Many of his client–patients begin to demand bottles of the cream when they consult him on other health issues. After a short time, Dorai starts placing ads for his product in *The Hindu*, the region's most important English-language newspaper. The ad stresses that "DR. DORAI'S MOONWHITE THYLAM MAKES YOUR FACE SHINE LIKE THE PONGAL MOON." It includes a rhyming "ditty" that runs:

> On the darkest night your face will gleam
> With Dr. Dorai's MOONWHITE CREAM
> A thylam which will make you glow
> Whiter than the whitest snow.

Caught unprepared for the massive response to his advertisement, Dorai is forced to transform part of the home of his predecessor in the business into a factory to produce Moonwhite Thylam. He also hires some nearby glassblowers to make the jars in which the cream is packaged. Owing to his advertising efforts, "pharmacies"[1] through much of south India begin selling Moonwhite Thylam. Over the next

---

[*] This paper has been presented in several locations including the University of Göttingen and Dartmouth College. The author wishes to thank attendees at these talks and especially the editors of this volume for their comments.

[1] The contemporary term for shops in which both local and foreign medicines were sold as well as for companies that produced indigenous medicine.

116

few years, Dorai goes on to become a very successful businessman. Davidar also highlights the perspective of a shopkeeper in Madras, who sells various kinds of medicinal product. The shopkeeper receives a dozen bottles of the thylam for sale from his local supplier soon after the advertisement appears. In spite of his own inclinations against skin lighteners, the shopkeeper feels compelled by the demand for the product to pressure Daniel for more stock. As Davidar represents the situation, the shopkeeper is, in effect, rendered helpless to resist the forces unleashed by the advertisement.

While the figures of Daniel Dorai and the shopkeeper are fictitious, they are clearly based on actual historical characters or on a close reading of newspaper advertisements from the early twentieth century. Davidar's account reflects an awareness of a form of business in India that was consolidating itself through the medium of advertising, one that I call "vernacular capitalism." By this term, I refer to new kinds of small, individual or family-run firm involving the manufacture of consumer products that advertised widely in the emerging print media, particularly vernacular newspapers. These businesses were involved in producing many commodities: cosmetics (like Dr. Dorai's Moonwhite Thylam), tonics (including sex tonics), hair oil, medicines, soap, matches, handloom and power loom saris, incense, and calendars. These types of firm were different from the big foreign multinational companies and Indian business corporations, which were also involved in catering to Indian consumers, in that they did not employ mass manufacturing techniques or have a corporate structure. In the initial stages of the formation of vernacular firms, the family members and sometimes a small clerical staff conducted all the roles of developing products and improving technology, supervising workers and production processes, marketing goods, and devising and placing advertising. By relying on the techniques of the modern mass media, vernacular capitalists developed demand for brand-name products throughout entire linguistic regions. When they placed ads in English or multiple vernaculars, they could even cultivate multiregional demand.

Modern business history on the early twentieth century has largely overlooked the development of vernacular capitalism, focusing primarily on the truly big business entrepreneurs in South Asia, such as capitalists in the textile industry and the large Marwari organizations that emerged after the Second World War (for instance, Roy 2018; Tripathi 2013). Both Tirthankar Roy (1999) and I (2012b) have looked at small-scale manufacturers engaged in the production of cloth, gold thread, leather, and several other products. Our works have high-lighted technological developments in these firms and the methods they used in recruiting and supervising labor, and they have stressed the importance of new markets for their products. But neither of us, nor, indeed, any other historian, discusses their marketing efforts to any significant extent. The works of Rajat Ray (for example, 1992), Chris Bayly (1983), and Anand Yang (1998) on the bazaar explore the spaces in which goods were sold and distributed, the character of transactions between merchants in these places, and the role of indigenous finance, but do not examine the new kinds of indigenous *producer* who were starting to enter these marketplaces after 1880 or the techniques they used to gain customers. Work on medical history (Berger 2013; Mukharji 2012; Schneider 2008; Sharma 2011, 2012) has drawn attention to advertisements run by small medical firms and has stressed how these firms became involved in commodity produc-tion but has not explored the implications of advertising for the busi-ness history of the subcontinent. Visual history has recently examined advertisements associated with commercial activity but has tended to focus on the most striking visual elements of this activity rather than their more quotidian aspects and their transformative role in the econ-omy (Haynes 2015; Jain 2007; various essays on the website *Tasveerghar*).[2]

This chapter seeks to place advertisement of vernacular firms in a business history of the subcontinent that takes the production of commodity images seriously. I argue here that advertisement became an important method used by manufacturing firms to develop markets, and that analysis of advertising highlights changes in the economy, including transformations in the character of the bazaar brought about by advertisements. A significant key to the emerging kinds of consumer-based business, I suggest, was to play a direct role in con-structing the cultural meanings of products sold far away from the place of manufacture, and in branding commodities so they would be distinguished from myriad other items in the same product categories. In so doing, these businesses sought *partially* to usurp the role of agents located in the bazaar who had been central to constructing consumers'

---

[2]   Recent exceptions are papers on advertising by Biswas (2016) and
    Venkatachalapathy (2014).

understandings of commodities. To adapt the language of this volume's introduction, their project was one of attempting to *disembed* the construction of meaning from a localized context. While the role of shopkeepers in the bazaar was never displaced completely, vernacular businesses increasingly concentrated the manufacturing and marketing processes under the same manager–owners.

The Emergence of Vernacular Capitalism

The rise of vernacular capitalists owes itself to their ability to take advantage of two new aspects of the early twentieth-century commercial environment: (1) the development of new consuming classes, particularly the urban middle class as well as other literate consumers willing to buy mass produced commodities in bigger cities and small towns, and (2) the wider dissemination of new print media, particularly in vernacular languages. Vernacular capitalists were entrepreneurs who devised new kinds of products for middle-class consumers and who discovered innovative methods of marketing their goods in print.

The formation of a small but growing middle class certainly facilitated the development of alternative forms of customership in India. The development of largely new occupational forms – government workers doing clerical and other jobs in the British administration, journalists, doctors, lawyers, the employees of larger multinational firms, and the clerks of local businesses – created a category of people who performed salaried work in the colonial economy. Individually, their incomes were often modest but the cash they controlled collectively for spending on consumer items was sufficient to attract the attention of many businesses. They typically acquired information about the goods they consumed through channels quite different from those associated with court culture in precolonial India or from localized sources of knowledge. For example, a writer in the journal *Kanara Saraswat* observed that elderly women in the Saraswat community, who had earlier possessed substantial knowledge about the value of herbs and other natural products drawn from the rural environment, lost touch with these forms of expertise as the community became increasingly urbanized (Chandavarkar 1938: 10). In some cases, middle-class Indians frowned on traditional knowledge about commodities as unscientific and backward. Persons deploying local medical practices might be dismissed as "quacks" whose preparations

relied on folk norms unsupported by scientific knowledge, while goods
sold by itinerant peddlers might be questioned for lacking uniform
quality. Members of the middle class looked to some new forms of
goods – for instance, packaged medicines, six-yard saris and soap – as
crucial markers of modernity. The fact that consumer-oriented vernacular businesses and global firms began to flourish in South Asia
around the same time as a category of people had emerged that identified itself as "middle class" is no coincidence. Most critically, members
of the middle class came to rely increasingly on advertisements as
a source of information about commodities.

At roughly the same time, the print media began to provide producers more direct channels for cultivating markets for commercial
goods. At present, our understanding of the ways commercial actors
established demand for their goods in distant locales before the early
twentieth century is limited. The picture we have seems to emphasize
the crucial role of "trading carriers" (Yang 1998: 227), who typically
purchased supplies at places of production and then transported them
to consuming regions by bullock carts, where they were sold to local
traders in larger regional towns and religious fairs. The local merchants
in turn often carried these goods into the smaller bazaars and periodic
markets, where they were sold by shopkeepers and hawkers. In the
religious fair of Maheji in Khandesh district, trading carriers brought
large quantities of commodities in caravans over the Ghats from centers spread over Maharashtra and Central India and sold these goods to
traders and itinerant peddlers who, in turn, took them into village
markets (Haynes 1999). These various figures were not just commercial actors in a narrow sense but were purveyors of the cultural meanings associated with these commodities. The original producer had very
limited means of transmitting commodity images directly to the consumer or even the shopkeeper at the local level, and products were
rarely marketed by brand name or their producers' names. Cloth
available in Maheji in the late nineteenth century, for instance, was
known by the *place* of its manufacture and not by the manufacturing
firm itself.[3]

---

[3] The practice of conveying the reputation of commodities by place name rather
than by brand has been widespread in the subcontinent, as Barbara Harris has
pointed out in a personal communication.

In this commercial environment, local merchants were crucial figures in constructing the understandings by which consumers made sense of different items. These meanings could differ radically from producers' intentions. An American advertising expert with experience in India recounted one example of such a wide divergence. To the expert's surprise, an American product intended to be used as a throat spray was acquiring a wide market in India. When he asked a Parsi merchant how this could be the merchant responded: "Ah yes, sahib! All the Eurasian girls buy it . . . . Three or four applications and the skin turns three shades whiter" (Eldredge 1930: 25). No doubt, the merchant in this instance was characterizing skin-lightening qualities that he and other shopkeepers were touting actively, rather than a perception generated just by the "Eurasian girls."

In a more contemporary exploration, Dulali Nag (1990) has examined the ways in which local shopkeepers describe the characteristics of *tangail* saris in Calcutta as customers sit in their shops. In this kind of system, the saris' qualities, rather than the reputation of their producers, became the key selling points stressed by the shopkeeper. Tomtom beaters and town criers, who are sometimes seen as representing preprint forms of "advertising" in India were typically hired by shopkeepers at the local level rather than by producers.

The possibility of print advertising rarely eliminated the role of intermediate figures in the marketing process, but it gave producers access to powerful means of shaping demand in places far from the manufacturing locale. An "imagined community" of largely middle-class consumers, who could read advertisements in towns spread widely over a region's landscape at the same time, could be conceived of and reached through newspaper advertising. With advertisement, the producing firm could create a more standardized set of commodity meanings that would, in effect, travel with the goods as they moved from the manufacturing establishment to wholesalers or other intermediaries and then into the bazaar shops, where goods were sold to consumers.[4] In effect, the use of advertisements allowed producers to contest the control of local shopkeepers and trading carriers over the construction of product meanings. Vernacular firms, sometimes very

---

[4] By using this concept, I deliberately invoke analogies to Benedict Anderson's concept of *Imagined Communities* (Anderson 1991), specifically his contrast between imagined communities and face-to-face communities.

modest ones, could try to influence the consumption of its commodities directly. Advertisement, in other words, facilitated the emergence of new types of small manufacturing firm that increasingly added a modern marketing dimension to their producing functions.[5] As they established demand for their products, these vernacular firms typically hired more workers on a wage labor basis to carry out production.

Our limited evidence indicates that demand was often built up through a process similar to that suggested in Davidar's book. The small manufacturing firms rarely sought to create new kinds of retail outlet themselves, but they funneled their products through shops in the bazaar. After designing new products, they typically encouraged local shopkeepers to stock an initial small supply of the commodities (perhaps by providing the items at low prices) as they began advertising in the locality. Once some customers purchased the item (and word had gone around about its qualities), the shopkeeper would hopefully seek to replenish his stocks.[6] As the firm did more business, it often developed more permanent arrangements with sales agents or wholesalers, who would be responsible for the local distribution of goods. Either the producing firm or the local agent would run advertisements to sustain customer interest. Advertising reinforced the message that was being transmitted by word of mouth. No producer could hope to achieve commercial success through advertising alone, so it could never completely replace the agency of local actors in constructing product meanings.

It is critical to emphasize that most retail sales continued to take place through the bazaar during the early twentieth century. At this time, new kinds of retail establishment – such as department stores and large showrooms – were being established in some of India's largest cities. Here goods were often sold at fixed prices, but these stores marketed their commodities mainly to European expatriates and wealthy Indian elites, not to wider sets of consumers (McGowan 2019). Only in a small number of cases did large companies create new retail outlets for their products; Godrej and Boyce's stores for its furniture is perhaps the best documented example (McGowan). But commodities produced by vernacular capitalists rarely made their way

---

[5] This section is influenced by the discussion of large enterprises in an American context in Alfred Chandler's classic work, *The Visible Hand* (1977).

[6] This process is described, for instance for multinational firms, in Eldredge (1930).

into these new kinds of commercial establishment. Instead their retail sales still took place in bazaar shops, which catered almost exclusively to Indians. Middle-class households sometimes sent their servants to the shops, providing them with old containers, labels, or advertisements so that the servants, often illiterate, would know what to purchase (U.S. Department of Commerce 1933: 8). Consumers could also make purchases by mail orders, paying for the goods on delivery (VPP) at their homes (U.S. Department of Commerce 1933: 8). These methods of merchandizing placed a premium on effective advertising and the development of distinctive trademarks.

Medical Advertising

The earliest and perhaps the most extensive form of advertising in Indian newspapers by vernacular firms was that for medical goods (hair oil might be its main rival). The early twentieth century witnessed the proliferation of medical firms. As Jeremy Schneider (2008: 15) has argued in discussing the rise of medical businesses in India:, "[T]he allure of an expanding market, the requirement of only small capital outlays and the proliferation of medical manuals spurred the entrance of many entrepreneurs into the manufacture and marketing of indigenous medical products." Medical advertisements often became critical to these newspapers' income, at least until the claims they made were regulated in the Drugs and Magic Remedies (Objectionable Advertisements) Act of 1954 (Gupta 2002: 66–83).

Medical notices typically alerted readers to the possibilities for self-diagnosis and self-treatment. By buying advertised medical commodities, middle-class consumers could hope to address their health problems without seeking intervention of medical specialists, thus saving themselves the awkwardness of revealing embarrassing personal details as well as the costs of paying doctor's fees that could strain their family budgets. Writing about the advertisement of Ayurvedic products during the early twentieth century, Schneider has argued (Schneider 2008: 39): "[N]o longer was the trained and the experienced *vaidya* (Ayurvedic practitioner) seen as the anchor and irreplaceable element necessary to achieve health and strength, rather the drug itself assumed overarching importance." The commodity advertised, Schneider suggests, displaced the balanced regimen of bodily practices – diet, exercise, the use of medicinal substances, and perhaps sexual restraint – that the indigenous practitioner might prescribe (Schneider 2008: 46–7). Advertisements similarly offered the possibility of bypassing professional doctors trained in Western bio-medicine at British India's universities (see also Daechsel 2006: 179).

Advertising proved particularly valuable when the product in question involved medical conditions that middle-class people would have been reluctant to discuss. Male sexual dysfunction, for instance, was a subject potentially surrounded by shame that middle-class men often were hesitant to talk about with their partners, their doctors, or their friends; ads sometimes referred to sex as a *gupt* or "secret" subject. Use of advertised tonics could displace reliance on traditional *gurus* or astrol-ogers, who had frequently been consulted when family members experi-enced sexual problems, such as the failure to produce offspring, and who prescribed appropriate charms and remedies.[7] Both indigenous medical specialists and doctors trained in Western medicine might have well-established relationships with the family or friends of a patient and could potentially leak damaging information into his social circle. Testifying to the *Drugs Enquiry Commission* around 1930, VK Parulkar, a Bombay doctor, specifically tied the role of medical advertisements to fears about revealing personal habits such as masturbation, widely believed to be the source of sexual dysfunction:

Specifically, these advertisements make great effect on men who have got weak nerves as a result of self-abuse [i.e., masturbation]. They are ashamed to tell their secret to doctors and expect doctors to find out the cause. In some cases therefore doctors are not able to find out the cause, in the absence of the clear history of which patients should give to medical men. Such patients therefore come to the conclusion that it is wise for them to try such remedies.

Impotency in such cases is very common. Such men spend tremendous sums of money for getting virile again. (Government of India 1931: 359)

For women, consultation with either a local specialist or a Western doctor might also involve revealing information about their physical conditions, such as infertility and irregular periods. Self-medication by using advertised products thus had the advantage of being discrete and less expensive but potentially "scientific" and "modern" in appearance. Sales through advertising permitted a certain anonymity on the part of the middle-class consumer that was missing when he or she relied on the medical specialist, whether "biomedical" or "indigenous." In other

---

[7] My thanks to Kaushik Bhaumik for this information about local practice.

words, vernacular capitalism through advertising contributed to (partially) loosening medical practice from the many social nexuses in which it had been embedded.

By the early twentieth century, a wide range of entrepreneurs had established medical businesses that relied on advertisements in western Indian newspapers. Most of their manufacturing establishments were located in the Bombay Presidency, but others were based elsewhere in India. In many cases, these firms' founders claimed to be well-qualified practitioners steeped in indigenous knowledge, such as Ayurvedic or Unani medicine, and asserted that they had discovered particularly effective medicines that would address a variety of ailments. Typically, they established a legal trademark for their commodities and began marketing them in areas close to their home bases. As demand for their products grew, they expanded the area of their activities; advertising in newspapers in distant locales became a crucial part of the commercial strategy of firms seeking to establish greater geographic reach. The examination of advertisements generated by three such firms illustrates this point.

Amritdhara

One firm that advertised widely in the English media of the Bombay Presidency during the interwar period was Amritdhara Pharmacy. The firm's ads mentioned that it had been founded in Lahore in 1901 by Vaidya Bhushan Pandit Thakur Datta Sharma, a *vaidya* from Lahore, whom one ad referred to as a "qualified Ayurvedic Physician with significant experience in treating patients" (Schneider 2008: 20). Evidence from a legal case that began in 1954 (and that has stretched into the current decade) indicates that the firm was originally called Amritki-Dhara (liquid of immortality), but Thakur Datta Sharma altered the trademark name in 1903 to Amritdhara. One source indicates that sales of Amritdhara had reached a lakh of rupees in 1911 (http://indiankanoon.org/doc/394080/). The company's original product was intended to address "headaches, diarrhoea and other complaints" (https://indiankanoon.org/doc/368264/).

By the second decade of the twentieth century, the firm was marketing its goods well beyond Punjab. Ads from Amritdhara can be found in the *Bombay Chronicle* from 1918 until well into the 1940s; the ads themselves mention that publicity for Amritdhara was available in

"English, Canarese, Telugu, and Marathi," as well as Hindi (May 18, 1918: 12; September 30, 1924: 11), suggesting an almost all-India focus to the company's campaign. The ads often included the postal address where the buyers could obtain a wider range of publicity materials; this information was perhaps meant to encourage readers to order the product directly from the company, with payment made on delivery by the postal service (although clearly many customers purchased it in local markets). Some ads picture customers picking up the product at a shop, perhaps indicating a presence in the bazaar (*Bombay Chronicle*, April 26, 1919: 14) (see Figure 5.1).

A 1936 *Chronicle* ad indicates that Amritdhara was distributed locally in Bombay by Chimanlal Shah of Princess Street. In 1938, the company had a clerical staff of twelve employees, including individuals who were involved in designing advertisements (http://indiankanoon.org/doc/368264/). Amritdhara products retained their distinctive trade-mark packaging well into the colonial period. Amritdhara became a limited liability company in 1942, transferred its operations from Lahore to Dehradun in 1947, continued to expand its operations after independence, and remains a significant Ayurvedic business to the current day (https://indiancaselaws.wordpress.com/2013/09/06/amrit dhara-pharmacy-vs-satya-deo-gupta/).

As it sought to establish markets outside its home region, Amritdhara made a series of bold claims for its products. To some extent, these claims used the rhetoric of the sidewalk hawker, with little grounding in the language of modern medicine (either of biomedicine or Ayurveda). In 1918, one ad in the *Chronicle* argued that Amritdhara was "INDIA'S infallible cure for all diseases," that it cured "miraculously all aches from head to foot" as well as a host of illnesses including indigestion, constipation, plague, cholera, and pneumonia (*Bombay Chronicle*, May 18, 1918: 12). Another ad referred to Amritdhara as the "TRUE ELIXIR OF LIFE, VITALITY AND HEALTH." "Among medicines," it insisted, "there is always only one that appeals to all sufferers. The most wonderful medicine in the world is the miraculous discovery of Kavi Vinod Vaidya Bhushan Pandit Thakur Datta Sharma, Vaidya of Lahore. Amazing cures are being wrought by it" (*Bombay Chronicle*, October 16, 1919: 11). Another stressed that the product was a "true panacea ... Hundreds of medicine chests are nothing compared with a small phial of this medicine." This ad also promised that Amritdhara could address

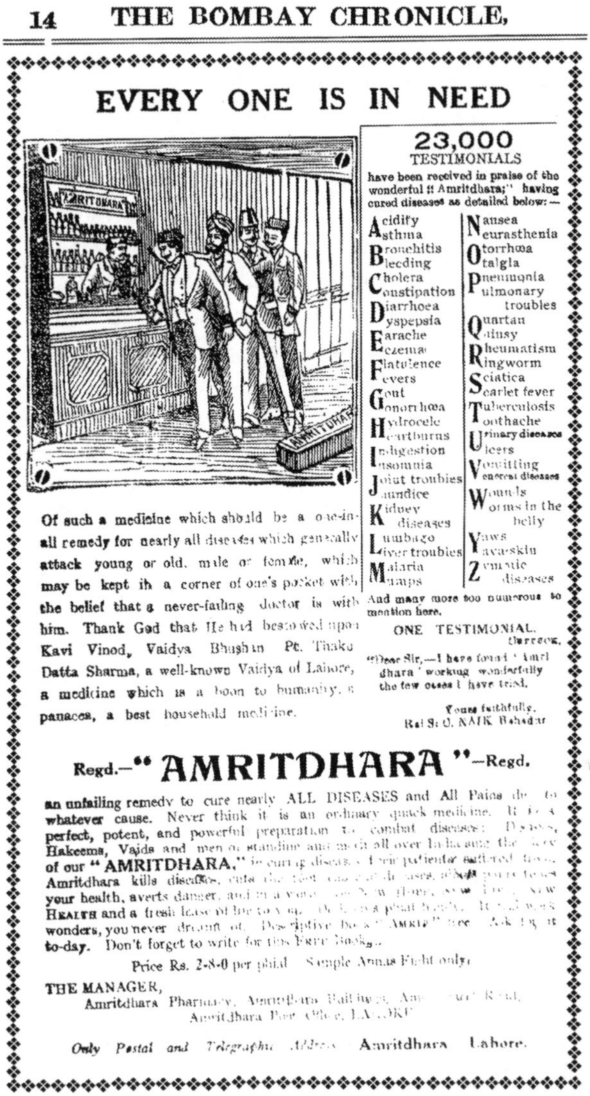

Figure 5.1 *Bombay Chronicle*, June 7, 1919, p. 14

diseases of animals and birds (*Bombay Chronicle*, December 19, 1918). Ads often touted thousands of testimonials the pharmacy had received, with one indicating that: "Doctors, Hakeems, Vaids, and men of standing and merit all over India sing the glory of our 'Amritdhara'

in curing diseases" (*Bombay Chronicle*, April 10, 1919: 3). Others
mentioned the endorsement of well-known professionals in government, the legal system, and education. Schneider argues that testimonials provided a crucial personal element in establishing customer trust
for commodities as firms moved from more local to national markets
(Schneider 2008: 20). Pictures in these early ads often featured
European characters, perhaps an indication that the ads were designed
by personnel working for the *Chronicle*.

In some ads, Amritdhara Pharmacy made arguments that its products possessed "tonic" qualities, a reference that usually suggested an
ability to improve male sexual function.[8] An ad for Amritdhara's
medicine Asugari, for instances, suggests the commodity was a herbal
product that "cures Diabetes of all kinds in all stages" and was "also
a great **Tonic** ... Vital Debility, Impotency, Sexual Weakness,
Spermatorrhea etc. are cured and the patient becomes an altogether
different man. It gives strength, increases life, digests food and
improves appetite. This medicine fulfils all the requirements of the
present day, and it is the king of the Aphrodisiacs." The notice added
that the product was "Cheap!" and gave a price of Rs. 4 for thirty-two
pills. Ads stressing the tonic properties of Amritdhara continued
throughout the interwar period (for instance, *Bombay Chronicle*,
November 12, 1923: 4; December 27, 1927: 7; February 7, 1928: 11).

In the 1930s, the central claims of the Amritdhara ads remained the
same, but the artwork was transformed significantly, reflecting increased
investment in designing and producing ads. A 1936 ad featured a snake
charmer (referred to as a "health" charmer) and promised that the
product's properties made it infallible in combating almost all diseases
(*Bombay Chronicle*, May 26, 1936: 9). Another ad from that year
mentioned a wide range of goods produced by the company, including
a medicine called *Makardhawaja*, a compound of which was portrayed
as an "aphrodisiac tonic as well as removes lack of retention [premature
ejaculation?]" (*Bombay Chronicle*, December 31, 1936: 11).

The ad claimed *Makardhawaja* was the only "Ayurvedic medicine
accepted by European and Indian Allopathy." Visually, the ad featured
a couple in a romantic pose, seemingly about to kiss. Advertisements

---

[8] The word itself has a broader meaning. According to *Webster's Third
International Dictionary of the English Language (2002), a tonic is "something
that invigorates, restores, refreshes or stimulates."

Who is not in
Danger
during the Epidemic
# of Cholera?

Heed you must for
the approaching
sickness and equip
yourself with

Amritdhara,
the world-renowned
never-failing remedy
and sure reventive
for this fell di-
sease; few drops of
Amritdhara will check
the further progress
at once and **three or four doses will completely cure** this
dreadful disease. Three drops daily in time of danger will
act as a potent and sure preventive. Millions of users
have declared it the

only infallible Remedy
in Cholera, Cholerine, Diarrhœa, Dysentery, Looseness of
the bowels, Constipation, Colic, Indigestion and kindred
ailments. It also cures Influenza, Fevers, Pneumonia and
Plague. A phial of the invaluable specific procured beforehand
would save many lives. For full particulars send for
booklet "Amrit" free.

Price Rs. 2-8 per phial, sample phial As. 8 only.

The Manager

AMRITDHARA PHARMACY,
**Table No. I Amritdhara Buildings, Amritdhara Road.
Amritdhara Post Office, LAHORE**
Postal and Telegraphic Address, "AMRITDHARA," Lahore.

Figure 5.2 *Bombay Chronicle*, February 27, 1919, p. 2

continued to stress Amritdhara's claims as a "panacea" throughout the
decade but now invoked values of conjugality and science, perhaps
reflecting the influence of ads for multinational products (see Figure 5.2).

Jadibuti

As the evidence from Amritdhara advertisement indicates, the sale of
tonics promising greater sexual potency was a major business during

the twentieth century. Some of these products achieved markets covering many regions of India. One such commodity was a tonic referred to
as "Jadibuti Manliness Set" from Ambala District in Punjab, which
was marketed by a businessman named SH Hussain. Unlike Thakur
Datta Sharma, Hussain claimed no special training in indigenous medicine. Jadibuti was actually a set of three items – a powder, an oil, and
a kind of pill – that were to be used in combination. Ads for Jadibuti ran
for roughly a decade in the *Mumbai Samachar*, Bombay's leading
Gujarati newspaper, but they were found in Marathi papers as well.
These ads typically give the address of the firm in Ambala, suggesting
the product might also be purchased by parcel post. But ads during the
1930s also mention that a local branch existed in Mumbai from which
Jadibuti could be obtained. Hussain himself seems to have traveled
around India publicizing Jadibuti, even occasionally staying in
Bombay – he clearly regarded the city as a major market.

To date I have found little information about the company's beginnings. One advertisement provides a myth about the firm's foundation
(*Mumbai Samachar*, January 6, 1928: 4). In this advertisement,
Hussain related an account of his life story. He confessed – taking the
anxious male reader into his confidence – to have had "bad habits"
(masturbation) during his childhood so that he was not fit for marriage
when he was twenty-five. He was ashamed of his nonperformance, and
after failing to find a remedy from local medical practitioners, he left his
home. During his travels, he met a *mahatma* (sage) in Kashmir who
took pity on him and gave him herbs to cure his problem. Within five
days, he indicates, the weakness in his penis was gone and his "youth"
had returned; his semen had become thick. He later set out to make
available to India's men the same product the holy man had provided
him.

The drawing featured in these ads illustrates Hussain's life account
(Figure 5.3 provides one version).[9] They feature a holy man and
a young man surrounded by a snake. Written in English on the snake
are the various causes of the young man's affliction: "masterbation
[sic.], spermatorrhea, premature ejaculation and nocturnal emission."
Above him are the phrases "no health, no happiness," "shyful dis-
grace," "anxiety," "no enjoyment," "dead life," and "dishonour of
family" – all supposed consequences of impotence. Three angel-like

[9] I have published the specific ad discussed here in Haynes (2012: 801).

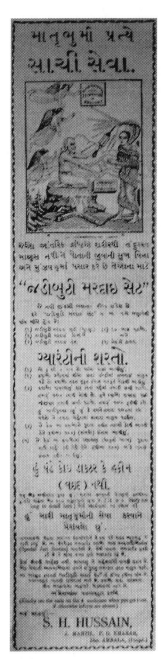

Figure 5.3 *Mumbai Samachar*, July 11, 1927, p. 13

figures with mustachios, one carrying a sign that reads "guaranteed extirpation of impotency," fly overhead. The three figures, seemingly representing the three elements of the "masculinity set," may have been drawn from the Parsi theater.[10] The subtext reads: "[T]he remedy that destroys the bitterest enemy of man's happiness, a message to provide new life for those who are living but who live as if they were dead." In the advertisement, Hussain guarantees his readers that that they would be restored to sexual health in ten days if they took the medicines: "[I]f there is any weakness in your sperm or genitals after using the product, then the medicine would be sent free." He also promises to mail Jadibuti in a package that would not allow others to know what was inside.

The headline in this ad ran "the true and faithful service for the motherland" and the ad was signed, "servant of the nation, SH Hussain." By suggesting his business was a "service for the motherland (*matrabhumi ni seva*)," Hussain in effect drew on a eugenic logic deployed through much of the late nineteenth century that linked physical capacities diminished through masturbation to national weakness (for instance, Alter 2011; Malhotra 2006). Seemingly, he saw himself as helping India's men to overcome shortcomings that plagued them individually, thereby making a more general revitalization of the country possible, presumably through enhancement of male reproductive capacities. Thus, Jadibuti ads promoted at one and the same time sexual intercourse, the generation of children, and the nation's welfare.

By the early 1930s, Hussain had added an appeal grounded in a conjugal logic. He ran a series of ads in *Mumbai Samachar* featuring a man and his wife (for instance, *Mumbai Samachar*, January 17, 1934: 5). Announcing that the products were an "astonishing remedy" for destroying "weakness [i.e., sexual dysfunction]," the ads' text suggested that the medicines would be found valuable by young males "who feared marriage after a childhood of bad habits, who were sterile, who had serious pains in their body, and who had failed to find any solutions from other doctors." Many men, it claimed, had used them successfully and had thus regained their honor. As a result, the ads went on, Jadibuti had become known as the "emperor" among all the medicines for weakness. The ad promised that the product would address weak nerves, thin semen, obstructions in semen, wet

[10] My thanks to Ramya Sreenivasan for this observation.

dreams, bodily weaknesses, jaundice, and frequent urination, evoking a medical logic in which a variety of bodily functions interacted together rather than one stressing symptom-specific remedies. Particularly important to the ad's resonance was the evocation of shame, a message that is conveyed through visual means. In the top image, a woman stands over a stressed husband, expressing compassion for his plight (a widely repeated trope). The wife's position above her husband seemingly heightened the sense of abjectness and humiliation in the situation of the dysfunctional man and the urgency of addressing his problem. In the lower image – after the man has used Jadibuti – the couple has a child and the man rests easily in an armchair, now a fulfilled and comfortable householder. Clearly, the ad addressed anxieties about the production of children, particularly sons, which was portrayed as key to the establishment of respectable adult manhood.

Some ads for Jadibuti in 1933 feature a photograph of Hussain; this image was one of the few photographs used in ads for goods made by vernacular capitalists (*Mumbai Samachar*, January 5, 1933: 5) (see Figure 5.4). Hussain is pictured in a suit and tie, clearly establishing his modern, scientific credentials. In the ad, he stated his desire to serve the people of Bombay, especially men whose engagement in "bad habits" during childhood had caused them to lose their strength, energy, and youth. He reported that he had recently developed a stronger formula of Jadibuti, which he was making available in Bombay without raising the price. He again mentioned that the product was available at a branch in Bombay. Clearly, the ad was drawn up locally, since it was printed in Gujarati and made regular reference to the city's people (as well as to those of Gujarat more widely). In the ad, Hussein in effect seems to have been involved in microtargeting a specific regional market far away from the place of production.

Both Amritdhara and Jadibuti advertisements reflect an effort by manufacturers to create commodity images that could be transmitted directly to consumers over considerable distances. In effect, they sought to impose on the product a set of meanings that remained fixed over space and thus sought to undercut (at least partially) the role of the bazaar trader in creating the meanings by which customers understood the project. Like the ads for Amritdhara, some of the claims made in the Jadibuti ads seem to reflect the logic and rhetoric that sidewalk hawkers used in selling such substances, now transposed into a print medium that could travel all over the landscape of Gujarati-speaking regions. At

Figure 5.4 *Mumbai Samachar*, January 5, 1933, p. 3

the same time, they included innovative appeals to the nation, to conceptions of modern conjugality, and to notions of modern science.

Dhootapapeshwar

The best documented example of the medical companies examined here was Dhootapapeshwar, an Ayurvedic firm headquartered in Panvel, now a distant suburb of Mumbai but then just a small town in the Konkan. The firm was founded by the Puranik family, originally Brahmin priests from Papeshwar in Ratnagiri district who were associated with a Shiva temple there – a visual image of the key shrine in this temple became the company's trademark. According to family records, the firm was established in either 1866 or 1872. In these accounts, the founder of the firm, Krishnashastri Puranik, an Ayurvedic practitioner with considerable experience in indigenous medicine, decided to make his preparations available to other practitioners so they could concentrate on diagnosing and treating customers:

One day at his clinic an incident happened which sparked the birth of a great enterprise. A prescription given by him was wrongly dispensed by an incompetent compounder. This brought forth the need for standardized Ayurvedic formulations, which would help Ayurvedic physicians to concentrate on patient treatment and save them from the time-consuming task of preparing medicines themselves at their clinics. Vaidya Krishnashastri Puranik knew the imperativeness of quality for the best treatment of Ayurved is as important as air for breathing. (http://sdlindia.com/index.php/about/history.html)

The firm's foundational account thus stresses the way the company's expansion involved the displacement of local practitioners from preparing medicines to the creation of more uniform products that would be purchased by consumers in standardized form.

Krishnashastri's son, Vishnushastri, introduced increasingly mechanized procedures for preparing larger batches of medicines; the firm's factory was established in Panvel around the turn of the twentieth century. Dhootapapeshwar became a limited liability company (Dhootapapeshwar Panvel Ltd.) in 1937 or 1938. Around 1947, the firm established three separate companies for different parts of its different activities: manufacture, sales, and publicity. The Puraniks sustained the family's knowledge of medicine through the *gurushishya* tradition, even as some members obtained an education in modern colleges and built up a major commercial enterprise.

By 1938, Dhootapapeshwar had developed a significant industrial establishment, with 225 employees (earning Rs. 8 to 45 per month, generally somewhat below those in the Bombay textile mills) and an output of Rs. 3–4 lakhs. The company obtained "herbs, minerals and animal products" from outside the area, spending Rs. 40,000 on these purchases. Another Rs. 25,000 was spent on buying bottles for packaging and preserving the medicines. No doubt, this created a significant business for glass suppliers, as in the case mentioned in Davidar's novel.

The company manufactured its medicines with machines using electric power, which had most likely been extended to this area only a few years ago (Report of the Bombay Economic and Industrial Survey Committee, 1938–1940 (1941)).

Advertising for the firm perhaps began in the early 1870s. An ad from the journal *Arunodaya* (February 22, 1880) from Thana town asks practitioners to get in touch with the company if interested in the products made by Dhootapapeshwar. This ad, however, was addressed to *vaidya*s, not the general public. The firm adopted its distinctive trademark in 1888. Around this time, it began to hire a set of commission agents in different parts of Maharashtra and elsewhere to sell its goods.

From at least the firm's beginnings, the Puraniks were strongly committed to promoting the standardization of Ayurvedic medicine and practice, no doubt partly because the adoption of uniform quality standards involved greater sales. In effect, Dhootapapeshwar's founders participated in the project of creating a modern Ayurveda that has been studied in analyses of twentieth-century intellectual discourse and new educational institutions, but that has been overlooked in discussions of commercial activities. In 1908, Dhootapapeshwar hosted a congress of 300 *vaidya*s from different parts of India; participants in the congress were urged to promote and propagate Ayurveda all over India.[11] In 1938, the firm began publishing a Marathi-language journal called *Arogya Mandir*, which was intended to inform *vaidya*s in the region about developments in Ayurvedic science and practice. The journal included articles on health, medicines and the Dhootapapeshwar business and advertisements for Dhootapapeshwar products. This journal has had a continuous run since that time and copies are preserved in excellent condition in the company's offices. In 1938, the firm established an Ayurvedic college in Panvel. This college's operations ended in 1944; according to Anand Puranik – head of the Puranik family when I visited the firm – the college's closing was caused by a government rule that dictated that medical colleges must provide instruction in dissecting dead bodies.

Sometime before 1900 (according to company employees), Dhootapapeshwar had established a depot in the neighborhood of Girgaon in Bombay to supply the urban market. By 1905, there were

[11] Interview with Anand Puranik, current head of the family firm, in 2016.
A picture of this conference is on the company's website.

six depots in northern and western India. The company also maintained a set of commission agents who would keep in touch with "customers" (that is, the shopkeepers who sold Dhootapapeshwar products). The 1938 report mentions the role of agents and dealers who distributed Dhootapapeshwar products throughout the Bombay Presidency and elsewhere in India. Anand Puranik mentioned to me that a sales staff of about a dozen individuals existed at the time; these people were men with some knowledge of Ayurvedic medicines. The firm, he said, distributed its goods through three types of outlets: "branches" (in several locations, including Bombay, Nagpur, and Lucknow), which were fully controlled by the company; "depots" (including one in Hubli), which were managed and controlled by outsiders but where the stock was owned by the firm; and "distributors," noncompany businessmen who owned both the physical location and the stock of goods under their control. Usually, each of these types of outlet would have arrangements with retail shops, where a *vaidya*, who provided medical advice, wrote prescriptions, and compounded various products would be in residence (he would not necessarily be the shop owner). Such Ayurvedic practitioners were mostly trained in the *guru-shishya* tradition (rather than in emerging educational institutions for Ayurveda). The firm's branch in Girgaon employed its own *vaidya*. *Vaidya*s from other Bombay shops would have regular dealings with these outlets, often obtaining a discount. Sales representatives met *vaidya*s from different shops as they traveled around. The whole distribution system, therefore, was based on personal interactions between company representatives on one hand, and the shopkeepers/ *vaidya*s on the other. The *vaidya*s, however, would also receive more regular information about the products from *Arogya Mandir* and advertisements. At least occasionally, the sales representatives organized exhibits at major public events. One image from *Arogya Mandir* shows a stall the company set up at the Haripura Congress in Gujarat (Surat district) in 1938; the sign is in Gujarati (March 1938: cover).

Dhootapapeshwar made two different kinds of commodity: preparations to be used in various shops by *vaidya*s, who would prescribe them to patients, perhaps after further compounding; and patient medicines for direct purchase by ordinary consumers for self-medication. Print advertisements were mainly intended for the second type. By the late 1930s, Dhootapapeshwar was involved in manufacturing and advertising a wide variety of commodities that did not require consultation with

Figure 5.5 *Stri Masik*, June 1986, p. 688

a *vaidya*. Its most prominently advertised product was *Baljivan*, a kind
of gripe water intended for babies (see Figure 5.5 for one such advertisement). It also produced *Makardhwajgujita*, a pill to enhance male
potency, *Shilapravang* (a men's tonic), *Abhraloha* (a medicine to promote women's health), and *Arvindasav*, an Ayurvedic drink that was

Figure 5.6 *Kesari*, July 16, 1937, p. 10

advertised as promoting the health of children. (Figure 5.6 advertises several of these commodities.) Its product range also comprised cosmetics such as Kanchan Snow and hair/body oil (*Brahmi Tel*).

The customers would carry ads from the newspapers to the shops and purchase the products without needing to consult the *vaidyas*. Dhootapapeshwar did not place these ads just in local newspapers and other publications intended for public consumption; it also printed ads in *Arogya Mandir*, a journal whose primary audience was the *vaidyas* and medical shop owners. In effect, these advertisements promoted standardized forms of medical practice and the stocking of Dhootapashwar products in medical shops. By the late 1930s, the company was *also* printing calendars that would be distributed by sales agents to shop owners and *vaidyas*.

Advertising in newspapers gradually became part of a much wider publicity campaign. By the 1930s, the company was heavily involved in printing the labels used on the bottles (which were critical in distinguishing the company's products from imitations), the journal *Arogya Mandir*, and other publications intended to inform *vaidya*s about the company's products and the calendars. The company set up its own printing press at the factory site (http://sdlindia.com/index.php/about .html#). Running this press became a major part of business operations.

Dhootapapeshwar ads at first were comprised simply of text, for instance the 1880 ad in *Arunodaya*. With time, the company added visual material. Advertisements were designed in several vernacular languages. I have found ads in both Gujarati and Marathi newspapers, although I have found none in any English papers. Clearly Dhootapapeshwar saw the imagined audience for its goods as stretching well beyond its own immediate area.

The personnel who designed Dhootapapeshwar's advertisements during the late 1930s were seemingly influenced by conventions in the emerging field of professional advertising, which, up to this point, was mostly associated with larger global firms and a very small number of big Indian corporations. In contrast to the ads produced for Amritdhara and Jadibuti, Dhootapapeshwar's advertisements avoided lengthy verbal treatments of the problems addressed by the product, the history of the company's founding figures, or elaborate discussions of the product's capabilities. Copy on the page was arranged to draw attention to the product's name and some key catch phrase(s); otherwise, type was used sparingly to establish the main claims of the commodity and to draw attention to the ad's key message. Images in the advertisements increasingly drew on conventions of the emerging profession of commercial art, associated strongly with formal advertising agencies. Unlike the publicity for Amritdhara, Dhootapapeshwar's ads avoided making claims to broad curative properties, and instead focused on the medicine's value in treating specific conditions. The advertisers often implicitly focused on themes of conjugality, then being stressed in professional advertisements. The ads for male tonics avoided highly explicit discussions of sexual problems but did rely on readers' understandings of such words as *shaktivardhak* (energy enhancer), *utejan* (enthusiasm), and *viryavardhak* (virility), words strongly associated with the concept of male potency. Almost every ad with any visual component included a picture of the trademark symbol of the Purnanik family shrine.

The publicity for Dhootapapeshwar elucidates the extent of the effort by newly emerging medical manufacturing firms to wrest control over the production of the cultural meaning of medical commodities from the hands of local practitioners. Before the advent of the medical firm and the rise of print advertising, *vaidya*s were no doubt involved in commercial activity, even if some of them were attached to specific patron families. In some cases, they may have relied on outside suppliers for the herbs and other necessary ingredients they used in their preparations. The development of larger manufacturers in effect displaced some of the *vaidyas*' role in gathering materials and preparing medicines (although the *vaidya*s still retained a central role in compounding). At the same time, especially for the class of goods intended for self-medication, the vernacular firms attempted to supplant the *vaidyas*' role in influencing the customers' understandings of the goods he or she consumed. A customer coming to an Ayurvedic shop with the ad of a product he or she wanted to buy already had some strong expectations of the commodity's capabilities, expectations shaped by the advertisement itself. When the customer purchased the commodity through the postal system or from a clerk at a medicinal shop, he or she could avoid contact with the *vaidya* altogether. Finally, the company sought to create standardized appreciations of Ayurvedic practices among the *vaidya*s themselves by organizing conferences, publishing a journal distributed among *vaidya*s throughout Maharashtra and printing a range of other information.

One, of course, should not exaggerate the transformative character of this effort; local practitioners probably still maintained much ability to influence their clients' perceptions, particularly for the medicines they themselves mixed and prescribed. But advertising clearly gave the vernacular capitalist an unprecedented role in manufacturing commodity images as well as the commodities themselves.

Conclusion

The examples of Amritdhara, Jadibuti, and Dhootapapeshwar clearly illustrate the importance of advertising to a category of medical manufacturing firms seeking to establish markets in early twentieth-century western India; hundreds of other firms were involved in similar efforts, although most not on the same scale. Vernacular firms typically began with very limited advertising budgets, refraining from significant expenditures that would require hiring specialists or using expensive techniques to produce high-quality images. Many of their ads were probably designed by family members and mostly comprised text, with little or no visual element. But as firms expanded their businesses, they often invested more heavily in the construction and projection of commodity images. They hired larger staffs to design advertisements, employed artists who supplied their services on an outcontracting basis, or paid specialists working for individual newspapers. Advertising art for vernacular firms in many cases was at first created in an ad hoc and eclectic fashion, drawing on a variety of local artistic genres and producing a great heterogeneity of appearances.[12] But increasingly, the firms hired a set of publicity designers who were influenced by the field of professional advertising. Their advertisements deployed the techniques of line drawing associated with the commercial art profession, developed short, punchier copy phrases, and used empty space on the page to capture the eye of the viewer. Here it makes sense to speak of the concept of interocularity, of the movement between one form of advertising art and another (Jay and Ramaswamy 2014: 44; Ramaswamy 2003: xvii). Increasingly as well they often sought to create associations of their products with authenticity, indigeneity, science, and conjugal fulfillment (the last being the major motif of professional advertising).[13]

Medicinal manufacturers were not the only vernacular firms using advertisement by any means. Small-scale powerloom manufacturers (like LV Tikekar of Solapur), soapmakers and hair oil producers, and a variety of other firms also submitted ads for their products. Advertisement is often the most crucial form of evidence we have for understanding the history of these businesses, which otherwise might be almost invisible to us. Unfortunately, we often cannot find in advertisements such basic information as the founding dates of firms or the number of employees. These ads do, however, provide a very concrete

---

[12] Holly Shaffer of Dartmouth College has been especially helpful in stimulating me to generate the arguments developed here.

[13] This point is a major argument of a book manuscript I am completing, *Brand-Name Capitalism, Advertising and the Making of Modern Conjugality in Western India, 1918–45.*

sense of the cultural meanings vernacular capitalists sought to attach to their products.

The expansion of print advertising is thus an indication of significant change in the character of South Asian approaches to marketing. Bazaars, of course, are places in which goods are exchanged, but historically, they have also often been the crucial locales in which commodity images were constructed. Before the late nineteenth century, the ability of commodity producers to influence the construction of meaning in the bazaar was very limited. Consumers who bought unbranded products in bazaars had little or no access to information about the original producers or their reputations; and producers had little way of directly influencing the perceptions of the ultimate customers. Typically, it was the intermediate figures who carried the goods of distant manufacturers to the consuming regions and towns and local traders in the bazaars – such as the *vaidya*s associated with medical shops – who were most involved in the construction of meaning.

For late nineteenth- and early twentieth-century vernacular capitalists, advertising provided a crucial opportunity to attach their commodities to specific claims, values, and visual associations despite the distances that separated them from the people who used their products. Through advertising, they contested the dominant place of mercantile figures in the construction of meaning; their project was, in effect, one of attempting to disembed meaning creation from its local context. For the small-scale manufacturers who invested in these new kinds of enterprise, the enhanced ability to influence how goods were understood by consumers was perhaps as central to shaping a new kind of small-scale industrial capitalism as was the introduction of new production technologies.

Bazaars, of course, themselves continued to be places of considerable exchange. With advertising, capitalists who sought to join both production and marketing functions together in a single enterprise came to play a new role in the bazaar, seeking to usurp some of the roles more localized actors had previously played. No doubt, shopkeepers, hawkers, and figures like local *vaidya*s continued to participate in the construction of meaning. Indeed, in the case of some commodities such as saris, foods, and cooking media, the role of advertisers submitted by producers in shaping consumer understandings was often rather limited compared with the roles played by shopkeepers and other local actors. And while the process of advertising was associated with a partial disembedding of marketing from their local nexuses, vernacular firms likely reembedded themselves in the bazaar by developing distributional networks that required sales agents to develop close relationships with the shopkeepers and other commercial actors (such at the *vaidya*s in the case of Dhootapapeshwar). Even big multinational firms at the time were often similarly engaged in trying to reconstitute their relations with small shopkeepers, wholesalers, and local agents rather than attempting to construct completely new retail networks, even when they hired large advertising agencies to conduct their publicity. The development of a brand-name capitalism associated with both global and local actors (such as vernacular capitalists) thus involved a reconfiguration of the social character of the bazaar but not its dissolution.

References

Alter, J 2011, *Moral Materialism: Sex and Masculinity in Modern India*, Penguin Books, New Delhi.

Anderson, B 1991, *Imagined Communities: Reflections on the Origin and Spread of Nationalism*, revised and expanded ed., Verso, London.

Arogya Mandir, *Marathi-Language Journal of Dhootapapeshwar*, 1938–present.

Arunodaya, 1880, Copy of Marathi Newspaper in Possession of Dhootapapeshwar, February 22.

Bayly, CA 1983, *Rulers, Townsmen, and Bazaars. North Indian Society in the Age of British Expansion, 1770–1870*, Cambridge University Press, Cambridge.

Berger, R 2013, *Ayurveda Made Modern: Political Histories of Indigenous Medicine in North India, 1900–1955*, Palgrave Macmillan, Basingstoke.

Biswas, P 2016, "Advertising and Enterprise in Colonial Bengal: Reflections on Hemendramohan Bose through a study of his Advertisements," paper written for the North American Conference on British Studies, November.

Bombay Chronicle, various dates, *English-Language Newspaper [Bombay]*.

Chandavarkar, GA 1938, "A Place for Home Remedies," *Kanara Saraswat*, XXII, 11.

Chandler Jr., AD 1977, *The Visible Hand: The Managerial Revolution in American Business*, Harvard University Press, Cambridge.

Daechsel, M 2006, *The Politics of Self-Expression: The Urdu Middleclass Milieu in Mid-Twentieth Century India and Pakistan*, Routledge, London and New York.

Davidar, D 2002, *The House of Blue Mangoes*, Harper Collins Ltd., New York.

Eldredge, FR 1930, *Advertising and Selling Abroad*, Harper & Brothers, New York and London.

Government of India, 1931, *India: Report of the Drugs Enquiry Committee*.

Gupta, C 2002, *Sexuality, Obscenity, Community: Women, Muslims and the Hindu Public in Colonial India*, Palgrave, New York.

Haynes, DE 1999, "Market Formation in Khandesh," *Indian Economic and Social History Review*, 36, 3 (August): 275–302.

Haynes, DE 2012a, "Selling Masculinity: Advertisements for Sex Tonics and the Making of Modern Conjugality in Western India, 1900–1945," *South Asia: Journal of South Asian Studies*, 35, 4: 787–831.

Haynes, DE 2012b, *Small-Town Capitalism in Western India: Artisans, Merchants and the Making of the Informal Economy, 1870–1960*, Cambridge University Press, Cambridge.

Haynes, DE 2015, "Advertising and the History of South Asia, 1880–1950," *History Compass*, 13, 8: 361–374.

http://sdlindia.com/index.php/about/history.html, viewed October11, 2015.

https://indiancaselaws.wordpress.com/2013/09/06/amritdhara-pharmacy-v s-satya-deo-gupta/, viewed October 12, 2015.

https://indiankanoon.org/doc/368264/, viewed October 12, 2015.

http://indiankanoon.org/doc/394080/, viewed October 12, 2015.

Jain, K 2007, *Gods in the Bazaar: The Economies of Indian Calendar Art*, Duke University Press, Durham.

Jay, M & Ramaswamy, S 2014, "Introduction," in M Jay & S Ramaswamy (eds.) *Empires of Vision*, Duke University Press, Durham.

Kesari 1937, *Marathi Newspaper [Pune]*, July 16, p. 10.

Malhotra, A 2006, "The Body as a Metaphor for the Nation: Caste, Masculinity and Femininity in the Satyarth Prakash of Dayananda Saraswati," in A Powell & S Lambert-Hurly (eds.) *Rhetoric and Reality: Gender and the Colonial Experience in South Asia*, Oxford University Press, New Delhi, pp. 121–53.

McGowan, A 2019, "Selling Home: Marketing Home Furnishings in Late Colonial Bombay," in P Kidambi, M Kamat, & R Dwyer (eds.) *Bombay Before Mumbai : Essays in Honor of Jim Masselos*, Hurst, London.

Mukharji, P 2012, "Chandshir Chikitsa: A Nomadology of Subaltern Medicine," in D Hardiman & PB Mukharji (eds.) *Medical Marginality in South Asia: Situating Subaltern Therapeutics*, Routledge, London, pp. 85–108.

Mumbai Samachar (MS) various dates, *Gujarati Newspaper [Bombay]*.

Nag, D 1990, The Social Construction of Handwoven Tangail Saris in the Market of Calcutta, PhD Dissertation, Michigan State University, University Microfilms International.

Ramaswamy, S 2003, "Introduction," in Sumathi Ramaswamy (ed.) *Beyond Appearances? Visual Practice and Appearances in Modern India*, Sage Publications, New Delhi.

Ray, R 1992, "Introduction," in R Ray (ed.) *Entrepreneurship and Industry in India, 1800–1947*, Oxford University Press, New Delhi, pp. 1–65.

Report of the Bombay Economic and Industrial Survey Committee, 1938–1940 [1941], Vol. II, Government Central Press, Kolaba.

Roy, T 1999, *Traditional Industry in the Economy of Colonial India*, Cambridge University Press, Cambridge.

Roy, T 2018, *A Business History of India: Enterprise and the Emergence of Capitalism from 1700*, Cambridge University Press, Cambridge.

Schneider, J 2008, Reimagining Traditional Medicine: Tracing the Emergence of Commodified Ayurveda in the Interwar Period, MSc thesis in economic and social history, Oxford University.

Sharma, M 2011, "Creating a Consumer: Exploring Medical Advertisements in Colonial India," in B Pati & M Harrison (eds.) *The Social History of Health and Medicine in Colonial India*, Routledge, London and New York, pp. 213–28.

Sharma, M 2012, *Indigenous and Western Medicine in Colonial India*, Foundation Books, New Delhi.

Stri Masik, *Marathi Journal* [Pune], June 1986, p. 688.

Tasveerghar: A house of pictures, digital archive of South Asian popular culture, most recently consulted February 9, 2018, www.tasveerghar.net.

Tripathi, D 2013, *The Oxford History of Contemporary Indian Business*, Oxford University Press, New Delhi.

U.S. Department of Commerce 1933, "Channels of Distribution of American Merchandise in India," *Trade Information Bulletin no. 817*, US. Government Printing Office.

Venkatachalapathy, AR 2014, "A Magic System? Print Publics, Consumption and Advertising in Modern Tamil Nadu," paper presented at the conference, The Long Indian Century: Historical Transitions and Social Transformations, Yale University, April.

Yang, A 1998, *Bazaar India: Markets, Society and the Colonial State in Gangetic Bihar*, University of California Press, Berkeley.

6 The Artifice of Trust: Reputational and Procedural Registers of Trust in North Indian "Informal" Finance

SEBASTIAN SCHWECKE[*]

Introduction

In 2007, the Allahabad High Court castigated a number of formal sector banks in harsh terms for employing business practices reminiscent of extra-legal (and illegal) moneylenders. Among other practices, the court expressed dismay at the use of private agents – who were "often anti-social elements" – for the recovery of loans as well as the affixation of signatures onto blank pages in credit contracts and the filling in of contract details in the absence of the debtor. The judgment made it clear that these were frequent infractions of business propriety in which the banks were "preying upon farmers in the modernized version of Shylock's pound of flesh."[1]

The court's linkage of "modernization" with propriety in business practices also figures in media reports in the wake of the Indian government's decision to devalue high-denomination rupee notes in late 2016 that highlighted deviations by the "formal" banking sector from expected behavioral norms in risk assessment. The practice of sending out teams by banks to inquire locally about the reputation of prospective debtors in contrast to employing prescribed risk assessment procedures is relatively common in contemporary India. In rare cases, the infraction of "modern" propriety by Indian banks has been more drastic, for instance, in a case highlighted by the eminent journalist

[*] I am highly grateful to my coeditors, Ajay Gandhi, Barbara Harriss-White, and Douglas E. Haynes, and to Andy Rotman for their comments to this chapter that pointed out all the various flaws (small or big) of earlier versions. Remaining errors are my own. My research would not have been possible without Michaela Dimmers, Rakesh Kumar Singh, Anoop Sharma, and Chandra Kishore Singh, and this is to let them know how much I appreciate their constant support!
[1] Allahabad High Court 2007, *Chander S. O. Buddhu v. State of UP.*

P Sainath in which the Osmanabad Bank used public shaming techniques reminiscent of itinerant moneylenders in colonial India (Sainath 2016).[2]

These cases highlight the underside of banking in India, especially problems in managing trust between the banks and their customers. For Indian finance, establishing trust between creditors and debtors has long been a central concern, one that was supposedly solved in the gradual shift toward "modern" finance since the nineteenth century. In breaching the procedural foundations of managing trust, banks were falling back on practices associated with moneylending and "indigenous" banking. Conversely, the use of these practices illustrates the multiplicity of manners in which trust can be handled. It underlines the necessity to rethink trust operating on markets as an artifact beyond the idiom of "modernization" – the pliability of markets as much as their social embeddedness and the reasons for the continued contestation of the state's jurisdiction.

Trust, it is argued here, forms an artifact that comprises a multitude of registers in its handling and creation, the most important of which, from the perspective of market participants in modern South Asia, relates to its procedural and reputational dimensions. The (originally) Weberian focus on rationalization and "formalization" through the employment of "proper" procedure serves to obscure more than clarify the nuances in the handling of trust that facilitate "informality" on Indian markets. Yet the registers of handling trust also constitute artifices: "clever tricks" marked by an ingenuity that resembles the Hindi term *jugaad* that "fix" markets in the face of significant difficulties and enable entrepreneurs to evade and transgress state regulations.[3]

---

[2] According to Sainath, the bank's public shaming included pitching tents in front of the homes of defaulting farmers and announcing the details of defaults among other techniques using bells and other musical instruments.

[3] My use of the term "artifice" here is originally derived from and is related to its use by Frank Perlin in a draft of his as of now unpublished monograph "The City Intelligible," where it is used to denote the uses of language to classify nature (and make it marketable). "Artifice" in this context should be read according to its meaning as a "clever and artful skill" and an "artful stratagem" (Merriam Webster English Dictionary), instead of being interpreted according to the term's negative connotation of false or insincere behavior, even though the latter may appear suitable when discussing the behavior of moneylenders.

Procedural and Reputational Registers of Trust

Writing in the backdrop of the recent global financial crisis, Paul Seabright (2010: 110–17) identified various notions of trust as among the main reasons responsible for the crisis, based on "false lessons" learned from the Great Depression, one of which was the mistaken imperative of maintaining confidence in the financial system rather than the conditions for this confidence; the assertion – seemingly magical in its tautology – that "if only *confidence* in the financial system could be maintained, the system itself could be *trusted* to survive and prosper" (Seabright 2010: 117; first emphasis in the original, second added).

The seeming magicality of the tautology stems from the difficulties in defining trust, which has spawned a significant body of sociological and anthropological literature on the subject (and its corollary, mistrust), demonstrating the complexity and opacity of trust as operating in social interactions instead of a concise semiotic consensus. Trust, according to Georg Simmel, forms an expectation of future behavior, "a hypothesis certain enough to serve as a basis for practical conduct" (Simmel 1950). The unspecifiable level of certainty to guide practical conduct distinguishes trust from hope, as argued by Liisberg and Pedersen, and instead trust bridges uncertainty among people based on concerns over "near and probable futures" (Pedersen & Liisberg 2015: 1–20) related to the experiential background of life histories. Trust, accordingly, forms a means of coping with ambiguities arising from probabilities and possible interpretations (Liisberg 2015: 158–76), but remains highly ambiguous itself.

The experiential foundations of handling the ambiguities inherent in the opaque character of trust and its handling, in turn, can be theorized with reference to Marcel Mauss (1970) and his concept of balanced reciprocity, underlying the nature of the gift as seeking to insure and maintain long-term relationships by sequences of giving and taking. The experience of the sequential character of exchanging serves to establish trust, and, therefore, facilitates the certainty needed for a practical conduct. Beyond the case of the gift, trust crucially hinges on experiencing sequences of exchanging nuanced and frequently minute details of information on one's conduct that can be interpreted by the recipient to gain higher levels of certainty over the giver's probable future behavior. The sequencing of this exchange of information is likely to be balanced over time, and works best if it is balanced.

Far from being restricted to (seemingly) less complex societies, the
experiential basis of trust in sequences of exchange relations remains at
the core of "modern" markets, although it may take different forms.
Corsin Jimenez, for instance, questions "how knowledge, responsibility and social relationality have been organized as epistemologically
distanced objects in contemporary capitalist regimes of audit and trust-
making" (Corsin Jimenez 2011: 178) and underlines the similarities of
technocratic, bureaucratic, and occult systems in their needs for the
certification of knowledge as robust, in order for it to *be* robust (Corsin
Jimenez 2011: 185). Certification, here, takes the place of direct interpersonal exchanges but nevertheless needs to be interpreted in
a transactional form, the sequence of which establishes the level of
certainty needed for a practice of trust that bridges uncertainty.

As argued by Carey, trust and mistrust do not form a binary opposition but are constitutive of each other (Carey 2017: 10) since uncertainty forms the basis on which the sequence of exchanges forming the
experience of trust and mistrust develop in parallel. In the process, the
experience of sequential exchange increases the levels of certainty constituting both trust and mistrust. Challenging the implicit correlation of
trust with familiarity and proximity, and with direct interpersonal
contact, Carey argues:

[T]rust amounts to confidence in *one's* expectations, and such
expectations ... must depend on a certain degree of familiarity with either
people, the world, or systemic representations of the real. (Carey 2017: 6)
    Proximity and familiarity [however] do not necessarily equate to know-
ability or certainty and cannot be used as a basis for generating expectations
and predicting future behavior. This point is critical, for it directly challenges
the very widespread notion that there is an umbilical relationship between
the holy trinity of proximity, familiarity, and trust. (Carey 2017: 8)

Rather than describing binaries of personal and system trust (Luhmann
1979), it is necessary to identify specific registers of trust based on the
experiential context of how trust and mistrust are predominantly
handled. The seeming tautology discussed at the outset – that in order
to trust a system, confidence in the system must be maintained – can be
extended to any register of trust. At the same time, it is the seemingly
magical character of trust in more abstract systems that differentiate
these systems from more directly knowable ones in obscuring their
experiential nature. The artifice of trust allows the handling of

uncertainties and ambiguities by various means that can be distinguished as registers of handling trust.

In India, a crisis of trust in the financial system emerged in late 2016, when the government decided to "demonetize" higher denominations of Indian Rupee banknotes. This led to a multiplicity of simultaneous crises of mistrust in both the formal and the informal segments of Indian finance at the same time as coping mechanisms – petty informal credit transactions – proved remarkably resilient. It is not my intention here to engage in greater detail with the "demonetization" misadventure yet the exercise's unfolding has formed a consistent backdrop for my research that needs to be spelt out. At the same time, "demonetization" needs to be seen as part of a longer project that has reinforced a segmentation within the capitalist class in India as outlined in a different context in the work of Barbara Harriss-White (for instance, Harriss-White 2018).

The history of capital in India from at least the last decades of the nineteenth century is marked by a complex web of processes: attempts to define and impose propriety in business procedure accompanied by the provision of significant incentives for adherence (cf. in the work of Ritu Birla 2009), followed by efforts of adjustment and/or evasion, in turn followed by newly designed measures of imposing "propriety." These processes were compounded by India's attempts to produce economic segments of "informality" through selective regulatory inclusion and – therefore – exclusion (cf. for instance Dietrich Wielenga 2016: 423–58). In its procedural focus on "formalization," the history and ethnography of Indian capital and entrepreneurship calls attention to the layers of abstraction and codification underlying "modernization" – the taxonomic grammar of what Appadurai in discussing the practices of contemporary global finance and its crisis has described as a "deep affinity between legal and magical proceduralism" (Appadurai 2015a: 481–5, 483; cf. Appadurai 2015b) in contemporary capitalism.

What makes the seeming tautology in the experiential foundations of trust depicted by Seabright "magical" is its procedural character, the fact that the sequence of exchanges follows a codified form guaranteed by the state as the regulator and therefore the final certifying agency. One end of the exchange relationship is not perceived by individual market participants as a (plausibly untrustworthy) person, but a "systemic representation of the real," whose actions can be anticipated, even if it is lacking the characteristics of proximity and (partially) of familiarity.

System trust, accordingly, is a register of trust that is exceptionally far removed from the forms of proximity that accompany other sequences of exchange that establish trust. Concerning Indian finance, more proximate registers of trust, especially those relying on the communication of family reputations, continued to remain the predominant forms underlying exchange relations to a greater extent than in the metropole. Yet the shift toward greater reliance on procedurally codified practices certified by the state marked these as not only superior but also "proper."

Ritu Birla has noted the increased stridency of state-led attempts to define propriety in business relations in line with this project of modernization – the definition of the "proper swindle" (Birla 2009)[4] – since the last quarter of the nineteenth century. Exchange relations that did not correspond to this definition of the proper swindle became marked as "improper" and gradually shifted toward extra-legal modes of operation rather than being discontinued, especially concerning moneylending transactions. I have described this process elsewhere as the production of a monetary outside (Schwecke 2018: 1375–419; cf. Harvey 2004; Luxemburg 1913).[5] It is important to keep in mind the availability of a multiplicity of registers of trust as opposed to a simple substitution of direct interpersonal sequences of exchange for a unified form of system trust.

In the following paragraphs, I will depict two important ways of adaptation to changes in the handling of trust as artifact and artifice in Banaras based on a study of trust in "organized" banking in the mid-twentieth century and in contemporary "informal" financial practices. Registers of trust have been described as procedural and reputational trust, respectively, to distinguish the two case studies from the binary of personal and systems trust.

[4] A concept originally used in the context of the introduction of limited liability under colonial rule, and the resulting crises of trust in the transactional grammar of Indian business.

[5] The concept of the production of monetary outsides describes the creation of enclaves within the capitalist economic order of India since late colonial times that deviate from many assumptions about capitalist entrepreneurial behavior, especially in the procedural dimensions relating to "modernization" and Weberian notions of rationalization, loosely making use of David Harvey's reinterpretation of Rosa Luxemburg's concept of the capitalist outside in which he attributes neoliberal capitalism with a capability to "invent" capitalist outsides.

The differences of these registers of trust from others are more visible concerning reputation. Reputation is, simply put, both more and less than personal trust. It is person-centric but already "systemic" to some extent in that reputation is far more than a mere track record of sequences of interpersonal exchange, thereby comprising a degree of unknowability and breaching the simplistic equation of trust with familiarity. Reputation assumes (based on the sequence of interaction between *other* persons) that persons with sufficient reputation will act according to the norms of an often vaguely defined systemic code. While an interpersonal track record starts from the assumption of pervasive mistrust, reputation already assumes a significant degree of trust between strangers, unless evidence of disrepute has been established by others. Furthermore, reputation is widely communicated. It relies on a network of information flows through gossip that overcomes the merely interpersonal and is, instead, based on the neighborhood or a similar spatial unit, or a form of group membership. Reputational trust, accordingly, assumes a high level of unfamiliarity and relies on the bridging of the unfamiliar by the embeddedness of strangers into a common transactional grammar though, crucially, it still presupposes that the sequences of interpersonal exchange that generate trust can be identified at need and that certification – when required – will involve knowable agents such as familiar and reputable persons vouching for the conduct of others by (partially) transferring their reputation onto the unknown person.

Procedure, in turn, is somewhat less than system trust. Procedural trust presupposes a general mistrust in the system either by the person trusting the efficacy of procedures, or by the institution (in this case, the state) mistrusting persons or other institutions (such as banks) that do not demonstrably follow specific procedural codes. It signifies that the codification of behavioral norms into bureaucratic processes creates levers of control to a "system" that is otherwise bereft of these. It presupposes the unknowable qualities of "systemic" agents, but it does not assume the knowability of the sequences of exchange generating trust and overcomes the risks inherent in the hypothetically flawed nature of strangers by the demonstration of adherence to codified procedures and their certification by a remote and only insufficiently knowable institution, the state. Yet, both the bank, as the institution demonstrating adherence, and the state, as the ultimate certifier of procedure, remain objects of mistrust, visible in "panics" (actually entirely rational behavioral sequences) that break out once procedural trust has been compromised to an extent that allows the inherent mistrust to overtake the tentatively posited trust into the enforcement of rule-bound behavior.

"Pristine Purity of Banking Conceptions": The Definition of the "Proper Swindle" in Twentieth-Century Indian Finance

I have argued elsewhere that the history of "informal" financial markets in twentieth-century Banaras can be depicted as the production of a monetary outside, marked chiefly by two intertwined processes of market framing and entrepreneurial responses (of adjustment or transgression of these rules) that produced procedural boundaries between "formal" and "informal" financial practices (Schwecke 2018). These processes brought about a transformation in the contractual basis underpinning debt relations. As opposed to David Hardiman's familiar argument that the abolition of usury laws in the mid-nineteenth century by bringing credit relations under the comprehensive purview of the Indian Contracts Act converted (more or less) harmoniously embedded village moneylenders and their urban counterparts into capitalist credit agencies (Hardiman 1996: 113–56), my argument is that the more important step in the development of what is capitalist in modern Indian finance was the removal of contractual law from the operation of moneylending but not banking, in the process defining the "proper swindle" in "organized" banking. The removal of contractual law from moneylending set into motion a process that resulted in the creation of a distinct monetary market comprehensively governed by notions of reputation instead of contractual and other regulatory law. Such notions of reputation had significantly changed from earlier mercantile ethics underpinned by moral codes related to community structures as depicted, for instance, by David Rudner (including in this book). Regulatory policy fed into the production of a thriving credit market segment catering to the needs of vast sections of Indian society, cut off from both the regulatory and the incentive structure defining Birla's "proper swindle." This supposedly residual and declining market segment continues to operate relatively smoothly, efficiently employing reputational registers of trust to stabilize highly exploitative transactional relations.

The corresponding codification of procedural propriety for "formal" or "organized" finance is of similar complexity. In between these two poles lies the history of "indigenous" banking and its demise. The dominant narrative, strongly influenced by modernization theory and cultural stereotyping, depicts the decline of "indigenous" banking in India as a failure of adjusting to modernity based on the intrinsic rootedness in traditional mercantile ethics, on a culturally derived incapacity to go with the times, ignoring the fluidity and sophistication of banking practices in India in the face of highly insecure credit market conditions. In the economics literature of the early postcolonial period, this position is shared widely (cf. Cirvante 1956: 47). At its core, it is frequently related to an interpretation of the unwelcoming response of many indigenous bankers to efforts by the Reserve Bank of India (RBI) to develop an integrated bill market under its auspices in the late 1930s. In strong contrast, the (in this context) politically ineffectual reports of the Shroff Committee and of the Study Group on Indigenous Banking in the 1971 Banking Commission Report squarely blamed the RBI for adherence to a notion of "pristine purity of banking conceptions"[6] that led to the failure of its efforts, underlining the aim of imposing procedural trust.

This procedural character of "modern" banking in India, however, evolved over a significantly longer period of time. The focus of Birla on the legal history of markets obscures the tardiness in the responses of business practice beyond the realm of law. "Organized" banking in India in the mid-twentieth century continued to follow modes of doing business that remained strongly reminiscent of the supposedly anachronistic world of "indigenous" banking. Indian finance capital, both petty and big, had tended to lean toward reputational rather than procedural registers of trust. In this respect, Rudner's work on Chettiar "indigenous" bankers (Rudner 1989: 417–58) is exemplary for demonstrating the resilience of supposedly nonmodern business practices. Nevertheless, the state-led "modernization" process of finance sought to impose adherence to new "procedural" codifications onto big business as a precondition to partaking in the incentive structures surrounding this political project: the credit structures that allowed banks to make use of

---

[6] Government of India, Banking Commission 1971, Report on Indigenous Bankers, p. 92.

central bank schemes, and the legal structure of contract enforcement through the courts.

As "indigenous" bankers handled transactions that were mostly too substantial to avoid detection by the state (in contrast to those by moneylenders), they needed to adhere to the procedural impositions by the state while continuing to handle trust in ways that reflected a "reputational" economy. While some mercantile communities outside Banaras that were engaged in banking were significantly more resilient, the major banking families of Banaras went into a terminal decline starting in the 1930s, in origin related to the effects of the Great Depression and the incipient decline of the economic importance of Calcutta, but compounded by the thrust toward "organized" banking. The failure of the bankers of Banaras to adjust is certainly correlated to business failure more generally. Yet it is the phenomenal scope of failure affecting the entire apex of the city's mercantile community, especially when contrasted to the relative success of other mercantile communities outside Banaras (Rudner 1989; Timberg and Aiyar 1980: 279–302) that necessitates a closer look at their inability to shift toward procedural registers of trust.

Conversely, "organized" banks in the city would be assumed to "have gone with the times," although many of their business practices reflected the continuity of reputational registers of trust. The history of the two main "organized" banks that originated from the city mirrors this development despite their legal constitution. Both banks can be depicted as business failures. The Bank of Benares (BoB) – which will be at the center of the subsequent analysis – was founded in 1904 and expanded its operations until the late 1930s, before abruptly entering bankruptcy in 1939 and being liquidated in early 1940. The State Bank of Banaras (SBB) was founded in 1946. The bank opened several branches across northern India but never became very profitable. After its nationalization, it remained ailing and was eventually merged with the Bank of Baroda in 2002 (Tiwari 2014: 35–48).[7]

---

[7] The respective banks need to be distinguished from earlier banks with similar names: the Bank of Benares was occasionally depicted as Benares Bank, similarly to an earlier bank of this name that had been operational from 1845 to 1849, and had been depicted as "*another striking example of unsound banking*" by Shirras. The State Bank of Banaras, in turn, was unrelated to the State Bank of Benares, the "central bank" founded for the princely state of Benares in the administrative reforms of the late 1930s. Cf. correspondence 132-S/106-B/38 between GVS Gillian at the Gwalior Residency and CG Herbert, I.C.S., Political Department,

Generating Trust as Procedure or Reputation: Banking Advertisements and the Artifice of Trust in Mid-Twentieth-Century Banaras

Trust is an ephemeral subject for a historian. One of the main sources that can be used for the study of trust for the purpose of this study, however, is banking advertisements. The following study of advertising patterns in mid-twentieth-century Banaras is based on an archive of newspaper clippings[8] covering media content related to finance between 1930 and 2011 from the respective leading newspapers in Banaras (defined by circulation) – until the early 1970s the newspaper *Aaj*, subsequently *Dainik Jagran*. The cases discussed here reflect general tendencies discernible throughout the period covered.

Broadly speaking, local banking advertising reached a spike in the 1930s and 1940s, and gradually declined in the 1950s, with very little advertising in the 1960s. It slowly grew in prominence after bank nationalization, and reached a new, if slightly lower peak from the 1970s until the late 1980s, declined again in the 1990s, and became noticeable only by its relative absence in the 2000s and early 2010s. Significantly, while the decline of newspaper banking advertising since the 1990s can be related to a shift toward visual media, the up- and downturns in print advertising broadly mirror periods marked by significant changes in the procedural grammar of banking operations. While other explanatory factors certainly need to be considered, it can be assumed that these changes necessitated efforts by the banks to reach out to the larger public in order to generate trust. This, in turn, is reinforced by a shift in the type of banking advertising that centered on the generation of trust in the banking companies until the mid-1970s and on product-based advertising reflecting consumer *aspirations* as opposed to consumer *mistrust* afterwards.

At the outset, it is important to identify to what extent banking advertisements include appeals to trust based on "procedural" and "reputational" registers. Banking advertising obviously attempted to

---

especially the "Rules of the Benares State Bank as revised from 1 October 1939," IOR V/10, India Office Records, British Library, London.

[8] In possession of the author. I wish to express my gratitude to Chandra Kishore Singh without whose help the digitization of this archive would not have been possible.

fulfill several objectives simultaneously, including creating awareness of the bank's brand and its specific products or special offers.

Reputational registers of trust differ from personal trust but crucially depend on the ability at need to identify the sequence of interpersonal exchanges creating trust. Bereft of an abstract, remote, and largely unknowable certification process, they rely on a knowable and familiar certifier whose personal reputation substitutes or vouches for the unknowable qualities of the bank as an institution. In procedural registers of trust, this need is replaced by a demonstration of adherence to codified procedural norms that create levers of control to be used by the remote and unknowable certifier. Under this assumption, appeals to trust based on the personal qualities of a bank's managerial staff form a straightforwardly reputational register of trust, as do appeals based on the bank's local social embeddedness. An intermediate category comprises appeals to trust a bank based on its relative standing in the market: the size of business constitutes a reassurance for the customer in that it (apparently) minimizes risks, but the need to impress on a bank's size also indicates a perceived lack of trust in the capacity of procedural adherence to ensure reliability. Straightforward instances of a procedural register of trust, in turn, comprise direct references to proper procedure, references to the bank's legal status, and advertising that implicitly presupposes "procedural" forms of trust. Following this broad categorization, banking advertisements in mid-twentieth-century Banaras demonstrate a combination of reputational and procedural registers of trust, although the predominance of procedural registers of trust in banking that is presupposed by their legal form is established unexpectedly late, that is, after the nationalization of banks in India in the late 1960s.

Figure 6.1 depicts the use of reputational registers of trust. It announces the decision of the Bank of Benares to reduce the commission for money transfers to Calcutta and Bombay for customers transferring money there frequently. While it may appear to be a reference to the bank's product range, this impression needs to be qualified: the advertisement does not give any details on the rate of reduction, or the definition of the term "frequent." Apparently, the bank – which commissioned the printing of half a dozen identical advertisements in paid-for advertising space in *Aaj* between 1933 and 1939 – did not perceive these details as important. It is plausible to conclude that the bank omitted these details as sufficiently "frequent" customers interested in

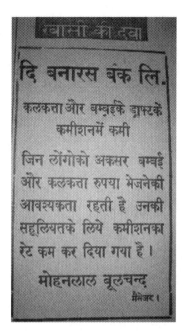

Figure 6.1 Bank of Benares, *Aaj*, April 1, 1936

the announcement of these policies would already have known the rates and target group of the scheme beforehand or at least were considered both capable of and willing to find out on their own. This interpretation is reinforced by the sequential character of the advertisements: being identical, it is not even clear whether the advertisements related to a succession of decreases in commissions, yet frequent customers must have been aware of these.

Yet this explanation raises the question why the scheme needed to be advertised in the first place. At the time of its first appearance in 1933, the bank did not have many competitors locally and including more detailed information would have been even more important in a context of competition. The advertisement can hardly be perceived as visually appealing. The lack of visual appeal cannot be interpreted as a demonstration of the value of thriftiness as potential customers may have plausibly questioned the need to spend the bank's money on a visually non-appealing *and* uninformative advertisement. The lack of visual appeal is also uncommon in newspaper advertisements of the time, as demonstrated profusely by Douglas E Haynes (2015: 361–74), including in this volume; nonbanking advertisements printed in *Aaj* throughout the 1930s tend to be far more elaborate.

The only detailed information given in the advertisement, in fact, was the manager's name, standing in for the bank's reputation and vouching for the validity of the policy in his personal capacity. The advertisement was thus highly reputational: its manager, Mohanlal Bulchand, was reinforcing the bank's standing with his own reputation. Bulchand was a highly respected banker at the time and was one of the most important informants for the United Provinces Banking Enquiry Committee Report (UPBECR) from Banaras. The cross-reference with the UPBECR reinforces the conclusion that the bank operated primarily through reputational registers of trust.

His testimony can be summarized as a strident appeal for the "formalization" of banking. Bulchand repeatedly stated his belief that the future of Indian banking lay in the system of joint stock banking. He also emphasized that all other forms of banking possessed sufficient facilities for carrying on their businesses and did not need any further assistance[9] and that, in contrast, the Imperial Bank needed to "assist [the joint stock banks] by the simplification of the procedure for realization of debts from defaulters, the imposition of restrictions on ... the Imperial Bank of India and the exchange banks to prevent them from competing with joint-stock banks and the starting of a State organization which should render financial assistance to these concerns in times of stringency."[10] In other words, while the future may have belonged to firms such as the Bank of Benares, they were clearly struggling in the face of competition not only from other banks but also from moneylenders and "indigenous" bankers who were "undesirable" or, respectively, did "not require any assistance."[11] Bulchand's oral testimony provided further evidence on the actual functioning of the Bank of Benares, which differed remarkably little from "indigenous" banking: The bank gave loans exclusively to "people who h[ad] good credit" – notably landlords, "indigenous" bankers, large-scale silk traders, and middlemen. The use of the term *credit* here refers to more than sound finances and should be interpreted rather as an English language expression for the Hindi term *sakh*, denoting social standing and individual reputation as well as the firm's standing in the market. In addition, the bank lent either on personal security – that is, on the respective debtor's reputation – for an approved

[9] UPBECR IV: 99.   [10] UPBECR IV: 100.   [11] UPBECR IV: 99.

list of customers or demanded vouching for bona fide credentials by a second (and known) person, without shared liability. It occasionally undertook inquiries in the neighborhoods and bazaars about the standing of local businesspeople, and sometimes gave loans to unknown debtors against collaterals. It dealt in *hundi* but did not work with "modern" financial instruments such as checks.[12]

While Bulchand may have believed that the future belonged to the *mufassil* joint stock banks, the extent to which the bank remained embedded in local reputational structures can also be seen from its chairman's letter to its shareholders, which highlights the bank's creditors' honor and social standing and humbly addresses their support through continued public expressions of confidence. It ends by expressing its gratitude for continued creditors' trust as a "question of the economic credit [*sakh*] of the nation."[13]

Returning to the generation of trust through advertising, the practice of highlighting the bank managers' names, lending their reputations to the banks, is a recurring feature of banking advertising well into the 1970s, although its frequency declines after the 1940s. Subsequently, it became an increasingly ritualistic feature as corporate identities gained prominence; the naming of its managerial staff diminished in importance to the level of being personal touches in the use of an otherwise increasingly procedural register of trust.

The most visually appealing banking advertisement in Banaras in the 1930s was also commissioned by the Bank of Benares and reinforces the impression of the advertisement shown in Figure 6.1. By late 1936, Bulchand had been replaced as the bank's manager. An identical advertisement was published four times between August and November 1936 by *Aaj*. An otherwise identical advertisement in black instead of red print was placed in *Aaj* another four times between January and September 1937, significantly after the change of management.

The advertisement does not announce any content other than the politely phrased intention of the new management to serve its customers well, and the names of its new chairman, manager, and secretary, reinforcing the employment of reputational registers of trust.

Apart from the six advertisements identical to the one shown in Figure 6.1 and the eight on the change of management, the bank commissioned twenty-seven more advertisements in *Aaj* from 1930 to

[12] UPBECR IV: 102.   [13] *Aaj*, December 19, 1939.

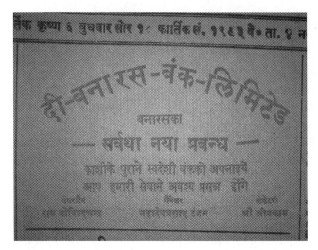

Figure 6.2 Bank of Benares, *Aaj*, November 4, 1936

1940. All of these were published in sections of the daily that were reserved for paid advertising space, although for some of these publications, it is not clear whether the bank intended these primarily as advertising or as fulfilling legal requirements, notably in the cases of the announcements of prior notice for withdrawals and withholding dividends.

Leaving aside the announcements on withholding dividends and the requirement of prior notice for withdrawals, Table 6.1 shows the extent to which the Bank of Benares continued to employ reputational registers of trust. Procedural registers were mostly absent. These registers only appeared to some extent in the advertisements specifying interest rates for fixed deposits and saving deposits, although they also included the manager's name as assurance, and, to a lesser extent, in the advertisements announcing details of the bank's equity and amount of deposits, although one of them also provided a comprehensive list of its directorate upfront. The remaining six advertisements in these categories deviated from the others by not including the names of managerial personnel. The relatively vague calls to deposit money in the bank as an assurance against theft, as saving schemes for educational purposes, or for gaining interest can hardly be interpreted as employing a procedural register of trust, especially as the bank's manager was clearly depicted as lending his reputation to the educational purpose of the advertisement.

Table 6.1 *Details of Bank of Benares advertising in the 1930s*[14]

Broad subject	Content	Number of ads
Exhortation against hoarding money	Hoarding cash at home is not safe Better to deposit in banks Name of manager	4
Nature of deposits	Deposits earn interest Rates unspecified Name of manager	3
Saving for education	Education for children is expensive Better to start saving early by depositing in bank Rates unspecified Name of manager	2
Nationalist advertising	BoB is a *swadeshi* bank and its commercial activities are serving the nation Name of manager	2
Details on company	Listing the names of the bank's entire board/directorate, the number and location of its branches, and details on the bank's equity	1
Branch opening ceremony	Opening of new branch Customers are invited to the ceremony Name of manager	1
Announcement of prior notice for withdrawals	Customers need to give BoB three-month's notice to withdraw higher amounts from its deposits (above Rs. 100) Name of manager	1
Specified interest rates	Interest is being paid on savings deposits Specified rates of interest for different savings schemes Name of manager	2

[14] Source: Advertisements by the Bank of Benares in the daily *Aaj*, 1930–1939 (in possession of the author). Newspaper editions are kept in the archive of the Nagari Pracharini Sabha, Banaras.

Table 6.1 (*cont.*)

Broad subject	Content	Number of ads
Interest having been paid on deposits	BoB has recently paid interest on different savings accounts Specified rates	3
Interest rates on fixed deposits	Details on interest for one-year fixed deposit Name of manager	1
Equity	Details on the bank's equity	2
Money deposited, equity, branches	Details on the amount of money deposited with the bank, on its equity, and the number and location of its branches	4
Withholding dividends	The bank regrets not being able to pay dividends to shareholders Name of chairman	1
Reduction in commission	Unspecified reduction of commission for regular customers transferring money to Calcutta and Bombay Name of manager	6
Change of management	Announcement of the names of its new management	8

This pattern of advertising needs to be contrasted with the efforts by other banks operating in Banaras to generate trust through advertising. As the Bank of Benares was the only bank of any significance with a local origin, it was in an advantageous position to use its local embeddedness for employing reputational registers of trust.

Banks entering the Banaras market from outside demonstrated an advertising pattern that managed to offset this comparative disadvantage to some extent, using both reputational and procedural registers. One common pattern was to increase the details on their banking operations, highlighting the bank's size and reliability through enhanced information on the bank's equity and amount of deposits but, crucially, also giving much more specified information on the bank's rates of interest. In early 1947, the Hindustan Commercial Bank went as far as to include details of staff bonuses paid in order to showcase business viability.[15] These indicate an incipient shift in advertising in which banks were competing for customers' trust based on highlighting the service provided, in contrast to appeals to customers to visit branches and find out for themselves. Banks from outside Banaras, in addition, did not advertise with an "educational" intent, with only one exception: in one of the first advertisements by banks from outside Banaras that appeared in *Aaj*, the Industrial Bank provided a highly detailed listing of its operational base, and concluded the advertisement with the slogan (translated from Hindi by me): "This is not a lottery. Many people have invested in lotteries, but few have benefited from them."[16] The perceived need for banks – who at the time were invariably targeting well-off and assumedly educated social strata – to elucidate fundamental aspects of "modern" banking business showcases the extent to which Bulchand's confidence in the future of joint stock banking was based on an awareness of a state-led "modernization" project rather than customer preferences.

While the competitors of the Bank of Benares frequently included the names of its managerial staff, the lack of familiarity of local customers with these bankers would have been much more extensive, so that the impact of a banker's name lending reputation to the bank was limited. In consequence, reputational registers were often employed less directly, seeking substitutes for familiarity. One prominent way to overcome this problem was to emphasize the number of branches across India and, frequently, the location of their headquarters in one of the metropolises. Bank headquarters in Calcutta or Bombay indicated business size and embeddedness in the "modern" Indian economy beyond the local economy of Banaras. In the 1940s, several banks went one step further in this process by highlighting the existence of agencies in New York and London and, in the case of the Kumilla Banking Corporation, in Australia.[17]

Demonstrating the relative decline of Banaras as an important financial center, several banks from the United Provinces/Uttar Pradesh started to follow this line after the mid-1940s by highlighting their

[15] Advertisement, Hindustan Commercial Bank, *Aaj*, January 24, 1947.
[16] Advertisement, Industrial Bank, *Aaj*, December 23, 1933. The term "lottery" here was likely meant to indicate a *chit* fund.
[17] Advertisement, Kumilla Banking Corporation Ltd., *Aaj*, January 10, 1947.

headquarters' locations in Kanpur and Allahabad. Conversely, the Bihar Bank Ltd. in the 1930s and 1940s followed a style of advertising reminiscent of the Bank of Benares, possibly reflecting the close commercial links between these regions.

Another noticeable feature of banks trying to enter Banaras was their choice of target clientele: as mentioned earlier, the Bank of Benares typically remained vague on this or preferred the term "frequent customers." In several cases, however, the bank became more specific, using the slogan (translated from Hindi): "gladly offering all kinds of banking services to persons of rank and status." Several banks from outside Banaras, conversely, advertised their willingness to serve all classes of customers, and in the late 1930s, the Bank of Benares for the first time also brought out an advertisement that omitted the class specification from the statement just cited.

However, even banks from outside the city regularly employed combinations of registers that tended to emphasize the reputational. A particularly interesting case is provided by the Tripura Modern Bank Ltd. in 1946.[18] The bank's advertisement was one of the first published in *Aaj* that specifically highlighted its legal status as a scheduled and clearing bank. The advertisement proceeded to list the names of its board, starting with the Maharaja of Tripura as the bank's guarantor and the Prime Minister of Tripura State as chairman. Although most of the content of the advertisement was used for a highly detailed description of the business, the Maharaja's involvement was repeated at the end of the advertisement in bold letters as the signee, thereby reinforcing the impression of lending his personal reputation to the bank.

A very similar pattern was followed by the State Bank of Banaras, which was set up by the city's most important banking families but included the Maharaja of Banaras as the bank's director. Other banks competed for reputation by announcing that opening ceremonies for branch offices would be attended by widely known Congress politicians.[19]

Starting in the 1940s but affecting the predominance of reputational registers of trust only by the early 1970s, banking advertisements began to demonstrate a pattern that presupposed customer confidence in

[18] Advertisement, Tripura Modern Bank Ltd., *Aaj*, October 10, 1946.
[19] Advertisement, Calcutta Commercial Bank, *Aaj*, January 25, 1939.

banking firms, indicating a greater reliance on procedural registers of trust. This shift was also related to the emergence of visual content and logos, and the images carried by them. The Economic Bank went so far as to encapsulate its legal form in the image of a rising sun.[20] Yet the advertisement still employed a strongly reputational register of trust through an invitation to join the opening ceremony of the bank's Jaunpur branch office that placed strong emphasis on the personal reputation of bank managers and notables attending the ceremony.

Logos started to be used by many banks in the mid-1940s, including by the State Bank of Banaras. Logos constituted one of the most easily recognizable procedural registers of trust in highlighting a "brand" rather than reputational features that allowed the tracing of the sequences of exchange to a knowable source. The frequency of their use was correlated to the disappearance of the names of managerial staff since the 1950s. In the 1930s, bankers lent their name to ensure the bank's reputation, but by the 1970s most advertisements were featuring logos and omitted bankers' names. Advertisements by State Bank of India from 1960s onward are particularly instructive, as many of these positioned the logo in the bottom-right corner, the typical position of the manager's name in earlier advertisements. The State Bank of Banaras formed an exception in this regard. While it frequently used its logo (typically in the top-left corner), it continued to use the names of managerial staff at the bottom or bottom-right corner well into the 1980s.

Extra-Legal Lending and the Reputational Economy of Debt in Contemporary Banaras

"Informal" financial practices in the city continue to flourish until the present – except for "indigenous" banking as outlined above. Signifying the most important step subsequently reinforced in a drawn-out process of legislation, the Usurious Loans Act of 1918 halted the incipient tendency to bring "informal" debt transactions under contractual law and reinforced the remodeling of petty debt transactions in pervasively extra-legal ways. Rather than falling back on a "moral" economy that was supposedly disrupted by liberal contractual law, what emerged as a consequence of entrepreneurial adjustments to the

---

[20] Advertisement, Economic Bank, *Aaj*, January 2, 1946.

need to evade the state-led "modernization" project should be portrayed as a "reputational" economy. Apart from being more precise, the differentiation is necessary to highlight the main feature of the markets' operational modes and their differences to the "moral" social orders reminiscent of "the Indian village" and its sociocultural construction, the obvious links between reputation and morality in general notwithstanding. To a significant extent, this development is already implicit in the description of Chettiar "indigenous" banking practices in the mid-twentieth century by Rudner (1989). It centered on the perceived need to visibly maintain a vaguely defined behavioral code bounded by caste membership. While this included obligations to assist or give preferential treatment to other, including less affluent Chettiars, the emphasis of Rudner's study is placed strongly on the demonstration of probity. In a tightly knit group of financial entrepreneurs, frequently operating in spatially dispersed locations, the emphasis on community membership in the employment of reputational registers of trust is hardly surprising. At the same time, given the longstanding process of reinforcing extra-legality in a commercial arena lacking the parameters described above, the reputational economy of debt that developed in contemporary Banaras is marked by the absence of a unifying social structure like community, strongly increasing the visibility of its foundations in the handling of reputational registers of trust.

The operational mode of Chettiar "indigenous" bankers depicted by Rudner needs to be identified as a reputational register of trust that supplements the generation of trust with the generation of obligation. Community – in this case, caste – plays a significant role in both and can be perceived to be particularly apt for this role, too. The combination of trust and obligation through community provided a bridge for the lack of direct interpersonal sequences of exchange as its experiential basis and in this way facilitated the creation of far-reaching mercantile networks. Similar forms of overcoming trust deficits in the absence of procedural registers of trust are prominently visible among other South Asian mercantile communities, for instance, as depicted by Claude Markovits for Shikarpuri trading networks (Markovits 2014) or by Bhaswati Bhattacharya for Armenian mercantile communities (Bhattacharya 2008: 67–98). The combination of trust and obligation also resembles the notion of credit (*sakh*) as portrayed by Bayly for banking families in early colonial Banaras, although in this case the reliance on caste and community structures is less direct, as the notion of *sakh* depended on local reputations that transgressed caste boundaries among select high-caste communities (Bayly 1983). Bayly perceived caste as an important element in the organization of mercantile strata, especially concerning long-distance trade and trading diasporas, but not as the main organizational element, instead emphasizing elaborate systems of mercantile ethics that centered on notions of credit, defined broadly to include noneconomic parameters (Bayly 2011: 99–121, 117). Correspondingly, everyday behavior and public scrutiny of the willingness to act as role models for an ideal merchant family gained in importance in upholding *sakh*. Instead of being specifically directed toward an intracommunity mercantile code, the notion of *sakh* remained strongly oriented toward patronage and the public display of piety and thrift. Conversely, Dalmia has demonstrated the attempts to control deviant behavior in her study of Harischand (Dalmia 1997). Traces of this notion, such as the relative importance attributed to association with notables like the kings of Banaras and Tripura whose socioreligious roles were of greater importance than their political authority, the restriction of banking operations to persons of "rank and status," and the low visual appeal in advertising that corresponds to a public display of thrift, are still discernible in bank advertisements in the mid-twentieth century.

It should be noted that in terms of adherence to mercantile codes of behavior, petty credit transactions in colonial India tended to be visibly distinct from the norms of "indigenous" banking and were frequently castigated in colonial sources for this.[21] At the same time, there is ample evidence that village moneylenders were frequently engaged in similar processes of patronage and the display of adherence to behavioral codes at lesser scales. The relative hostility toward "outsiders" as moneylenders – whether this refers to small-town Marwari lenders in the Deccan in the second half of the nineteenth century as depicted by Hardiman (1996), "Hindu" moneylenders in the early twentieth century Sinkiang[22] or Hyderabad[23] or, for that matter, Kabuli lenders in

---

[21] Cf., for instance, the derisive depiction of petty lenders in the classification of lending professions in the United Provinces by the Upper India Chamber of Commerce (UPBECR IV, 45).

[22] Sinkiang. Proposed exclusion of Hindu moneylenders not engaged in legitimate trade. Dated May 18, 1932. File no. IOR L/PS/12/2343, India Office Records, British Library, London.

[23] "Moneylenders' Act Amendment. Hyderabad State Move," *Times of India*, April 29, 1946.

the Indian countryside – can at least partially be attributed to their unwillingness to follow these codes in the locations of their businesses, although they might have followed similar codes in their places of origin. In early twentieth-century Banaras, the combination of trust and obligation in credit transactions was exploited by Harhias, a group of itinerant lenders especially from rural Bihar, whose recovery practices were strongly defined by tactics of public shaming, very similar to the already cited practice of the Osmanabad Bank as depicted by Sainath in 2016.[24] Their methods centered on staging a *dharna*, frequently sitting on the doorsteps of the homes of defaulting debtors and loudly proclaiming the injustices done to them by the breaches of contractual obligations.

The reliance on reputational registers of trust in extra-legal petty debt transactions in contemporary Banaras has since changed significantly. Given the ubiquity of petty debt transactions in the locality, debtors at times undertake great efforts to avoid familiarity as much as possible, seeking out lenders in far-away neighborhoods to conceal the shame that goes with public visibility of the need to approach moneylenders.[25] Of course, given the pervasive need within a system of finance operating through reputational registers of trust to identify the sequence of exchanges at need, this strategy is partially futile in its intention to avoid public detection as lenders will need to conduct inquiries in the debtor's neighborhood. Yet there is a face-saving difference between local gossip on indebtedness to a moneylender that involves familiarity – and is therefore supposed to be locally known – and gossip on debts that are supposedly hidden by a lack of proximity.

However, most petty debt transactions take place within the neighborhood, bazaar, or commercial arena where gossip carries information on reputations. As an ordering element within the market, the neighborhood has clearly eclipsed the importance of caste and kinship ties. Even within a restricted geographical arena such as the neighborhood, however, reputation needs to be distinguished from familiarity. While it is certainly true that many debt transactions occur within ties of friendship or kinship, these tend to be concentrated on either very

[24] UPBECR I: 51–3; III: 460–61, 464.
[25] There is a clear contrast here to the tendency of openly discussing debt remarked by Isabelle Guérin (2014). However, it should be noted that while shame can be an important reason for people to avoid public knowledge of debt, the majority of debt transactions in Banaras take place in relatively high public visibility.

small or very large principals (relative to the socioeconomic standing of the debtor), and they frequently do not remain viable options for repeated cases of indebtedness. For the "standard" extra-legal debt transaction, the basis of trust lies in the indirect experience of the sequences of exchange carried by local gossip that establishes reputations. By the standards of "formal" credit markets, trust between strangers in extra-legal finance is high in that a significant level of trust is assumed unless a high level of disrepute is known through local communication flows. As reputations (or notions thereof) can be identified at need by a skilled market participant, the need for a debtor to showcase socioeconomic standing and solvency – as required in "formal" finance – is rarely of central importance in negotiations. In turn, the debtor's need to *maintain* reputation by adhering to the terms of the extra-legal contract as much as possible and by making amends in case of temporary incapacity to do so is of paramount importance to avoid future sanctions by the creditor (and other lenders), and by local society in general.

This places a heavy obligation on the debtor to maintain trust, in contrast to the systems of mercantile ethics described by Rudner or Bayly in which the debtor's obligation is (at least partially) accompanied by a corresponding obligation of the creditor to operate in certain manners. This circumscription of the creditor's behavior is not entirely absent but has become internalized to the transaction. Relying on extra-legal practices and being associated with notions of greed, exploitation, and a failure to comply with the suppositions of "modernity," a moneylender's public image is relatively low in any case, and it is further lowered by association with poorer clients, partially out of class prejudice and partially through the (typically justified) public equation of lending to the poor with enhanced forms of exploitation as well as intimidation, at times comprising petty violence. In these circumstances, the lender's conduct is publicly scrutinized and communicated through gossip just as much as the debtor. But this scrutiny is restricted almost entirely to the lender's handling of the recovery process: a "good" lender in contemporary Banaras is one who displays lenience in times of need and manages to recover interest and principals with as little recourse as possible to intimidation, public shaming, and other behavioral transgressions. But there is hardly any sanction on the "level" of exploitation through interest, with interest rates falling into widely known ranges according to the lenders' assessments of what can possibly be extracted from their clients as opposed to individual circumstances involved in the transaction or even as incentives, offering preferential treatment in return for a debtor's "good" reputation. Similar to the high level of trust in the debtor, unless gossip establishes disrepute, the use of reputational registers of trust in contemporary extra-legal finance includes a high level of trust in creditors, in the value-neutral sense of an expectation of future behavior providing a basis for practical conduct.

Andy Rotman's contribution in this volume demonstrates how bazaarism centers on trust and reputation. Notably, the Hindi term used most frequently to describe trust in this context (*vishvaas*) is used more frequently in ways denoting reputation when discussing informal financial transactions. There is a clear understanding that trust and reputation are inextricably linked. While trust and reputation – in the bazaar of Banaras – are certainly not identical, the "half-forgotten dialect" of the bazaar that Rotman identifies as a stumbling block in understanding the ordering of this particular socioeconomic regime implicitly equates trust with the reputational registers of its handling. For the commercial entrepreneur in the bazaar as Rotman shows, trust in the reputational register of its handling – trust in the reputation of a shop, a shopkeeper, or even a shopkeeper's ancestors – can assign positive qualities to the products sold and thereby serve as a substitute for "brandism." The experiential character of trust in this context needs to be built, and the possibility of "alienation" from the social embeddedness of commercial relations in the bazaar provides a distinct form of punishing behavior that compromises this trust, albeit not always entirely.

The extra-legal character of moneylending in contemporary Banaras prevents "informal" financial entrepreneurs from following this route of using *vishvaas* in assigning positive values to their services. Instead, reputation in petty extra-legal finance remains highly preoccupied with either direct interpersonal ways of negotiating trust or with the communication of reputations through neighborhood gossip. Where "organized" banks in Banaras needed to showcase their reputations in order to gain trust in the mid-twentieth century, but afterwards were increasingly able to shift toward the advertisement of products, within some limits even creating brands, informal financial entrepreneurs are stuck in the reputational economy that Rotman identifies as bazaarism without being able to make use of the virtues of *vishvaas* in generating positive images that could replace "brands."

What is striking in observing "informal" financial negotiations is the low level of acrimony between debtors and creditors, which appears to be at odds with the public perception of the business. Beyond the possibility of "alienation" as well as explanations through a fatalistic acceptance of socioeconomic status, this apparent contradiction can be partially resolved by distinguishing between the relationship of (relatively high) trust between the transactional parties and the public image of moneylenders in general: once a person enters into a debt relationship, the need to build and maintain reputation frequently creates the conditions under which the former perception takes centerstage, relegating the latter to a secondary concern that is likely to remain subdued unless the relationship of relatively high trust breaks down to a significant extent. According to most lenders I spoke to, it is not the instance of defaulting that leads to the collapse of trust from the creditor's point of view but rather the act of miscommunicating the likelihood of default. In turn, in the debtor's perception it is not so much the act of pressurizing the debtor that generates mistrust but the breach of unwritten conventions of "acceptable" behavior by the creditor. Given the ubiquity of defaults on payments and repayments in "informal" finance, a strict handling of reputational registers of trust in the manner of a financial track record would not serve the needs of either debtors or creditors in preserving the conditions for a relatively high level of trust. The "moral" aversion of debtors to moneylenders may still be pronounced – it frequently is, although primarily among poorer debtors and much less so in the trade credit segment where debtors often times are lenders simultaneously. The lack of open revolt reflects not only a fatalistic acceptance of the need to engage with moneylenders in the absence of better alternatives but an (often implicit) understanding that the maintenance of high-trust relationships with the lender offers small, yet tangible benefits for the debtor as well, so that "playing to the rules" remains preferable even in a context of moral revulsion.

Reputation as a register of trust in "informal" finance in contemporary Banaras is constantly renegotiated, and the results of these negotiations are communicated through gossip. At the higher levels of the market, the likelihood of default on the original contractual terms needs to be communicated to the creditor. The latter, in turn, is

expected to demonstrate lenience to a significant extent. In an improvised discussion group between lenders and debtors at the level of the
market that can be characterized as the main bazaar a consensus
emerged that having been notified of imminent default, the creditor
was to offer a moratorium on repayment for the duration of two
months, including a moratorium on interest payments for this period
in order to handle the default keeping in view the respective reputational obligations. While this result certainly cannot be taken as an
unwritten rule for the entire market, it is clear from interactions with
other lenders and debtors that the "reputable" response to an open
communication of difficulties in repayment required the lender to
accept deferments, in this way safeguarding the trust imposed in him,
but also demonstrating to market participants the willingness and
capability to handle any difficulties arising within the extra-legal transaction. For the creditor, the display of lenience decreases returns on
investment over time, yet these are compensated by increases in reputation through the demonstration of an avoidance of undue pressure. For
the debtor, while the ability to pay on time provides proof of financial
solvency, the loss of reputation that is involved in defaulting can be
offset by "playing straight," taking the creditor into confidence. In this
way, the incidence of default can even be beneficial in establishing
reputation, even if only in cases of actual payment difficulties and in
finely calibrated ways.

   At the level of lending to the poor, levels of mistrust are significantly
higher than in the trade credit segment, yet still lower than in the
"formal" financial sector, which, up to the present, has not been able
to develop credit practices targeting the poor since these rely on relatively high levels of trust that cannot be handled through procedural
registers. The latter is evident even in microfinance practices that
impose purpose and other restrictions on the targets even in cases in
which the microfinance scheme operates as a savings account rather
than as a credit scheme (cf. Shetty 2013). While the highly exploitative
(and largely illegal) character of moneylending to the poor presents
obstacles for the smooth functioning of the market based on high levels
of trust, reputation is still communicated in similar ways than in the
case of trade credit. The main difference between the practices of
lending followed in contemporary Banaras is in the relevance of direct
interpersonal exchange. Characterized by high levels of (temporary)
defaulting, reputations necessarily involve relatively high levels of

mistrust between the two transactional parties, and these need to be bridged through interpersonal interaction. The requirement of relatively high trust levels in this comprehensively extra-legal section of the market reinforces a performative character of negotiations in which both parties frequently employ well-rehearsed behavioral practices to counter the respective opposing claims: of supplication and protest against the inequity of contractual obligations, and of intimidation and protest against the extent to which lenience is sought.

The performance of interpersonal renegotiations of contractual terms centers on the extraction of a price for lenience. Moneylenders are highly aware that they simultaneously need to show their willingness to be lenient and reinforce the perception that lenience is difficult to obtain, and that their conduct will be publicly scrutinized. This scrutiny makes it difficult to maintain a reputation that carefully balances trust and mistrust in order to facilitate continued business activities. Reputational registers of trust, accordingly, operated much more smoothly in the "traditional" system of indigenous banking where they still relied on a broader social embeddedness and targeted relatively affluent clientele. In contemporary Banaras, they continue to provide a fully functional alternative to the "formal" sector of finance, in spite of the lack of complementary social structures other than the neighborhood, and information flows through gossip.

Conclusion

The discussion of the reputational registers of trust employed in petty extra-legal finance in contemporary Banaras demonstrates one of the major problems faced by "organized" local banks in the mid-twentieth century. In order to comply with the intentions of the state-led "modernizing" project for financial markets, banks were supposed to switch to procedural registers of trust before their use was fully established in the locality. More importantly, they needed to do so before their own standing in the reputational registers of trust still pervasively employed on the city's financial markets could have been consolidated. Recollections of "organized" banking practices by descendants of the great indigenous banking families of the city and, in one case, of the last living person involved in founding these firms portrayed these banks as facades under the guise of which "indigenous" banking practices were supposed to continue. Rather than being an accurate description of intentions – the failure to "go with the times" – these depictions demonstrate the quandary in which "organized" banks were placed, and the failure of businesses to shift to procedural registers of trust while simultaneously establishing themselves in the reputational economy of debt.

The use of reputational registers of trust may appear anachronistic when seen in a modernizing idiom, yet these registers provide their users advantages that cannot be replicated easily through procedural registers of trust. The most important comparative advantage of reputational registers lies in the high level of trust employed. This facilitates transactions that in more mistrustful financial regimes can take place only with major difficulties. For debtors, the negative fallout of this – placing obligations inherent in the debt transaction almost exclusively on the debtor – is compensated to some extent by the facilitation of access to credit, especially in cases where credit would otherwise be restricted to "safe" cases, that is, to "persons of rank and status." While there are comparative advantages commensurate with the employment of procedural registers of trust, these are not *inherently* superior – as envisaged in the state-led "modernization" project – especially since the superiority is more pronounced in large debt transactions and in much more stable conditions than faced by the emerging business sector of "organized" banking in the late-colonial Indian hinterland. In addition to studying the legal form of the shift toward procedural registers of trust and therefore the process of defining the "proper swindle" or creating the magicality of procedural propriety in capitalist socioeconomic orders, business history and economic anthropology need to look beyond the well-documented legal structure of Indian businesses and highlight the pragmatic adjustments that reinforced "informality" or facilitated the circumvention of "the formal."

References

Appadurai, A 2015a, "Afterword. The Dreamworld of Capitalism," *Comparative Studies of South Asia, Africa and the Middle East*, 35, 3, 481–5.

Appadurai, A 2015b, *Banking on Words. The Failure of Language in the Age of Derivative Finance*, University of Chicago Press, Chicago.

Bayly, CA 1983, *Rulers, Townsmen, and Bazaars. North Indian Society in the Age of British Expansion, 1770–1870*, Cambridge University Press, Cambridge.

Bayly, CA 2011, "Merchant Communities: Identities and Solidarities," in MM Kudaisya (ed.) *The Oxford India Anthology of Business History*, Oxford University Press, New Delhi, pp. 99–121.

Bhattacharya, B 2008, "The 'Book of Will' of Petrus Woskan (1680–1751): Some Insights into the Global Commercial Network of the Armenians in the Indian Ocean," *Journal of the Economic and Social History of the Indian Ocean*, 51: 67–98.

Birla, R 2009, *Stages of Capital. Law, Culture, and Market Governance in Late Colonial India*, Duke University Press, Durham.

Carey, M 2017, *Mistrust. An Ethnographic Theory*, HAU Books, Chicago.

Cirvante, VR 1956, *The Indian Capital Market*, Geoffrey Cumberledge Oxford University Press, London.

Corsin Jimenez, A 2011, "Trust in Anthropology," *Anthropological Theory*, 11, 2: 177–96.

Dalmia, V 1997, *The Nationalization of Hindu Traditions. Bharatendu Harischandra and Nineteenth-Century Banaras*, Oxford University Press, New Delhi.

Dietrich Wielenga, K 2016, "Repertoires of Resistance. The Handloom Weavers of South India, c. 1800–1960," *International Review of Social History*, 61: 423–58.

Guérin, I 2014, "Juggling with Debt, Social Ties, and Values. The Everyday Use of Microcredit in Rural South India," *Current Anthropology*, 55, Supplement 9: 40–50.

Hardiman, D 1996, "Usury, Dearth and Famine in Western India," *Past and Present*, 152: 113–56.

Harriss-White, B 2018, "Awkward Classes and India's Development," *Review of Political Economy*, 15 May (https://doi.org/10.1080/09538 259.20181478507).

Harvey, D 2004, "The 'New' Imperialism. Accumulation by Dispossession," *Socialist Register*, 40: 63–87.

Haynes, DE 2015, "Advertising and the History of South Asia, 1880–1950," *History Compass*, 13, 8: 361–74.

Liisberg, S 2015, "Trust as the Life Magic of Self-Deception: A Philosophical-Psychological Investigation into Tolerance of Ambiguity," in S Liisberg, EO Pedersen, & AL Dalsgard (eds.) *Anthropology and Philosophy*, Berghahn, New York, pp. 158–76.

Luhmann, N 1979, *Trust and Power*, Wiley, Chichester.

Luxemburg, R 1913/2003, *The Accumulation of Capital*, Routledge, London.

Markovits, C 2014, *Merchants, Traders, Entrepreneurs. Indian Business in the Colonial Era*, Permanent Black, Ranikhet.

Mauss, M 1970, *The Gift. Forms and Functions of Exchange in Archaic Societies*, Cohen & West, London.

Pedersen, EO & Liisberg, S 2015, "Introduction: Trust and Hope," in S. Liisberg, EO Pedersen, & AL Dalsgard (eds.) *Anthropology and Philosophy*, Berghahn, New York, pp. 1–20.

Rudner, D 1989, "Banker's Trust and the Culture of Banking among the Nattukottai Chettiars of Colonial South India," *Modern Asian Studies*, 23, 3: 417–58.

Sainath, P 2016, "In Marathwada, a Bank's Humiliating 'Gandhigiri' Tactics Tighten the Squeeze on Desperate Farmers," *The People's Archive of Rural India* (https://ruralindiaonline.org/).

Schwecke, S 2018, "A Tangled Jungle of Disorderly Transactions? The Production of a Monetary Outside in a North Indian Town," *Modern Asian Studies*, 52, 4: 1375–419.

Seabright, P 2010, *The Company of Strangers. A Natural History of Economic Life*, rev. ed., Princeton University Press, Princeton.

Shetty, SL 2013, *Microfinance in India. Issues, Problems, and Prospects, a Critical Review of Literature*, Academic Foundation, New Delhi.

Shirras, GF 1920, *Indian Finance and Banking*, Macmillan & Co, London.

Simmel, G 1950, *The Sociology of Georg Simmel*, Free Press, New York.

Timberg, TA & Aiyar, CV 1980, "Informal Credit Markets in India," *Economic and Political Weekly*, 15, 5/7: 279–302.

Tiwari, BK 2014, "A Case Study of Benares State Bank Ltd. (BSB) with Bank of Baroda (BoB)," *Asian Journal of Management Studies and Education*, 3, 1: 35–48.

7 Mandi *Acts and Market Lore: Regulatory Life in India's Agricultural Markets*

MEKHALA KRISHNAMURTHY

Introduction

The Agricultural Produce Marketing Committees (APMC) Act remains among the most widely commented on and one of the most deeply misunderstood laws governing Indian economic life. APMCs – more commonly known as *mandi*s – are notified, physical primary markets designated as the main, and in some cases, the only, state-sanctioned sites for the regulation of the critical "first transaction" between the primary producer and the buyer of his or her agricultural produce. But we are already mixing up our terms. In fact, the APMC is *not* the regulated market itself, but stands for the local market committee constituted to oversee the regulation of a given market area. Depending on the region and commodity in question, an active *mandi* or wholesale agricultural produce market may or may not come under the oversight of an APMC. Conversely, depending on where you are in the country, it is quite possible, even likely, that one would find an APMC on paper or a notified regulated marketyard on the ground with no sign of an actually existing market on its premises.

Then there is the nontrivial matter of whether this is a state or central legislation. At the level of national policy, across political parties, one would be forgiven for thinking the "APMC Act" is a binding central law. To take one recent example, consider this line: "Congress will repeal the APMC Act and make trade in agricultural produce – including exports and inter-state trade – free from all restrictions" (Indian National Congress 2019: 17). This was a declaration in the manifesto of the Indian National Congress (INC) in the run-up to the national election in 2019. Five years ago, in 2014, the Bharatiya Janata Party (BJP) had also promised to reform the APMC Act in its own manifesto for change. But, there is no such thing as a single, applicable "APMC

Act" that the central government has the power to reform or repeal. There are only individual state-level agricultural produce marketing acts that include but are not restricted to the functioning of market committees – and several states currently do not have any such APMC Act in force at all. Moreover, even when there are acts in place, we find significant differences in content and even wider variations in the extent of implementation and enforcement – across states, within states, and across commodity systems.[1] This is precisely the reason that the central government has had to take the route of repeatedly producing and promoting a Model Act (2003, 2017) in the hope that states can be persuaded to adopt it in letter and spirit.

Finally, even when policymakers and expert commentators are well aware of the division of powers in Indian agriculture, the overwhelming sense is that the processes of regulatory reform across states have been virtually static and entirely captured by vested local interests as if they are a singular force of resistance and have no rational role in the regulatory life of agricultural markets. A keyword search on this act would lead with the terms "delisting," "reform," and "repeal." These calls for reform and repeal are almost invariably framed in terms of "freeing the farmer" from the clutches of the APMC monopoly so that he may sell wherever, whenever, and to whomsoever he chooses. All this while simultaneously acknowledging that at least half of all commodity trade and much more when it comes to specific states and commodity markets do not flow through regulated markets and that village-level exchange between petty producers and petty commodity traders still remains the reality across a significant proportion of the country. Indeed, in many contexts, it is not so much that farmers are denied the right to transact outside *mandi*s, but that they are constrained to do so. Instead of being bound to sell to licensed traders in *mandi*s, many Indian farmers are not yet free to step foot inside the regulated market, even if such a market exists within reach. This last condition, that is, the presence of an accessible regulated physical market is in itself is a major assumption given the agrarian structure and the highly uneven spread of marketing infrastructure across the country.

As a result, the actually existing reality of regulation is persistently unclear and confounding in terms of its intentions and effects. Is the so-

---

[1] On regional diversity of agricultural markets, see Krishnamurthy (2015).

called APMC Act a case of inappropriate and regressive regulation, a "bad" law that has actually been effectively implemented and sedimented over time? Or is it a robust regulatory marketing model that has failed to practically materialize where farmers have needed it most? Is it a regulatory protection under assault or a regulatory perversion that is being ruthlessly defended? A safeguard for vulnerable producers or a shelter for exploitative traders and intermediaries? What, then, does its stubborn survival actually facilitate: the potential realization of a promise of fair conditions of agricultural exchange or its perpetual evasion? Unfortunately, instead of clarification, the generalizations and contradictions only seem to abound and multiply, while a vast, vital, and visible sector of the Indian economy and market life remains astonishingly unspecified.

This chapter is a modest effort at conceptual and empirical illumination. It begins by returning to the origins, intentions, and instruments that have animated the state regulation of primary agricultural markets in India over the past century and to the competing imperatives that make any effort at disciplining the first transaction in agrarian exchange such a fraught exercise. It then draws on long-term ethnographic and archival research in and around an agricultural market in the central Indian state of Madhya Pradesh (MP). Here it traces out some of the major changes in the regulatory life and life history of a single *mandi*, attending to the diverse narratives and experiences of both state-level legislative amendment and marketyard-level activism and market reform over a span of five decades.

What might a regulatory biography of a local market offer us in the context of such a vast territorial and technical challenge? First, drawing on instruction from the grounded and generative field economics of Barbara Harriss-White, we know that empirical specification is simply a general requirement in any serious attempt at understanding how agricultural markets actually work.[2] But, given the comparative diversity, internal complexity, and institutional dynamism of these markets across India, even adequate specification is a genuinely (and perhaps even impossibly) difficult task. In this context, a *mandi* presents one with a scale of market organization intimate enough for the ethnographic immersion and observation required to illuminate market

---

[2] On Tamil Nadu, see Harriss (1984), Harriss-White (1996) and Harriss-White (2016). On West Bengal, see Harriss-White (2008).

structure, institutions, and the changing relations of exchange. At the same time, it is so inextricably and relentlessly interconnected and interactive with larger political, administrative, commercial, and social systems and networks that one is compelled to track a range of connections and movements, and follow their diverse effects if one is to have any grasp on market dynamics as they play out in the field.

The "local" and "locality" is therefore here both an empirical site and an analytical approach (Harriss-White 2008). As the anthropologist, Jane Guyer, illustrates in the case of food regulation in Britain and Nigeria:

Local arenas are pieces of a complex global mosaic of socio–technical models, constructed from diverse elements in one context, reconfigured for application to others, and subjected to constant amendment. They are punctiliously defined and redefined by technical terminologies and implemented by specialized functionaries. Understanding any part of this process then, however small, entails an understanding of the dynamics of multiplicity without losing sight of the differential power that allows some intentions and definitions to prevail over others, some boundaries to hold strong and others to open up. (Guyer 2016: 41)

It is through this kind of engagement with a local market arena that I hope the close study of a *mandi* in central India might enable us to better understand the complex and contested nature of regulatory processes more generally and the very real stakes involved in their holding and unfolding over time.

The Origin of the Species: A Brief History of the Model of Regulated Markets in India

Over the past century, a particular vision of what it means to have "properly organized" and regulated agricultural markets has come to occupy and preoccupy the Indian policy and planning imagination. This ideal has also been enshrined as the centerpiece of state marketing legislations, where it has proved itself as hard to dislodge from the page as the proverbial middleman it has tried so resolutely to banish outside it. At its core is the belief that a network of regulated local physical primary markets is the best option to discipline the critical first transaction between rural producers and the first buyers of agricultural produce.

We can trace this model back to its articulation in the report of the Royal Commission on Agriculture (1928), which declared that the countrywide establishment of regulated markets for a wide variety of agricultural produce "would confer an immense boon on the cultivating classes of India" and must form "an essential part of any ordered plan of agricultural development in the country" (Royal Commission on Agriculture in India 1928: 289). It seems quite certain that its presence here was, at least in part, a transplant. The immediate "prehistory" of this recommendation takes us to regulatory initiatives directed at reigning in the unruly wheat and meat markets of early twentieth-century Britain. There, "as part of the late Victorian predilection for municipal order and hygiene, acts controlling piecemeal the conduct of colorful but squalid urban markets" had begun to "pepper the Statute Book." By 1920, "there were 32 such acts, mainly concerned with the sale and slaughter of cattle and transactions in wheat, in markets run by local sheriffs or stewards" (Harriss 1984: 72). In 1922, a committee was constituted to investigate and comment on the "prevailing legal chaos" that raged around British agricultural markets, and, in 1924, based on its review, the Markets Branch was formed in the Ministry of Agriculture. This British committee was presided over by none other than Lord Linlithgow, who only four years later, in 1926, was appointed chairperson of the Royal Commission in India, bringing with him many unimplemented ideas from British markets (Harriss 1984: 72). From within India, the Commission also drew extensively on a quarter-century of pioneering provincial legislation – primarily, the Berar Cotton and Grain Markets Act 1897, the first law of its kind in India, and the Bombay Cotton Markets Act 1927.

The common feature of these regulatory interventions across metropole and colony, Berar and Bombay was the establishment of local market committees to actively oversee the management and regulation of primary agricultural markets. The Commission's report justifies this statutory emphasis on local control and autonomy by describing in detail the extent of inter- and intra-district variation in the structure and organization of specific commodity markets. Therefore, even as the question of representation posed persistent procedural and political challenges, market committees run by local stakeholders were considered the only regulatory structure capable of handling the contextual diversity and social embeddedness of agricultural exchange. Today's much vilified APMCs are its offspring. At the same time, however, the

Commission also expressed the view that the proper functioning of
these local markets could only be secured under a dedicated provincial
legislation and should not be left vulnerable to the urban orientation
and vested interests of municipal councils and district boards. Thus, the
dual imperatives of *localization* and *standardization* formed
a constitutive – and enduring – tension in the framing of agricultural
marketing regulation in India. More generally, any legislative act at this
level of the marketing system faced the unwieldy task of balancing and
reconciling multiple regulatory imperatives, each involving different
market actors and interests in relations that sometimes positively reinforced one another while regularly coming into conflict.

At the outset, regulated marketing acts epitomized a "producerist"
approach to the state regulation of agricultural markets. Instead of
favoring the maximization of consumer welfare (the explicit function
of other legislation governing essential commodities), these acts built
on a legal approach that prioritized producer security "not as a matter
of ex post compensation but rather as intrinsic principles to organize
agricultural and retail markets" (Cohen 2013: 83). Regulated markets
were therefore intended, first and foremost, to protect primary producers from the wide range of exploitative practices – or what ML
Dantwala, writing a decade after the Royal Commission, evocatively
referred to as the many forms of "evil" – that farmers routinely experienced at the hands of intermediaries and traders. These include everything from collusive and secretive price setting, mixing, watering, and
other forms of adulteration, to fraudulent weighment, idiosyncratic
quality assurance, customary deductions, delayed payments, and
more (Dantwala 1937: 252). Regulated markets were to systematically
take steps, including information dissemination, open auctions, and
standardized weights and measures, to address these "defects" in market practice. Stacking the committee with bona fide farmer–members
was also expected to help ensure that producers participated on fair
terms of exchange in regulated markets and that there were processes in
place for the formal settlement of disputes.

Ultimately, however, even with the most robust safeguards, farmers
were unlikely to realize fair prices for their produce in uncompetitive local
markets. Therefore, the second imperative for regulated markets was to
create conditions to attract, incentivize, and oversee the different kinds of
buyer needed to encourage and sustain a competitive local market for
agricultural commodity trade. Here, the licensing of new traders,

processors, and intermediaries, and the granting of shops and warehouses in the marketyard was to play a critical role in the regulation – and restriction – of competition, both inside and outside the regulated market.

Finally, in order to maintain and support itself, the new system of regulated markets had to continuously generate fiscal returns to the state. Its primary means of revenue extraction were through the collection of market fees, taxes, and fines. In turn, the logic and logistics of revenue generation itself both necessitated and at least partially sustained a dedicated marketing bureaucracy deployed at various levels of the regulatory apparatus, sometimes in coordination, but all too often in conflict with other state agencies involved in myriad capacities in agricultural markets. State marketing acts were thus charged from their very conception with delivering a balancing act that would have tripped up even the most light-footed of weighmen. Populated with diverse, divided interests, straining against competing regulatory imperatives, and exposed to a range of external forces, their implementation in different states across the country was never going make for a straightforward story.

Mandi Acts and Regulated Markets in MP

While regulated markets were enshrined as key sites in the agricultural system in colonial provincial legislations that multiplied during the 1930s, there were in fact only seventy-three officially regulated principal markets across undivided India by 1940 and only 286 across independent India by 1950.[3] The faith in the fundamental role of regulated agricultural markets, however, remained central in the postcolonial policy and planning imagination, and was expressed through new targets for their expansion in each of the Five Year Plans that followed. They formed a critical part of a national and international development vision but were to be sanctioned and regulated under different, autonomous state-level agricultural marketing acts. Today, it is estimated that there are around 6,746 regulated markets operating under the different acts in force across India, of which, 2479 are principal wholesale marketyards.[4]

---

[3] National Council of State Agricultural Marketing Boards (COSAMB): www
.cosamb.org/markets.html.
[4] Ibid.

In the erstwhile state of Madhya Bharat, the state government enacted the Madhya Bharat Agricultural Produce Markets Act 1952 and for a period of time, around 1956, when the state was reorganized into MP and Maharashtra, different acts were in effect in different regions of the newly formed administrative territories (Gupta 1973: 25). Four years later, repealing the older provincial laws and consolidating the newer ones, regulation in MP was brought under a single act and renamed the Madhya Pradesh Agricultural Produce Markets Act (APMA) 1960. A decade later, the National Agricultural Commission recommended that all states establish apex institutions to direct and oversee the regulation of local agricultural markets within their respective state boundaries. The Madhya Pradesh State Agricultural Marketing Board, generally referred to as the Mandi Board, was created in 1973 with its headquarters in the state capital, Bhopal. The Mandi Board was established under the 1972 edition of the APMA (also known as the Mandi Act), which is the same act that continues, with important amendments, to remain in force today.[5]

Harda Mandi 1969–2019: A Regulatory Biography

The *Krishi Upaj Mandi*, or Agricultural Produce Market of Harda, was officially notified under the Madhya Pradesh State Agricultural Produce Marketing Act 1960 on December 1, 1969. At the time, it was one of 116 wholesale markets to be brought under state regulation across MP[6] and was already well-established as a small but prominent trading center for marketing of cotton and oilseeds. Over the years, the number of regulated markets in MP has grown to 241 principal marketyards and a further 275 submarketyards. Each principal market is supposed to function under the regulatory oversight of an elected *mandi* committee or APMC. Harda Mandi is among the fifty largest (Class A) *mandi*s in the state and is a major market for soybean, wheat, and gram. But Harda town itself remains classified as a small Tier-II town with an urban population of around 74,000 surrounded by an irrigated agrarian hinterland with

---

[5] Madhya Pradesh State Agricultural Marketing Board: http://mpmandiboard .org/.
[6] RP Gupta, *Agricultural Prices in a Backward Economy*, p. 26. The state of Madhya Pradesh at the time included the territory that is today the separate state of Chhattisgarh.

a notable proportion of medium and large landowners. There are 195 villages that fall directly within the *mandi*'s notified catchment area.

For the first three years of its official regulatory life, Harda Mandi did not have a Market Committee. Its inaugural Committee was only elected in 1973 after the establishment of the MP State Mandi Board. But the Committee lasted only until 1975 when it was dissolved, along with almost all elected institutions in the country, with the imposition of the Emergency. The next committee almost managed to run its five-year term but fell short when it was suspended by the state government in 1982. Subsequently, a committee did run through the second half of the eighties; but from 1991 onwards, *mandi* elections were once again suspended, this time for the rest of the decade. At the turn of the century, however, the state government brought elected market committees back into action for two consecutive terms: 2000–2005 and 2005–2010. In recent times, elections were last held after a delay of two years in 2012 and were once again running late at the time of writing.

How should we characterize and chronologize this half-century of regulatory life in Harda Mandi and the activation, dissolution, and suspended animation of its Market Committee? How has the *mandi* changed in scale, commodities, structure, and organization over this time? How were different interests expressed in the agricultural market, and to what extent and with what effect did they shape market practices and the terms of exchange for different market actors? How might we grasp the dynamics of regulatory reform and revision as they played out in this central Indian market and what might it tell us about the political economy of Indian agricultural markets more generally? The rest of this chapter is an attempt to sketch out the regulatory biography of Harda Mandi, drawing on ethnographic observation, official records, and personal accounts of farmers, traders, laborers, market functionaries, committee members, politicians, bureaucrats, corporate leaders, and regional agro-commercial capitalists involved in the making and management of the market every day and at specific periods in time.

Mercantile Interests, Political "Camp-ism," and Market Control: The 1970s and 1980s

For the first two decades after notification, the elected *Mandi* Committee in Harda was effectively controlled by dominant local mercantile interests and by one particular commercial and political power center. To be fair, the first Committee did in fact demonstrate the incipient possibilities for protecting the interests of producers in a regulated market. Its chairperson was a rich Jat farmer, a part of a famous Jat–Gujjar duo that stormed Harda's political landscape in the 1960s. Both men came from large, well-established landowning families, with the Gujjar leader serving as the elected representative – Member of the Legislative Assembly (MLA) – to the state legislative assembly from this constituency for two terms. His Jat partner was appointed the first chairperson of the *Mandi* Committee and is remembered for having successfully abolished the *jholi pratha*, the practice of bagging grain using large, expertly tied sheets of cloth. The *jholi* was a well-known aid in grain theft. When using a *jholi*, grain could be partially spilled into the vests and pajamas of the *hammal*s (*mandi* laborers) as they swept it up in the cloth and transferred it deftly into gunny bags. Old *mandi* people recalled the tragicomic sight of wiry *hammal*s, their loose clothes stuffed with produce, waddling to the dark corners of the *mandi* to relieve themselves of their ill-gotten g(r)ains! During its first term, the *Mandi* Committee passed an order banning this technique and replacing the cloth *jholi*s with tin scoops. Decades later, this would be recalled as the first of a series of activist measures that sought to put in place fairer practices of exchange for farmers in the *mandi*-yard. But, before the Committee could take up any further causes, it was dissolved with the Emergency in 1975.

When it was reconstituted in 1978, the *Mandi* Chairperson, the first of two successive Bishnoi farmers appointed to head the Committee over the next decade, was handpicked by a man who had emerged as the most powerful political figure in Harda. He held the popular title of *Nagar Seth*, the town merchant/magnate. When residents simply referred to "the *Seth*" without adding the name of a trader or a firm, one could safely assume they were talking about him. The *Nagar Seth* belonged to the oldest and largest trading firm with its cotton trading and processing businesses well-recognized across the regional market. But it was his political power as a leading figure in the Congress Party, known for his close ties to Indira Gandhi and to state leaders, that made him such an influential political force. Moreover, his was precisely the kind of power that comes from wielding influence without directly contesting political office: he was known to be a large man who cast an even larger shadow on the life of local commercial and political institutions. During this period, Harda Mandi was firmly in his grip.

The extent of his control over the *mandi*'s management is illustrated by the recruitment and allegiance of *mandi* staff. The few posts sanctioned to manage local market activities and records were all appointed by the *Mandi* Committee. They were therefore personally selected by its Chairperson, often from among young men close to him, and by extension, were quickly conscripted into the service of furthering the political and business causes of the *Nagar Seth*. From the peons to the clerks, market inspectors to accountants, the local functionaries – a number of who were still employed in the *mandi* when I conducted fieldwork – recounted the innumerable small and large tasks that they were allotted in the course of their official duties in the *mandi*. For instance, they recalled being instructed to routinely divert produce from one trader's shop to another's, fix figures, manipulate *mandi* electoral rolls, and manufacture grounds to disqualify opponents from contesting elections.[7] Their presence and pressure was felt in villages around Harda, while the most loyal among them accompanied delegations on important market business to Bombay (now Mumbai) and were dispatched on sensitive political errands to Bhopal.

Of course, as one might imagine, the *Nagar Seth* did not go unchallenged, both by commercial rivals in the market and by political rivals in the constituency. Indeed, rampant political factionalization, often described in colloquial political commentary as *goot-baazi* or "campism" was is a well-known feature of the Congress Party in MP, a feature that continues to this day. Politics in Harda was no exception and was marked by a fierce political rivalry within the Congress between the *Nagar Seth* and his intra-party arch rival. During the eighties and through the early nineties, the *mandi* was among the prominent local arenas that was affected by the internecine political battles between two fiercely opposed camps within the Congress: one used the market to consolidate local political and economic power through its trading interests; the other deployed state power whenever in political favor to

---

[7] For instance, holding a *chakki* license would indicate that you were involved in small-scale processing and retailing activities and could therefore disqualify a farmer from being considered for election to the *Mandi* Committee. In the run-up to *mandi* elections, functionaries recall being ordered to issue a number of these licenses to eliminate opponents from contesting.

try to undermine his political rival's commercial interests in the local agricultural market.

The Mid-1980s and the "Revolutionary" Reorganization of the _Mandi_ Order

During the first decade and a half of state regulation, _mandi_s like the one in Harda, although formally notified, were, for all intents and purposes, left to local management and this meant that the market was essentially in the hands of private traders. While the considerable economic and political influence of the _Nagar Seth_ loomed large and asserted itself in myriad ways through the local _Mandi_ Committee and market functionaries, the day-to-day processes of exchange in Harda, as elsewhere in MP and in many other states, were run by a category of specialist commission agents known as _kaccha arhatiya_s, who operated between primary sellers and buyers and were responsible for the auctioning and sale of farmers' produce. Farmers were typically tied to particular _arhatiya_s in long-term credit-based relationships, often cultivated over generations. The _mandi_-yard itself was a crowded three-acre plot, taken on rent and was entirely managed by forty-odd commission agents and their private staff. Their shops lined the perimeter of the _mandi_, where the auction proceeded by rotation until the end of the market day. All market infrastructure was in private hands and the locally appointed market functionaries were neutral and ineffective at best and more generally engaged in the bidding of the most powerful traders.

Against this backdrop, in the early 1980s, the state government decided to launch a program to dismantle this system of commission agents – _mandi_ by _mandi_ – across MP. Given the prevailing structure of markets and the grip that _kaccha arhatiya_s exercised in local credit-and-commodity markets, this was an extraordinarily ambitious move and one that was highly unlikely to succeed if discharged by mere legal and administrative fiat. But Digvijay Singh, the Congress politician who led the charge as state minister for agriculture, had a distant horizon in sight. Politically, he felt that the action to eliminate the _kaccha arhatiya_s would serve as an attack on the rival BJP's "_bania_ base," a political base that has historically been heavily dominated by the traditional trading castes. At the same time, Singh framed the "liberation" of the _kisan_ from the clutches of the _arhatiya_ as part of a wider strategy to try to broaden expand the Congress Party's own narrow political base by favoring the middle-caste landowning farmers, who would eventually stand to gain from this reform. But, of course, as we have already seen, the Congress was also deeply involved in the fortunes of the local and regional agro-commercial elite and going after their interests was a political risk. Singh reasoned that the political risk would be counteracted by fiscal rewards. Here, he was counting on the timing: the state was in the early phases of an agricultural transformation driven by the rapid spread of soybean, a new cash crop, in what has come to be known as MP's Yellow Revolution. If the state wanted to support farmers while extracting a portion of the expanding cultivation and trade in this protein-rich, export-oriented oilseed as revenue, it had to first bring the marketing system more firmly under state regulation and management. Removing the *arhatiya*s from local *mandi*s was a critical step in this process.

This was a tense encounter between *arhatiya*s and state functionaries on the ground. For those familiar with the long history of such local battles between traders and the state, the events in Harda illustrate many textbook elements. The state government first suspended the trader-controlled *Mandi* Committee. Local authorities then proceeded with territorial displacement: forcefully relocating the *mandi* from the private three-acre plot that the *arhatiya*s rented and controlled to a massive sixty-four-acre public marketyard across the road. For their part, the *arhatiya*s sought recourse in familiar tactics of dispelling and stalling: conjuring spirits (ghosts, they claimed, haunted the desolate new marketyard), petitioning the court (the marketyard was completely unsuitable for agricultural marketing), and going on strike. But, the local district officials, led by a short yet formidable District Collector, were well-prepared to stand day and night in the marketyard and to buy all the farmers' produce until the *arhatiya*s returned to the *mandi*. When they did, a new market order was put in place: commission agent licenses were cancelled, the auction was taken over by state-appointed auctioneers, all lots were lined up along a platform for direct sale to the highest bidder, and all buyers had to pay farmers directly in cash by the end of the marketing day. Putting these changes in place was by no means easy, but it *did* indeed happen. Perhaps most surprisingly, farmers continued to come to the *mandi* to market their produce, while credit relations moved out to the villages and to the town bazaar.

Stepping back, it is important to recognize that the reasons for the "successful" elimination of *kaccha arhatiya*s from the *mandi* cannot be simply explained by the force of the state's regulatory action. It must be understood instead by considering the changing dynamics of agricultural production in Harda around the same time. In the mid-1980s, this major market reform coincided with the expansion of canal irrigation and the cultivation of soybean, a new short-duration crop, which had demonstrably different marketing dynamics from the time- and input-intensive unirrigated, long-duration cotton that soybean had begun to replace. It was this *conjunctural dynamic* that was vital to the delinking of credit and commodity marketing and to the reorganization of the *mandi* in Harda during this period.

The Post-Revolutionary Reality: Distress and Dynamism in the Marketyard, 1985–2000

The abolition of the system of *kaccha arhatiya*s is remembered as the most "revolutionary" reform in the *mandi*'s regulatory life. Today, farmers who are old enough to remember their family's *arhatiya*s, recall their dependence on the old commission agents during the long, lean seasons of cultivation and for marketing of their produce later in the year, when the harvests came in. They also laugh heartily at the visible decline and disappearance of this group of once-powerful intermediaries. By the end of 1980s, the majority of the original *kaccha arhatiya*s, who had depended primarily on their credit-and-commission businesses in the old *mandi*, had gradually exited the scene. Only a handful of firms from the old guard who had well-established commodity trading networks and agro-processing concerns, took up licenses to operate on their own accounts in the new marketyard. Along with them, a new crop of younger, ambitious trading firms entered the market hoping to cash in on the rapidly expanding soybean trade.[8]

Given all this churn and dynamism in the composition of *mandi* traders, I had somewhat naively assumed that the abolition of the old commission agents, the entry of new buyers, and greater oversight by the state must have heralded a period of substantial improvement in

[8] For a more detailed analysis of the changing composition of *mandi* traders in Harda, see Krishnamurthy (2013).

marketing practices in the *mandi*. Instead, I found that even as Harda's farmers experienced significant increases in production, now from the cultivation of two crops – soybean and irrigated wheat – marketing life for the newly "liberated" farmers in the *mandi* seemed to hit a historic low. This appeared ironic, to say the least. But the farmers who experienced the change in the *mandi* had a common explanation. In the old *mandi*, farmers were treated by the *arhatiya*s as their *grahak*s or "customers" with whom they had to maintain long-term relationships. Under that system, while farmers were acutely conscious of the exploitation associated with interlocked exchange, they were also quick to acknowledge the strength and security of the social and economic ties with commission agents, who after all had personal stakes in the futures of their farmer–customers. In the new *mandi*, farmers found that in the absence of long-term relations of credit and commission, they now ceased to matter personally to the traders with whom they only engaged in one-time exchange during the marketing season. Their produce, however, was more attractive than ever before. What followed, all market actors unanimously agreed, was an exponential increase in the extent of grain theft by traders and laborers, who were known at this time for routinely manhandling farmers and their grain. Conjuncture, then, was followed by disjuncture and for farmers a sense of both loss and humiliation in the marketyard.

At the same time, however, outside the *mandi*, other movements were underway as new political ambitions were being sown and irrigated in Harda's fields. Indeed, the shift from cotton to soybean was often remarked on as a new phase in local political power in Harda, a transition from the mercantile grip of the *Nagar Seth*, a Marwari cotton trader associated with the Congress Party to the growing prosperity and political aspirations of a Jat soybean farmer rising up within the BJP. Notably, the young Jat's election as MLA in 1993, the first of four consecutive terms in power, coincided with the almost complete replacement of cotton by soybean in Harda. It should come as no surprise by this point that the *mandi* was the site that the young Jat leader chose to launch his political campaign by waging a series of protests against various malpractices committed by traders. In the years that followed, Jats became an increasingly activist presence in the *mandi*-yard, spearheading the activities of the two major farmer organizations in Harda, the BJP-affiliated Bharatiya Kisan Sangh (BKS) and an independent local group called Kisan Panchayat (KP).

These actions culminated in a turn-of-the-century battle to install an electronic weighbridge in Harda Mandi. Although widely recalled as a collective demand of farmers, the credit for spearheading this campaign was usually given to the leader of the KP, another enterprising Jat, who farmed ninety acres of irrigated land and had recently returned to Harda with an MSc in agriculture. On the back of this victory, he would soon be elected as the chairperson of the *Mandi* Committee and would serve as a popular leader among farmers for five years (2000–2005). He would eventually be ousted and undone by an intra-caste feud with the MLA that matched the intraparty rivalry of the earlier era and outdid it in terms of violence, landing both Jat leaders in jail at different periods of time. But, let us return to the question of weight. It should come as no surprise that the introduction of an electronic weighbridge was fiercely resisted by the traders who benefited illegitimately from the manual system of weighing. Undeterred, the Jat activist was able to convince the District Collector to institute a one-month trial period. In the marketyard, he supervised the entire process and ensured that it did not break down or erupt in violence. Eventually, the trial period was extended and Harda became the first *mandi* in MP to switch entirely to electronic weighment of farmers' produce. This ended the rampant theft of grain associated with manual weighment, reordered the flow of vehicles and produce in the marketyard, significantly reduced marketing time, and reorganized *mandi* labor. But, as importantly, the electronic weighbridge served as a sensitive indicator of changes in the agrarian economy and its politics.[9]

In Harda, then, roughly fifteen years after its notification as a regulated market, the state formally stepped in to eject a layer of commission agents and to delink credit and commodity marketing. As a result, new traders were able to enter the market and buy directly from farmers in open auctions. But, simultaneously, weighment practices suffered further deterioration. It then took another fifteen years for a group of activist farmers to successfully fight for fair weighment as their right in the regulated marketyard, an action that the state had no plan to initiate on its own at this time. If anything is clear at all from this, it is that the various elements of agricultural exchange (even when they are steps in the same basic transaction) rarely yield completely to

---

[9] For a more detailed analysis of the changing practices of weighment and its effects, see Krishnamurthy (2018: 28–52).

a single regulatory authority or synchronize in any self-evident direction.

Fiscal and Functional Consolidation in the 1990s: Market Fees, Fines, and Functionaries

From 1991 to 2000, *mandi* committees in MP were once again placed in a state of suspension. Digvijay Singh was now chief minister (serving from 1993 to 2003), and he continued to view the *mandi* as a key site for intervention and reform. This time, the decade-long suspension minimized local interference while the grounds were prepared for the initiation of a further series of market reforms.

The State Mandi Board, headquartered in Bhopal, was the main institutional site for these initiatives and efforts were made to strengthen its capacities to undertake such a process. Senior officials involved at the time described how special personnel from within the administrative service, select officers from cooperative, procurement, and marketing agencies, as well as information technology specialists were deputed to the Mandi Board to assist with different aspects of the reform agenda. The process of regulatory revision was a long and detailed exercise, attending to the many minute aspects of agricultural marketing and the unpredictable political process of legislative change.

Unsurprisingly, one of the first orders of business for the state was to bring about changes to the regime of *mandi* fees and fines. In 1986, the state removed a double taxation provision that levied fees both at the time of purchase and on movement and sale in another *mandi*. Now, a fee would only be levied at the point of purchase, as long as proof of fee payment issued by the *mandi* accompanied the moving consignment. This was applied first to processors in 1986, and subsequently, to all buyers in the market in 1990. At the same time, the fine imposed on evading parties was increased substantially to five times the cost of the fees evaded, with a provision to levy an interest payment at the rate of 24 percent per annum if fees were not paid for stocks purchased within fourteen days. As market prices and volumes traded in key commodities began to rise and *mandi* authorities started monitoring cases by increasing the targets set for inspection and action against evading parties, the risks of being caught and the costs associated with it also increased significantly. In time, many *mandis*, including the one in Harda, also instituted an advance fee collection system based on the estimated volumes to be purchased each month by major buyers in the market.

The *mandi* fee itself after experimentally being reduced from 1 percent to 0.5 percent in 1999 was hiked to 2 percent in 2000. This rise was justified on the grounds of directly promoting rural development as, in addition to improving *mandi* infrastructure, a proportion of this fee was allocated toward the construction of rural roads, especially approach roads between villages and market towns under the Farmers' Road Fund. Notably, a small percentage was also dedicated to the upkeep of local *goshala*s (cow sheds), an open political "concession" to the religious and cultural "sentiments" of the Hindu population, especially, the Marwari trading communities that have historically collected donations for the maintenance of local *goshala*s in their market areas. With the growth in agricultural production, incomes across the major *mandi*s of MP have grown substantially over time. In Harda Mandi, fees rose from Rs. 52 lakh in 1991–92 to Rs. 90 lakh in 1995–96, multiplying by over five times to the range of Rs. 5–8 crore annually between 2007 and 2010.[10]

These moves to increase state revenue through *mandi* fees not only raised the profile of the Mandi Board among state institutions in the capital but were also accompanied by significant improvements in both the stature and size of the staff assigned to man the local marketyards. During the suspension of elected committees, officers-in-charge (OICs) were stationed in *mandi*s across the state, including in Harda. In a few cases, these officers were even drawn from the elite ranks of the Indian Administrative Service (IAS), young men, who as the experienced superintendent of Harda Mandi recalls, brought both status and strict enforcement into *mandi* management during their stints. Under them, he explained, the *mandi* gradually changed from being privately and locally run to a more *prashasnik* or state-infused institution, empowered with state administrative authority. The staff also grew in number, from only four or five low-level appointments in the mid-1970s, to twenty to thirty-five in the 1980s and 1990s, currently standing at forty-five *mandi* functionaries in Harda, still short of a mandated total of sixty full-time positions. Over time, the Mandi Board also inducted and trained an experienced cadre of

[10] Harda Mandi records.

mandi secretaries, capable of managing a variety of *mandi*s of different sizes and political dimensions across the state during the course of their careers.

Importantly, even as the government expanded the administrative capacity of the agricultural marketing bureaucracy, it intended not only to revive the suspended local market committees but also to deepen democratic participation in *mandi*s on the ground. In this regard, *mandi*s can be seen as part of a larger state agenda championed by Digvijay Singh towards democratic decentralization in MP during this decade (see, for instance, Manor (2010)). In 2000, the state government introduced "direct elections" for the post of *mandi* chairperson (*adhyaksh*). Previously, landowning farmers in a market area only voted for the ten farmer–members of the Committee. The chairperson, who also had to be a farmer, was nominated by the Committee, including the trader–member, representative of licensed weighmen and laborers, MLA's nominee, and other local department nominees (cooperatives, agriculture, land, and *panchayat*). Given that the chairperson was the key signatory in routine *mandi* work and in the passing of orders, the nomination process was often captured, as we have already seen, both through political pressure and monetary inducement by powerful trading parties. By mandating the direct election of the chairperson by all the landowning farmers in the market area, it was hoped that even under the inevitable influence of party politics and trader financing in the highly contested *mandi* arena, there would still be greater potential for the emergence of genuine farmer representatives at the helm of *mandi* committees. At the same time, given the improved fiscal health of local *mandi*s and the scope for political graft from all manner of market regulation and "maintenance" activities, the *mandi* bureaucracy also knew that the local markets would become sites of intensified party-based contestation, political pressure, and financial leakage. Having worked hard to consolidate its grip on the *mandi* system, the Mandi Board was therefore careful to impose new limits on the powers of the elected chairman and to ensure that its own cadre of appointed functionaries retained significant control on *mandi* management. They were well aware that, in the words of a seasoned Mandi Board official: "Handing power back to the people after the Emergency is an exercise in itself."

Competition and Concession in the *Mandi* System: Private Procurement Hubs in the 2000s

Until this point, *mandi* reforms in MP had focused, albeit erratically and unevenly, on the implementation of agricultural marketing regulation to put curbs on the exploitation of farmers by commission agents and traders while enhancing revenue collection by the state. Now, in the early twenty-first century, state and national policy priorities shifted towards more fundamental regulatory reform to "open up" the *mandi* system to competition from alternative sites of exchange.

Under the original MP Mandi Act, the officially designated market-yard – and where relevant, sub-marketyard – was the only site within any state notified market area where agricultural commodity exchange was properly regulated under the law. Outside the marketyard, petty commodity exchange and trade (i.e., low volume, retail level buying and selling) was allowed under permissible limits; it would, in any case, be virtually impossible for the state to oversee village traders and itinerant aggregators, although *mandi* inspectors did conduct spot-checks occasionally on some of the larger *phutkar* or "retail-level" establishments and looked into their stocks. Any entity interested in substantial purchasing of agricultural produce within the market area had to either take a *mandi* license and bid directly in the auction or buy through a licensed trader either on a fixed commission, through a broker, or in a bilateral trading arrangement. Large agribusiness enterprises – regional, national, and multinational – had long participated in the *mandi* trade both by taking individual licenses and operating via licensed agents. But corporations had a long litany of complaints about the *mandi* system, its vested interests, and infrastructural deficiencies. APMC-ruled *mandi*s, it was increasingly argued by national policymakers and economic advisors, were an anachronistic market institution and impeded large-scale private investment in agricultural commodity trade and processing in India. Accordingly, a new Model APMC Act released in 2003 and an updated edition in 2017 encouraged states to allow private procurement yards and private markets to operate outside the regulated *mandi*-yard.

MP was a forerunner in this process. In 2002, after a lengthy negotiation, the state government formally amended the Mandi Act, to allow the establishment of "single license yards," the official term for private procurement centers located *outside* the *mandi*-yard where the license holder could buy produce directly from farmers. This major reform was introduced to facilitate the Indian corporate conglomerate ITC's *e-choupal* initiative, which involved the creation of a network of soybean and wheat procurement "hubs" across western MP. Under the new amendment, corporations could now apply for individual licenses from the *mandi* committee under whose notified market area they planned their procurement activities. A few years later, in 2007, provisions were made to grant corporations single licenses, issued by the Mandi Board, allowing them to bypass individual *mandi* committees and operate freely in any market area in the state. Further, another amendment was made in the Act in 2009 allowing the entry of national electronic spot exchanges to be integrated into existing *mandi*s, anticipating, nearly a decade in advance, the push for the creation of a larger national agricultural market.

Notably, these regulatory changes have been brought about by state governments under both major national parties – the Congress Party until 2003 and the BJP from 2003 to 2018. In fact, in 2004, *mandi* traders across MP shut down *mandi*s in a month-long strike hoping that the new BJP government would make a U-turn to appease their traditional *bania* base and rollback the decision on private yards. They were sorely disappointed by the BJP's support for the reform and pointed to this moment of continuity as a sign of a broad political consensus in favor of corporate capital versus local and regional traders. There was much talk of big fish and small fry, and a common refrain that the country would later rue what they described as the *mandi*'s East India Company moment.

For ITC and state-level reformers, however, it was the concessions made in favor of the *mandi*s that were seen as most significant. First, licenses were still granted by *mandi* committees for private marketyards in their notified market areas. Second, it was agreed that single-license holders would have to pay regular *mandi* fees to the APMC on transactions within the private marketyard. Since fees were justified on the basis of the use of the *mandi* premises and its facilities, this was actually an unfair imposition on private firms who put up and used their own procurement infrastructure. However, it was eventually considered to have been a masterful "concession" that, on the one hand, gave the *mandi* the sense of fiscal gain while opening it up to competition, and on the other, gave the corporation a license to operate outside the *mandi*, while keeping it under regulatory oversight. A few

years later, a third concession was granted in favor of *mandi* traders in
the issuing of orders to the effect that a minimum distance of eight
kilometers was to be maintained between the *mandi* and the private
marketyard. This was intended to deter farmers from moving conveniently between the two sites in search of better prices and to also
prevent them from cancelling *mandi* transactions if the private procurement price for the day was more favorable.

Described as necessary "course corrections" and enabling "concessions" by some and mischievous "restrictions" and regrettable "roll-
backs" by others, these measures are illustrative of the kinds of
negotiation and revisionary movement that characterize complex and
multifaceted processes of market reform. For all their apprehensions,
looking back today Harda's traders would largely agree, to borrow
a popular phrase, that the rumors of the *mandi*'s impending demise
were indeed greatly exaggerated. Instead, the presence of the private
yard (*choupal*) does appear to have provided some price competition
and a serious alternative marketing channel to at least a group of
farmers associated in the ITC network. Perhaps even more significantly, it forced the *mandi* to upgrade its own infrastructure and
improve critical (nonprice) processes such as improved weighment,
timely payment, and the speed and conduct of daily activities. As the
seasons progressed, both farmers and traders also came to realize that
seasonal single-buyer procurement hubs were not the same species as
multi-buyer, multi-commodity, permanent, publicly regulated marketplaces. In the process, the *mandi* came to further realize its distinctive
character and comparative advantage.[11] It is ironic, therefore, that by
the end of this decade, the *mandi* found itself reduced in one major
season to the equivalent of a single-buyer procurement center. Only, as
it happened, this time, the market was not taken over by a private
corporation but by the state.

The State Takes Over the Marketyard: Public Procurement
of Wheat from 2008

Historically, farmers in central India, unlike their counterparts in the
North Indian granaries of Punjab and Haryana, had never benefited

---

[11] For a more details about the differences between hubs and *mandi*s, see
      Krishnamurthy (2011).

from centrally declared minimum support prices (MSPs) via public procurement of wheat and paddy, which are major crops in MP and Chhattisgarh, respectively. This changed dramatically in the late 2000s, when the two BJP chief ministers bet on the political gains to be made by launching large-scale grain procurement programs. In MP, Shivraj Singh Chouhan, much like Digvijay Singh before him, understood the potential political gains from a deep engagement in agricultural markets and was ready to galvanize the state machinery to deliver on the ground. From the 2008 *rabi* (winter crop) marketing season, Chouhan made a substantial wheat "bonus" over and above the MSP, an annual fixture, ensuring that wheat prices in MP were among the highest in the country. This move was backed by a massive decentralized procurement operation led by state agencies with Primary Agricultural Cooperative Societies (PACS) deployed to buy directly from farmers across the state. Within a short span of five years, in what was a remarkable feat, MP had catapulted ahead of Haryana in wheat contributions to the central food-grain pool (see Krishnamurthy 2012).

Prominent wheat *mandi*s such as the one in Harda were key sites for public procurement and between March and May, the state virtually took over the marketyard. Within this window, as arrivals grew to epic proportions, private trade was effectively sidelined and the entire *mandi* staff was engaged in managing the rising temperatures, and relentless volumes, both literally and metaphorically. Although some of the more prominent functionaries, including the proactive Mandi Secretary thrived in the thick of the action, from a regulatory point of view, they were the first to admit that state procurement compromised some of the *mandi*'s most cherished processes. First, the auction was suspended as the state was effectively the only buyer in the *mandi* and no private actor could compete with the MSP *plus* bonus price. Traders were reduced to bidding only on the few lots of high-quality grain that came in and on the small number of poor-quality food-grain lots rejected by the PACS. As a result, numerous private corporations restricted procurement and moved their buying operations to other states. For once, local traders and private corporations were united in dismay; the state, they both predicted, would "kill" the market for wheat in MP, just as it had done in Punjab, and destroy grain varieties and qualities while increasing the dependence of farmers in the process. Second, the strictly enforced *mandi* rule requiring same-day cash settlement of the full payment to farmers also had to be relaxed as state agencies were well-known for delays in processing payments and would make direct transfers to farmers' bank accounts. Third, state agencies also had to be exempted from paying *mandi* fees in advance unlike all the other regular licensed buyers in the *mandi*. Finally, the entry of the state agencies and especially the village-based PACS into the *mandi* as procurement agents opened the gates to greater political pressure and the activation of a whole range of rural social and political "settings" that played out and strained existing relations in the market-yard (Krishnamurthy 2012).

The economic and agro-ecological effects of large-scale public wheat procurement in MP will require another, longer discussion. What is striking for our purpose here, however, is the manner in which different levels and limbs of the state coordinate, mal-coordinate, compete, and come into conflict at any given time as government policies are implemented. In this case, the state's price support and public procurement policy undermines state regulation of agricultural markets, changing, at least seasonally, the very structure and character of the *mandi* as a market site.

The Survival of the Fittest? The Limits and Possibilities of Regulatory Evolution in Agricultural Markets

As I reach the statutory word limit of my contribution to this volume, I am acutely aware of all the threads dropped, those still to be picked up, and the further twists in the tale of the regulatory life and life histories of a half-century of Harda Mandi. Over the past two decades, there have been three *mandi* elections in 2000, 2005, and 2012, two of which have seen women being elected as chairpersons of the *Mandi* Committee, in both cases as proxies for powerful Jat men on different sides of a fierce inter-caste feud. During this period, the negotiations between the political and bureaucratic heads of the *mandi* intensified and cooled off, yielding a mix of conflict, coordination, coercion, corruption, and competence, often in some combination at the same time. Having focused on the major market for grain and oilseeds, I have not even begun to describe the state's attempts to regulate and deregulate local fruit and vegetable markets and the failure to eliminate commission agents there. Similarly, the regulation of electronic futures markets and the ambiguous and anxiety-provoking relations between spot and futures markets and physical and electronic platforms will require a chapter to itself. And finally, there remains much more to be said about the everyday practices and changing relations of commodity exchange in the *mandi*: on information, price discovery, and auctions, on labor wages and welfare, and on cash and electronic payment and settlement, especially in the aftermath of demonetization.

Even so, we have managed to traverse and trace a century of regulatory visions and revisions that have shaped and unsettled the organizational structure, institutional dynamics, and relations of exchange and trade in Indian agricultural markets. In particular, we have focused on the origins, evolution, and adaptation of one of the most important and enduring regulatory species in the agrarian economy: the APMC and the notified market or *mandi* that it oversees. We then followed the fraught processes of regulatory enforcement and evasion, legislative amendment and local activism, and a series of revolutionary and routine acts of reform and resistance as they played out in a major agricultural state (MP) and within a single APMC *mandi* (that in Harda). What emerges is an understanding of how deeply contextual and contingent the regulation and management of agricultural markets are in practice. This specificity, however, it should be equally clear is not particular to a historical period or place – or to a method of study – but is a general, structural feature of agricultural markets.

Agricultural markets are populated with multiple, competing interests, racked with internal divisions and competing sources and centers of market power and authority, and are embedded and exposed at all levels to social, political, and economic forces and relations both internal and external to the marketing system. From the outset, not only does state regulation in India have little illusion that this is a condition that can be overcome through centralized legislation, but by constitutionally charging agricultural markets with provincial/state powers and infusing them with local statutory authority, it becomes an intrinsic element in the system of agricultural markets. As a result, state regulation is inherently limited by the deep and structural inequalities that persist in the system of agricultural production, exchange and consumption, and operate between its multiple actors and their highly differential and differentiated powers and interests. But, precisely for the same reason, regulatory principles and institutions have also at specific times and places expanded and intensified the spaces for contestation between these unequal market actors – including the different, often competing elements and entities that represent the state in market life. As we can see from the racy and routine regulatory life and life history of Harda Mandi, this generates a whole range of possibilities – expected and unexpected, intended and unintended – for regulatory reform that both subtly and substantially shift the balance of powers in the market over time. Foresight and short-sightedness, hubris and hesitation, regulatory loopholes that are lifelines and regulatory tenets that become tentacles: little wonder then the *mandi* itself is invariably both the hero and villain of its own story.

References

Cohen, A 2013, "Supermarkets in India: Struggles Over the Organization of Agricultural Markets and Food Supply Chains," *University of Miami Law Review*, 68, 19: 83.

Dantwala, ML 1937, *Marketing of Raw Cotton in India*, Longsman, Green & Co. Ltd., Calcutta.

Gupta, RP 1973, *Agricultural Prices in a Backward Economy*, National Publishing House, New Delhi.

Guyer, J 2016, "Toiling Ingenuity: Food Regulation in Britain and Nigeria," in J Guyer (ed.) *Legacies, Logics, Logistics: Essays in the Anthropology of the Platform Economy*, University of Chicago Press, Chicago.

Harriss, B 1984, *State and Market: State Intervention in Agricultural Exchange in a Dry Region of Tamil Nadu, South India*, Concept Publishing Company, New Delhi.

Harriss-White, B 1996, *A Political Economy of Agricultural Markets in South India: Masters of the Countryside*, Sage Publications, New Delhi.

Harriss-White, B 2008, *Rural Commercial Capital: Agricultural Markets in West Bengal*, Oxford University Press, Oxford.

Harriss-White, B 2016, "From Analysing 'Filieres Vivrieres' to Understanding Capital and Petty Production in Rural South India," Journal of Agrarian Change 16, 3: 478–500.

Indian National Congress 2019, *Congress Will Deliver*, All India Congress Committee, New Delhi.

Krishnamurthy, M 2011, Harda Mandi: Experiencing Change in an Agricultural Market in Central India, unpublished PhD thesis, University College London, chapter 5.

Krishnamurthy, M 2012, "States of Wheat: The Changing Dynamics of Public Procurement in Madhya Pradesh," *Economic and Political Weekly, Review of Rural Affairs*, 47, 52: 72–83.

Krishnamurthy, M 2013, "Margins and Mindsets: Enterprise, Opportunity and Exclusion in a Market Town in Madhya Pradesh," in N Gooptu (ed.) *Enterprise Culture in Neoliberal India: Studies in Youth, Class, Work and Media*, Routledge, London, pp. 206–21.

Krishnamurthy, M 2015, "The Political Economy of Agricultural Markets: Insights from Within and Across Regions," in IDFC Foundation (ed.) *India Rural Development Report 2013–2014*, Orient BlackSwan, Hyderabad, pp. 61–79.

Krishnamurthy, M 2018, "Reconceiving the Grain Heap: Margins and Movements on the Market Floor," *Contributions to Indian Sociology*, 52, 1: 28–52.

Manor, J 2010, "Beyond Clientalism: Digvijay Singh's Participatory, Pro-Poor Strategy in Madhya Pradesh," in P Price & AE Ruud (eds.) *Power and Influence in India: Bosses, Lords and Captains*, Routledge, New Delhi, pp. 193–213.

Royal Commission on Agriculture in India 1928, *Report: Royal Commission on Agriculture in India*, Government of India, Central Publication Branch.

8 | The Market and the Sovereign: Politics, Performance, and Impasses of Cross-LOC Trade

ADITI SARAF[*]

A citation from Abu Fazl's edicts of Akbar, reproduced in Sudipta Sen's *Empire of Free Trade* visualizes the Mughal body-politic as the domain of a divinely ordained emperor, traversed by people likened to flows of Galenic humor (Sen 1998: 21). Warriors are likened to fire, people of learning to water, peasants and cultivators to the earth, and merchants and professionals to air. Consequently, Sen argues, *movement* was seen as essential for merchants, and the ruler's province was to safeguard routes and venues of trade in return for revenue in the form of taxes. Under Mughal administration, a set of privileges, obligations and duties were conceived under *Sair-o-Jihat* – literally, the "facets of travelers/wanderers/passersby" – and set apart as distinct from the revenue obtained from settled cultivation in land. Precolonial marketplaces thus served as an extension of the king's patrimony, materialized in a knot of rituals, customs, overlapping claims within a tiered, scalar system of patronage. The East India Company's colonial intrusion, Sen argues, disrupted and transformed this commercial landscape, consolidating power through the "permanent settlement of marketplaces," forcefully establishing a new regulatory frame for "free trade" that set apart colonial marketplace for imperial commodities, speculation, and investment (Sen 1998: 119).

[*] I am grateful to the editors, Ajay Gandhi, Barbara Harriss-White, Douglas Haynes, and Sebastian Schwecke for inviting me to contribute to this volume and for their astute and insightful comments that were invaluable for developing my argument. I also thank Swayam Bagaria, Veena Das, Jane Guyer, Penelope Harvey, and Naveeda Khan for helpful comments on various presentations of my work that are reflected in this chapter. The Social Science Research Council, the Wenner-Gren Foundation, and the European Research Council funded fieldwork for this research.

Writing in a similar historical arena, the transitional epoch from Mughal to colonial British rule in the eighteenth century, Christopher Bayly conceptualizes society of the time as a "great machine for sacrifice" in which the king is named as "sacrificer-in-chief" (Bayly 1998: 59). For Bayly, relations between merchants and the sovereign were organized along the ritualized separation and interdependence of spheres. While the king's display of pomp, consumption, and gift giving asserted forms of legitimacy in which "trade goods in India had a specific cultural value unique to its polity," the commercial elite carefully maintained the separation of spheres: the private austerity of their homes contrasted with the pomp and ceremony of the courts. Bayly foregrounds the cohesion and solidarity of the commercial classes as a bulwark against the dramatic shifts and tussles of the eighteenth-century political arena, an environment which, according to him, blurred the line between legitimate "profit" and "plunder." In this context, he places the advent of the East India Company as one force among several vying for a piece of the trading landscape and territorial power. The ascendance of the Company is viewed not as an indomitable event but the result of particular arrangements of power and alliances in the political playing field.

I begin with these two related counterpositions to mark the distinct lines along which the historical relationship between commerce and sovereignty in South Asian markets is usually envisioned. One strand of scholarship emphasizes the enforced insertion and imprint of ruling authority in marketplaces, both through formal structures of law and ceremonial practices of gift giving, reciprocation, and delegation. Another strand differentiates the order of the sovereign from that of merchants, framing relations between the two spheres as one of interdependence rather than hierarchy, built on varying and ritualized degrees of distance and association. Without committing to either approach – one that views the relation between markets and sovereigns as that of ebbs and flows, or one that insists on a hierarchy – I examine the complex entanglements of commerce and sovereignty in contemporary trade across Kashmir's Line of Control (LoC).

Assembled as a double row of fencing entwined with electrified concertina wire, the LoC separates Indian-administered from

Pakistan-administered Kashmir at South Asia's most bitterly disputed border. Cross-LoC trade was established in October 2008, and unilaterally and indefinitely suspended by a diktat from the Indian Ministry of Home Affairs in April 2019. While the official notification framed the decision in the interest of national security, citing that the trade routes were being "misused by the Pakistan based elements for funneling illegal weapons, narcotics and fake currency etc." (MHA notice, April 18, 2019), it was strongly disputed by traders and workers who suffered tremendous economic loss and anguish (Zargar 2019). In this chapter, I focus on the significance of cross-LoC trade as a regulatory fabrication for unpacking potentials that question and disrupt the power of states over the markets they seek to control, in this case for overtly political projects. "Cross-LoC trade" was conducted under the watchful eyes of several state security agencies, in a highly surveyed and militarized zone. Statistically speaking, the actual commerce was negligible, but the exchange suffused by outsize symbolism and performance. Its effects sharpened the disputed legitimacy of the state and its fictions of sovereignty, while simultaneously opening out sites for traders and other political-commercial actors to articulate contesting sovereign decisions and actions that stood out within the narrow confines of cross-LoC trade. The symbolic politics around cross-LoC trade is therefore much more relevant than the volume of goods for assessing its significance.[1]

Jammu and Kashmir (J&K), India's only Muslim majority state at the northernmost boundary, has been the site of intense political and territorial rivalry between India and Pakistan since 1947. In the Indian-administered Kashmir Valley, a popular movement for self-determination or freedom (*Azaadi*) was launched in 1989, which resulted in more than a decade of armed insurgency and brutal reprisals by the Indian state. For decades thereafter, the Indian state exercised control in the Kashmir Valley through the

---

[1] This chapter was written before the indefinite suspension of cross-LoC trade in April 2019. My contention is that the continued suspension of cross-LoC trade and the recent abrogation of J&K's special status under the Indian Constitution in August 2019 enhances the struggles over sovereignty detailed in this chapter – pushing them beyond a lethal threshold – rather than rendering them outdated or irrelevant.

exercise of emergency laws and the enduring installation of armed forces, causing deep-rooted anger and resentment. Since 2008, the *Azaadi* movement had taken on renewed urgency with massive popular protests that inaugurated what scholars called the "new Intifada [uprising]" in Kashmir (Kak et al. 2010). These protests intensified in 2016 after the killing of a charismatic militant leader, Burhan Wani, by state forces, resulting in a state of siege imposed through curfews, cordon-and-search operations, communications blackouts, and the use of injurious force against crowds including the use of high-velocity pellets. In August 2019, the Indian government unilaterally revoked the state's autonomous status under the Indian constitution – the basis on which J&K acceded to the Indian union after Independence. The announcement came amid a communications blackout, the house arrest of prominent leaders, and the mass deployment of additional troops in what is already one of the world's most densely militarized zones, pushing the dispute beyond a new, lethal threshold.

Against this background, cross-LoC trade was established in 2008 as a highly formalized commercial exchange at the de facto border between the Indian- and Pakistan-administered parts of Kashmir. In contemporary international relations parlance, cross-LoC trade is referred as a confidence-building measure (CBM) – a diplomatic artifact that forms part of what is known as "Track II diplomacy," defined as "non-governmental, official, and unofficial contacts and activities between non-state actors." Undertaken to manage conflict outside official diplomatic channels, CBMs were collectively viewed as a mechanism put in place to improvise a way around the impasses of the supposedly "intractable" Kashmir dispute. Cross-LoC trade was devised as a nontaxable, nonmonetized form of barter, and a bizarre set of customs evolved to ensure that the trade was defined as neither "internal" nor "external" (Kira 2011). This care with language was significant for avoiding the acknowledgement of the LoC as an "international border" where import and export duties would apply, which would belie both India and Pakistan's territorial claims on the former princely state. The conflict management template for cross-LoC trade lines up against other enactments of cross-border trade as a "conflict mitigating" mechanism with varying degrees of failure, for instance in South Sudan/Uganda and Palestine/Israel (Kira 2011). The ground operations of cross-LoC trade, however, disrupt assumed relations between the market and the sovereign as conceived in the language of commercial regulation, or in images of wild cross-cutting frontier commerce, or even trade as a technique of conflict mitigation. Rather, the paradoxical protocols of cross-LoC trade demonstrated that commerce continues to be terrain for the exercise of overlapping authority and multiple political markers, and that it is impossible to sanitize the market and turn it into a neutral arena for free trade. Drawing on historical scholarship that analyzes contesting sovereignties in commercial spaces, and the emergence of markets as sites of political claims making, I examine recent boundary wars around customs, commodities, and the idea of community as manifested in cross-LoC exchange. I show how both traders and the state continually improvised laws and practices in order to reshape commerce as a site that manifested distinct notions of sovereignty at odds with one another, thus constituting cross-LoC trade as a field in which state control was both performed and punctured. But, first, a discussion on the singularity of the LoC and cross-LoC trade is necessary.

Crossing Lines of Control

From 1846 to 1947, the Kashmir Valley was part of Jammu Kashmir the largest of the princely states in the British Indian Empire.[2] In October 1947, two months after the end of the British Raj and the creation of India and Pakistan on the basis of religious demographics, the Hindu Dogra king of the Muslim majority princely state controversially acceded to India after seeking assistance to quell what the Indian government termed a "tribal invasion" from Pakistan. The war that followed between India and Pakistan came to an uneasy pause in January 1948, and the Ceasefire Line brokered by the UN divided the lands of the former princely state into sections controlled by both Pakistan and India. Subsequent wars in 1965, 1971, and 1999 entrenched the division of the lands between India, Pakistan, and China with increasing rigidifying of the militarized boundaries.

---

[2] I will use the shorthand "Jammu Kashmir" to refer to the lands of the former princely state as well as the aspiration for a reunited Jammu Kashmir as a future political entity.

Presently, Jammu and Kashmir (J&K) is administered by India, and Pakistan administers the region of Azad Jammu Kashmir (AJK) and Gilgit-Baltistan. The uninhabited northeastern region of Aksai Chin is presently under Chinese control.[3] In the Muslim majority Kashmir Valley, J&K, where I conducted fieldwork, a popular movement for liberation – *Azaadi* – from Indian rule has been ongoing since 1989, resulting in armed militancy, brutal state reprisals, and tremendous human suffering. The Valley is flanked on the south by the Hindu majority district of Jammu, an extension of the Punjab plains separated by the Pir Panjal mountains. To the Valley's east lies the vast and thinly populated region of Kargil–Ladakh with a slim majority population of practicing Tibetan Buddhism and a significant minority comprising Shi'i Muslims. The LoC, which is what the UN Ceasefire Line negotiated in 1949 was renamed as, divides Indian-administered J&K from Pakistan-administered AJK. After the 1971 war between India and Pakistan, the LoC became the de facto political and military border. Increasingly built up, militarized, electrified, and mined, the LoC interrupted and criminalized prior crossings between villages and communities on either side. Although it has become increasingly immutable, the LoC paradoxically indexes the incompleteness of the cartographic consolidation by the nation-state, as both India and Pakistan stake claim on the entire territory through distinct framings. Kashmiri self-determination is thus wedged within "concern for (and dispute over) a Jammu-and-Kashmir that is both a former and a not-yet or never-to-be political entity" (Robinson 2013: 32). Contradictions around customs, commodities, and community in cross-LoC trade serve to dramatize these antinomies of sovereignty.

Cross-LoC trade was inaugurated at the LoC following massive protests in the summer of 2008. The trigger was a decision by the J&K government under Indian administration to transfer about 100 acres of forest land to the Amarnath Shrine Board for the construction of temporary facilities for Hindu pilgrims. This caused the Muslim majority in the Valley to erupt in protests, which became a rallying point for opposition to colonization and aggressive religious politics by the Indian state. Since centuries, Hindu pilgrims have undertaken the

---

[3] My research was conducted entirely in the India-administered Kashmir. For a summary of the shared political and historical predicament of the regions of Kashmir, Jammu, Ladakh, Azad Jammu Kashmir, Gilgit-Baltistan, and its diverse inhabitants, see Sökefeld (2013).

Amarnath pilgrimage for a few weeks in summer to a cave-shrine high in the mountains that hosts an icy stalagmite resembling the iconic *Shivaling*. The scale of the pilgrimage expanded exponentially under the Hindu nationalist Bharatiya Janata Party (BJP), whose previous rule from 1998 to 2004 marked the reassertion of control by the Indian state in Kashmir as armed militancy declined. In 2008, however, opposition to the temporary land transfer united Kashmiris in an unprecedented way, cutting across class lines and combining political arguments about identity with ecological ones about protecting the fragile mountain landscape. The ferocity of Kashmiri protests resulted in the decision to revoke the land transfer, which triggered further protests and communal tension in the neighboring Hindu majority region of Jammu. People in Jammu led massive protests and an "economic blockade" on the Valley by cutting off all transport and cargo on the Jammu–Srinagar highway, the main vehicular channel connecting the Kashmir Valley to the rest of India. As the Kashmir Valley's main point of contact with the outside world remained choked, AJK, under Pakistani administration, lay adjacent yet politically inaccessible to the west of the LoC.

Following the economic blockade from Jammu, protestors from the Kashmir Valley took out huge marches to the LoC chanting slogans of *Muzaffarabad Chalo* ("Let's go to Muzaffarabad") and *Hamari Mandi Rawalpindi* ("Our market is in Rawalpindi," in Pakistan). The protests were powerful, public assertions of the intention to "break the LoC" and the right to cross to the other side. Trade and traders' collectives entered the political sphere with renewed and urgent demands that interlaced with the movement for Kashmir's independence (*Azaadi*). The issue of "cross-LoC trade" became important not only as a condition for Kashmiri self-sufficiency but also to challenge the restrictions placed by the Indian state on Kashmir's ability to trade freely with all partners, notably, those across the LoC in Pakistan. In August 2008, scores of people were killed when police and paramilitary opened fire on one of these processions to "break" the LoC at the border town of Uri.

The attention generated by such marches and their repression hastened the opening of cross-LoC trade, under the headships of Manmohan Singh and Pervez Musharraf in India and Pakistan, respectively, that had been mooted in 2005 as a CBM. Cross-LoC trade was launched with the establishment of a joint chamber to promote economic interaction, with representatives from both India- and Pakistan-administered parts of the former princely state. Previously, because of the Amarnath protests and the economic blockade in the Indian-administered state of J&K, internal relations between the respective chambers of commerce in the Kashmir Valley and Jammu region had deteriorated to the point where its members had stopped talking to each other (personal communication, February 2013). Allegedly, it took the arrival of a trade delegation from AJK and the persuasive powers of AJK's business leaders to mediate between the two. Then consultations were held through the intervention of a third party – a British NGO – in a third country, Turkey, with stakeholders from both parts of divided Jammu Kashmir. Following talks with the Indian and Pakistani governments, two trade facilitation centers (TFCs) were opened on one of Asia's most hostile borders – one connecting Chakan da Bagh in the Jammu sector to Rawalkot in AJK, and the other connecting Uri in the Kashmir sector to Muzaffarabad in AJK. In Uri, the passage of cross-LoC transport and exchange officially and ceremoniously takes place on the Kaman Bridge or *Aman Setu* – the "Bridge of Peace" owned equally by India and Pakistan, linking Indian-administered Kashmir with Pakistan-administered AJK. The inauguration of the cross-LoC trade was welcomed with fanfare across the board as a "pragmatic" and "normalizing" gesture to enhance goodwill and interaction across the LoC. Symbolically, it was in line with the official stances of both India and Pakistan of "allowing" interdependence between the nominally semi-autonomous but divided parts of the state without having to change their respective positions. While many of my Kashmiri interlocutors did not buy into the fiction of trade creating peace, cross-LoC exchange was a long awaited first step of making connections across their divided homeland, holding out hope that eventually, the "iron curtain of barbed wires, bunkers, trenches, and hostile militaries" would, at the very least, transform into a "linen curtain between self-governing regions of Indian and Pakistani Jammu and Kashmir" (Kira 2011: 18).

What does it mean to take up commerce as an arena for political negotiations? Stepping back skeptically from discourses that pit cooperation and commerce against war and conflict, the idea of combining trade with diplomacy has a long history in the geographical space of the south-central Asian frontier, in which Kashmir was an important regional center. Entwinement of trade and diplomacy was strikingly materialized, for instance, in tributary exchange between the various sovereigns who governed the heterogeneous political geography of the frontier: the last trans-Himalayan caravan carrying the customary tribute left from Leh, in Ladakh, for Lhasa, in Tibet, in the 1950s, at the cusp of the Chinese occupation. The partition of the Indian subcontinent in 1947 closed off historical trade routes extending west, south, and north from the Valley into lands presently under the territorial jurisdiction of Pakistan and China. The Jammu–Srinagar national highway, connecting the Valley to mainland India emerged as the sole land outlet for trade and mobility. Subsequently, India's territorial control over the Kashmir Valley has been closely associated with economic integration through massive aid packages and development spending (Schaffer 2005), currently materialized in Kashmir's massive debt to Delhi.[4]

Against this background, I use this chapter as an opportunity to discuss the emergence of the market as an arena where transactions of a public, political nature may be observed (Chakrabarty 1992; Gandhi 2016). Significantly, cross-LoC trade is staged neither in the public space of the marketplace nor as a mass spectacle. On the contrary, it occurs in a highly securitized and cordoned-off space. The artifact of cross-LoC trade and the space in which it is conducted partakes both in political performance through its symbolism, and becomes a politically significant parody of the association between states and markets. By parody, I mean a reworking of different elements that undergird the relationship between the market and the sovereign – namely customs, commodities, and community – into bizarre and novel compositions. Such reworkings mimic in an exaggerated manner what the relations between the market and the sovereign *should be*, but result in upending notions of legitimate authority through tensions – one might say, absurdities – of juxtapositions such as that of nonmonetized "barter" with "taxes." To apprehend the regulatory paradoxes of cross-LoC trade, the next section engages the distinct investments of states and communities in the emergence of the marketplace as a major public arena under colonial rule for forging political communities and their lines of relatedness and rupture. The

---

[4] The total liabilities of the state to the center stood at over US$8 billion in 2015–2016, amounting to 60.27 percent of the gross state domestic product (Annual Report on State Finances, Government of Jammu & Kashmir, 2016).

merchant community, encompassing both the newly empowered commercial elite and the numerically preponderant petty *bazaaris* emerge as important subjects, actors, and links in these developments. This picture of the bazaar as quintessentially "public" and *bazaaris* as agential, intentional political mediators is undermined in cross-LoC trade. Yet, being framed by historical and anthropological scholarship helps understand cross-LoC trade arrangements not simply as eccentric by-products of a violent dispute but as a continuation of broad and enduring conversation on the entanglements of states and markets in South Asia.

The Emergence of the Market as a Public, Political Arena

The space of the market has been, historically and imaginatively, the scene of seduction and spectacle. Sen (1998) describes the precolonial marketplace square or the *chabutra* as the site for the authorized display of power and punishment. Much like the scene described in the opening pages of *Discipline and Punish* (Foucault 1979), the power of the sovereign was publicly inscribed in these settings on the bodies of its condemned subjects through open whippings, torture, parading, and hangings. The morally suspect yet irresistible spaces of artistic performance, itinerant mystics, and pimps and prostitutes formed another form of spectacle, all of which called for both patronage and sanction. The most recognizable imprint of ruling authority, single or multiple, was through the imposition of taxes – different forms of customs and *octroi* – for safeguarding trade venues and the passage of goods. The tussle between the late Mughals' and the English East India Company's authorities over trade extended beyond raw power and profit into the discursive realm, and discrete forms of overlapping political authority and plural genealogies of the markets clashed wildly with notions of free trade that accompanied the consolidation of liberal political economy and mercantile trade in England. The effort to "free" indigenous capitalists from the "cultural" pressures of functioning within an extended kin network, so that they may develop into modern economic subjects, became an important preoccupation for colonial commercial law (Birla 2009; Martin 2012; Schwecke 2018; Washbrook 1981). Yet, in spite of being disengaged from customary authorities after the "permanent settlement of markets" (Sen 1998), and purportedly emerging as a more "neutral" arena, marketplaces remained deeply embedded in local milieus of power, accommodation, and ritual display. The potential of the marketplace as an arena of ritual display or protest was continually activated for political activities. Far from appearing as a space of "disorder" or spontaneous *communitas*, strong, supple, and enduring lines of association and allegiances left their imprint on market events, rituals, and activities, offering "the occasion and place for expressing the legitimate order and simultaneously providing opportunities for channeling competition and conflict" (Freitag 1989: 36). I want to take up the public arena of the marketplace as a site of articulation of community interests and their relations to the state – patterns and movements that have been analyzed as precursors to postcolonial performances of communal identity, sectarianism, and nationalism (Hansen 2004; Haynes and Prakash 1992; Jaoul 2007; Pandey 1990). In both the past and the present, marketplaces have staged political performances where new relations of community and sovereignty have been imagined, enacted, and sometimes undone (Chatterjee 2016). Such histories cast long shadows on the present workings of cross-LoC trade, indexing the incomplete nature of national integration in regulatory paradoxes around the distinction between licit and illicit commodities, customs and communities.

Focusing on the marketplace in nineteenth-century Banaras, Sandria Freitag (1989) writes how publicly staged ritual events and performance genres (such as the enactment of *Ramlila* performances or *Muharram* processions) became occasions for readjusting power relations, both within communities and between communities and the state. While the important identifiers of the community did not initially express themselves as "Hindu" or "Muslim," but as different groups within such putative communities (such as "Marathas," "Rajputs," and "Julahas"), all of them struggled over ritual positions in such events to consolidate their status as the natural leaders of the community. Initially fragmentary, "fundamental community identities based in caste, occupation, place of origin of immigrants, and even mother tongue became channels for mobilizing competition for cultural dominance in urban areas" (ibid.: 41). Strongly contesting the dismissal of bazaar protests, *mohalla* politics, and "riots" as parochial, Freitag's account spotlights markets as places in which values are contested, links forged between formal and informal worlds, and where disorder and order are both instantiated.

Colonial state structures also appear in a more varied and interesting relationship to the publics that they governed (Haynes 1991; Yang 1998). While imperial state officials initially saw themselves as mediators during urban disturbances, they subsequently withdrew from activities such as face-to-face interactions that symbolically expressed relations between the sovereign state and local communities. Importantly, Freitag attributes the dramatic expansion of the public arena mainly to this real or presumed absence of state. Yet, while state authorities often stood apart in the face of volatile intercommunal riots, the colonial government replicated community identities in state structures by drawing allies and intermediaries from persons prominent within the traditional hierarchies of communities, whom they called "natural leaders." Intersecting lines of association across religion and occupation led to the ascendance and solidarity of the Hindu commercial elite along a range of urban voluntary associations such as literary *samiti*s, *ramlila* committees, and self-governing neighborhood (*mohalla*) committees. David Gilmartin's account of urban politics and communal sentiment in Lahore and Amritsar complements Freitag's account, showing how urban commerce emerged as significantly distinct and predominant from rural institutions that revolved around Sufi *sajjada nashin*s as well as the corporate *qasbah* society (Gilmartin 1988). While bazaars, mosques and *madrasa*s were the mainstays of urban Islamic religious and social life in South Asia, colonial North Indian cities such as Lahore were also imperial administrative centers whose ideology was founded on relations between rural kin-based communities and "natural leaders" in the city – the latter usually comprising property-owning magnates with networks of credit and control known as *ra'is* (patron or boss). Below the top tier, the urban *ra'is* exercised control through contacts with "neighborhood leadership" supported typically by heterogeneous factions with cross-cutting alliances around local caste and religious groupings, the *ulama*, petty merchants, and bazaar factions. As the growth of the city attracted migrants and developed the middle class with increased positions within law and bureaucracy, new interest-based associations that went beyond local patronage networks became dominant and began to assert distinctive religious identities. Prominent among the Muslims were the *anjuman*s (voluntary cultural associations), *tanzim*s (literally "associations"), which focused on communal and defensive political organization with a commitment to Shariat and Islam, and the *biradari*s (brotherhoods), which, although based on an ideology of tribal/ethnic blood/descent, dispensed with the vertical hierarchy of descent politics to serve as a powerful idiom of horizontal solidarity in the cities. The Kashmiri *biradari*s, comprising mostly migrant petty merchants, artisans, and laborers became one of the most numerically and politically dominant urban *biradari*s in Punjab. They occupied a distinctive political center within the urban landscape, their ideology voiced by figures such as the poet–philosopher Mohammad Iqbal and Saifuddin Kitchlew of the Khilafat movement. Espousing translocal Muslim solidarities, articulating Kashmiri identity as inseparable from the commitment to Islam, and directly opposing colonial authority through opposition to the Hindu Dogra ruler of the princely state of Jammu Kashmir, urban Kashmiris became the force behind the "symbolic, public assertion of Islamic identity" (Gilmartin 1988: 88).

These new forms of publicity articulated with older patterns of commerce and sovereignty materialized in trans-Himalayan trade networks in Kashmir to set up trade as a potent arena for political negotiation. During my fieldwork in the Kashmir Valley, it was evident that economic and commercial elements did not feature as impressions that were epiphenomenal to the political question but inextricably entwined with the latter. Such dynamics were discerned in the political activism of trade and traders' collectives, as well as the symbolic value accorded to certain forms of trade, such as cross-LoC exchange, that far exceeded its statistical significance. I have circled back to colonial historiography to frame marketplace encounters of commercial and sovereign authority against this history. In the present workings of cross-LoC trade, such political elements appear at a tangent to their discussion in the archive. While marketplaces emerge as vibrant public arenas within cities, cross-LoC trade is relegated to Uri, a remote and highly militarized border town that is cordoned off from the bustle of everyday spaces of exchange. While one hears whispers and/or unconfirmed rumors of illicit and complicit cross-border smuggling at the LoC, the most strikingly visible spatial characteristic of Uri is a sense of militarized overregulation. Uri is hemmed in by Pakistan-controlled territory. Currently, this border is the only point in the Kashmir sector in which official exchange takes place, and therefore while geographically vulnerable, shelling seldom takes places here. In the initial decades after Partition, the LoC as a social boundary used to be permeable, fluid, and often rendered immaterial by cross-cutting community, occupational, and kinship ties, until the stiffening of the boundary line criminalized such exchanges by associating them with terrorism and spying (Robinson 2013). But, as Robinson points out, the reticence around these movements and laws does not mean that such patterns have died out. That borderlands are neither simply boundaries nor stable spaces is poignantly true of the LoC districts: unlike frontier-badlands that are viewed as escaping sovereign regulation, they are subject to violent and militarized structures of surveillance, regulation, and boundary making. However, as the official point of border-crossing, Uri is also a precarious site of bilateral cooperation – for example, during relief activity that followed the 2005 earthquake, and until recently, in overseeing the acutely surveyed flows across the Kaman Bridge. On Mondays, the cross-border Muzaffarabad–Srinagar bus service, evocatively named *Karwan-e-Aman* (the Caravan of Peace) ferried civilians clutching immigration documents verified on both sides, their identity and kinship ties across the LoC duly proved. From Tuesday to Friday, trucks laden with goods plied the cross-LoC trade. For five days a week, the synchronized movement of the bus and trucks moving to and fro engaged a number of drivers, officials, and laborers, fostering a precarious form of "people-to-people" contact. The last extension of India-controlled territory on the Kaman Bridge has also been curated as a tourist site (Saraf 2019) Cross-LoC exchange participates in this curation. Security clearance is required to visit the Kaman Bridge. The Indian army checkpost at the bridge has the slogan "Saviours of the Valley" emblazoned across it. A faded billboard featuring photographs of what appeared to be ceremonial greetings and feastings announced: "Indian Army welcomes you to Jammu & Kashmir." The optics are favorable for public consumption and media reports – the train of colorful trucks flanked by denuded peaks, gleam-ing white gates opened by smartly dressed soldiers, the bright blue of the TFC signage, all make for visually attractive but homogeneous tableaus. This ceremonious semiotics, however, routinely confront the everyday snags of sustaining this cumbersome form of exchange.

Cross-LoC Trade: Customs, Commodities, Community

I conducted ethnographic research in Srinagar's markets for twenty-four months between 2009 and 2016. During the early days of field-work, talk would often turn toward the topic of cross-LoC trade, supplemented with excerpts read out from reports in local newspapers, often bought by one person from the corner stationery store and then passed down the row of shops. Questions around cross-LoC trade that I encountered in those preliminary weeks persisted during the course of my fieldwork and were reflected in a spate of articles in local newspapers and magazines. Particularly, the Valley-based *Kashmir Life* carried a series of reports between 2010 and 2013 that identified the absurdities that assailed cross-LoC trade, because of the political nature of the endeavor and the conflicting interests of various parties involved. Much of what follows is drawn from these reports, interviews with various traders and trade leaders involved in cross-LoC trade, and a visit to the TFC in Uri in 2018. The magazine reports dwelt on the strange customs that were evolved to ensure that the trade did not legally crystallize the LoC as an international border, something that the government of India, the government of Pakistan and the Kashmiri businessmen who comprised the Joint Chamber for cross-LoC exchange did not officially want, albeit for different reasons. Therefore the trade was devised as barter trade only with special care towards language – goods were "traded in" or "traded out" and not "imported" or "exported," the exchange was not monetized, and the US dollar (USD) was not officially adopted as the standard of exchange (although the 2011 research monograph on cross-LoC trade by the Kashmiri scholar Altaf Kira demonstrates that some traders did indeed peg currency conversions to the dollar). The standard operating procedures (SOP), updated in 2012 and accessible at the J&K government's Department of Commerce and Industries website, spelled out a limited number of commodities – "Agreed Items" on an "Agreed List" – that may be bartered at each TFC: namely, primary produce or handicrafts manufactured in either part of the former princely state of Jammu Kashmir only. Twenty-one local items, including carpets and other handicrafts, fresh fruits and vegetables, saffron, aromatic and fruit-bearing plants, coriander, black mushrooms, honey, herbs, papier-mâché products, etc., were allowed to be bartered between the India-administered and Pakistan-administered parts of Kashmir. The list of items coming in from the other side also included twenty-one items, with some marginally differentiated objects such as *gabba*s and *namda*s (rugs), Peshawari leather slippers, and prayer mats (*jahnamaz*). Most other items are more or less the same as those on the outgoing list. Thus, instead of the diversified commodities of the bazaar we find the artifice of limited lists. Furthermore, cross-LoC exchange was conditional on the stipulation that "products of third-country origin" would not be allowed for nontaxable barter trade. Rates of exchange would be set by the Government Director for Industries, based on prevailing market prices as communicated by a committee comprising the Commissioner for Sales Tax and representatives from the departments of Agriculture and Food and Civil Supplies. All traders, transporters, drivers, workers, and staff at the TFC were to be stringently checked and verified (although it appears that the projected establishment of a "biometric database" does not currently exist), and the TFC custodian was to maintain an account for each trader and report any suspicious increase in "positive balances" to the police, intelligence bureau, as well as the State Home Secretary. Numerous annexures to the SOP spelled out detailed protocols for receiving, checking, securing, and dispatching goods and trucks from the "other side," as well as the duties of the various agencies involved – police, border security personnel, and TFC Custodian and Trade Facilitation Officer. The plethora of forms to be filled for every consignment of goods included the truck entry form, the "cargo manifest" form (including description, number, weight, sender, and recipient of goods), the release or rejection order, a checklist for the required treatment of primary products, an application for permit of entry of plant products for consumption, and finally the Plant Health Certificate (or "quarantine certification") along with its accompanying application.

As magazine reports from the early years detailed, a multitude of security arrangements were often unable to meet the rush of trade traffic, often resulting in hostile standoffs with the armies of India and Pakistan closing their gates and refusing to let the convoys from their counterpart's side return. There are no banking facilities that link the divided region, no landline phone communication between traders on either side. Communication is possible via cellphones but avoided due to the harassment it would attract from intelligence agencies, and traders continually complained about having to conduct "blind trade" through barter without face-to-face interaction or regular communication with their counterparts. Reportedly, many traders engaged in cross-LoC trade have relatives across the de facto border who often stand as guarantors but that itself can become a cause for increased scrutiny and suspicion (Mir & Gattoo 2018; Qadri 2013). In fact, throughout its tenure the suspicion under which this trade was

conducted has been its most noteworthy aspect. Members of the joint
chamber have not been able to meet to draft the proposed "constitution" since their first meeting in Turkey,[5] and traders from Uri, where
the TFC is located, anonymously complained of being repeatedly summoned by the police. The security procedures, lack of storage, banking,
and communications facilities, and the delays and setbacks they caused
were repeatedly evoked to describe the unsustainable nature of this
trade and the impossibility of its fulfillment – embodied in customs
arising from the in-between nature of a trade that is neither "internal"
nor "external." Yet, reports and studies also mentioned that despite
such obstacles, trade not only persisted but had also grown, although
not to the degree that had been initially and optimistically projected
(Kira 2011). In any case, the reported numbers are quite disparate:
while newspaper reports in 2017 lamented that cross-LoC trade was all
but dead, reports from 2018 pegged its expansion in the decade since
2008 between US$100 million and US$700 million.[6] The official trade
figures since 2008, from the government of J&K's Industries and
Commerce Department, states the values of goods "traded out" as
Rs. 3744.507 crores (just under US$540 million) and those "traded
in" as Rs. 3343.084 crores (just over US$481 million).[7]

A major discrepancy that has plagued trade politics is that nonlocal
items soon started forming the bulk of the trade. Since no duties are
charged in this form of barter, the checkpoints rapidly became nodes
for the movement of profitable nonlocal commodities such as garlic,
onion, coconut, bananas, and green *moong* lentils. Initially, local traders apparently alerted authorities that larger business houses operating outside J&K had appointed local agents to save duty and
transportation costs. Soon after, traders' collectives working at the
official India–Pakistan border at Attari Wagah in Punjab lodged formal

[5] A group of cross-LoC traders reportedly met in "neutral" Azerbaijan in
January 2019 to discuss trade-related issues, but in a personal and non-official
capacity.
[6] "Cross-LoC trade marks ten years," *The Nation* (Pakistan), October 22, 2018
(https://nation.com.pk/22-Oct-2018/cross-loc-trade-marks-10-years); and
"Border Business: Where Kashmir unites India, Pakistan via trade," Mir Ehsan,
The Hindustan Times (India), May 29, 2018 (http://www.hindustantimes.com/
india-news/border-business-where-kashmir-unites-india-pakistan-via-trade/stor
y-0QtjXon1LAd4MupcEk3N7N.html).
[7] J&K Trade and Export Policy 2018–2028, Government of J&K, Industries and
Commerce Department, 2018.

complaints with their respective governments about traders at the LoC taking undue advantage of the "goodwill gesture": that is, importing commodities without paying tax and servicing larger markets in both India and Pakistan. The governments of India and Pakistan took note after the prices of commodities in both countries were affected. In 2011, Pakistan banned the export of green lentils to J&K after prices were raised in Pakistan, and India banned the export of cardamom and coconut. Other South Asian countries also weighed in – for instance, Sri Lanka objected to duty-free coconuts being imported into Pakistan from across the LoC that were selling at almost half the price of what Pakistan was importing them for from Colombo (Irfan 2011). It became obvious that the most popular and profitable commodities traded at the LoC were those that also injected volatility into their markets, thus attracting repeated interventions by the state in the enforcement of the original mandate that decreed exchanging local origin goods produced in either part of divided Jammu Kashmir.

The enforcement of this "origin clause" obviously impacted the volume of LoC trade. However, it remained contested, circumvented, or simply ignored, throwing into sharp relief the contradictions between the interests of commerce and that of politics. In 2013, the former president of the joint chamber for cross-LoC trade, a prominent businessman from the Kashmir Valley resolutely insisted that he wanted divided J&K to be treated as a "free economic zone," where trading entailed no imposition of taxes on any commodity coming in from the "other side," or, to borrow from cross-LoC traders' speech, moving between "LoC-east and LoC-west." In a personal interview, he recounted how he told representatives of the government as well as national-level business organizations that Jammu Kashmir was one economic entity. Since India had a parliamentary resolution declaring that the "other side" is theirs, he argued, one could not ask for customs duty within the territory of Jammu Kashmir since that went against the parliamentary resolution. Besides, he maintained that Kashmiris would not like any taxes to be imposed on any commodity from the "other side, whether it is pro-duced or not produced there." Some other traders adopted a more conciliatory tone: one trader from Jammu was cited as urging the larger trade bodies not to get upset over cross-LoC trade. He explained: "It is less business and more emotion because this nominal trade is helping us unite somehow – the idea is to produce trust and not wealth" (Irfan 2012).

Yet trust is rare in trade conducted under intense suspicion and inspection. In January 2014, trade was suspended for nearly a month after army personnel in Uri allegedly seized several packets of heroin from a truck carrying almonds from AJK. The driver was arrested, and the Kaman Bridge was closed off from both sides. The trader named as the receiver of the consignment insisted that another trader had used his invoice and that the consignment was meant to advance to another state. The driver claimed to be a last-minute replacement for the regular driver, such substitutions being common to everyday running of cross-LoC trade, and that he was entirely unaware of the contents of the truck. The month-long standoff between India and Pakistan regarding jurisdiction, with both governments trading accusations of conspiracy, caused about fifty drivers to be stranded on either side as involuntary "guests." Following the "brown sugar" incident, governments of India and Pakistan reportedly held a joint working group meeting to discuss streamlining cross-LoC trade, but subsequent incidents in 2015 and 2016 of drugs and small arms being found in trucks have frequently stalled cross-LoC trade.

Through these snapshots of the unsettled nature of cross-LoC exchange, I want to draw attention to the contradictions that arise in the attempt to align mobile networks of trade with the intransigent diktats of a militarized border. The mode of the CBM demarcates commerce as a domain of goodwill for tentatively drawing out a future conception of an "interdependent" Kashmir. But in so doing, the state appropriates an improviser mode that aims towards deemphasizing violence, accrediting "trust" to the future, and eventually deferring the political question of the Kashmiri demands for self-determination. This stance is at odds with Kashmiri nationalist aspirations that envision Jammu Kashmir as a single economic entity, suggesting intimations of an undivided political entity. Presently, such articulations are expressed in the articulation of a free trade zone that would "benefit from being at the strategic crossroads in the region" eventually connecting directly to Central Asia. During my fieldwork in 2017, traders also voiced aspirations of connecting cross-LoC exchange to the China–Pakistan Economic Corridor (CPEC) being established under China's Belt and Road Initiative (BRI). In the last few years, since the establishment of a Hindu nationalist government in 2014 and its aggressive suppression of the self-determination movement in Kashmir, cross-LoC trade has become more vulnerable to political machinations. Right-wing politicians lobbying for its closure have attacked cross-LoC trade as a threat to national security, a conduit for drugs as well as informal *hawala* transfers that fund anti-state activities from Pakistan. Since demonetization in November 2016, which rendered illegal tender 85 percent of the cash circulating in India in the alleged attempt to counter "black money" and "terrorist finance," financial intelligence and antiterror agencies became particularly active in Kashmir and Uri, subjecting a large number of traders both at the LoC and elsewhere to increased scrutiny, investigations, and arrests. In a newspaper report carried by *The Economic Times* in 2017, an anonymous trader engaged in cross-LoC trade bemoaned that even medical and electricity bills and the mobile phones of their wives had been seized by security officials.[8] Traders at the LoC have to manage the borderlines between the trade and crime, between being "subjects with agency" and "subjects of authority" (Birla 2011) in real and pressing ways.

Displaying Trade

Despite setbacks and obstacles cross-LoC trade endured, sustained mostly by inhabitants of the border districts. In February 2018, with the kind help of a businessman and interlocutor engaged in cross-LoC trade, I was able to visit the TFC in Uri. Along with some Kashmiri friends, I drove up from Srinagar in a hired Innova taxi. The mood inside the car was festive: other than Haider,[9] a social worker who had lived in Uri after the devastating earthquake in 2005, none of us had ever been to the Kaman Bridge. Approaching Uri there was growing excitement about being proximate to the other side, from imagining ourselves caught in the crosshairs of guns pointed at us by invisible soldiers. Javed, our driver was speeding a bit because we did not want to miss the passage of the goods-laden vehicles from Pakistan, adorned with famously vibrant "truck art" (Elias 2003; Sökefeld 2008), released into Indian-administered territory at the Kaman Bridge. In the town's main street, we were joined by our police escort, Salim.

---

[8] *The Economic Times*, "Why barter trade is considered biggest confidence building measure between India and Pakistan," October 27, 2017.

[9] The names of all persons have been changed.

His company made the process of acquiring permission to visit the Kaman Bridge quicker and easier. Salim and Haider fell into an easy conversation: the former was native to Uri and the latter had spent several months there conducting earthquake relief: "There are four to six garrisons here in Uri," said Haider. "Each garrison has several battalions, and each battalion has approximately 1,200 soldiers, so you can imagine the number of men stationed here." While I was unable to verify this statement, Uri demonstrated none of the conspicuous features of what Janet Roitman calls the "garrison-entrepôt" (Roitman 1998). Roitman defines the garrison-entrepôt as a site for the overlap and intersection of military and commercial practices. Violent forms of accumulation that reinscribe and redistribute licit and illicit economies and authority are instantiated in such spaces. In the Chad basin, the physical frontier of several nation states, Roitman notes a visible proliferation of unregulated economic activity that contributes in surprising ways to the vitality of state power itself – drawing in urban merchants, border officials, and other state and non-state personnel into an assemblage of commercial actors. Cross-border commerce in Uri appeared far more muted and mundane, despite the periodic newsflash about drugs or arms smuggling. Undoubtedly the most spectacular aspect was the train of gorgeous trucks that passed us while we were waiting for security clearance. Javed, our driver, took countless selfies as they moved past us towards the TFC.

When we disembarked at the TFC, the trucks that had passed us by were parked neatly side-by-side, cornucopias of color and trimmings. We stopped to admire them before watching the goods being unloaded at the "Cargo Point." The pace of work was brisk but without any ostensible tension or anxiety (see Figure 8.1). Drivers from the other side were distinguished by neon-orange safety vests, usually worn by roadworker crews, and that now served as markers of foreignness. They were milling about inside the boundary of the TFC, apparently forbidden from leaving its premises. A canteen, toilets, and a resting area for the "guests" were provided within. At the boundary wall, civilians and waiting drivers of trucks from the Indian-administered side lined up to watch the activity below. The consignment for the day consisted of delicious nectarines, locally known as *kinnu*, and almonds. We were plied with these commodities, some of which we ate and the rest we pocketed as souvenirs for friends or family back in Srinagar. The TFC overlooked the reservoir of a dam identified simply

Figure 8.1 Unloading at TFC; photo by author 2018

as "Uri 2." Two small girls were playing at the outer boundary, burning up the discarded cardboard crates, ashes fluttering towards the water below.

Later in the car, I joked with Salim about what would happen if a driver from the other side were to just take off his neon-orange jacket and leave the TFC. Salim simply smiled, and Javed quipped that those who want to be troublesome would find ways to do so. Trucks from the other side had to cross a swathe of civilian territory to reach the TFC. They were escorted on this journey from the Kaman post by a local police officer who served as both keeper and co-passenger for that short distance. Salim had been on escort duty several times, and I asked whether they did *baat-cheet* (made conversation) on these journeys and he nodded. He told me that a team of officials from both sides would meet at the Kaman Bridge daily. A line would be drawn smack in the middle, and each side would take care not to step over the line. The team consisted of an official from the army, the police, and a customs and trade representative on each side, and they met daily to exchange notes and resolve trade-related issues. We drove past the burnt stumps of houses where militants, who had sneaked into Uri and attacked an army post six months ago in September 2016, had taken shelter. Later that month the Indian government had announced the successful accomplishment of highly publicized "surgical strikes" by the Indian army, allegedly inflicting "significant casualties" on militant camps across the LoC in Pakistan-administered Kashmir. This military action formed the subject of a 2017 Bollywood patriotic blockbuster named *Uri: The Surgical Strike.*

Beyond intermittent limelight and TV publics, cross-LoC trade in Uri plodded on viewed primarily by drivers, laborers, state officials, and security forces, amidst a precarious sense of equilibrium maintained on a heavily militarized border. Occasionally, the border was breached, but not all crossings were equally dramatic. As we drove away, Salim told us a story of a madwoman (*paagal aurat*) from "Bihar–Bengal" who had recently wandered to the other side. Her supposed provenance indicated that she belonged to the migrant labor community that is often recruited for infrastructure and road development projects in Kashmir. "One day the army headquarters in Uri got a call from the other side, saying that someone from our side had gone over, and they were preparing to send her back," he explained. It took a lot of paper-work and coordination to enable her to return, said Salim, but even-tually she came back laden with gifts of clothes, blankets, and sweets. "How did she get over there? What route did she take?" Javed asked. "No one knows," replied Salim, "no one can understand what she says" (*uski zubaan koi nahin samajhta*).

The unintelligibility of the border-crossing madwoman under-scored the illegibility of the most ordinary and unspectacular aspects of the cross-LoC trade. Knowledge about how equivalences are conceived and reciprocities established in this form of barter remained obscure to me. As an outsider to Uri and cross-LoC trade, alert to the charged potential for political suspicion, I refrained from asking questions and likewise traders refrained from divulging the details of connections and practices that enabled "blind trade" but could anytime be criminalized or made punishable. The ethno-graphic murk around the ordinary workings of trade contrasted starkly with the stylized theater of its display – the synchronicity of crossing vehicles, the tactical visibility of colorful trucks and neon vests, and elaborate scripted lists and protocols for exchange. The webbed sociospatial relationships that made such exchanges possible were submerged by the thin theatrical displays. In this sense, the visible and invisible, the legible and illegible were part of the same spectrum of performance.

Conclusion: Incongruous Imaginaries

The merging of political and commercial activity demonstrated in historical scholarship is renewed in the outsized symbolism and overdetermined framings of contemporary cross-LoC trade. Given its nominal, and somewhat unaccountable, commercial value, the trade's distinction lay in how it staged disparate imaginations of sovereignty. In both precolonial and colonial eras, the relation between the market and the sovereign was in no way neutral, monolithic, or exclusionary despite claims or aspirations to the contrary. Rather, scholarship shows how the two spheres of power were embroiled and overlapped in a multitude of ways, whether in Mughal notions of ritual and patronage or in colonial officials imposing and trespassing on the supple forms of authority in the bazaar. In other words, neither form of sovereignty could be enacted without participating in the performances of commercial exchange, despite symbolic and bureaucratic attempts to separate the two. The artifact of cross-LoC trade recasts this aspect with tremendous irony in the context of the postcolonial states' aggressive rhetoric of absolute and exclusive claim on Kashmir. The ludicrous list of items, checklists, police escorts indicated that commercial exchange is always subject to political pressures from the "other side." Despite the intense deployment of political and military resources to direct trade along nationalist geographies, and the zero-sum politics that suffuses mainstream political discourse on Kashmir in both India and Pakistan, the trade depends precisely on both states acknowledging the others' presence, legitimacy, and authority. However emphatically cross-LoC trade protocols ritualize nation-state narratives, they cannot prevent stark intrusions from the "other side." The wider point about the fiction of bounded national economies or putatively "free" markets notwithstanding (Mitchell 1998), the cross-LoC trade artifact emerged from the specific historical and military calculations that suspend the fundamental question of Jammu Kashmir's political self-determination. In view of the perpetual provisional status of Jammu Kashmir and the fraught nature of state legitimacy, the rituals of cross-LoC trade inaugurate a subjunctive space for the precarious creation of competing "as-if" worlds (Puett 2008): *as if* the state mitigates violence and builds confidence by "allowing" people-to-people contact; *as if* circumventing lists and denying custom payments activates Kashmir as an undivided political entity. Much like the public, political arena of the bazaar, the space of cross-LoC exchange gets bound up in the spectacle of this as-if quality. The bureaucratic nomenclature imposed by the state, figuring exchange as nonmonetized barter, the demands of cross-LoC traders and the absurdities the assail cross-LoC trade are generated from conjuring a divided Kashmir "united" by trade, thereby suppressing the history of the violent dismemberment of Kashmir as an already-given. While competing pictures of sovereignty conspicuously perform the overlap between illegal (formally prohibited) and licit (socially sanctioned) exchange (van Schendel & Abraham 2005), the hurly-burly of cross-LoC trade further muddles such distinctions – not contraband drugs and arms but mundane items such as coconuts and bananas become hotly contested. However even in this parodic state, cross-LoC trade remains significant, even as a narrow site, for the potential articulation of Kashmiri sovereignty through assertions of choice of trading partners and decisions on who and what *not* to tax. In the overwatched and overregulated space of Uri, hosting many layers of army, police, and intelligence personnel, this form of exchange makes available a space of expression of longstanding alliances, channels, and connections for traders, drivers, and workers who ply cross-LoC trade. This is not an outright subversion of state sovereignty – at best, it punctures and plays with state hegemony by unsettling the authority to impose customs and in circulating "nonlocal" commodities that inject volatility into larger markets, forcing states to reckon with the incomplete nature of their own regulation and surveillance. Sometimes the sequence of potential disruption and subsequent reinstatement of state authority serves to strengthen rather than subvert the intrusive state. The fiction that trade produces trust and creates "peace" is tested in the periodic political belligerence that threatens the very existence of cross-LoC trade, perceived as a risk to national integrity. Yet as the state attempts to craft an artifact that enables it to reassert control in a space of disputed legitimacy, that artifact itself becomes a site where contesting ideas of sovereignty find limited articulation.

The weird protocols of cross-LoC trade thus become comprehensible as being devised and enforced primarily to repress older geographies of contiguity and commerce in the borderlands for establishing the self-presence of nation states. In this functional-farcical role of managing conflict and promoting "trust," cross-LoC trade falls into an arena of political-economic negotiations over – and performances of – sovereignty; thus partaking in the history of political control through trade in the frontier-borderlands. However, for traders who engage in cross-LoC commerce in all its absurdity and elasticity, its artifactual form serves as an opportunity for activating transversal ideas of autonomy, community, and profit that are not permissible under the national regulatory regimes of rival states. Perhaps precisely for this reason, cross-LoC trade endured for more than a decade despite all odds, and its "effectiveness" cannot be assessed from a perspective confined to the present moment.

References

Bayly, CA 1988, *Rulers, Townsmen and Bazaars: North Indian Society in the Age of British Expansion, 1770–1870*, Cambridge University Press, Cambridge.

Birla, R 2009, *Stages of Capital: Law, Culture, and Market Governance in Late Colonial India*, Duke University Press, Durham.

Birla, R 2011, "Law as Economy: Convention, Corporation," *UC Irvine Law Review*, 1, 3: 1015–37.

Chakrabarty, D 1992, "Of Garbage, Modernity and the Gaze," *Economic and Political Weekly*, 27, 10–11: 541–7.

Chatterjee, M 2016, "*Bandh* Politics: Crowds, Spectacular Violence, and Sovereignty in India," *Distinktion: Journal of Social Theory*, 17, 3: 294–307.

Elias, JJ 2003, "On Wings of Diesel: Spiritual Place and Religious Imagination in Pakistani Truck Decoration," *RES: Anthropology and Ethics*, 43, Islamic Arts: 187–202

Foucault, M 1979, *Discipline and Punish: The Birth of the Prison*, Vintage Books, New York.

Freitag, SB 1989, *Collective Action and Community: Public Arenas and the Emergence of Communalism in North India*, University of California Press, Berkeley.

Gandhi, A 2016, "The Hermeneutics of the Bazaar: Sincerity's Elusiveness in Delhi," *South Asia: Journal of South Asian Studies*, 31, 1: 126–48.

Gilmartin, D 1988, *Islam and Empire: Punjab and the Making of Pakistan*, University of California Press, Berkeley.

Hansen, TB 2004, "Politics as Permanent Performance: The Production of Political Authority in the Locality," in J Zavos, A Wyatt, & V Hewitt (eds.) *The Politics of Cultural Mobilization in India*, Oxford University Press, New Delhi, pp. 19–36.

Haynes, DE 1991, *Rhetoric and Ritual in Colonial India: The Shaping of a Public Culture in Surat City, 1852–1928*, University of California Press, Berkeley, Los Angeles, and Oxford.

Haynes, DE & Prakash, G (eds.) 1992, *Contesting Power: Resistance and Everyday Social Relations in South Asia*, University of California Press, Berkeley.

Irfan, S 2011, "Mess of a Trade," *Kashmir Life*, 25 April.

Irfan, S 2012, "Barter's Fear Factor," *Kashmir Life*, 25 July.

Jaoul, N 2007, "Dalit Processions: Street Politics and Democratization in India," in JC Strauss & DC O'Brien (eds.) *Staging Politics: Power and Performance in Asia and Africa*, I.B. Taurus, London and New York, pp. 173–93.

Kak, S (ed.) 2011, *Until My Freedom Has Come: The New Intifada in Kashmir*, Penguin, New Delhi.

Kira, AH 2011, Cross-LoC Trade in Kashmir: From Line of Control to Line of Conquest, Working paper, Indira Gandhi Institute of Development Research, Mumbai.

Martin, M 2012, An Economic History of the Hundi, 1858–1778, dissertation submitted to the Department of Economic History, London School of Economics.

Mir, KF & Gattoo, MH 2018, "Cross LOC Trade Between India and Pakistan – Contours and Dynamics," *Pakistan Business Review*, 19, 4: 843–60.

Mitchell, T 1998, "Fixing the Economy," *Cultural Studies*, 12, 1: 82–101.

Pandey, G 1990, *The Construction of Communalism in Colonial North India*, Oxford University Press, New Delhi and New York.

Puett, M 2008, "Ritual and the Subjunctive," in AB Seligman, RP Weller, MJ Puett, & B Simon (eds.) *Ritual and Its Consequences: An Essay on the Limits of Sincerity*, Oxford University Press, Oxford and New York.

Qadri, A 2013, "India Pakistan Hostility Kills Trade on Kashmir Border," *New York Times*, October 23.

Robinson, C 2013, *Body of the Victim Body of the Warrior: Refugee Families and the Making of Kashmiri Jihadists*, University of California Press, Berkeley.

Roitman, J 1998, "The Garrison Entrepôt," *Cahiers d'Etudes Africaines*, 38, 2–4 : 297–329.

Saraf, A 2019. "'Interference: Terror, Tourism, Trade,' Contribution for Collection on 'Volumetric Sovereignty,'" *Environment and Planning D: Society and Space* blog (https://societyandspace.org/2019/03/03/interference/).

Schaffer, T 2005, *Kashmir: the Economic of Peace Building*, The Center for Strategic and International Studies (CSIS), Washington, DC.

Schwecke, S 2018, "A Tangled Jungle of Disorderly Transactions? The Production of a Monetary Outside in a North Indian Town," *Modern Asian Studies*, 52, 4: 1375–419.

Sen, S 1998, *Empire of Free Trade*, University of Pennsylvania Press, Philadelphia.

Sökefeld, M 2013, "Jammu and Kashmir: Dispute and Diversity," in P Berger and F Heidemann (eds.) *The Modern Anthropology of India: Ethnography, Themes and Theory*, Routledge, London and New York.

Van Schendel, W and Abraham, I 2005, *Illicit Flows and Criminal Things: States, Borders, and the Other Side of Globalization*, Indiana University Press, Bloomington.

Washbrook, DA 1981, "Law, State and Agrarian Society in Colonial India," *Modern Asian Studies*, 15, 3, 649–721.

Yang, AA 1998, *Bazaar India : Markets, Society, and the Colonial State in Gangetic Bihar*, University of California Press, Berkeley.

Zargar, S "'Our Lives and Property are at Stake': As Cross-Loc Trade Halts, Kashmiri Traders Lament Losses," *Scroll.in* May 04, 2019 (https://scroll.in/article/921849/our-lives-and-property-are-at-stake-as-cross-loc-trade-halts-kashmiri-traders-lament-losses).

9 | Brandism vs. Bazaarism: Mediating Divinity in Banaras

ANDY ROTMAN[*]

In August 2017, an advertisement for Jawed Habib hair and beauty salons with the slogan "Gods too visit JH salon" appeared in Indian newspapers (Figure 9.1). It featured various gods at a JH salon, under the watchful gaze of their traditional "vehicles" (*vāhana*), presumably getting ready for the upcoming Durga Puja. We see the goddess Durga, astride her lion, surrounded by family members. The goddesses Saraswati and Lakshmi are applying makeup, as their vehicles (swan and owl, respectively) watch intently; the god Kartikeya, with curlers in his hair, is reclining, his peacock looking on; and Kartikeya's brother, Lord Ganesha, with his mouse at his shoulder, is counting money, perhaps preparing to pay for the treatments.

Jawed Habib, owner of the enormous salon franchise, with its nearly 800 outlets, was accused by some of hurting religious sentiments and mocking Hindu deities. Twitter provided an excellent means for trolling: "u belong to '#religion of peace' but need to portray Hindu Gods in a salon?? U don't think ur Prophet wud like ur salon?"[1] And this: "Can't do much else, not like I can issue a fatwa, but at least I can vow to never visit your salons again ... Despicable," which had 1,341 retweets.[2] Shortly after the advertisement blew up on Twitter,

[*] For their support and suggestions, my thanks to Abhishek Agrawal, Sumiran Caprihan, Naindeep Chann, Lewis Davis, William Edelglass, William Elison, Rick Fantasia, Rabindra Goswami, Arun Himatsingka, Sandy Huntington, Sunila Kale, William Mazzarella, Anne Mocko, Christian Novetzke, Ajay Pandey, Ramu Pandit, Christopher Pinney, Dhrub Kumar Singh, Rakesh Singh, Janna White, and to audiences at Cornell University and Union College. A special thanks as well to the editors of this book for their insightful comments.
[1] Rajalakshmi Joshi, September 4, 2017 (twitter.com/rajalakshmij/status/904893969359712258).
[2] Nupur J Sharma, September 4, 2017 (twitter.com/unsubtledesi/status/904930874776403968).

@JH_JawedHabib u belong to " #religionofpeace " but
need to portray Hindu Gods in a salon?? U don't think ur
Prophet wud like ur salon??

10:28 PM · Sep 4, 2017 · Twitter for Android

Figure 9.1 "Gods too visit JH salon" (Embedded image has been cropped and lightened for clarity.)

a complaint was lodged against Habib in Hyderabad, and one of his salons was vandalized.[3] Habib promptly issued numerous apologies.[4]

---

[3] See "Case Registered Against Jawed Habib for 'Insulting' Hindu Gods," *The Hindu*, September 8, 2017 (www.thehindu.com/news/cities/Hyderabad/case-registered-against-jawed-habib-for-insulting-hindu-gods/article19644025.ece); "Jawed Habib Salon Vandalised In Unnao District, Uttar Pradesh," *NDTV*, September 9, 2017 (www.ndtv.com/cities/jawed-habib-salon-vandalised-in-unnao-district-uttar-pradesh-1748051).

[4] Jawed Habib, September 4, 2017 (twitter.com/JH_JawedHabib/status/9049516 64519430144); September 4, 2017 (twitter.com/JH_JawedHabib/status/90495 9342058733568); September 4 2017 (twitter.com/JH_JawedHabib/status/9049 61724276654080); September 5, 2017 (twitter.com/JH_JawedHabib/status/ 905011953864646656); September 5, 2017 (twitter.com/JH_JawedHabib/ status/905021957787140096); etc.

Not everyone, however, was offended. One person on Twitter pointed to similar Durga Puja ads from previous years and noted that they had caused no controversy.[5] Another person posted a similarly sassy Habib salon advertisement that appeared in *The Telegraph* in Calcutta just before Durga Puja in 2009. The goddess Saraswati – hair disheveled and eyes askew, veena in her left hand and gesticulating with her right, her swan slightly exasperated – explains her consternation in the caption: "We can't get our hair styled at Habib's. We have to wear it long and loose for four days." That advertisement caused no controversy at all. Could it be, the author notes, that the outrage for Jawed Habib is "because he has an Islamic name?"[6]

This last author has a point about the cause of the outrage, but, in what follows, I want to focus not on what allows such advertisements to be construed as "deliberate and malicious acts, intended to outrage religious feelings."[7] Instead, I want to focus on the practice of using gods in Indian advertising as a way of asking deeper questions about the nature of certain visual and market systems in India, their relationship with one another and with the moral economies that undergird them, and the complex ways that markets can be moralized and moralizing, as well as sacralized and sacralizing.

In addressing these issues, much of my data comes from ethnographic research in the main bazaars of the Pakka Mahal area in the city of Banaras – also known as Varanasi and Kashi – which has been both a religious and commercial center, for the city and the nation, for centuries.[8] Since 2001, I have been interviewing merchants and consumers, religious leaders and devotees, pilgrims and politicians, often

---

[5] Saileena, September 6, 2017 (twitter.com/saileenas/status/905334952681553920).
[6] Deepanjan Ghosh, "Goddess Durga has Starred in Bengali Ads for Years – So Why Is Jawed Habib in Hot Water Now?," *Scroll.in*, September 12, 2017 (scroll.in/magazine/850250/goddess-durga-has-starred-in-bengali-ads-for-years-so-why-is-jawed-habib-in-hot-water-now). See too "Hairstylist Jawed Habib Gets Trolled for Hindu Gods Ad Ahead of Durga Puja," *The Indian Express*, September 6, 2017 (indianexpress.com/article/trending/trending-in-india/jawed-habib-hairstylist-trolled-for-hindu-gods-ad-ahead-of-durga-puja-4831338/).
[7] The complaint lodged in Hyderabad was registered under section 295A of the Indian Penal Code: "Deliberate and malicious acts, intended to outrage religious feelings or any class by insulting its religion or religious beliefs." For more on the history of section 295A, see Adcock (2016).
[8] In the past, people in Banaras distinguished between the Pakka Mahal and Kacca Mahal, the traditional upmarket and downmarket sections of the city (Bayly 2011: 115; Kumar 1988: 63). The latter term has now lost currency.

repeatedly, in an effort to understand the complex and constitutive relationship in the area between religion and commerce, and how these interactive and evolving systems affect the social life of the city. Over the years, many of my informants have become friends and teachers, and their insights inform much of what follows.

Advertising Before the Era of Brand

India is filled with companies named after the goddess Durga, and their advertisements, bearing the goddess's name, and even image, generally circulate with little fanfare, and certainly without causing a Twitterstorm. There is Durga papad and Durga pickle, Durga matches and Durga mustard oil, Durga pipe fittings and Durga sodium bicarbonate, Durga hotels, Durga restaurants, and Durga medicine stores. And there are also companies not specifically named after Durga but that routinely depict her image on their products. This is a common practice for companies that sell "materials for religious ritual" (*pūjā sāmagrī*), such as incense and camphor. As a result, the numerous shops in the Pakka Mahal that sell these commodities often line them up so that they appear both as objects for sale and rows of icons, blurring the line between store and shrine, commodity and divinity, and helping make their shops look like the temples that they serve.

And Durga isn't even the most popular of the gods when it comes to advertising; Lakshmi reigns supreme. Lakshmi-named businesses proliferate throughout India, with local general stores, such as *kirānā* markets, often bearing the goddess's name, especially in small towns like those on the outskirts of Banaras. Lakshmi is also very popular on the Indian stock exchange, where there are dozens of businesses named after her, such as Lakshmi Auto Components, Lakshmi Cement and Ceramics Industries, Lakshmi Energy and Foods, and Lakshmi Precision Screws.

To be sure, naming one's company (or child) after a Hindu god has long been a common practice in India. Likewise common has been the practice of creating advertisements for one's company that feature Hindu gods, as is evident by even a cursory look at old matchboxes, packaging for cloth, wrappers for fireworks, or promotional calendars.[9] In fact, it is still a common practice in some sectors –

---

[9] See, for example, Datawala (2007); Dotz (2007); Giannuzzi (2000); Jain (2007); Uberoi (2003).

sweetshops in Banaras are a good example – and within the domain of ritual-related items, it is closer to a norm, with the company name often barely visible.

But India's ideas about commerce, and its de facto rules, are changing; the uproar regarding the Habib salon advertisements is a case in point. One crucial intervention in these conceptions of commerce began in 2002. At that time, India embarked on a plan to promote itself for investment, trade, and tourism with its "Incredible India" campaign, which brought together "every possible government sector" to market the nation (Kant 2009: xii). The campaign was an extremely successful exercise in "nation branding," asserting India's cultural and economic power in global markets and raising awareness of corporate and product brands in domestic ones.[10] This was the beginning of "Brand India."[11] Now, after a huge influx of multinational products and advertising and a proliferation of shopping malls that feature them – from three in 1999 to more than 600 at present, with nearly 100 in and around Delhi – global capitalism has transformed India's commercial culture.[12] Nation building is morphing into nation branding, and earlier ideas about advertising and national identity are being reconfigured, along with the proper role of Hindu gods in each.[13]

Yet "brand" itself is not a stable concept. Much like "religion," it designates a phenomenon that has changed considerably in conception and practice over time. Also like "religion," it shares a history of periodic powerplays, as countries have been compelled, politically and economically, to find (or invent) its modern incarnation in their homelands, leading to sweeping changes in indigenous conceptions of morality, culture, and the nation-state.[14] Once reified (if not deified), in other words, both "religion" and "brand" have histories of coercion

---

[10] For more on the "Incredible India" campaign, see Bolin & Stahlberg (2010); Edwards & Ramamurthy (2017); Geary (2013); Harish (2010); Kerrigan et al. (2012). See too the abundance of materials on nation branding – in Estonia (Jansen 2008), Latvia (Dzenovska 2005), Macedonia (Graan 2013), Poland (Aronczyk 2007), Qatar (Mattern 2008), and so on.
[11] See Mongia (2005); Rangnekar (2005).
[12] For more on the impact of "the Great Indian Mall Boom" (Puri 2018), see Gooptu (2009); Kalhan (2007); Sen (2017: 215–20); Voyce (2007); Wyatt (2005).
[13] For more on the juggernaut of nation branding, see Comaroff & Comaroff (2009); Kaur (2012); Van Helm (2001); Volcic & Andrejevic (2016). For more on its effects in India, see Mazzarella (2003); Nanda (2011); Parameswaran (2014).
[14] See, for example, Josephson (2012); Smith (1988); likewise, Burke (1996); Domosh (2003); Koehn (2001).

and imperialism, and likewise, faith and devotion, unquestioned truths and unquestionable allegiance.

In other words, "brand" in its current form did always not exist in India.[15] There was advertising, even various kinds of trademark, and businesses promoted their reputations, but "reputation" was not "brand" in the modern sense of the term.[16] Hence, to assess earlier advertising in India using modern brand logic would be a misconstrual, like reading early Indian *dharmaśāstra* texts and applying our modern divisions of "religious" and "secular," or "public" and "private," to ascertain their spheres of meaning and application.[17]

Helpful for making sense of this distinction is Hans Belting's *Likeness and Presence: A History of the Image Before the Era of Art*, which traces a parallel phenomenon. Before the Renaissance and Reformation, holy images were treated not as "art" but as objects of veneration that possessed the tangible presence of "the Holy." The idea and category of "art" simply wasn't present at the time, and to read these images as "art" is to misread them. To view a thirteenth-century image of the Virgin as "art" is a kind of category mistake; so too viewing as "brand" an early twentieth-century advertisement for the Standard Cigarette Company that featured Gandhi (Figure 9.2).

The connection between Minerva, Roman goddess of strategic warfare; Gandhi, pacifist icon; and cigarettes needs to be understood through an alternate logic to ascertain its original power.[18] Just as "religion" has a history and a prehistory, so too do "art" and "brand," and it takes some work to understand the rules of these dispensations whose arbitrariness has now been naturalized into Bourdieuean *doxa*, and taken for granted as always already there. As such, it becomes hard to imagine a world in which these phenomena don't exist, and to resist the temptation to conjure their presence even in their glaring absence.

[15] Douglas Haynes argues – implicitly in his chapter in this volume and explicitly in his forthcoming book – that modern branding began in India in the 1920s or 1930s, if not earlier. My focus is on the shift in branding in India that happened as a result of neoliberalism, beginning in the 1980s.

[16] For a comparison, see Douglas Haynes's chapter in this volume, which examines early twentieth-century advertisements by "vernacular capitalists" and how they "facilitated the emergence of new types of small manufacturing firm that increasingly added a modern marketing dimension to their producing functions."

[17] For some sense of the dauntingly broad and evolving semantic range of *dharma*, see Halbfass (1988: 310–33); Hiltebeitel (2011).

[18] For more on this alternate logic, see Rotman (2010). For more on brand logic and "Gandhian publicity," see Mazzarella (2010).

Figure 9.2 The Standard Cigarette Company featuring Gandhi

Also helpful is Ashis Nandy's insightful article, "The Discreet Charms of Indian Terrorism," in which he analyzes accounts of various Indian hijackings in the 1970s – or what could be called "takeovers before the era of hijackings" – and in the process shows how "the clash between the dominant language of the nation-state system and the residual traditional language of rebellion" renders the latter "virtually inaccessible to those who speak the first language" (Nandy 1995: 24–5). From the perspective of the dominant language, the residual language is "immature … inefficient, anarchic, and irrational," while it self-identifies as modern, secular, and rational (Nandy 1995: 23–4). What remains is a "half-forgotten dialect" – which is "an indication of another moral universe"; facilitates dialogue, collaboration, communion, and trust among disparate stakeholders; and keeps violence at bay – and to which the now dominant language has little access (Nandy 1995: 22).

The now dominant language in today's global capitalism is what I refer to as "brandism" – akin to what Constantine Nakassis (2013: 116–19) calls "brand neoliberalism," in recognition of the ways that, since the 1980s, brands have spearheaded the neoliberal project,[19] producing among consumers specific identities, affiliations, emotional entanglements, and social imaginaries.[20] And signaling a different moral universe is a local form of Indian commerce, a half-forgotten vernacular that fosters wider solidarities, which I refer to as "bazaarism." Here I follow Arang Keshavarzian (2007: 70) in understanding the bazaar as a "series of ongoing and socially embedded networks that are mechanisms for the exchange of specific commodities," while also recognizing the bazaar as a moralized and moralizing entity with concomitant institutions, value systems, and products.[21] From brandism's perspective, bazaarism is for the most part "immature … inefficient, anarchic, and irrational."[22] And it is indeed rebellious, especially in the ways that it imagines the gods and our relationship with them. But what is this alternate "moral universe" that bazaarism embraces? And what exactly does it facilitate? And why might brandism want to displace it? One way to address these questions is to examine something that both bazaarism and brandism promote although in different forms and with divergent ends: the franchise.

---

[19] Dating this shift in "brand" to the 1980s is less problematic than defining what the shift entails. According to Arvidsson (2006: 3): "Although brands have a long history as a commercial institution, reaching as far back as the eighteenth century … their position as central components of the social fabric was established in the 1980s. Brands now became something of an omnipresent tool by means of which identity, social relations and shared experiences (like spending a night in bed talking about Apple products) could be constructed. They were spun into the social fabric as a ubiquitous medium for the construction of a common social world." According to Nakassis (2013: 117): "Although the brand predates these shifts [in the 1980s] in capitalism, it is precisely since the 1980s that the brand has been more intensively used as a kind of abstracted rentier capital laminated onto a structure of production capital, a site of investment and speculation and a form of value addition that derives profit not *from* its commodity vehicles but *through* them – more precisely, through the ways brand image (and the premiums it extracts) commodify *access* to brand imaginaries (as mediated by moments of purchase) through a continual relationality with, or leasing of, the brand."

[20] See Arvidsson (2005); Coombe (1998); Foster (2007); Lury (2004). See also the cluster of articles on "brand neoliberalism" in *Cultural Anthropology* (2013), 28, 1, 110–79.

[21] See Bayly (1983); Jain (2007); Yang (1999).

[22] In nineteenth-century Banaras, in what might be seen as a similar pitting of languages, local merchants "bitterly resisted the standardization of weights and measures," which infuriated outsiders. "According to Agra merchants Banaras resisted out of 'self-willed ignorance and intolerance of all change'" (Bayly 1983: 450).

Brandism, Bazaarism, and the Franchise

According to *The American Marketing Association Dictionary* (2017), a brandism bible of sorts, "brand" is "a name, term, design, symbol, or other feature that *distinguishes* an organization or product *from its rivals* in the eyes of the customer."[23] And as the dictionary, along with the current flood of management textbooks, makes clear: brands are unique; they set one apart; they are necessary for product differentiation; and they have individual identities, which are fundamental to consumer recognition and symbolize the brand's differentiation from competitors.[24] Differentiation is key; without it, the blur of similar products and stores creates a kind of homogeneousness that makes brand loyalty – the holy grail of branding – an impossibility.[25] It also forecloses the possibility of franchising, that most ubiquitous form of corporate expansion, which has flourished under global capitalism.[26]

Within brandism, there is a very recognizable franchise model. Think McDonald's. Put simply, a corporation allows individuals to use its brand and business model with the proviso that they follow certain rules and regulations and offer a portion of their earnings back to the host corporation. For these individuals, the goal of opening a McDonald's franchise is not differentiation; it is affiliation. One wants to be affiliated and associated with all of the host corporation's power and glory.[27] Affiliation is also one of the selling points of a franchise (e.g., "Billions and Billions Served"). By consuming its products, you get to join a like-minded cohort of consumers – even

---

[23] Emphasis added. The dictionary has recently updated it definition: "A name, term, design, symbol, or any other feature that identifies one seller's good or service as distinct from those of other sellers." Available at www.ama.org/reso urces/Pages/Dictionary.aspx.

[24] See, for example, Kotler and Armstrong (2016: 274–91).

[25] See *American Marketing Association Dictionary*, s.vv. *differential advantage, distinctiveness*. See too Kotler and Armstong (2016: 248–53).

[26] "In the United States alone," Kotler and Armstong (2016: 82) note, "some 770,000 franchise outlets account for more than $830 billion of economic output. Industry analysts estimate that a new franchise outlet opens somewhere in the United States every eight minutes and that about one out of every 12 retail business outlets is a franchised business."

[27] As a former McDonald's board member explained: "If every asset we own, every building, and every piece of equipment were destroyed in a terrible natural disaster, we would be able to borrow all the money to replace it very quickly because of the value of our brand. . . . The brand is more valuable than the totality of all these assets" (Greenberg and Naím 2001: 30–31).

when the corporation itself sells you on its differentiation. "Think different," urged Apple's classic advertisements, along with billions of others (Grainge 2000).

Within bazaarism, there is likewise a very recognizable franchise model, although it differs from its counterpart in brandism in that is constituted as something like a divine dispensation.[28] Think general stores named after Lakshmi. Individuals make use of a brand, and to some extent business model, with the proviso that they offer a portion of their earnings back to the divinity. Think "religious ritual" (*pūjā*). For these individuals, the goal of opening a Lakshmi store (or a Lakshmi temple) is likewise not differentiation; it is affiliation. One wants to be affiliated and associated with all the god's power and glory. It isn't that one expects enormous differences between the proprietor of a Lakshmi store or a Durga one; rather, consumers have a sense that such proprietors are more-or-less god-fearing and law-abiding. To name a shop after a god is a bit like making a vow of adherence to a general moral code – the mercantile equivalent of putting one's hand on a bible and testifying to one's honesty.

Affiliation with Lakshmi is especially easy, for there are few requirements for entry into her dispensation. Each Diwali – the proverbial festival of lights – most Hindu businessmen in Banaras (and across India) install new small, inexpensive statues of Lakshmi and Ganesha in their stores, and this establishes them within Lakshmi's fold. As such, one might choose Lakshmi because she doesn't demand veneration that is particularly onerous. Or one might choose Lakshmi because she is one's "family deity" (*kula-devatā*) or "personal choice of deity" (*iṣṭa-devatā*). Or one might choose her simply because she is regarded as a goddess of wealth, prosperity, and good fortune – not only in

---

[28] "Franchise" in bazaarism adheres closer to a much earlier meaning of the term: "a special privilege or exclusive right to perform some public function, granted by a sovereign power to any person or body of people" (*Oxford English Dictionary*, 3rd edition, s.v. *franchise*). In this case, the "special privilege" is something like a prerogative of faith, or even a divine injunction, and franchises are akin to a decentralized version of the multisite church (Surratt et al. 2006). Others, however, might recognize such a prerogative as an action "initiated unilaterally by a single executive acting beyond the bounds of ordinary (human) laws" and observe that "exercises of prerogative are often attended by a degree of secrecy and opacity that make an executive's genuine motives as inscrutable as God's purpose, which makes it difficult – morally and epistemologically – to critique the actions of an executive cast in the role of savior" (Fatovic 2008: 488).

Hinduism but also in Buddhism and Jainism. Or one might also choose her because there is a known association between the god in question and the product – for example, Lakshmi with general stores, Saraswati with books and stationery, and Ganesha with sweets.[29]

A businessman, might, however, choose (or feel compelled) to follow a more rigorous protocol. In *Amar Akbar Anthony* (1977) – one of the most popular Indian films of all time – a local bigman named Anthony (played by megastar Amitabh Bachchan) tithes 50 percent of his earnings to a Catholic church, for he considers Jesus his business partner. As Anthony explains: "Whatever He gives to me, I give back fifty percent for the poor. That's an understanding between us." In other words, Anthony's business works because of Jesus's grace, so with Jesus he has a fifty-fifty profit-sharing arrangement.[30]

While affiliation is the most obvious feature of the legions of Lakshmi stores and other divine franchises, there is nevertheless differentiation. Perhaps the most obvious form of differentiation is created visually: the oft-occurring array of images of gods and/or photographs of deceased family – usually patriarchs – that constitute a sociogram and de facto shrine within these stores.[31] The images of gods create a divine nexus within which one is situated, and the images of deceased family create a familial lineage, such that the store and its owner are located in both divine and human terms. This matrix of affiliations functions, to some extent, as a store's bona fides.

So what happens within these respective franchise models when an affiliate screws up? Or, put another way, what prevents a franchisee from engaging in impropriety or just deviating from company standards? Within brandism, stringent rules of behavior are put in place by

---

[29] There are also many examples for which the connection between company and deity is more tenuous. In Banaras, such stores abound – the Saraswati Saw Mill, Sri Har Har Gange Lamp Shed, Shri Gopal Bags, Vishwanath Alankar Mandir, and countless others – and generally cause no consternation.

[30] For more on Anthony's logic, see Elison et al. (2015: 123–6).

[31] Similarly, in Bourdieu's (2004: 601) analysis of the social uses and meaning of photographs in a peasant society in southwestern France, "photos are read and appreciated not in themselves and for themselves, in terms of their technical or aesthetic qualities, but as lay sociograms [i.e., figural representations of one's social relationships] providing a visual record of extant social roles and relations; and they are typically stored away in a box as it would be indecent or ostentatious to display them in one's home." To display such "lay sociograms" in one's store in the bazaar is not "indecent or ostentatious"; it is expected, as is the regular veneration that they receive.

the parent corporation, for if one store within the franchise screws up, all stores within the franchise may be taken to task. If one McDonald's serves tainted hamburgers that lead to a salmonella outbreak, all McDonald's may then be suspect. Within bazaarism, there are likewise stringent rules of behavior, but transgressions by one errant franchisee don't usually reflect poorly on the rest. A single sinner doesn't somehow compromise the god's other devotees; neither does he damage the god's reputation.

Nevertheless, an errant franchisee can expect harsh penalties, whether divine or human. Crossing a Hindu goddess can have severe repercussions. In *Jai Santoshi Maa* (1975), an Indian mythological superhit, a tainted offering – spiked with lime juice as opposed to salmonella – leads to disastrous consequences: the goddess kills a group of children in retribution.[32] Popular Hindu "vow" (*vrat*) literature is likewise filled with such accounts: follow the rules prescribed by the deity, and she will favor your family with blessings of health, wealth, and prosperity. Disobey her rules, and she will punish your loved ones without mercy.[33]

The bazaar itself likewise punishes infractions, generally not through litigation but through forms of alienation. The mercantile world is so fully embedded in the social world that financial ruin can lead to a kind of social death, or worse. In the "tight, face-to-face society [of the bazaars of Banaras in the eighteenth and nineteenth centuries], the failure of one's credit in the bazaar was a sentence of commercial and sometimes physical death" (Bayly 1983: 219).[34] To defy a bank or a creditor (or the gods or one's ancestors) was quite literally to take one's life in one's hands. Nowadays, the penalties aren't as severe but stories abound of lawbreakers ostracized not only from the higher realms of commerce but from the more quotidian realms of sociality, unable to rent a room or buy a home, get their children into the right schools or married.[35] Breaking the norms, be they legal or moral,

---

[32] For more on this retributive logic, see Lutgendorf (2005).

[33] For more on *vrat* materials and practices, see Menzies (2004); Pearson (1996).

[34] Bayly (1983: 461) makes the same point elsewhere: "There were cases in ... Benares ... where great merchants who had participated in the business of state lost their credit and died of starvation."

[35] "Lawbreakers" in this context is seemingly a fuzzy term, for the ethical rules of the bazaar are not codified in an official code. They are more tacit than explicit – difficult even for residents to articulate in propositional form although they regulate many aspects of their behavior (cf. Gerrans 2005). Moreover, these

rendered them functionally excommunicated, with exile the only logical course of action.[36]

Brandism in the Bazaar

While doing research in the main bazaars of Banaras and watching the ongoing tensions between bazaarism and brandism, the idea of a "brand" has been something of a moving target, from the nonexistent, to the ill-defined, to the quotidian, sometimes exacerbating and sometimes alleviating the struggle between these two systems. Consider these three accounts from 2003, 2006, and 2010.[37]

In 2003, I was doing research on the world of jute bags with images and text silkscreened on them, which were quite common at that time. An estimated 90 percent of these bags were *gift-wālā*, adorned with promotional logos and given away by businesses as a form of advertising, and the remaining 10 percent were *cālū-wālā*, "crappy" bags bearing some form of *apparent* commodity image or branding and sold inexpensively in the bazaar. To a person, vendors and customers resisted ANY reading of the *cālū* bags. To read those bags in the conventional sense of the term was to misread them as well as to misunderstand the visual economy in which they operated. All of my

> rules are not applied equally to everyone in all circumstances; there is no "one law for all," either by design or practice (Menski 2009). Rules may vary according to one's gender, stage of life, social class, and religious position, just as they do in normative Hindu configurations of dharma (Rocher 1978: 1284–9). Once again the film *Amar Akbar Anthony* offers a helpful parallel. The world of the bazaar is much like "Anthonyville" (*Anthony Nagar, Anthony Wadi*) – the area around Anthony's bar that functions as sovereign territory, with rules that seem sensible (if not moral) to its denizens and random (if not illegal) to both church and state (Elison et al. 2015: 38, 55–6, 125–6). In the film, as in the bazaar, law is like a rivulet of water, adapting to circumstances and obstacles. Being fluid, however, is not the same as being arbitrary. Nevertheless, Sebastian Schwecke's (personal communication) observations about his own ethnographic work in Banaras are telling: "There are no hard and fast rules, allowing ambiguity, enabling people to transgress rules with only mild repercussions in many cases, while leading to severe sanctions in different, though broadly comparable instances. The management of reputations through communication flows is chaotic and unpredictable, necessitating caution but still allowing leeway in a non-systematic way."

[36] For more on "law and order" in Banaras, see Medhasananda (2002: ii, 855–935).

[37] Some of what follows is excerpted from Rotman (2010), which offers a more detailed account of the image worlds of Indian jute bags.

informants – more than forty regular interviewees – agreed that the graphics imprinted on the bags had no "meaning" (*matlab*). These included the street vendors who hawked jute bags from positions along the main road near the Ganga River, the wholesalers of jute bags who sold their goods in bulk from one of the industrial bazaars in the Pakka Mahal, and the shopkeepers who sold a variety of bags in a mostly middle-class neighborhood.

For example, the street vendors I spoke with were eager to praise the merits of the jute bags they sold, but they were unwilling to interpret the images and text emblazoned on them. Repeatedly I was told that the graphics didn't mean anything, even in cases when the meaning seemed clear to me. For example, I assumed that "OSCAR: A BEAUTIFUL MIND" referred to the Russell Crowe film that won four Oscar awards and "US-64" referred to the infamous failed mutual fund that was bailed out by the government (Figure 9.3). I guessed that the man pictured in the latter was lunging after the fund, and his money invested in it, although both proved elusive, outside the purview of his spectacles and beyond his grasp. Yet my attempts at reading the images were met with bewilderment by vendors and customers alike.

I was told that people didn't buy bags because of their graphics. People bought bags because of their perceived quality and durability. This was also borne out by my observations. In choosing a bag,

Figure 9.3 Jute bags

customers would test the strength of the jute and the handle, which was made of either bamboo or plastic, but they rarely examined the graphics closely. When I did question a customer as to why she was buying a particular bag, the answer invariably concerned practicality, not aesthetics. Questions about the particular meaning of an image or a bit of text were met with incredulity. It was as though the graphics on the bags were somehow unreadable – resistant to interpretation by virtue of existing below a certain threshold of observability, like my own reaction to the proprietary tartan and check patterns on Scottish woolens (Harrison 1968) or the designs on hospitality carpets in hotel lobbies. They remain seen-and-yet-unseen, witnessed but not noticed.[38]

In a conversation with a retailer of jute bags named Amitabh, I remarked that no one – not street vendors, wholesalers, or customers – ever seemed to pay attention to the graphics on jute bags, even though the graphics were made up of recognizable images, such as cuddly bears, and recognizable phrases, such as simple tag lines in English (e.g., Style, Freedom, I Love India). Like my other informants, he too said that he never paid attention to these graphics, and his good friend who was listening concurred. So I asked them, since nobody seems to notice the graphics on jute bags, if they could, what graphics would they put on these bags to make them more desirable to customers. The friend explained that he would put the name of their neighborhood in Hindi on the bag – in this case, Dal Mandi – to appeal to local pride. But Amitabh disagreed. He explained that the bags needed graphics, but the graphics weren't meant to be understood. Presumably, if they were understood, they would be less desirable. But, I countered, I could often grasp the "meaning" of the images and the text. I could often understand them. Then he said: "There isn't any meaning to be grasped. If you can understand the *printing* on a bag, then you didn't understand it."

Amitabh's critique can perhaps be better understood by considering, for a moment, Abelam art in Lowland New Guinea. Anthony Forge describes how Abelam painters do not distinguish figurative and abstract elements in their work. Even when figuration is "apparently" present in their painting, as in the likenesses of men's faces, these

---

[38] As a point of comparison, see descriptions of the "invisibility" of Dalits in Indian public life (Baudh 2017).

painters vigorously deny any figurative intent or figurative content to their work: "Two-dimensional painting for the Abelam," Forge (1973: 177, 189) explains, "is a closed system having no immediate reference outside itself." And within this system, "graphic elements modified by colour, carry the meaning. The meaning is not that a painting or carving is a picture or representation *of* anything in the natural or spirit world, rather it is *about* the relationship between things." As Diane Losche (1995: 59) observes, "To ask what a sign means is irrelevant to the Abelam. . . . Asking the Abelam what this particular design means is akin to asking, 'What does your refrigerator mean?' or, to reverse the issue, 'What does your painting do?' For the Abelam this separation between meaning and function is an inappropriate basis on which to ask a question."

Now this isn't to say that the graphics on jute bags were meaningless to their local Indian audience. The words and images that they contain were recognizable, as most of my informants claimed, and they did constitute a system of meaning. But the power of these graphics was generated by their words and images being slightly incomprehensible: recognizable but not fully readable. It was through this discursive disjunction that these graphics generated their allure, or as my informants would say, their "exotic" or "foreign" quality. To the brand-trained eye, the bags seemed mostly discursive and barely figural, but to the producers and consumers in the bazaar, the opposite was the case. The graphics were not texts to be read or images to be decoded; they were icons that testified to a highly affective awareness of a globalized commercial world. To own such an icon was to have bought into a world of Westernized consumer culture and to begin to possess the cultural capital, if not financial capital, of participants in that economic field.

I use the term "icons" here first and foremost in a Peircian sense. Charles Peirce ([1885] 1993: 243) famously identified the triad of symbols, icons, and indexes, with symbols being arbitrary and conventional, icons exhibiting a similarity or analogy to the object of discourse, and indexes having some natural relationship of contiguity with the referent that then "forces the attention to the particular object intended without describing it."[39] In brandism, brand markers are

---

[39] For other applications of Peirce in the study of South Asia, see (most famously) Daniel (1984) and (most recently) Elison (2018).

intended to function as indexes, leading the viewer back to the company or product with a kind of "stern fidelity" (Pinney 1997: 20). At this time in the bazaar, however, Amitabh and others didn't view these objects as referring to specific corporate or commercial entities, which could then be discerned through "reading." Instead, they recognized these images as gesturing to a world of exotic and foreign power and capable, seemingly or otherwise, of "passing on supernatural favors" (Belting 1994: 47).

Recent work, in fact, has shown that viewers have the same neurological response to strong brands as they do to religious icons (Lindstrom 2008). Brand loyalty and religious faith are neurological twins, likewise Nike the goddess and Nike the swoosh, transcendence and "brandscendence" (Clark 2004). Perhaps, then, by reading these commodity images as icons – that is, by bypassing the expected reading of commodity image as index – my informants had, in fact, read them with the desired intent, perceiving them as something akin to "strong brands" even without knowledge of the brand itself. This, too, has corollaries in the more overtly religious practices of the bazaar, where numerous shrines are venerated as powerful icons and yet their precise provenance and referent is unknown. These include nondescript stones smeared with vermillion paste that are venerated as Hindu icons, and which may be Ganesha or Hanuman, or could even be a "found" *swayambhū liṅga* of Shiva, but whose precise referent is of no great concern to those who do offer veneration. As I was repeatedly told, a *mūrti* – a divine statue or idol – is powerful regardless of which god it designates. Likewise, there are tiny unnamed *mazār*s whose provenance is unknown or forgotten but which are venerated by a wide cross-section of the bazaar's residents, their "blessing" (*barkat*) in no way contingent on knowing the shrine's index.[40] Perhaps it was inevitable that brands would eventually take hold in the bazaar, especially when one realizes that "veneration" often entails "donation," with cash being a standard offering.

[40] Lukas Werth (1998: 78, 80) makes a similar argument about small shrines that are "ubiquitous in the Pakistani landscape." It is "not necessary in Pakistan to know the name or even the life of the *pir* of a small shrine: the fact that he is supposed to belong to a holy category is sufficient to qualify him to be prayed to, even though the personality of the saint has been almost effaced and is of very little importance."

In 2006, after a new brand consciousness had made inroads in the Indian marketplace – moving from the realm of the barely comprehensible exotic to almost signifying – I had another conversation with Amitabh, the bag retailer, in which I asked him to define the word "brand." Perusing his stock, Amitabh explained to me that Popeye, Harry Potter, Scooby Doo, and Pokémon were brands. Yet when I asked about his other bags, which were inscribed, respectively, with "Diesel," "Armani," "Polo," and "Adidas," he explained that these were "styles" not "brands." The manufacturer of the Diesel bag was Donex, and the manufacturer of the Armani bag was Mayur, but neither, according to Amitabh, was a brand. So, I asked, within his world of merchandise what constituted a brand? "Brands," he explained, "are really films and shows you see on television." Another shopkeeper told me that branded goods are the best quality products; that they are exclusively foreign; and that they are only available in shopping malls. The bazaar, he said, sells no brands.

In 2010, brandism had made such extensive inroads into India's malls and mainstream media that a successful silk merchant, who had lived his whole life in the bazaar, said to me, with only a hint of irony, "brand loyalty has become this generation's religious faith." He then lamented that soon, it seemed, all of India would turn into one big mall and everything would be branded – except, of course, the gods. "But can't a god be a brand?" I asked. Everyone recognizes the Hanuman image from the Sankat Mochan Temple, with his tilted head and gentle smile. The image is everywhere in the bazaar, on posters and postcards, statues, and paintings. "Couldn't the temple copyright that image," I asked, "and charge licensing fees if people wanted to used it?" "No, no, no," he said. "They wouldn't do that." But neither of us was sure if he was right.

Reputation and Trust

While the shopkeepers in the bazaar whom I interviewed struggled to make sense of brand, often second-guessing and revising their definitions, they were invariably forthright and articulate about the connection between themselves, their companies, and their advertisements, and why customers shop with them, whether once or repeatedly. One might think of this as a vestige of "reputation before the era of brand," echoing Belting's idea of image before the era of art, and functioning something like Nandy's idea of a half-forgotten vernacular. And nearly all the shopkeepers with whom I spoke focused on one key term: *viśvās* (trust).

This parallels Sebastian Schwecke's insights (in this volume) about the importance for the banking industry in mid-twentieth-century Banaras of "reputational registers of trust" rather than "procedural" ones. The former, Schwecke explains, "rely on a knowable and familiar certifier whose personal reputation substitutes or vouches for the unknowable qualities of the bank as an institution." The procedure of banking is somehow unknowable (and hence untrustable), and so the locus of trust is on a particular individual, generally the manager, who functions as a certifier – or perhaps, "certifier before the era of brand ambassador" (cf. Mazzarella 2002).

Once again, the respective franchise models of brandism and bazaarism offer some clarification. In brandism's franchise model, the locus of trust is the corporation, not the individual owner. Think McDonald's. It would be rare for a consumer to even know the owner of a particular McDonald's, although becoming an owner requires one to jump through an enormous number of proverbial hoops and make an initial down payment of a *minimum* of $500,000, which must come from non-borrowed personal resources.[41] In this top-down model, an owner of an individual store is subsumed within the corporate body, so trust is directed toward an inanimate construct not an animate person.

In bazaarism's franchise model, however, the locus of trust is the individual owner, not the corporation. Think Lakshmi general stores. While customers might, to some extent, know Lakshmi – as in, they are her devotees – their trust is generally directed toward individual shopkeepers. In this bottom-up model, owners of an individual store are not subsumed within the corporate body, so trust is directed toward an animate person – a human being – and not an inanimate construct.

Even now in the bazaars of Banaras – even when the procedure of a business is knowable, as per Schwecke – personal reputation is of paramount importance. For example, Kalu's shop in Chowk, considered by many to sell the finest samosas in the area, has no signboard; in fact, it has no name at all. Kalu's shop is simply known by the name of the original proprietor, even though the eponymous Kalu has now passed away and his sons run the store. The shop has generic statues of Lakshmi and Ganesha and images of Shiva, rendering the space even

---

[41] See corporate.mcdonalds.com/corpmcd/franchising/faq.html.

more anonymous than would their absence. The samosas are made elsewhere and only sold at the shop, so it isn't possible to observe the procedure of their making. The locus of trust is in the product – "taste and see for yourself" (*khā ke dekho*), one is told – and this trust is augmented by the Kalu's "good name," which his sons have inherited and augmented. Such named-yet-unnamed shops are common in the Pakka Mahal. And considering that divine affiliates have generic names, like Lakshmi General Store, rather than ones that offer the "differentiation" or "distinctiveness" prized by brandism, they might be similarly classed as named-yet-undernamed.

As my informants in the bazaar repeatedly emphasized, trust (in the reputational register) is the most crucial commodity in the city; it is the substratum that allows for much of the business in the city to take place. Trust, in fact, is even more than this: it is an active element, crucial for cultivating and maintaining networks that tie the city and its inhabitants together (Rotman 2014). When one enters Raj Bandhu, one of Banaras's premier sweetshops, located in the heart of the Pakka Mahal, one is greeted with a sign: *keval āp kā viśvās chāhiye*, "Your trust is all that matters." It could also be the city's motto.[42]

Perhaps this isn't surprising. In the bazaars of Banaras, there is little reliance on police or courts, as neither of them functions particularly well,[43] and since brandism has yet to make great inroads, there are few nationally recognized brands to rely on. And so in a world where the quality and price of products are not enforced by formal law, and where one has little recourse to the offices or officers of the state to provide assurances, some form of "trust" is essential to facilitate commerce.

---

[42] The idea that trust is crucial for the proper functioning of a social order is hardly new in India. It is evident in the *Mahābhārata* (Bowles 2007: 252–62), where the idea is also wonderfully parodied when a cat and a mouse try to outfox each other. As the mouse explains to the cat: "The teachings on politics are best summarized by the word 'distrust.' Therefore, distrust your fellow man. It's your own best policy" (Sukthankar et al. 1933–1959: xii 136.187; cf. trans. Fitzgerald 2003: 522).

[43] For example, Jolie Wood (2013: 84) notes that in Banaras "institutions of the state, such as the administration and police, effectively encourage the use of agitation to make demands by ultimately making or at least promising concessions" rather than encouraging individuals to follow "normal procedural channels. ... The Hindi proverb recited by several respondents, *jab tak bachha nahin rota, ma usko doodh nahin pilati hai* [As long as a child isn't crying, a mother isn't going to give him milk] is evidently true."

Figure 9.4 Hara Gaori Bhander

And this is one reason why shopkeepers are so keen to affiliate themselves with divinity. The locus of trust is oneself, but a key component of one's trustworthiness is one's devotion, for reputation in the bazaar is inextricably linked to religiosity. For example, near Kedarnath, one of the most revered Shiva temples in Banaras, which itself is thought to be Shiva's city, there is a famous sweet shop called Hara Gaori Bhander (Figure 9.4). The original proprietor's name was Hari, and his wife's name was Gaori, so the shop is named almost eponymously, but not quite. The owner switched his name from Hari (which is a name for Vishnu) to Hara (which is a name for Shiva) to better appeal to the neighborhood's Shaivite customers. Notice, too, that his wife's name, Gaori, is also a name for Shiva's wife, so the shop becomes yet one more divine affiliate.

"Studies of Indian traders in general," Jonathan Parry (1989: 70) notes, "suggest that a reputation for piety is a hard commercial asset essential for establishing a merchant's credit-worthiness." In other words, one is more likely to extend trust and credit to those traders who are presumed to be pious – like Hari/Hara above – for their trustworthiness and creditworthiness are correlated with their piety. Not surprisingly, then, *viśvās* is closely affiliated with *śraddhā* – "faith," "piety," or "belief" – with the former frequently being used to define the latter,[44] and both terms articulating "an economy of exchange" (de Certeau 1985: 192).[45] One extends

---

[44] This is the case in the Vedānta tradition of Śaṅkara (Sawai 1987) and Gauḍīya Vaiṣṇavism (Edelman 2015). Elsewhere the two are paired, as in they are in the benedictory verses to Tulsidās's *Rāmcaritmānas* (Lutgendorf 2016: 2, verse 2).

[45] Michel de Certeau (1985: 195) posits a contractual nature for forms of belief such as *viśvās* and *śraddhā*. As Donald Lopez (1998: 239) explains, "under this contract, the believer, in a position of inferiority to the object of belief, gives

"trust" and "faith" with the expectation of some future gain, be it money or merit, goodwill or grace. *Viśvās* is distinguished from *andhviśvās* – "blind faith" or "superstition" – for it comes with a sense of surety that one will recoup one's investment, and with interest. And considering that *viśvās* derives from *vi-* plus root *śvas*, "to breathe," one can surmise that this surety allows one to "breathe a sigh of relief."

But having too much piety or misplaced piety may be viewed with suspicion or distrust, indicative of zealotry or bad faith. There is some expectation that there should be a match between one's piety and one's practice, between one's interior religious life and one's external religious deeds. In the bazaarism of Banaras, piety allows for certain form of ritual "play" (*līlā*), which includes dressing up as the gods and dramatically re-enacting important moments in their lives, as with Ram Lila and Ras Lila, which celebrate the deeds of Rama and Krishna, respectively. The month-long performance of Ram Lila in the suburb of Ramnagar is especially esteemed, and for many of the actors and attendees, it "is not a theatre of make believe but of hyper-reality" (Schechner 1993: 133).[46] The pious, as it were, can play at and with divinity, all in good faith.

In brandism, however, the parameters for public displays of piety are more narrowly conceived and more rigorously policed – legally, with regard to brand and trademark infringement (Gangjee 2008), and morally, with charges of "insincerity" (Haeri 2017)[47] and "hurt religious sentiments" (Vishwanath 2016).[48] From such a perspective,

something away in the hope of getting something back, not now, but in the future. In order for the contractual relation to be maintained, there must be the expectation of some return on the initial investment, a surety of some salvation, and this in turn depends on the presumption of the ability of the object of belief to guarantee the loan." For more on *śraddhā* as such a practice, see Rotman (2009: 23–62).

[46] For more on the Ram Lila at Ramnagar, see Hess (1983); Lutgendorf (1991).

[47] Following Haeri (2017: 123–4): "Sincerity, a concept held to be central to the formation of the Protestant liberal subject, is achieved when feelings, thoughts, and intentions are matched by exterior, spontaneous speech that expresses that interiority without the mediation of persons, things, and other people's words. . . . Defined in this way, sincerity is therefore centrally concerned with the relationship that the *individual* constructs with the divine."

[48] Such policing is often both legal and moral. Vishwanath (2016: 352, 360), for example, traces "the regulation of what Indian legal language describes as 'hurt religious sentiments' to its colonial origin, demonstrating that historically, the mandate of rulers has been to favor the powerful by reinforcing their capacity to silence the weak." And in certain recent cases, such as the case against Wendy

bazaarism's ritual play, like its commercial logic, is likely to seem perverse or even hypocritical. To be a merchant in Banaras in the eighteenth and nineteenth centuries, "one had to submit to the discipline of the relations of the bazaar, and this involved accepting the sumptuary and religious as well as commercial practices of its inhabitants." Foreign observers were thus "inclined to describe their behavior as 'queer' or 'irrational'" (Bayly 1983: 453). In the bazaars of Banaras, such forms of submission and acceptance are still the norm, as are the critiques of outsiders.

Generally missing from such critiques is the recognition that ritual and play are often, in fact, useful:

Counterintuitive to most senses of Enlightenment thought and sentiment . . . ritual acts and practitioners are not after all hypocritical because they give external signs for an internal state that might not be present. . . . As structured duality, ritual encompasses the ambiguity of life much better than [the anti-ritualistic mode of] sincerity can. It allows one to "play" with such ambiguity in a manner precluded by sincerity's undue concern with the authenticity of one's actions and beliefs. (Seligman et al. 2008: 113)

Bazaarism, in other words, has a logic and practice that works, and maybe even works well, even if from the outside it seems "queer" or "irrational," "counterintuitive" or "insincere." And hence the need (and likely failure and futility) of rejoinders and apologies on its behalf. Attempts to bridge (or defy) the gap between brandism and bazaarism and explain the "half-forgotten vernacular" are likely to fall short. Sometimes words fail.

In the end, Jawed Habib never tried to explain the logic of his "Gods too visit JH salon" advertisement; instead, in a video of himself that he posted on Twitter, he blames the advertisement on a franchise partner in Calcutta that printed it without his permission. The sentiments of many were hurt, he observes, so, of course, it was a mistake. He has been working for twenty-five years, he continues, signaling his long-standing reputation. The errant deed of one franchisee has clearly put his reputation, and the reputation of the whole franchise, at risk. Then he explains that he has, in fact, only one religion – that of scissors. No mention is made of Islam or Hinduism, but his piety is nonetheless

Doniger's *The Hindus: An Alternative History*, "those sentiments are deployed to preserve high-caste, Hindu majoritarian prerogatives by means of the implicit threat of violence." See also Nussbaum (2014).

confirmed.[49] And then he apologizes, making clear that he had no intention of hurting anyone.[50] A few minutes later, he Tweeted again, reiterating his intentions and his sincerity: "Dear All, we respect your sentiments as we apologize sincerely. It was not to hurt you at all."[51] The religion of scissors picks no sides and picks no fights.[52]

The Network of Bazaarism

So why not replace bazaarism with brandism, informal law with formal law, trust with seeming surety? Why not abandon the "irrational" and "counterintuitive"? I asked a variety of people in the bazaar the following question: "If the bazaar could be governed by an honest, efficient, and well-regulated police force and court system, would you embrace the change?" The large majority said "no," and many were forceful in their refutations.[53] As one silk merchant told me, the bazaar creates a situation

[49] Habib comes from an elite lineage of barbers – his grandfather was the official barber to the President of India and cut the hair of many dignitaries – and his education was distinctly nonparochial. He studied French at Jawaharlal Nehru University (JNU) and then, at his father's bidding, hairdressing at the Morris International School in London. In presenting himself and his company, Habib focuses not on religion but on science, as both his culture and method, as in his online Company Profile: "We've evolved together as a family over the last three generations and have espoused a culture of science and understanding that is used to style hair. Our employees are our assets who are meticulously trained on the innumerable scientific methods of hair cutting and styling that would directly benefit our treasured customers. To be even more specific, the methodology that we follow is what we call science-based styling and not just styling based on products" (jawedhabib.co.in/company-profile/).

[50] Jawed Habib, September 5, 2017 (twitter.com/JH_JawedHabib/status/905021957787140096).

[51] Jawed Habib, September 5, 2017 (twitter.com/JH_JawedHabib/status/905024087168212992).

[52] Until recently. On April 22, 2019, Jawed Habib joined the Hindu nationalist Bharatiya Janata Party (BJP). Referencing the party's campaign slogan "I too am a Watchman" (*Main Bhi Chowkidar*), he said, "Until today, I was a watchman of hair. Now I have become a watchman of the nation" (*Aaj tak main baalon ka chowkidar tha. Aaj mein desh ka chowkidar ban gaya hoon*). See *Asian News International*, April 22, 2019 (twitter.com/ANI/status/1120313719689502720/photo/1).

[53] And yet many of inhabitants of the bazaar have now embraced Prime Minister Modi and what Schwecke (personal communication) calls his "well-policed but highly interfering system of state authority into Indian markets." Again following Schwecke: "Power had been perceived to be in the hands of distant elites, as it was in eighteenth century Banaras, when Delhi was far-away, the representative of Delhi was sitting in Lucknow, and the local strongman was

in which people must interact with one another and must find "trust" in order to survive. This means that people must make common cause with others, and this is the basis of the social order. Amitabh, the bag seller whom I mentioned previously, was more apocalyptic: "If formal law replaces trust in Banaras," he said, and then paused, contemplating that possibility, "it is the end of humanity."

To put a more academic gloss on their comments, one might say that in the bazaar trust engenders (and is engendered by) so-called "associational engagements," which are informal and voluntary, and these create a form of cohesion and solidarity among otherwise unaffiliated shopkeepers and residents. These affiliations are not based on preexisting solidarities, such as affinities of caste or ethnicity; they are diverse and constitutive, forging solidarities where there was none. They are a heterogeneous outlier among the many "ethnically homogeneous communities who have built prosperous networks of commerce without relying on formal court ordering," like orthodox Jewish diamond merchants in New York (Richman 2006: 409), Chinese family businesses in Southeast Asia (Weidenbaum & Hughes 1996), and Shvetambar Jains in the emerald industry in Jaipur (Babb 2013). Writing of the bazaars of Banaras in the eighteenth and nineteenth centuries, Bayly (2011: 117) offers this explanation:

It is difficult to see how caste in any sense could have been the prime parameter of mercantile organization in complex cities [such as Banaras]. Forms of arbitration, market control, brokerage, neighbourhood communities, and above all conceptions of mercantile honour and credit breached caste boundaries, however construed, and imposed wider solidarities on merchant people.[54]

Imposing "wider solidarities" fosters community ties, not communal ones, building heterogeneous networks of mercantile trust rather than

kept out of the bazaar as much as possible and restricted to [nearby] Ramnagar. What changed was that Modi was supposed to be *their* man, and the rules he would make were supposed to be in *their* favor." Instructive here are the reactions of bazaar residents to the building of the Kashi Vishwanath Temple corridor and the more than 250 buildings that have been razed in the process. See, for example, Agarwal (2019); Srivathsan (2019).

[54] Even if caste is not "the prime parameter of mercantile organization," it still plays an important role in Banaras, as it does throughout most of India, in the organization of long-distance trade and credit networks (Damodaran 2008; Harriss-White 2003; Munshi 2016) and in the development of camaraderie if not civil society (Basile 2016; Basile & Harriss-White 2000; Chari 2004).

simply coopting the trust that already exists within a community and extending it to mercantile activities.[55] Furthermore, this kind of trust network – in an example of what Mark Granovetter (1983) calls "the strength of weak ties" – has been shown to be an effective bulwark against communal violence:

"Why does communal violence take place?" Varshney (2002) sought to answer the question by comparing Hindu–Muslim relations in six cities of India. Substantively, the main conclusion was that the presence or absence of inter-ethnic, or inter-communal, civic organizations – business associations, professional organizations, labor unions, political parties, reading clubs, sports clubs, film clubs, nongovernmental organizations (NGOs), and poli- tical parties – was critical to explaining why some cities had chronic ethno- communal violence, while others, despite huge provocations, remained always, or nearly always, peaceful. Integrated associational life allows strong ties to be formed across communities, acting as a serious constraint over the polarizing strategies of those groups that would benefit from violence, including political parties and organizations. (Varshney & Gubler 2013: 156)[56]

So maybe Amitabh's apocalyptic warning wasn't so far off. While communal violence has recently torn apart many communities in North India, Banaras has remained largely unscathed.[57]

---

[55] Francesca Trivellato examines a forty-two-year business partnership (1704–1746) between two Sephardic Jewish families, Ergas and Silvera, and as their activities show, "in order to work effectively, C. A. Bayly's 'communities of mercantile trust' did not have to be homogenous in ethnic or religious terms. Even among Sephardim, a pledge or a threat was only believable when expressed in a context that lent it credence. In fact, it may be better to refer to 'networks of mercantile trust' to dispel the consensual overtone that the term *community* carries" (Trivellato 2009: 273).

[56] Shashi Tharoor (2002), in a review of Varshney's book, offers a telling example: "Varshney has no illusions about how riots are instigated and manipulated: whatever the proximate trigger for violence, there is always a politician with an axe to grind, pulling the strings, inflaming passions, exploiting the victims for purely political ends. But his point remains that the chances for success of such politicians (he calls the breed 'riot-entrepreneurs') would be remarkably lower if there is vigorous and communally-integrated civic life, not just through everyday casual contact but through formal associations that consolidate the mutual engagement of the two communities. The Hindus of Varanasi would not attack the Muslim artisans who make the masks and effigies for the annual Ram Lila, even if an irresponsible and bigoted politician egged them on to do so."

[57] As Engineer (1992: 510) notes: "There were practically no communal riots in Benaras from 1947 to 1966 but from 1966 to 1991, i.e. 25 years, there have been about 12 communal riots." And yet since then there has been none, even as the

But there are also more prosaic benefits to such trust networks. Ajit, a middle-aged professional in Banaras, recently explained to me how he encourages his wife to shop at a variety of local stores, developing a relationship with numerous shopkeepers so that she can extend her and, by association, their social network. But she is an introvert and finds serial shopping and socializing tiring, and wishes instead to patronize a single store, preferably one that would afford her more anonymity. Ajit claims that the investment of time and energy is worthwhile to create a social safety net; his wife demurs, claiming that she doesn't need its benefits. "But how can she know for sure?" Ajit asked rhetorically. "So many things can happen! And there are some things money can't buy."

Like this, for example. In an article describing his father's demise from a brain hemorrhage, Siddharth Mukherjee (2018: 30–32) offers a vivid account of the extraordinary dividends an investment in the bazaar's social network can yield:

Oh, and he loved markets. Malls, particularly American ones, depressed him: to shop without confrontation was to die without a battle. When signs reading "FIXED PRICE" began to appear in Delhi's shopping arcades – mainly to fend off inveterate bargain hounds like him – he saw it as a symbol of the impending end of civilization. But he never met a man with a pushcart whom he didn't give his heart to. Perhaps it was fated, then, that the first of his falls, more than a year earlier, occurred as he made his way back from the neighborhood market with a bag of onions in each hand; that the first responders were fruit and vegetable venders who knew him by name and knew exactly where he lived; that they brought him home, like slightly banged-up royalty, on a repurposed fruit cart.

[And when he could no longer go outside] the fruit and vegetable sellers began to turn up at home. The daytime nurse – a scraggly young man nicknamed Bishnu: the god, among other things, of maintenance and preservation – made a habit of propping him up in his rocking chair on the balcony every morning, and having the various venders congregate below like a worshipful throng. My father was delighted to be back among the believers. He would banter with them from above – a king under house arrest, but a king nonetheless berating them about their prices; protesting the abysmal quality of the eggplants; asking why he, at his age, must suffer the sins of their bruised cauliflowers; and why the

population has more than tripled and the city has become a center for Hindutva politics (Rehman 2018). For more, see Malik (1994); Raman (2010: 134–98); Williams (2007).

fish was never quite fresh. It was a small miracle: Mr. Mukherjee could no longer go to the market, and so the market came to Mr. Mukherjee.

Robert Orsi (2005: 6) proposes configuring religion as "a network of relationships between heaven and earth involving humans of all ages and many different sacred figures together." And, in that case, Siddharth Mukherjee's reflections need not be taken metaphorically. His father had faith in the bazaar. He engaged "the believers" who worked there in the give-and-take that constitutes the bazaar's central rite, gaining admission into a network that is embedded in an alternate "moral universe" with its own "economy of exchange," and made to feel like royalty, blessed with retainers who served with devotion. This is bazaarism as a religion unto itself, and it hasn't yielded to brandism, and perhaps never will. A small miracle indeed.

References

Adcock, CS 2016, "Violence, Passion, and the Law: A Brief History of Section 295A and Its Antecedents," *Journal of the American Academy of Religion*, 84, 2: 337–51.

Agarwal, K 2019, "In Modi's Varanasi, the Vishwanath Corridor Is Trampling Kashi's Soul," *The Wire*, March 8 (thewire.in/politics/kashi-vishwanath-corridor-up-bjp).

Aronczyk, M 2007, "New and Improved Nations: Branding National Identity," in C Calhoun & R Sennett (eds.) *Practicing Culture*, Routledge, New York, pp. 105–29.

Arvidsson, A 2005, "Brands: A Critical Perspective," *Journal of Consumer Culture*, 5, 2: 235–58.

Arvidsson, A 2006, *Brands: Meaning and Value in Media Culture*, Routledge, London.

Babb, LA 2013, *Emerald City: The Birth and Evolution of an Indian Gemstone Industry*, State University of New York Press, Albany.

Basile, E 2016, "Impact of Caste on Production Relations in Arni: A Gramscian Analysis," in B Harriss-White (ed.) *Middle India and Urban Development: Four Decades of Change*, Springer India, New Delhi, pp. 29–64.

Basile, E & Harriss-White, B 2000, "Corporative Capitalism: Civil Society and the Politics of Accumulation in Small Town India," Working Paper, no. 38, Queen Elizabeth House, Oxford University.

Baudh, S 2017, "Invisibility of 'Other' Dalits and Silence in the Law," *Biography*, 40, 1: 222–43.

Bayly, CA 1983, *Rulers, Townsmen and Bazaars: North Indian Society in the Age of British Expansion 1770–1870*, Cambridge University Press, Cambridge.

Bayly, CA 2011, "Merchant Communities: Identities and Solidarities," in MM Kudaisya (ed.) *The Oxford India Anthology of Business History*, Oxford University Press, New Delhi, pp. 99–121.

Belting, H 1994, *Likeness and Presence: A History of the Image Before the Era of Art*, trans. Edmund Jephcott, University of Chicago Press, Chicago.

Bolin, G & Sthålberg, P 2010, "Between Community and Commodity: Nationalism and Nation Branding," in A Roosvall & IS Moring (eds.) *Communicating the Nation: National Topographies of Global Media Landscapes*, Nordicom, Goteborg, pp. 79–101.

Bourdieu, P & Bourdieu, MC 2004, "The Peasant and Photography," trans. and adapted by Loïc Wacquant and Richard Nice, *Ethnography*, 5, 4: 601–616.

Bowles, A 2007, *Dharma, Disorder and the Political in Ancient India: The Apaddharmaparvan of the Mahābhārata*, Brill, Leiden.

Burke, T 1996, *Lifebuoy Men, Lux Women: Commodification, Consumption and Cleanliness in Modern Zimbabwe*, Duke University Press, Durham.

de Certeau, M 1985, "What We Do When We Believe," in M Blonski (ed.) *On Signs*, Johns Hopkins University Press, Baltimore, pp. 192–202.

Chari, S 2004, *Fraternal Capital: Peasant-Workers, Self-Made Men, and Globalization in Provincial India*, Stanford University Press, Stanford.

Clark, KA 2004, *Brandscendence: Three Essential Elements of Enduring Brands*, Dearborn Trade Publishing, Chicago.

Comaroff, JL & Comaroff, J 2009, *Ethnicity, Inc.*, University of Chicago, Chicago.

Coombe, R 1998, *The Cultural Life of Intellectual Properties*, Duke University Press, Durham.

Damodaran, H 2008, *India's New Capitalists: Caste, Business, and Industry in a Modern State*, Palgrave Macmillan, Basingstoke.

Daniel, EV 1984, *Fluid Signs: Being a Person the Tamil Way*, University of California Press, Berkeley.

Datawala, S 2007, *Matchbook: Indian Match Box Labels*, Tara Publishing, Chennai.

Domosh, M 2003, "Pickles and Purity: Discourse of Food, Empire, and Work in the Turn-of-the-Century USA," *Social and Cultural Geography*, 4, 1: 7–26.

Dotz, W 2007, *Light of India: A Conflagration of Indian Matchbox Art*, Ten Speed Press, Berkeley.

Dzenovska, D 2005, "Remaking the Nation of Latvia: Anthropological Perspectives on Nation Branding," *Place Branding and Public Diplomacy*, 1, 2: 173–86.

Edelmann, J 2015, "The Cause of Devotion in Gauḍīya Vaiṣṇava Theology: Devotion (*bhakti*) as the Result of Spontaneously (*yadṛcchayā*) Meeting a Devotee (*sādhu-saṅga*)," *Journal of the American Oriental Society*, 135, 1: 49–69.

Edwards, L & Ramamurthy, A 2017, "(In)credible India? A Critical Analysis of India's Nation Branding," *Communication, Culture & Critique*, 10: 322–43.

Elison, W 2018, *The Neighborhood of Gods: The Sacred and the Visible at the Margins of Bombay*, University of Chicago Press, Chicago.

Elison, W, Novetzke, C, & Rotman, A 2015, *Amar Akbar Anthony: Bollywood, Brotherhood, and the Nation*, Harvard University Press, Cambridge.

Engineer, AA 1992, "Benaras Rocked by Communal Violence," *Economic and Political Weekly*, 27, 10/11: 509–11.

Fatovic, C 2008, "The Political Theology of Prerogative: The Jurisprudential Miracle in Liberal Constitutional Thought," *Perspectives on Politics*, 6, 3: 487–501.

Fitzgerald, J 2003, *The Mahābhārata, vol. 7: 11. The Book of the Women, 12. The Book of Peace, Part One*, University of Chicago Press, Chicago.

Forge, A 1973, "Style and Meaning in Sepik Art," in A Forge (ed.) *Primitive Art and Society*, Oxford University Press, New York, pp. 169–92.

Foster, R 2007, "The Work of the New Economy: Consumers, Brands, and Value Creation," *Cultural Anthropology*, 22, 4: 707–31.

Gangjee, D 2008, "Polymorphism of Trademark Dilution in India," *Transnational Law and Contemporary Problems*, 17, 3: 611–30.

Geary, D 2013, "Incredible India in a Global Age: The Cultural Politics of Image Branding in Tourism," *Tourist Studies*, 13, 1: 36–61.

Gerrans, P 2005, "Tacit Knowledge, Rule Following and Pierre Bourdieu's Philosophy of Social Science," *Anthropological Theory*, 5, 1: 53–74.

Giannuzzi, L 2000, *Cock: Indian Firework Art*, Westzone Publishing, London.

Gooptu, N 2009, "Neoliberal Subjectivity, Enterprise Culture and New Workplaces: Organised Retail and Shopping Malls in India," *Economic and Political Weekly*, 44, 22: 45–54.

Graan, A 2013, "Counterfeiting the Nation: Skopje 2014 and the Politics of Nation Branding in Macedonia," *Cultural Anthropology*, 28, 1: 161–79.

Grainge, PD 2000, "Advertising the Archive: Nostalgia and the (Post) National Imaginary," *American Studies*, 41, 2/3: 137–57.

Granovetter, M 1983, "The Strength of Weak Ties: A Network Theory Revisited," *Sociological Theory*, 1: 201–33.

Greenberg, J & Naím, M 2001, "The FP Interview: McAtlas Shrugged," *Foreign Policy*, 124: 26–37.

Haeri, N 2017, "Unbundling Sincerity: Language, Mediation, and Interiority in Comparative Perspective," *Hau: Journal of Ethnographic Theory*, 7, 1: 123–38.

Halbfass, W 1988, *India and Europe: An Essay in Understanding*, State University of New York Press, Albany.

Harish, R 2010, "Brand Architecture in Tourism Branding: The Way Forward for India," *Journal of Indian Business Research*, 2, 3: 153–65.

Hariss-White, B 2003, *India Working: Essays on Society and Economy*, Cambridge University Press, Cambridge.

Harrison, ES 1968, *Our Scottish District Checks*, National Association of Scottish Woolen Manufacturers, Edinburgh.

Hess, L 1983, "Ram Lila: The Audience Experience," in M Thiel-Horstmann (ed.) *Bhakti in Current Research*, Dietrich Reimer Verlag, Berlin, pp. 171–94.

Hiltebeitel, A 2011, *Dharma: Its Early History in Law, Religion, and Narrative*, Oxford University Press, Oxford.

Jain, K 2007, *Gods in the Bazaar: The Economies of Indian Calendar Art*, Duke University Press, Durham.

Jansen, SC 2008, "Designer Nation: Neo-Liberal Nation Branding – Brand Estonia," *Social Identities*, 14, 1: 121–42.

Josephson, JA 2012, *The Invention of Religion in Japan*, University of Chicago Press, Chicago.

Kalhan, A 2007, "Impact of Malls on Small Shops and Hawkers," *Economic and Political Weekly*, 42, 22: 2063–6.

Kant, A 2009, *Branding India – An Incredible Story*, HarperCollins, Noida.

Kaur, R 2012, "Nation's Two Bodies: Rethinking the Idea of 'New' India and its Other," *Third World Quarterly*, 33, 4: 603–21.

Kerrigan, F, Shivanandan, J, & Hede, AM 2012, "Nation Branding: A Critical Appraisal of Incredible India," *Journal of Macromarketing*, 32, 3: 319–27.

Keshavarzian, A 2007, *Bazaar and State in Iran: The Politics of the Tehran Marketplace*, Cambridge University Press, Cambridge.

Koehn, N 2001, *Brand New: How Entrepreneurs Earned Consumers' Trust from Wedgwood to Dell*, Harvard Business School Press, Boston.

Kotler, P & Armstrong, G 2016, *Principles of Marketing (Global Edition)*, 16th ed., Pearson, Harlow.

Kumar, N 1988, *The Artisans of Banaras: Popular Culture and Identity, 1880–1986*, Princeton University Press, Princeton.

Lindstrom, M 2008, *Buyology: Truth and Lies about Why We Buy*, Doubleday, New York.

Lopez, D 1998, *Prisoners of Shangri-La: Tibetan Buddhism and the West*, University of Chicago Press, Chicago.

Losche, D 1995, "The Sepik Gaze: Iconographic Interpretation of Abelam Form," *Social Analysis*, 38: 47–60.

Lury, C 2004, *Brands: The Logos of the Global Economy*, Routledge, London.

Lutgendorf, P 1991, *The Life of a Text: Performing the Rāmcaritmānas of Tulsidas*, University of California Press, Berkeley.

Lutgendorf, P 2005, "Who Wants to Be a Goddess? Jai Santoshi Maa Revisited," *Chakra*, 3: 72–112.

Lutgendorf, P 2016, *The Epic of Ram, vol. 1*, Murty Classical Library of India, Harvard University Press, Cambridge.

Malik, D 1994, "Three Riots in Varanasi, 1989–90 to 1992," *South Asia Bulletin*, 14, 1: 53–6.

Mattern, S 2008, "Font of a Nation: Creating a National Graphic Identity for Qatar," *Public Culture*, 20, 3: 479–96.

Mazzarella, W 2002, "Cindy at the Taj: Cultural Enclosure and Corporate Potentateship in an Era of Globalization," in DP Mines & S Lamb (eds.) *Everyday Life in South Asia*, Indiana University Press, Bloomington, pp. 387–99.

Mazzarella, W 2003, *Shoveling Smoke: Advertising and Globalization in Contemporary India*, Duke University Press, Durham.

Mazzarella, W 2010, "Branding the Mahatma: The Untimely Provocation of Gandhian Publicity," *Cultural Anthropology*, 25, 1: 1–39.

Medhasananda, S 2002, *Varanasi at the Crossroads: A Panoramic View of Early Modern Varanasi and the Story of Its Transition*, Ramakrishna Mission, Institute of Culture, Kolkata.

Menski, W 2009, "Indian Secular Pluralism and Its Relevance for Europe," in R Grillo et al. (eds.) *Legal Practice and Cultural Diversity*, Ashgate Publishing Limited, Aldershot, pp. 31–47.

Menzies, R 2004, "Lucky You; Lucky Me: Revival Based on Women's Ritual Power in Vrat Kathas," *Chakra*, 2: 58–69.

Mongia, S 2005, *Brand India*, B.R. Publishing Corporation, New Delhi.

Mukherjee, S 2018, "My Father's Body, at Rest and in Motion," *The New Yorker*, January 8: 28–35.

Munshi, K 2016, "Caste Networks in the Modern Indian Economy," in SM Dev & PG Babu (eds.) *Development in India: Micro and Macro Perspectives*, Springer India, New Delhi, pp. 13–37.

Nakassis, CV 2013, "Brands and Their Surfeits," *Cultural Anthropology*, 28, 1: 111–26.

Nanda, M 2011, *The God Market: How Globalization Is Making India More Hindu*, Monthly Review Press, New York.

Nandy, A 1995, "The Discreet Charms of Indian Terrorism," in *The Savage Freud and Other Essays on Possible and Retrievable Selves*, Princeton University Press, Princeton, pp. 1–31.

Nussbaum, M 2014, "Law for Bad Behaviour," *Indian Express*, February 22 (indianexpress.com/article/opinion/columns/law-for-bad-behaviour/).

Orsi, RA 2005, *Between Heaven and Earth: The Religious Worlds People Make and the Scholars Who Study Them*, Princeton University Press, Princeton.

Parameswaran, A 2014, *For God's Sake: An Adman on the Business of Religion*, Portfolio, New Delhi.

Parry, J 1989, "On the Moral Perils of Exchange," in J Parry & M Bloch (eds.) *Money and the Morality of Exchange*, Cambridge University Press, Cambridge, pp. 64–93.

Pearson, AM 1996, *Because It Gives Me Peace of Mind: Ritual Fasts in the Religious Lives of Hindu Women*, State University of New York Press, Albany.

Peirce, CS 1885 [1993], "One, Two, Three: Fundamental Categories of Thought and of Nature," in CJW Kloesel et al. (eds.) *Writings of Charles S. Peirce: A Chronological Edition, vol. 5*, Indiana University Press, Bloomington, pp. 242–7.

Pinney, C 1997, *Camera Indica: The Social Life of Indian Photographs*, University of Chicago Press, Chicago.

Puri, A 2018, "The Rise and Growth of Indian Malls," *Deccan Herald*, June 14 (www.deccanherald.com/business/economy-business/rise-and-growth-indian-malls-676834.html).

Raman, V 2010, *The Warp and the Weft: Community and Gender Identity Among Banaras Weavers*, New Delhi, Routledge.

Rangnekar, SD 2005, *Realizing Brand India: The Changing Face of Contemporary India*, Rupa and Company, New Delhi.

Rehman, M 2018, "Explaining the Inconvenient Truths of Indian Political Behavior: Hindutva, Modi, and Muslim Voters in 2014," in M Rehman (ed.) *Rise of Saffron Power: Reflections on Indian Politics*, Routledge, New York, pp. 168–90.

Richman, BD 2006, "How Community Institutions Create Economic Advantage: Jewish Diamond Merchants in New York," *Law & Social Inquiry*, 31, 2: 383–420.

Rocher, L 1978, "Hindu Conceptions of Law," *Hastings Law Journal*, 29, 6: 1283–305.

Rotman, A 2009, *Thus Have I Seen: Visualizing Faith in Early Indian Buddhism*, Oxford University Press, New York.

Rotman, A 2010, "Baba's Got a Brand New Bag: Indian Jute Bags and Exotic Others," in A Sinift (ed.) *5 year Plan: Literary Supplement*, Krishna Printers, Jaipur, pp. 31–55.

Rotman, A 2014, "In Varanasi We Trust," in *The City and South Asia*, Harvard South Asia Institute, Cambridge, pp. 53–5.

Sawai, Y 1987, "The Nature of Faith in the Śaṅkaran Vedānta Tradition," *Numen*, 34, 1: 18–44.

Schechner, R 1993, "Striding Through the Cosmos: Movement, Belief, Politics, and Place in the Ramlila of Ramnagar," in *The Future of Ritual: Writings on Culture and Performance*, Routledge, London, pp. 131–83.

Seligman, AG, Weller, RP, Puett, MJ, & Simon, B 2008, *Ritual and Its Consequences: An Essay on the Limits of Sincerity*, Oxford University Press, New York.

Sen, S 2017, *Colonizing, Decolonizing, and Globalizing Kolkata: From a Colonial to a Post-Marxist City*, Amsterdam University Press, Amsterdam.

Smith, JZ 1988, *Imagining Religion: From Babylon to Jonestown*, University of Chicago Press, Chicago.

Srivathsan A 2019, "Varanasi, by Design; Vishwanath Dham and the Politics of Change," *The Hindu*, March 23 (www.thehindu.com/society/varanasi-by-design-vishwanath-dham-and-the-politics-of-change/article26607193.ece).

Sukthankar, VS et al. (eds.) 1933–1959, *Mahābhārata*, Bhandarkar Institute, Pune.

Surratt, G, Ligon, G, & Bird, W 2006, *Multi-Site Church Revolution: Being One Church in Many Locations*, Zondervan, Grand Rapids.

Tharoor, S 2002, "Violence and Its Manifestations," *The Hindu*, June 7 (www.thehindu.com/thehindu/mag/2002/07/07/stories/2002070700140300.htm).

Trivellato, F 2009, *The Familiarity of Strangers: The Sephardic Diaspora, Livorno, and Cross-Cultural Trade in the Early Modern Period*, Yale University Press, New Haven.

Uberoi, P 2003, "'Unity in Diversity?' Dilemmas of Nationhood in Indian Calendar Art," in S Ramaswamy (ed.) *Beyond Appearances? Visual Practices and Ideologies in Modern India*, Sage Publications, New Delhi, pp. 191–232.

Van Ham, P 2001, "The Rise of the Brand State: The Postmodern Politics of Image and Reputation," *Foreign Affairs*, 80, 5: 2–6.

Varshney, A 2002, *Ethnic Conflict and Civic Life: Hindus and Muslims in India*, Yale University Press, New Haven.

Varshney, A & Gubler, J 2013, "The State and Civil Society in Communal Violence: Sparks and Fires," in A Kohli & P Singh (eds.) *Routledge Handbook of Indian Politics*, Routledge, New York, pp. 155–66.

Viswanath, R 2016, "Economies of Offense: Hatred, Speech, and Violence in India," *Journal of the American Academy of Religion*, 84, 2: 352–63.

Volcic, Z & Andrejevic, M 2016, *Commercial Nationalism: Selling the Nation and Nationalizing the Sell*, Palgrave Macmillan, London.

Voyce, M 2007, "Shopping Malls in India: New Social 'Dividing Practices,'" *Economic and Political Weekly*, 42, 22: 2055–62.

Weidenbaum, M, & Hughes, S 1996, *The Bamboo Network: How Expatriate Chinese Entrepreneurs Are Creating a New Economic Superpower in Asia*, Simon & Schuster, New York.

Werth, L 1998, "The Saint Who Disappeared: Saints of the Wilderness in Pakistani Village Shrines," in P Werbner & H Basu (eds.) *Embodying Charisma: Modernity, Locality and Performance of Emotion in Sufi Cults*, Routledge, London, pp. 77–91.

Williams, P 2007, "Hindu Muslim Brotherhood: Exploring the Dynamics of Communal Relations in Varanasi, North India," *Journal of South Asian Development*, 2, 2: 153–76.

Woods, JMF 2013, "Protest, Politics, and the Middle Class in Varanasi," *Economic and Political Weekly*, 48, 13: 78–85.

Wyatt, A 2005, "Building the Temples of Postmodern India: Economic Constructions of National Identity," *Contemporary South Asia*, 14, 4: 465–80.

Yang, AA 1999, *Bazaar India: Markets, Society, and the Colonial State in Bihar*, University of California Press, Berkeley.

10 Black Money in India: Fighting Specters and Fostering Relations

AJAY GANDHI

Introduction

On a nondescript, cramped lane in central Mumbai, across from a construction-goods store stacked with plastic tubing, is Mr. Jayakar's shop. Next door, at a grains and pulses mill, a noisy, rumbling machine produces a perpetual cloud of flour that hovers, mist-like, in the street.[1] These establishments in a neighborhood called Matunga Labour Camp – or simply Labour Camp by residents – serve a lower-middle-class population. Most residents are migrants from other Indian states and work in the metropolis's many informal trades. Humble in size and features, the shop remains indispensable to their everyday lives. The man I call Mr. Jayakar operates this publicly subsidized ration shop, one of millions to be found throughout the country. They frequently sell staples such as flour, sugar, and lentils to those deemed under a state income threshold, i.e., "below the poverty line." Jayakar's establishment focuses on kerosene, usually used for lighting in rural areas without electricity and as cooking fuel in cities. Invariably, long lines of residents – generally women, elders, and children – wait with hard, dented plastic jugs for their allotment. Sometimes, because the shop's opening hours fluctuate at the operator's will, residents leave their jugs in a multicolored queue and depart to conduct other chores. They rematerialize on hearing rumors of imminent disbursement.

[1] The Max Planck Institute for the Study of Religious and Ethnic Diversity in Göttingen supported fieldwork for this project. Earlier versions of this chapter were presented in Leiden, Göttingen, and Zurich. I am grateful to the following for their constructive engagement with this material: Sebastian Schwecke, Leilah Vevaina, Radhika Gupta, Sanjukta Sunderason, Nira Wickramasinghe, Jens Zickgraf, Kushanava Choudhury, Geert de Neve, Henrike Donner, Douglas Haynes, Barbara Harriss-White, Suzanne Naafs, Daniela Vicherat-Mattar, Atreyee Sen, Olga Sooudi, Peter van der Veer, Maja Vodopivec, and Nate Roberts.

269

India's vast infrastructure of ration shops – termed the Public Distribution System (PDS) – comprises institutionalized and parallel systems of exchange, ambivalently tethered to money. Ration-card holders are prescribed, on a household basis, a monthly allotment of publicly procured goods. These are collected by beneficiaries, free or at a subsidized rate, on presentation of one's ration card or booklet.

Ration shops are typically thought to be unsavory places that are full of corruption (Gupta 2012: 96; Michelutti 2019: 186–7). Operators may be seen to divert state-procured and subsidized goods for sale in the open market. Reports abound of shops demanding higher rates for goods than is officially mandated, and bribes to access shortages of certain commodities. Cultural discourses reaffirming such tropes saturate popular film and documentaries. Films such as *Special 26* (2013), *Gulabi Gang* (2012), and *Raid* (2018) luxuriate in tax-evading profiteers exploiting public resources.

Some residents complain that Jayakar's attendants will not distribute their entitlement without a small bribe. Their sense is that they do not receive their kerosene entitlement, in quality or quantity, and that the operator, rather than the public, benefits most. Others tell of ration goods circulating in the locality in exchange for cash or something else. In an Indian ration shop, money and nonmonetary exchange intersect unpredictably. This constellation of official and unofficial transactions blurs the public-rational and secret-invisible.

Locals claim that Jayakar siphons off a part of state-subsidized kerosene and sells it on the black market, where it is mixed with higher-cost automotive fuels and lubricants. In this way, Jayakar seems to make "black money" out of his privileged access to a nonmonetized public good. This term encompasses income tainted by its illegitimate source, undeclared nature, and, when sent abroad, extra-territorial location. Whatever color Jayakar's money is, he has plenty of it, and he distributes it widely.

During my thirteen months of fieldwork in Labour Camp, between 2011 and 2017, I was exposed to equivocal readings of black money. As a moral critique rooted in notions of injustice and corruption, the area's residents understand it in spectral and pernicious terms. Here, money is spoken of as immaterial and illegitimate (Appadurai 2000; Dodd 2014). Yet a different perspective is provided when looking at Jayakar's various exchanges, investments, and donations. Money here serves as a hinge between transactional orders and therefore as a tangible expression of relational ties and social outcomes (Guyer 2004; Parry & Bloch 1989).

For example, I learned that Jayakar's money underwrites participation in speculative games, real-estate investments, the funding of family businesses, campaign support for municipal politicians, and donations toward religious temples and festivals. Labour Camp's ration-card holders, naturally, see unfairness in Jayakar's flexibility and freedom. Their sentiment echoes the national refrain about black money. It is associated with immorality and blamed for subverting development.[2] Money here serves a speculative discourse of ill-gotten wealth. Beyond the abstract moralism surrounding the rhetoric of black money, however, we need to probe how it is embedded in transactional life. From that vantage point, Jayakar's income lubricates a wide array of collaborations and commitments. His proceeds, we will see, underwrite kinship ventures, business ties, neighborhood festivities, and political investments. In this sense, black money fosters, rather than undermines, the unfolding of social relations.

Given this, we might ask some questions about this most elusive and inscrutable yet routinized and quotidian monetary form. What is black money, and why does it have such ubiquity and publicity? Is it best understood as a semiotic sign, whose relevance is primarily discursive and representational? Or is it more aptly understood as a medium, a value form whose significance lies in the domain of exchange and circulation? What are the moral, temporal, and spatial dimensions of black money? And how does it mediate between relational domains, transactional orders, and temporal horizons?

I seek to address these questions by outlining black money's pervasiveness in national debates, political finance, and ordinary exchange. In the following section, I discuss how it provides a window onto a cultural theory of money in India, shaped by nationalist and developmental discourses. At issue here is the semiotics of money. Black money, as a sign, may denote wealth that has tangible, material form, and simultaneously be conjured as a spectral, immaterial hoard. Although a symbolic or discursive approach illuminates cultural anxieties attending money, it is limited by a circularity that restricts a deeper

---

[2] See the language in government reports on black money described in detail in the next section (Acharya et al. 1985; Indian Ministry of Finance 2002; Wanchoo 1971). In the reports, black money is synonymous with superficial showiness and declining solidarity.

understanding of money's relationship to relationality, morality, and temporality.

To glean such details we might move, I suggest, to the arena of exchange, namely, the relational domains and transactional orders implied in its production and circulation. An ethnography of Jayakar's kerosene business and his other monetary activities illuminates the benefits of an exchange-based approach. In so doing, this chapter argues that black money, understood from one vantage point as a subversive threat to moral conduct and collective thriving, may also be seen as a hinge between transactional orders, and as indispensable to the maintenance of social, political, and religious life.

The Semiotics of Black Money: National and Moral Dimensions

Since the 1950s, public discourse in India has been replete with references to black money. This term denotes liquidity that is undeclared. Its common material expressions are cash, property, and gold. It can include capital obtained through illicit irregularities, such as large-scale bribery. It also obtains from routine, if dubious, forms of commerce, such as smuggling, gambling, and prostitution. In its most exaggerated iteration, black money suggests profits siphoned out of the country into offshore bank accounts.

Black money has mainly been studied with a view to policy. Some have tried to define its contours, often artificially excluding or simplifying income that is, in practice, used to refer to myriad forms simultaneously. For example, one study distinguishes between the realms of black income within a set time period, wealth that is immobile, and turnover that is extra-legal (Acharya et al. 1985: 6). In contrast, I show that black money's rapid circulation, and movement in and out of relational domains and transactional orders, makes this categorization somewhat artificial. Black money may refer to proceeds associated with various activities, moved across distinct geographies, and manifested in different forms. I seek to keep its polyvalent character intact, insofar as it is inherent to a wider sensibility surrounding money.

Black money can thus be thought of as a value form that differentiates and mediates. It can distinguish or connect subject and object, national and extra-territorial, moral and immoral, and spectral and material. For example, black money may signal the material and immaterial. Gold nuggets, penthouse apartments, and Bollywood films are tangible manifestations of its existence. Yet it is also an elusive specter, countless zeroes attached to a proxy offshore account. The discourse of black money further marks a regulated spatial sphere of exchange defined by the national border.[3] Finally, it specifies a distinction in moral character, between the upstanding and disreputable. In the class jockeying of India's urban elite, for example, status distinctions separate the salaried "professional" who earns taxed "white money," and the dubious "businessman" who lubricates his dealings with untaxed cash (Searle 2013: 273). In this stream of middleclass self-identification, the salaried professional's humility and sincerity are prized over the businessman's greed and recklessness.

Given all of this, in anthropological terms, we can comparatively categorize black money among a vast array of "adjectivally marked moneys" – hot, liquid, dirty, fast, bitter, polluted – used to parse certain types of liquidity (High 2013; Maurer 2006: 24; Shipton 1989). I focus on black money (*kala dhan* in Hindi) as the most ubiquitous articulation of such marked money in India. There are, however, terms that overlap with it. One such term is "speed money." This refers to bribes given by businesses or individuals to officials so as to expedite bureaucratic approvals and hasten public service delivery (Berenschot 2010: 889; Weinstein 2014: 128). Another expression, used for one-off and smaller bribes, is "money for tea and water" (*chai-paani ka paisa*). Synonyms for black money are similarly marked, such as "number-two money" (*do number ka paisa*).[4]

---

[3] It is worth emphasizing that the normative overlap between monetary circulation, territorial borders, and the nation-state is a historically contingent formulation. The notion of India (or *Bharat*) as a bounded national territory and homogenous financial and transactional space emerged in the late nineteenth century in both nationalist discourse and colonial bureaucratic and representational practices (Goswami 2004). Yet monetary flows exceed the imagined contours of a delimited India. For example, Indian merchant communities have long had an imprint elsewhere. Sindhis in Central Asia and Chettiars in Southeast Asia engaged in elaborate trading and moneylending activities that were transregional in scope, during the precolonial and colonial eras (Amrith 2013: 130; Markovits 2000: 82–3). As such, Indian monetary transactions have a longstanding mobility belied by putatively natural national borders.

[4] There are other suggestive Hindi terms for ill-gotten income. Young guides and commission brokers in North India, seen to engage in disreputable work, evoke talk of "bad money" (*galat paisa*), "cheating money" (*cheating ka paisa*), and "wicked money" (*haram ka paisa*) (Huberman 2012: 167).

Commentators suggest that black money first acquired public significance in India during the Second World War.[5] During this period, merchants and traders were thought to have amassed significant shortage-induced profits that remained hidden. As with previous instances of political emergency during colonial times, such as during famines, this war catalyzed accusations of hoarding and inspired government vigilance. Notably, state regulation of markets increased significantly during this late colonial period; quite likely black money does not appear in the archival record with any significance before this period because the state's regulatory interventions were not as intense before (Tomlinson 1979). This enhanced regulatory regime, distinct from early colonial rule, meant that a sphere of capital could be demarcated as illegal, and thus a whole swath of national capital termed black money could come into existence. As historians of twentieth-century India have shown, market players navigated a proliferating set of regulations, controls, permits, and licenses that were qualitatively different than those of the economic landscape prior to the 1940s (Chibber 2003; Das Gupta 2016).

After 1947, black money surfaced in terms of access and ability. Those with access to publicly controlled goods, the channels by which they were circulated, and other restricted, valuable, and non-monetized things (permits, licenses, jobs, student admissions, exams) could derive black money from their unauthorized sale. And those with the ability to skillfully circulate and convert money – often requiring networks of finance professionals, brokers, and smugglers – could invest, hide, launder, and thus transmute income.

In the 1950s and 1960s, black money acquired a prominent presence and was used to circumvent excise taxes, unfavorable exchange rates, and onerous import controls. It became ubiquitous in commercial transactions and national discourse. This was especially true after the late 1960s with the ascendance of left-wing populism within the dominant Congress party. During this period, a significant portion of exchange was done off the books. A segment of a transaction was conducted with

[5] The term "black money," given overlapping political histories and cultural affiliations in South Asia, is prevalent throughout the region. In Pakistan, Bangladesh, and Nepal, black money is a recurring feature of reports about corruption, illegal trades, and money laundering. At an analytical level, my argument about the equivocal evaluation of black money in India is echoed by Arild Ruud's ethnography (2011: 66) in rural Bangladesh. There, black money is seen as illegitimate and evidence of wider corruption, but also as an instrument that enables action and is integral to power's efficacy.

"white money," that is, bank drafts and taxable receipts. The larger balance was settled with black money, or undetectable cash transfer. Certain swaths of the economy were notoriously shaped by these conversions. For example, the burgeoning Hindi film industry, centered in Mumbai, expanded considerably after the 1940s, partly because it proved conducive for money laundering. Those with access to income gleaned in other markets – such as jewelers, property developers, commodity tradesmen, and brokers – could back particular filmstars, directors, and production houses. Capital generated elsewhere and invested in films thereby turned into white money (Booth 2008: 97–9). Indeed, black money has helped infuse the "speculation, solicitation, risk, and violence" that mark Bollywood (Appadurai 2000: 633).

During economic crises and periods of political upheaval, the state targeted those suspected of having black money. For example, during the 1975–1977 Emergency – a nearly two-year period when democratic conventions were suspended – the specter of black money loomed large. Laws were passed that mandated stiff penalties for black money holders, and tax collectors were empowered accordingly (Hewitt 2008: 128). Crackdowns on tax evaders, smugglers, hoarders, and profiteers figured prominently in state propaganda. *Yojana*, the Planning Commission periodical, for example, featured a government advertisement entitled "Drive against Black Money" which trumpeted efforts to uncover and declare hidden wealth (July 1, 1976: 30). This was a period of heightened inspections and audits, targeting those conducting unsanctioned forms of exchange.

Simultaneously, black money became indispensable to democratic politics. During the late 1960s, business regulations tightened, and, in 1969, amid populist measures such as bank nationalization, corporate contributions to political parties were banned. The Congress Party, then unchallenged, was a beneficiary of quiet strategic donations from large industrial houses (Chibber 2011: 284). This form of "briefcase politics" involved the exchange of government licenses or permits required for business in return for contributions ("number-two money") to the party coffers (Kochanek 1987: 1290). In the 1970s and 1980s, the discrepancy between legal election expenditure limits and the actual money spent during polls ballooned, with the deficit filled, to a great extent, by black money (Acharya et al. 1985: 239–40).

The evolution and expansion of this semiotically burdened form of money has converged, since the 1980s, with other developments. These include the fragmentation of the political landscape, the growth of new political parties, the ever-increasing sizes of constituencies, the creation of new elected positions at the local, state, and central levels, and the growth of the mass media. Voluminous streams of capital accumulation in urban real estate mean election finance flows significantly from "builders" or property developers (Kapur & Vaishnav 2011). These factors have amplified election expenses for political contestation, from municipal ward to parliamentary seat.

Today, the earlier architecture for political financing remains intact. Governmental approvals and discretionary decision making are still essential to the economy. Thus, black money remains indispensable for political visibility and ordinary exchange. Black money is routinely employed for campaign advertisements, and for the distribution of goodies and freebies among voters – saris, alcohol, cash, meals, etc. – before elections (Piliavksy 2014). Expensive purchases, such as urban property and contemporary art, have precisely negotiated white and black ratios (Appadurai 2000: 639; Sooudi 2012: 134). By conducting property or art transfers substantially in black, buyers and sellers evade capital gains and wealth taxes, and stamp duty and registration fees. In estate planning, insurance, and tax accounting, undeclared wealth and foreign transfer can emerge. *Hawala*, the longstanding, non-institutional vehicle of international money transfer, popular throughout the Indian Ocean, and often braided with decentralized credit instruments termed *hundi*, also entails black money (Jaffrelot 2010: 626; Martin 2009: 909).

In public discourse, however much one is complicit with its production and circulation, black money is invariably lamented, sometimes in hyperbolic terms. This likely reflects the widespread sense that the state has failed to prevent ostensibly nonmonetized public goods from having fixed price points. For example, government jobs and services in the state sector, which is vast and supports many tens of millions, are often contingent on monetary inducements (Gupta 2012). The monetized, instrumental, and self-interested inflections of an arena suffused by a liberal discourse of merit, justice, and development are keenly felt. For example, many low-income Indians pay for state services that are ostensibly provided on citizenship and residence grounds. As Emma Tarlo observes: "[T]he poor in Delhi relate to the state principally through the market. Basic amenities, such as land jobs, electricity, water and paving are things, not provided, but purchased in exchange for votes [and] money" (2003: 11).

This frustration at monetary exploitation provides one strand of the public antipathy towards black money, and intersects with another strand, concerning its purportedly extra-territorial location. It is worth pointing out that this anxious refrain likely exaggerates the black money that is abroad. For example, during the lead-up to the 2009 general elections, a senior figure in the Communist Party of India stated in parliament that Rs. 1.45 trillion in Indian deposits was parked in Swiss banks (Madsen 2011). This figure, ostensibly based on a Swiss Banking Association report, was widely circulated in political circles and repeated in news commentary, acquiring an outsized facticity (ibid.: 90). Yet no Swiss association had published or verified this figure, and researchers later found it to be grossly exaggerated (Kar 2011: 51). This illustrates how talk of black money acquires the dimensions of speculative myth. Such stories narratively verify the pervasive but secretive corruption that accompanies the monetization of public goods.

These two realms are distinct, insofar as routine, if illicit, monetary transactions around public goods and services do not end up in Swiss accounts. At a discursive or symbolic level, however, they can be conflated. The corruption deriving from privileged access to restricted vehicles of value blurs with the spectacular sums of public outrages. Since India's economic liberalization in the 1990s, numerous scandals have involved outsized irregularities. Some involve well-connected brokers of armaments, mobile spectrum, and mineral resources. The media-fed righteous anger inflecting these episodes amplifies the resemblance between everyday monetization of public goods and the more lucrative and television-ready kind.

Public figures continue to invoke black money's existence elsewhere as an urgent problem. For example, in 2012, Baba Ramdev, a yoga and lifestyle guru popular among the middle classes, carried out a massive protest fast in Delhi. He condensed grievances about governance and corruption into the slogan "Save the Country, Bring Back the Black Money" (*desh ko bachao, kala dhan wapas lao*). During India's 2014 national election campaign, various candidates – from Arvind Kejriwal, a public-minded reformer, to Narendra Modi, leader of the "Hindu-first" BJP – vowed to retrieve all black money stashed in Swiss accounts.

As Prime Minister, Modi made repeated public promises towards sourcing and retrieving such income. This is best exemplified by his government's surprise move in November 2016 to withdraw 500- and 1,000-rupee denomination banknotes. This unforeseen and far-reaching effort was termed "demonetization" (*notebandi* in Hindi). While demonetization implies an erasure or withdrawal of cash, the Hindi term more acutely captures the process, conjoining the everyday term for cash (*note*) with the word *bandi* for restricting or tying. With this abrupt top-down intervention, roughly 86 percent of all Indian currency was withdrawn from circulation. Currency holders were given a short period to exchange them for newly issued notes. The state indicated that demonetization was implemented to both force hoarders of illicit income to come clean and to counter counterfeit currency, the existence of which is regularly blamed on Pakistan. As Modi said when announcing the venture, demonetization was a "decisive step" to counter "black money," helping "curb the evil of corruption holding the country back in its race towards development. ... Enemies across the border running their operations using fake notes" would correspondingly suffer. In this rationale, we see the conjunction of antagonism vis-à-vis external enemies, anxiety about corruption, and the idea that black money hinders development. Demonetization's aim, in part, was acting on the speculation that dormant wealth could become activated when recirculated; holders of black money could in one adamant gesture be dispossessed. However, studies suggest that this intervention fell far short of its goals; the informal economy, which runs mainly on cash, was badly affected, and the promised boost to the monetary supply from returned black money did not materialize.

In this nationalist discourse, black money is understood as hidden and unproductive. While white money (or official income) circulates freely and is usefully employed, black money is seen as stagnant. The connotation is of a secret store of something valuable but idle. Yet black money's seemingly stationary and underutilized nature is belied by research. Studies of Indian monetary inflows and outflows suggest that black money is frequently circulated into the country from abroad, a practice known in finance circles as "round-tripping" (Kar 2011). These notions, in sum, reveal more about moral anxieties and speculative discourse, than what money actually does.

The public discourse traced above suggests that black money is an elusive specter and a moral outrage; that an inalienable part of the national essence is being laundered, converted, corrupted, and disguised. Here, the symbolism of black money is akin to anthropological discussions of the hoard (Weiner 1992). In many places, certain repositories of wealth – such as cattle, land, or adornments – constitute a form of inalienable wealth. The rhetoric of black money has striking continuity through recent decades, irrespective of the political inclinations affecting markets. It repeatedly conjures up inalienable wealth – a national hoard – that is being ransacked.

This helps explain the urgency, alarm, and stigma attached to black money. In government reports, policy documents, and academic papers, black money frequently indexes the absence or distortion of public morality. In 1970, for example, a government committee was chaired by a retired Supreme Court justice and dedicated to black money and the underground economy. Its final report explains the proliferation of tax evasion by way of the "general deterioration in moral standards of our people" (Wanchoo 1971: 10). A later official investigation on black money echoed this formulation, seeing in black money a "precipitous drop in public morality" blamed on "new, moneyed elites with little to offer except their example of material success" (Acharya et al. 1985: 241). A later government report on black money echoed this formulation: "The fight against the menace of black money needs to be fought ... at ethical level, we have to reinforce value/moral education in the school curriculum and build good citizens ... the thrust of public policy should be to discourage conspicuous and wasteful consumption/ expenditure, encourage savings, frugality and simplicity" (Indian Ministry of Finance 2002: 65). Academics studying black money generally adopt this pejorative, disciplining language. One analyst talks of how "the black economy is eating away at the innards of Indian society" (Kumar 2002: xxii).

At this point, it is apparent that black money is a vexed symbol. A nationalist discourse that privileges monetary productivity and territorial sanctity is pervasive. Alongside it is a moralizing tone that disparages the selfishness and disloyalty of those with black money. In this rhetoric, black money is – the dark twin of legitimately earned money – itself potentially spectral, hidden, and immaterial. Of course, black money can have a "thingness" about it, given that it is manifested in gold adornments or contemporary art or high-rise apartments.[6] Yet

---

[6] A further exploration of this theme, the materiality of black money, lies outside the scope of this chapter. A study of the habits and notions that attend cash

it is mostly inscrutable, abstract zeros lying somewhere just out of reach.

Such dimensions accorded to black money reflect the equivocal nature of money in general. Money acquires its charge from both publicity and secrecy; what is hidden from view may be as efficacious as that which is publicly flaunted (Robbins & Akin 1999). The idea that Indian wealth lies in underground Zurich vaults therefore reflects social critique. For, howsoever wealth is generated and distributed, many find it to occur in an unjust, asymmetrical, and secretive manner. Amidst much wealth creation is the sense that some are doing unduly well. In other words, the discontent surrounding black money may reflect the disorienting incommensurability between what one sees – the endless construction of buildings in urban India – and the puzzle as to who can afford them and how they pay for them. Speculation, about value and wealth, is here an effort to narratively domesticate the inexplicable, contingent, and improbable variety of fortunes (Puri 2014). The much-hyped, much-rebuked, ever-persistent notion of offshore black money thus represents money's irresolvable semiotic tensions. It draws attention to "the gaps between representation and reality and sign and substance" (Maurer 2006: 30).

In the remainder of this chapter, I bracket aside this discussion of black money. Howsoever much it illuminates a broader cultural attitude towards money, further inquiry into these symbolic and representational aspects may merely restate stigma and anxiety. At this altitude, we know very little about black money's trajectory as it moves across social spheres and generational horizons, or its presence in relational domains and transactional orders. In the following sections, I shift our analytical attention towards these realms.

marked as black money would no doubt illuminate, as has been done elsewhere, how "money is contextually differentiated and restricted in its convertability" (High 2013: 677). Studies have shown that common forms in which black money is held include residential and commercial property, as well as precious metals and gemstones (Acharya et al. 1985: 302). More recently, India's art market has seen an influx of capital from those laundering black money. Property, art, and precious metals and gemstones, as asset forms, offer obvious advantages. Depending on the market price, they spur the creation of higher investment yields than cash lying dormant. Further, in case of detection or government raids, their ownership and provenance can be fudged. Property purchases or business ownership, for example, is often done in *benami* form, whereby formal registration is done through proxies such as friends and family.

To pivot to analyzing black money within circuits of exchange is to better understand how the circulation of money bridges different transactional orders and social horizons. Black money's production and circulation entails various obligations with their own relational ends and temporal duration. As we shall see, black money is most visible in routine and euphemized exchanges, such as that between a businessman and the state official or politician and constituency. To comprehend black money beyond its symbolic or representational character, one might follow it as it is produced, transferred, donated, and invested. By doing so, we productively qualify some reigning assumptions attached to black money.

In the following sections, we shall see how black money is generated and disseminated in a Mumbai neighborhood. On the one hand, residents' moral critique of a ration shop operator's illicit proceeds invokes a wider discourse of black money subverting social thriving. Yet on the other hand, black money, from the perspective of the possessor, enables execution on social commitments. From the vantage point of those having black money, such capital stitches together relational domains, transactional orders, and temporal horizons of familial, political, and religious kinds. Black money, seen within transactional circuits and not as a pejorative discourse, can be understood in equivocal terms as simultaneously spurring moral critique and as saturating and buttressing social aims.

Channeling Black Money

Labour Camp is located between a middle-class suburb, Mahim, and is adjacent to Dharavi, the city's largest and best chronicled slum. The neighborhood overlaps in terms of economic activity and social profile with Dharavi. Still, many residents distinguish their area from the somewhat notorious mega-slum. Labour Camp had by the mid-twentieth century a concentration of working-class Maharashtrians working in the city's textile mills. Also residing were low-caste Valmikis, some employed in municipal waste collection (Sharma 2000).

Today, Labour Camp's demographic is less tied to industrial labor or to the rest of Maharashtra state. Most of the families I came to know – mostly migrants, from other Indian states such as Andhra Pradesh and Uttar Pradesh – worked and lived in fragile, fluid milieus. Many earned income from more than one job, lent capital or hands for a cousin or friend's enterprise. Others rented, sewed, sorted, drove, and collated for piecemeal jobs outsourced from nearby Dharavi. Their sources of income were tied up as much in kin relations as one-off opportunities. For example, the men might work one job during the day, but have a side income driving or delivering or brokering in the evening or weekends. Similarly, Labour Camp's women were, alongside their domestic duties – cooking, cleaning, childrearing, home maintenance – seen in the outdoor lanes. There, alongside bundles of freshly stitched clothing, they were sewing or cutting threads or checking zippers for clothing exporters based in Dharavi.

These families, seeking to defray expenses, made considerable use of ration shops. Many Labour Camp families had one member with a ration card. At various times during the day or evening, household members (generally mothers, the elderly, and children) queued for food-grains and petrol goods. Unforeseen happenstances brought me to one of these shops, a nondescript outpost with blackened, sooty walls. It belonged to Jayakar, a member of the Pathare Prabhu caste, a Hindu community with well-established roots in Mumbai.

Jayakar's shop is an undeniable component of the neighborhood economy. Labour Camp households use subsidized kerosene as a cooking fuel; before electrification, it was also used to light interiors and outdoor lamps. Those entitled to a kerosene subsidy (known as *subsidy-wale*) may also leverage their allotment. Ration-card holders conduct a parallel web of exchanges alongside the formal one between state patron and citizen supplicant. Some residents sell their allotted kerosene to neighbors or barter the fuel for items they lack.

The shop is also important to Jayakar. Licenses to distribute subsidized kerosene are scarce and correspondingly valued. His family holds three such licenses across central Mumbai, which sustain yet other family members who manage these distribution shops. The social life of subsidized kerosene looks like the following. In its "neat" or pure form, kerosene is shipped from refineries to state oil depots. A blue dye is added to prevent its diversion and adulteration ("white oil" is the term for kerosene purchased on the open market). Tankers bring the fuel to Labour Camp's ration shops; sometimes, these are large motorized trucks and, at other times, bulls hauling small carriers pull up curbside. There, the shop's helpers pour the liquid – the lurid color of an enthusiastically named energy drink – into metal barrels. Outside, a queue of hard plastic jugs of various colors snakes along the road. When kerosene is to be disbursed, residents emerge and track their container in the queue; given shortfalls and delays, grumbling and sharp words are invariably heard. The shop attendants, using metal funnels, pour the liquid into the jugs, splashing messily as they grow tired, distracted, or aggravated.

In Labour Camp, it is public knowledge – if not empirically verifiable fact – that Jayakar siphons and sells a part of the subsidized kerosene he gets on the black market. Complaints about the quality, quantity, and unpredictable allotment of fuel abound. Residents feel that the fuel they receive is diluted and adulterated; many rarely get their full allotment. Jayakar's staff are said to spin tall tales – refinery shutdowns, truck mafias, distribution issues, equipment breakdowns – to stall or defer giving the public their due. The shop opens erratically at odd hours and sometimes on only one day per week. Many residents thus purchase kerosene at market rates, nearly double the cost of subsidized fuel.

When I asked how such seeming diversion persists in spite of public knowledge, residents spoke of shadowy nexuses. One Labour Camp resident, Sonu, operated a handcart and sold fried snacks. He previously employed a pressurized kerosene lamp because of uneven and dim street lighting. This kind of Petromax lamp is still used by roadside vendors in India. Sonu often purchased his kerosene on the open market. With rates rising, and subsidized kerosene scarce, he switched to a battery-operated florescent lamp. But this was a transition of evident reluctance; whereas the Petromax radiates a warm yellowish glow, the new lamp imparts a harsh white glare. Asked about kerosene diversion and the seeming impunity with which it occurs, Sonu replied that "the police and shopkeeper work together hand in glove" (*police aur dhukandar ki mili-bhagat hai*). His assessment echoes a broader interpretation of state complicity in illicit profiteering. Kerosene and subsidized good siphoning is widely narrated as unfolding through official complicity (Gupta 2012: 96). Thus, anticorruption movements invoking ordinary people feed off a sense that vested state interests perpetuate public property's capture.

If Jayakar diverts government-allotted kerosene for private profit, he is hardly an outlier. Most kerosene intended for residential use is thought to end up with commercial and transport users. A high percentage is mixed with more expensive automotive fuels, such as diesel and automotive lubricants. Reports suggest that between 30 and 50 percent of the kerosene provided to Indian ration shops is diverted to open markets, resulting in proceeds, or black money, of billions of dollars (Shenoy 2010: 6).

Given the neighborhood's sentiment of his business, and the routine pilfering afflicting subsidized kerosene, I assume that Jayakar – to a degree – pockets a certain surplus. If correct, this is a not atypical example of how black money is generated. Whether it is the customary extraction of an unofficial self-reward or the more lucrative scams around spectrum licenses and mining allotments, black money is often gleaned via privileged access to public goods.

Let us turn to examine how money, sociality, and morality intersect in this milieu. As narrated earlier, Labour Camp's residents employ derogatory moral language about Jayakar's business. His money, in other words, is differentiated by disdain and disapproval. Ravi, a migrant from Vishakhapatnam who works for a company selling paint and chemical additives, describes Jayakar's business as "black market profiteering" (*kala bazaari*). The term denotes monetary benefit acquired from inflationary hoarding and selling. Sushil, a Marathi man whose grandfather migrated to Mumbai from Pune, puts Jayakar's income in the same category as the bribes demanded by police. As opposed to "work done from blood and sweat" (*khoon-pasaine ki kamai*), Sushil terms Mr. Jayakar's income as "black earnings" (*kali kamai*).

Here, the invocation of black (*kala/kali*) symbolically manifests what is murky and dangerous about wider market activity. In Labour Camp, even beyond the realm of money, income and trades encompassed by blackness are seen as morally dubious. Illicit activity proliferates in the vicinity in prosaic items such as meat and cement, as well as in drugs. Men who sell stolen electrical cables, for example, are said to be involved in an "illegal trade" (*kala dhandha*). The blackness of money is symbolically related to its temperature: prostitution or gangsterism involves "hot money" (*garam paisa*). Finally, the blackness and heat of certain income streams is linked to their secondary status. Money earned legitimately is "white" (*safed*) and "number one" (*ek number*). Black money, in contrast, is "number two" (*do numbri*). The latter taints Jayakar's income in this comparative taxonomy. As Prashant, a leather-goods salesman from Meerut, claims, Jayakar's wallet is full of "number-two money" (*do number ka paisa*). Thus, there is a symbolic and discursive blurriness that obscures the specificities of black money with those of illicit markets. They get associated with nefarious blackness, a raised temperature, and a secondary status, and therefore clumped into a differentiated ethical category.

Labour Camp's residents therefore view the subsidized kerosene shop's monetary exchanges as inseparable from market and moral transactions. Jayakar's income is conflated with disreputable or illicit income-generating activities. Can we complicate this binary between upstanding and illegitimate, clean and dirty, and white and black money? True enough, Labour Camp residents heap disdain on Jayakar's illegitimate proceeds. Yet, as we shall see, his income is funneled through relational domains, temporal horizons, and transactional orders. His money flows through neighborhood traders, local politicians, family relations, and religious institutions. Coursing through these different collective units, timescales, and lines of reciprocity and obligation, Jayakar's money is fused to the prospective prosperity of others. Thus far, we have seen how, from the perspective of Labour Camp residents, black money is spectral and immoral. This is symbolic discourse that differentiates types of market activity and monetary extraction. In the following section, we swivel from the external speculations of discourse to the internal actualities of Jayakar's exchange. There, I will suggest, black money, far from parasitically subverting public life, may actually reproduce social ties, relational obligations, and transactional orders.

Relational Ties and Transactional Orders

As my time in Labour Camp continued, I accumulated residents' impressions of Jayakar. Yet to avoid him remaining an analytical cipher, I needed to ingratiate myself with him. The way to do so was circuitously, for he was a fleeting presence at his shop and not directly approachable. Like many people in Mumbai, he was constantly on the move, attending to entrepreneurial and family duties. He was, however, publicly known in Labour Camp; he sponsored local politicians and festivities, for example. Therefore, I thought to approach him in terms of his larger profile. I contacted him via another Labour Camp trader specializing in PVC construction materials. Balding and compact, he has a cautious bearing. He deferred a longer conversation, but after I persistently rang him, he agreed to meet at another of his businesses in Dadar, also in central Mumbai. This was a store selling mobile phones and accessories.

By then, I saw how his ration shop functioned on different occasions. Naturally, I wondered what his men did to the barrels of kerosene behind a partition in the shop. I was also curious about the friendliness between his shop attendants and the kerosene delivery employees. But I instead asked Jayakar about his social networks in Labour Camp.

The Labour Camp trader who gave me Jayakar's number told me that they both participated in a "chit fund." This is a prominent vehicle of informal cash circulation in India, also known as a "kitty" or "bisi" (Schwecke 2018: 1412–14). Social intimates with good trust bonds put forward an equal amount on a regular, usually monthly, basis. The pot of money is pooled and collected by one member during each succeeding round, depending on the format's gambling, raffle, and auction elements. Over a single year, each party knows that he can expect a one-time windfall. Entrepreneurs may use this for investments or to back another business venture. Jayakar, when asked what traders did with their chit fund proceeds, noted examples of pressing need. A store renovation or expansion, he said, would require upfront outlays. Or if one of his sons required a top-up for an investment in property, he could direct proceeds there. Sitting in the Dadar shop full of mobiles, cases, and accessories, he mentioned that the last time his "ticket" was called in this chit fund, he had revamped the store's signage and lighting. The glossy mirrors and bank of overhead illumination magnified a sunglasses-necessary glare. The store radiated the fruits of this investment.

The chit fund's reliance on interpersonal trust and its constant cash circulation undercuts the notion that black money is dormant and unproductive. During my time in Mumbai, I heard stories about how despite the city's housing crunch, hundreds of thousands of apartments were lying unused. In these urban mythologies, the property, like the black money used to buy it, is spectral. High-rise apartments are the architectural embodiments of black money; an idle resource unfairly lying beyond access.

When Jayakar spoke about his business ventures, it was apparent that they were interrelated with kin ties. He told me about property investments he had made in Nagpur, another city in Maharashtra, with two of his cousins. With other businessman dabbling in real estate, they bought land in the vicinity of a new airport and special economic zone.

Seeing my curiosity about these investments – and perhaps miscalculating an anthropologist's average income – he hinted at his willingness to dispose of these assets. Here, Jayakar was betting on his family – in the intergenerational reproduction and wealth of his kin group – and also conducting an instrumental transaction.

I was intrigued to learn that Jayakar's financing extended to the arena of the state and of political parties. In a 2012 municipal election, he backed the local candidate for the National Congress Party. Local hoardings showed pictures of him and his fellow Labour Camp traders wishing the candidate well, a feature typical of Indian election campaigns. Having strong political support is essential for his business. A public ration shop license can be investigated or revoked. Indeed, Jayakar recalled a period, which lasted some weeks, when insufficient kerosene was delivered to his shop. Government inspectors were rechecking his shop license and ordering suppliers to defer delivery. Labour Camp residents saw this as an outcome of his deliberate diversion for profit. Jayakar read this disruption as harassment directed towards extracting bribes from him. State officials were, in this reading, using the guise of verifying documents to extort cash. Asked how this standoff ended, Jayakar stated plainly that it was only after the local MLA intervened that the investigation petered away and his supplies resumed.

This account helps us make sense of how the state is at one level invested in eliminating the generation of black money and at another creates incentives for it. High-level committees seek to stem the generation of black money in the marketplace; low-level functionaries create the conditions for many to engage in coercive and asymmetric exchanges for their survival. We have not a monolithic state but contested jurisdictions within, at one level working to combat pilfering and at another level creating incentives for its furtherance. As a government report notes: "[E]nterprises are motivated to generate black income in order to meet certain costs which cannot be shown on the books. Such costs may range from petty bribes to low-level government functionaries to substantial 'political contributions'" (Acharya et al. 1985: 11).

This oblique reference to political contributions echoes Jayakar's engagement with electoral parties. He speaks euphemistically of his financial backing of political candidates as "help" (*madad*). This echoes the wider Indian context, where the quid pro quo of black money in the political arena is formulated as a "gift" or "donation"

(Kapur & Vaishnav 2011: 7). Money is one of the most pliable ways that social action is manifest. In particular, it can be transformed from self-interested, short-term, and instrumental uses to other-centered, public, and transcendental usages. Such transmutation is key to the symbolic conversion necessary for money to bridge different transactional orders (Parry & Bloch 1989: 25). Money's morality is thus not intrinsic or absolute but shifts with conditions of generation and circulation. What we see in Jayakar's investments and donations is a keen appreciation of the social matrix and political context within which his market activities are embedded. No doubt Labour Camp's residents might see this formulation as a cynical rationalization. Yet from his vantage point channeling funds to political supporters is necessary for relational domains and transactional orders to be sutured together.

Note here the spatial and temporal dynamics of black money: Jayakar's kerosene business helps to underwrite traders' chit fund circles, family businesses and investments, and neighborhood politics. Thus, his black money is located in circles of embedded and spatial immediacy instead of being vaporous and disembodied. This echoes research within economic anthropology on how money is a value form that expands and contracts along lines of physical and ascribed proximity (Zickgraf 2017). Black money is embedded not just within different time horizons – for immediate favors as well as transactions conducted in the indeterminate future – but can be located differentially, in terms of closeness and distance.

There is yet another social spectrum at work here, that of the religious order. Jayakar, speaking about his public activities, mentioned donations to a Pathare Prabhu temple in Dadar. Presumably, the support of a religious institution adds to his stature and contributes towards his social esteem. Later, I learned that Jayakar also donates money each summer towards an annual *Dahi Handi* festival celebrating Krishna's birth. Market operators commonly transact significant sums in religious spaces and festivities in India.

Indeed, the nexus of everyday finance and religious patronage finds expression in ethnographies of how entrepreneurs, alongside their illicit or illegal enterprises, transform into social patrons. Adjacent to Labour Camp, in Tamil-dominated parts of Dharavi, there is the still-remembered example of Vardhabhai. From the 1950s, he ran a criminal organization involved in illicit alcohol production when prohibition was in force, land acquisition and property development, and gambling and prostitution. Like many metropolitan "big men," he was a community benefactor, helping residents to access utilities and government services, and sponsoring religious festivals (Weinstein 2014: 48–9). This constitutes a not unusual blurring of criminal, strongman, fixer, patron, and politician in contemporary India. There is a well-defined template of monetary acquisition that reproduces unequal wealth, and the performance of magnanimous gestures towards the community (Hansen 2005). In this feedback loop, community patronage enhances one's reputation and trustworthiness, facilitating further exchange of and access to capital and credit.

The anthropological notion that money mediates between different moral evaluations, relational domains, and transactional orders is echoed elsewhere. For example, the distinction between consumption, on the one hand, and savings or investments, on the other, obscures how monetary transactions are oriented towards prospective outcomes. The exchange of money is a "performative conversion, a devotion of present income to the hope of future gains" (Guyer 2004: 99). We have seen this in Jayakar's income flows: whether investing in property with his kin, or donating money to a temple or festival, he projects his current wealth towards possible results. These outcomes are not simply to do with personal wealth accumulation, but encompass political patronage, familial well-being, and religious festivity. These manifestations of black money unfold at different temporal scales: from the family-linked investments of Jayakar's current calculations, to the multiyear cycle of political campaigns, to the religious donations that will presumably linger for decades.

Important here is the equivocal character that marks the production and circulation of black money. An anthropological comparison with another milieu suffused by an "adjectivally marked money" (Maurer 2006) is instructive. Among Luo farmers in Kenya, "bitter money" is primarily generated by selling land or crops such as tobacco or cannabis (Shipton 1989). Because these are linked to community ownership and ancestral spirits, and involve unfairness and injustice, such traffic is seen with moral disapproval. Natural disaster, personal misfortune, and supernatural vengeance are seen to potentially accompany reinvestment in family marriages, lineage property, and livestock purchases that shore up male power. The resolution of this quandary is not possible, because of the irreducible ambivalence that attends money's generation and distribution. Notably, bitter money can become good money through purification rituals, as black money might become white. This helps shed light on how black money is enveloped in both vexed disapprobation and routinized complicity.

I have suggested here, via the case of a Mumbai ration shop operator, that his purported black money serves as a hinge between different relational domains, temporal horizons, and transactional orders. In anthropological terms, black money proliferates – beyond its practical necessity – as a resource that may reproduce the intergenerational, political, and religious order. Pumped into family reproduction, collecting neighborhood esteem, cultivating political backing, and supporting the eternal gods, Jayakar's seemingly dirty money is, in this manner, neutralized and cleansed.

Conclusion

In this chapter, I have suggested an answer to the question: what is black money? Initially dwelling on symbolic and discursive readings, I have argued that the persistent nationalist refrain about illegitimate and offshore wealth in postcolonial India is foremost a moral question.

What makes money black is the critique of those possessing the capacity to produce it. Those who inveigh against its existence broadcast a socialized anxiety about the ethical conduct and civic selflessness of others.

Beyond its semiotic facets, black money's exchange dimensions show that as it is generated and circulated, this differentiated form of money retains a complex potential. It can simultaneously undermine and underwrite social relations, temporal horizons, and transactional orders. Jayakar's case shows that black money, while thought of as immoral, spectral, and extraterritorial, can be understood as productive, tangible, and held in close proximity. By funneling funds to favored politicians during elections or participating in a communal chit fund or buying into a collective land investment, Jayakar is, from one perspective, self-interested and law breaking. Yet the money is being spread along webs of obligation and reciprocity that implicate his family, professional intimates, kinship networks, and political authorities. In this sense, black money serves as a hinge between family and neighborhood, present and future, and market and politics. While thought of as a selfish scourge, black money also underwrites society's endurance itself. The irony of this most disreputable form of money is that its blackness colors the most esteemed and highly reputable.

References

Acharya, SN &Associates 1985, *Aspects of the Black Economy in India: Report Submitted to the Ministry of Finance*, Government of India, National Institute of Public Finance and Policy, New Delhi.

Amrith, S 2013, *Crossing the Bay of Bengal: The Furies of Nature and the Fortunes of Migration*, Harvard University Press, Cambridge.

Appadurai, A 2000, "Spectral Housing and Urban Cleansing: Notes on Millennial Mumbai," *Public Culture*, 12, 3: 627–51.

Berenschot, W 2010, "Everyday Mediation: The Politics of Public Service Delivery in Gujarat, India," *Development and Change*, 41, 5: 883–905.

Booth, G 2008, *Behind the Curtain: Making Music in Mumbai's Film Studios*, Oxford University Press, New York.

Chandavarkar, AG 1983, "Money and Credit (1858–1947)," in D Kumar & M Desai (eds.) *The Cambridge Economic History of India*, vol. 2: C.1757–C.1970, Cambridge University Press, Cambridge, pp. 762–803.

Chibber, P 2011, "Dynastic Parties: Organization, Finance and Impact," *Party Politics*, 19, 2: 277–95.

Chibber, V 2003, *Locked in Place: State Building and Late Industrialization in India*, Princeton University Press, Princeton.

Das Gupta, C 2016, *State and Capital in Independent India: Institutions and Accumulation*, Cambridge University Press, Cambridge.

Dodd, N 2014, *The Social Life of Money*, Princeton University Press, Princeton.

Goswami, M 2004, *Producing India: From Colonial Economy to National Space*, University of Chicago Press, Chicago.

Gupta, A 2012, *Red Tape: Bureaucracy, Structural Violence, and Poverty in India*, Duke University Press, Durham.

Guyer, J 2004, *Marginal Gains: Monetary Transactions in Atlantic Africa*, University of Chicago Press, Chicago.

Hansen, TB 2005, "Sovereigns Beyond the State: On Legality and Authority in Urban India," in TB Hansen & F Stepputat (eds.) *Sovereign Bodies: Citizens, Migrants, and States in the Postcolonial World*, Princeton University Press, Princeton.

Hewitt, V 2008, *Political Mobilisation and Democracy in India: States of Emergency*. Routledge, Oxford.

High, M 2013, "Polluted Money, Polluted Wealth: Emerging Regimes of Value in the Mongolian Gold Rush," *American Ethnologist*, 40, 4: 676–88.

Huberman, J 2012, *Ambivalent Encounters: Childhood, Tourism, and Social Change in Banaras, India*, Rutgers University Press, New Brunswick.

Indian Ministry of Finance 2002, *White Paper on Black Money*, Ministry of Finance, Department of Revenue, Central Board of Direct Taxes, New Delhi.

Jaffrelot, C 2010, *Religion, Caste, and Politics in India*, Primus, New Delhi.

Kapur, D & Vishnav, M 2011, *Quid Pro Quo: Builders, Politicians, and Election Finance in India*, Center for Global Development, Washington.

Kar, D 2011, "An Empirical Study on the Transfer of Black Money from India: 1948–2008," *Economic and Political Weekly*: 45–54.

Kochanek, S 1987, "Briefcase Politics in India: The Congress Party and the Business Elite," *Asian Survey*, 27, 12: 1278–301.

Kumar, A 2002, *The Black Economy in India*, Penguin, New Delhi.

Madsen, ST 2011, "Ajit Singh S/O Charan Singh," in ST Madsen, KB Nielsen, & U Skoda (eds.) *Trysts with Democracy: Political Practice in South Asia*, Anthem, London, pp. 73–102.

Markovits, C 2000, *The Global World of Indian Merchants, 1750–1947: Traders of Sind from Bukhara to Panama*, Cambridge University Press, Cambridge.

Martin, M 2009, "Hundi/Hawala: The Problem of Definition," *Modern Asian Studies*, 43, 4: 909–37.

Maurer, B 2006, "The Anthropology of Money," *Annual Review of Anthropology*, 35: 15–36.

Michelutti, L 2019, "The Inter-State Criminal Life of Sand and Oil in North India," in B Harriss-White & L Michelutti (eds.) *The Wild East: Criminal Political Economies in South Asia*, UCL Press, London, pp. 168–93.

Parry, J 1989, "On the Moral Perils of Exchange," in J Parry & M Bloch (eds.) *Money and the Morality of Exchange*, Cambridge University Press, Cambridge, pp. 64–93.

Parry, J & Bloch, M 1989, "Introduction: Commodities and the Politics of Value," in J Parry & M Bloch (eds.) *Money and the Morality of Exchange*, Cambridge University Press, Cambridge.

Piliavsky, A 2014, "India's Demotic Democracy and Its 'Depravities' in the Ethnographic Longue Durée," in A Piliavsky (ed.) *Patronage as Politics in South Asia*, Cambridge University Press, Cambridge, pp. 154–75.

Puri, SS 2014, *Speculation in Fixed Futures: An Ethnography of Betting in Between Legal and Illegal Economies at the Delhi Racecourse*, University of Copenhagen, Copenhagen.

Robbins, J & Akin D (eds.) 1999, *Money and Modernity: State and Local Currencies in Melanesia*, University of Pittsburgh Press, Pittsburgh.

Ruud, AE 2011, "Democracy in Bangladesh: A Village View," in ST Madsen, KB Nielsen, & U Skoda (eds.) *Trysts with Democracy: Political Practice in South Asia*, Anthem, London, pp. 45–70.

Schwecke, S 2018, "A Tangled Jungle of Disorderly Transactions? The Production of a Monetary Outside in a North Indian Town," *Modern Asian Studies*, 52, 4: 1375–419.

Searle, L 2013, "Constructing Prestige and Elaborating the 'Professional': Elite Residential Complexes in the National Capital Region, India," *Contributions to Indian Sociology*, 47, 2: 271–302.

Sharma, K 2000, *Rediscovering Dharavi: Stories from Asia's Largest Slum*, Penguin, New Delhi.

Shenoy, B 2010, *Lessons Learned from Attempts to Reform India's Kerosene Subsidy*, International Institute for Sustainable Development, Winnipeg.

Shipton, P 1989, *Bitter Money: Cultural Economy and some African Meanings of Forbidden Commodities*, American Ethnological Society Monograph Series no. 1, American Ethnological Society, Washington.

Sooudi, O 2012, "Art Patron as 'Taste Scapegoat'? Complicity and Disavowal in Mumbai's Contemporary Art World," *Etnofoor Anthropological Journal*, 24, 2: 123–43.

Tarlo, E 2003, *Unsettling Memories: Narratives of the Emergency in Delhi*. Hurst & Company, London.

Tomlinson, BR 1979, *The Political Economy of the Raj 1914–1947: The Economics of Decolonization in India*, Macmillan, London.

Wanchoo, KN 1971, *Direct Taxes Enquiry Committee Final Report*, Ministry of Finance, Government of India, New Delhi.

Weiner, A 1992, *Inalienable Possessions: The Paradox of Keeping-While-Giving*, University of California Press, Berkeley.

Weinstein, L 2014, *The Durable Slum: Dharavi and the Right to Stay Put in Globalizing Mumbai*, University of Minnesota Press, Minneapolis.

Zickgraf, J 2017, "Becoming Like Money: Proximity and the Social Aesthetics of 'Moneyness,'" *HAU: Journal of Ethnographic Theory*, 7, 1: 303–26.

11 Market Making in Punjab Lotteries: Regulation and Mutual Dependence

MATTHEW S. HULL[*]

Introduction

It is easy to find lottery shops in Punjab, India. Large, overhead signs say "Punjab State Lottery" in Hindi and/or Punjabi scripts (Figure 11.1). But the products these shops sell are more varied than their signs suggest. The Punjab state lottery (PSL) acts as a front. The main business of these shops is the selling tickets from the lotteries of several northeastern states and the illegal lotteries that operate using their organization and infrastructure. Regulations and the business organization they foster have made the PSL, the northeastern states lotteries, and illegal lotteries unexpectedly dependent on one another. As they vie for market share they must also share the market. If any lottery drove another out of the market, its own business would collapse. The key to understanding this is to see how variably regulated practices entangle to make the lottery market.

The differences in regulation within the lottery market could be characterized in terms of the distinction between formal and informal, "representing bureaucracy and popular self-organization" (Hart 2006, 2008). As Keith Hart argues, the formal–informal distinction, while questionable, has its uses. However, in this article, I avoid binary characterizations of differential market regulations such as formal–informal and legal–illegal for two reasons.

First, the institutional agents, targets, and practices of regulation vary considerably within what we might call the formal or legal lottery

[*] I am greatly indebted to the insights and assistance of Shiv Kumar and DP Singh. This article benefited immensely from the observations of Jatin Dua, Krisztina Fehérváry, Barbara Harriss-White, Douglas Haynes, Andrew Haxby, Gustav Peebles, and especially Stine Puri, Ajay Gandhi, and Sebastian Schwecke. Finally, I would like to express my thanks to the editors of this volume for their perceptive and patient efforts to bring it together.

Figure 11.1 Lottery shop in Mohali, near Chandigarh

market. Within some kinds of economic practices, we can fruitfully distinguish functionally complementary markets (legal and illegal, formal and informal) or segments of a single market. In her wonderful work on horserace betting in Delhi, for example, Stine Puri shows a "parallel" illegal market "lying in the shadows of legal betting and finance" (Puri 2014: 217; see also Puri 2015). In contrast, the legal market for lotteries in Punjab is subject to the varying regulatory practices of several Indian states, the central government, a consortium of lottery corporations, and police. The binary distinctions of formal–informal and legal–illegal make it more difficult to grasp how the interplay among regulating institutions and their regulations shapes markets and market segments.

Second, as Janet Roitman observes, economic activities characterized as informal often use highly organized systems of labor, financing, and authority: "The only way in which one can demarcate these activities from the official economy and official state administration is with respect to a particular shared characteristic: that is, circumventing state economic regulation" (Roitman 2004: 19). Instead of "informal," she analyzed such activities as "unregulated" and we can extend her argument beyond a binary characterization to highlight the variability of regulation.

Roitman's point is especially relevant to the Punjab lottery market, where legal and illegal lottery activities are almost identical and organizationally fused. As Peebles observed, in highly regulated economies transactions alike in every other respect are delineated "between legitimate and illegitimate" by "the use of a receipt" (Peebles 2011: 70). In the case of the Punjab lottery market, legal and illegal transactions are not distinguished by *whether* a receipt is used, but *how* it is used. As I describe in more detail below, machine-printed ticket receipts marking a regulated transaction are used in illegal transactions – lottery sellers scrawl the terms of illegal bets on cast-off losing tickets littering their shops. In a kind of mockery of the regulatory role of ticket receipts, they are used to flout the tax regulations of the state of Punjab and the business agreements with corporate ticket agents. The legal and the illegal are two sides of the same paper, the difference between them paper thin.

This similarity and operational dependence among different lotteries is not new. Since the establishment of the PSL in 1968, various legal and illegal lotteries in the state have been borrowing and trading properties of one another as their operators attempt to capture their competitors' share of the lottery market. This essay charts this history, inspired by Jane Guyer's call for the study of forms of regulation, their succession, and combination (Guyer 1993). She shows how different "models" of regulation, defined in terms of their key goal (guarantee of fixed relationships, protection of purity, provision of welfare, arbitration of social costs), both succeeded and (to a lesser degree) supplemented one another in the regulation of food in Britain and its colonies.

The two dominant models of lottery regulation in India have been the "protection of economic welfare," especially of the poor, and the "appropriation of the profits" of the lottery industry. Central and state governments implemented these different models through a variety of rules and institutions. My focus is less on what Guyer calls the "ideological rubrics" of forms of regulation than the way they interact in practice to make a market in a particular shape. The increasing regulation of the lottery market in India is not a straightforward modernization story of the incorporation of informal economic activities into formal economic arrangements. Efforts to increase the regulation of lotteries fostered the growth of new, less regulated activities, including outright illegal ones. Specifically, intersecting regulations prompted the creation of an innovative, loosely regulated lottery product that was easy to distribute in parallel black market sales. The market for lotteries in Punjab shows how regulation can significantly format even activities that escape one or another component of its regulatory apparatus.

This article focuses on lotteries to examine how different government entities and corporations can shape markets in India. As I argue below, technical infrastructures and business organization play regulative roles in the lottery market. However, legal regulation has a particularly strong role in shaping lottery markets for two reasons. First, in India and elsewhere, lotteries are intensely legally circumscribed because they are commonly condemned on moral grounds and as a tax on the poor. Second, lotteries – the legal ones, at least – are especially amenable to legal regulation because they are games constituted largely by formal rules, which are easily targeted by law. For example, as I describe below, a simple 2010 central government rule that banned two- and three-digit lotteries suddenly remade the industry.

This article concentrates on the features of lotteries that figure in its regulation. It is not intended to be a comprehensive treatment of lotteries in India or lotteries as a particular kind of practice found in many places. Therefore, it does not address many important issues thematized in scholarship on lotteries such as the moral and political debates concerning lotteries, the sociocultural orientations that make certain lottery games appealing, the calculative and speculative practices of lottery players, and the links between lotteries and a variety of practices that address risk and uncertainty and invite fortunate events – from astrology and prayer to moral living.[1] Finally, my ethnographic work to date has concentrated on the PSL department and the corporate agents who distribute its tickets.[2] Further research will explore in more depth the perspectives of the lottery officials of northeastern states, low-level lottery sellers, and those who play the lottery, but

---

[1] For ethnographic work on these issues with respect to lotteries (see Casey 2003; Davis 2006; Klima 2006; Krige 2011; Mosquera & Garcia de Molero 2004; Selby 1996; Van-Wyk 2012, 2013).

[2] This chapter is based on ethnographic research conducted in Ludhiana and Chandigarh/Mohali for six months in 2014 and for two month-long periods in 2015 and 2016. I gratefully acknowledge the American Institute of Indian Studies for its generous support of this research.

unfortunately, they are not well-represented in the account I present in this chapter.

Prohibition

The kind of numbers games now called "lotteries" have old roots in South Asia. But the modern market for them developed in response to the regulatory practices of the colonial state. A thorough history of numbers games waits to be written, but we can trace their development through late nineteenth- and early twentieth-century colonial regulations. The changes in regulations register a move away from betting on the timing or measure of actual events to the abstraction of the digits used to express them.

What are today called "lotteries" did not emerge from what were called lotteries in the colonial period. (I return to the implications of this terminological shift in the next section.) From the early seventeenth century, lotteries had become an established form in England for raising funds for public goods, including roads and bridges, educational and medical institutions, and colonial adventures such as the Virginia Company. The identification of lotteries with projects of general welfare distinguished them from "gambling," which was subject to a variety of regulations. In India, from the late nineteenth century, what Puri characterizes as a "fusion of lottery and betting" (Puri 2014: 17) was practiced in relation to horseraces, with tickets being sold as far away as London (Frith 1976: 18, cited in Puri 2014: 17).[3]

The Government of India's Public Gambling Act of 1867 did not even mention lotteries and the Bombay Prevention of Gambling Act of

---

[3] Puri describes the practice as follows: "As the race club culture developed, 'lottery dinners' were organized on the night before the races for members. At these events, people could buy tickets for a fixed sum on a particular horse. The tickets were then put up for auction – and could be sold for an even higher amount, depending on the popularity of the horse – and were put into a barrel (Frith 1976: 18). The winner would be the ticket drawn with the right horse number and the prize was the total pool of ticket money" (Puri 2014: 17). Interestingly, this same fusion of horserace results with lotteries was the beginning of the return of legal lotteries in the United States. Begun in 1964, the winning numbers of the "New Hampshire Sweepstakes," operated by the US state, were based on horseraces rather than selected through a method of chance to avoid violating the US anti-lottery statutes.

1887 explicitly excluded lotteries from its definition of gambling. The colonial regulation of gambling was aimed less at curtailing gambling than curbing the disorderly public behavior that accompanied it. Regulation of gambling tended to attach itself to places and focused on controlling gaming houses where people would gather to use "cards, dice, tables or any other instruments of gaming" (Public Gambling Act of 1867, s. 1).

Anne Hardgrove (2007) shows that by the late nineteenth century, presidency governments increasingly focused on the practice of rain betting. Different accounts date the beginnings of betting on the rain to either the 1820s or the 1880s, but it was thriving by the late nineteenth century. Bettors would wager on the amount of rain that would fall in a three-hour afternoon period. The morality and social consequences of rain betting were cited in 1890s' bans, but the legislation likely had other goals. Ritu Birla (2009) sees it as an effort to distinguish illegal and legal markets for speculation. Hardgrove argues that the government's aim was also to take a piece of the gambling action itself: "Shutting down rain gambling was a way of pushing people to speculate on the official opium exchange, and not informally, as in rain gambling shops, where the state could not gain any profit" (Hardgrove 2007, para. 328).

By 1900, however, "gambling" on the price of opium through speculative purchase transactions taxed by government gave way to betting on the final digit of the daily sales price of opium, no longer tied to the movements of the overall price as in the futures market. Such a wager could return five to nine times the amount of the wager. This kind of betting was open to a much wider range of people, because it required no knowledge of or connections with the movements of the opium market. Moreover, because it did not involve the actual purchase of opium, these bets could be placed for as little as one *anna*. "This daily *satta* was said by the government to 'attract the idle riff-raff of the town, the labourer, the servant, and the mill-hand'" (Hardgrove 2007, para. 322).

As the opium trade declined in the first decades of the twentieth century, the practice of betting on the final digit of a commodity price spread to cotton and jute (Birla 2009). Reflecting the expansion of international trade and communications, betting increasingly used the prices on British and American spot and futures markets in London, New York, and New Orleans.

By the 1920s, amendments to the 1867 Act began to take account of the varieties of numbers games, focusing on digits as a central feature in addition to the measures of the phenomenon speculated on. In 1926, the Public Gaming Act of 1926 in the United Provinces was amended to prohibit gambling on the digits of a number indicating the price of cotton, opium, and other commodities, as well as the amount of rainfall. Central Provinces Act of 1927, prohibited "gaming-houses" defined as places where there was "gaming":

(a) on the market price of cotton, opium, or other commodity or on the digits of the number used in stating such price; or
(b) on the amount of variation in the market price of any such commodity or on the digits or the amount of such variation; or
(c) on the market price of any stock or share or on the digits of the number used in stating such price; or
(d) on the occurrence or non-occurrence of rain or other natural events; or
(e) on the quantity of rainfall or on the digits of the number used in stating such quantity.

(Central Provinces Act 3 1927, s. 2)

The account of "*dara* gambling" in a 1938 book on gambling law in India by the attorney SMA Sami registers a move completely away from using natural or market events as a source of digits. Sami was careful to point out that "*dara* gambling has no connection whatever with the price of any commodity" (Sami 1938: 71). He wrote that the "modus operandi" of "*dara* gambling" was "well known" and he quoted a description of it from a 1933 court decision:

The owner of the house who may be conveniently called a book-maker accepts bets from individuals, bets on digits ranging from 1 to 100. After he has got a sufficient number of bets he makes small slips of papers from 1–100, puts those slips in a jar and then after rolling about extracts three out of the jar. The numbers mentioned on those slips are added together and after eliminating the first digit there remain in the majority of cases a number consisting of two digits. The whole of that number is called the *dara* and an individual who has bet on that number gets a fairly large amount, whereas the individual who has bet on the last digit of that number gets a comparatively smaller amount. Such a digit is known as *baraf*. (Sami 1938: 71)

The likely derivation of the name for this kind of gambling from *dar*, the Hindi word for "rate," suggests that the game itself developed from the kinds of commodity price betting that the government had banned. Sami suggested that the use of papers in a jar was used to get around the ban on betting on events and commodities, drily observing: "The failure on the part of prosecution to establish by definite evidence that slips of paper had any connection with the sale-price of any commodity is not a fatal defect for sustaining a conviction under section 3." (Sami 1938: 71).

Nevertheless, the practice of betting on the final digits of commodity prices continued into the 1960s. By the 1950s, a huge numbers business had grown in Mumbai that used the opening and closing spot price of cotton on the New York market. The evidence is not solid, but it seems that the last three digits of the opening and a closing price were added to produce a single digit for each price. What came to be called *matka* (Hindi for "pitcher" or "earthen jar") grew out of a shift away from using these prices. There are various and irreconcilable reports about why. The five-day schedule of the NY market did not allow for weekend draws. The Bombay cotton market might have stopped receiving the price information from NY. In another account, the prices ended in zero for several days in a row, generating suspicions that someone was perhaps manipulating the NY cotton market to win the numbers game, which prompted the betting community to adopt the open and close rates of wholesale cotton traded on Bombay's cotton exchange at Siwri. The most banal, and perhaps hardest to make sense of, comes from the Vinod Kalyanji, son of Kalyanji Bhagat, the man considered the originator of Mumbai *matka* (also known as *Kalyan matka*). Vinod Kalyanji claimed that, in the mid-1950s, his father decided that the cotton figures were becoming too predictable to bet on (Mujumdar & Patel 2007). According to Vinod, his father began to study the American numbers game in the late 1950s and started a new game, and "the name *matka* is because the idea occurred to my father while seeing people bet on numbered chits drawn from a pot." From the start, *matka* was based on drawing three cards from a deck. The game succeeded in Bombay and spread quickly to all of India, in part because it had high odds (from 1:9 for bets on a single digit) and could be played for as little as one rupee. Furthermore, the similarity of *matka* to a lottery also probably discouraged authorities from controlling it very aggressively.

Bhagat is credited with the invention of *matka*, but the game itself closely followed the way commodities prices were used. Bhagat's new game evolved in its early years, but it soon settled into a structure that is still used today. There are two draws of three cards each every day, respectively known as the "opening" and "closing" draw, which traditionally take place at 9 pm and midnight. The cards correspond to numbers 0 to 9. So, a draw might be 9, 5, 4. These numbers are added up, in this case, to 18. The last digit of this sum is used as the opening number, so it would be 8 and the draw would be represented as "954 8X." The closing draw works in the same way: if 3, 6, and 8 are drawn, from the sum of 17 you would get a closing digit of 7. The full draw would be represented as "954–87–368." Bookies take bets on all these outcomes, but most of the bets are on the opening and closing digits (in this case, the single digits of 8 and 7) or the pair (here 87). Picking the single digit pays nine times the wager, double digits pays ninety times. Accomplished through many media, the single-digit game, whether called *dara*, *matka*, or lottery, has proved to be the most successful game in India.

Appropriation

State lotteries were an effort on the part of state governments to take over parts of a thriving illegal lottery business. According to the Directorate of Punjab State Lotteries (DPSL), the state lottery "was established in the year 1968 as a wing of the Finance Department with a view to curbing illegal lotteries like *satta*, *matka*, etc. by organizing lotteries at regular intervals and also to mobilize resources for the state exchequer" (Directorate of Lotteries, Punjab n.d.). Although curbing an illegal industry was the key aim, we can look at the establishment of the PSL as related to the nationalization of private banks in 1969. And the move is even more closely aligned with efforts of colonial governments to capture existing betting markets, like attempting to push rain bettors into speculating with purchases on the opium market.

Although many states operated lotteries for some period in the 1970s and 1980s, the number of lotteries exploded in the early 1990s as states struggling to meet their budgets were drawn to a method of raising funds without increasing taxes. Lotteries are a concurrent matter under the Indian Constitution, so both states and the Union have the authority to frame laws to regulate the conduct of lotteries. The role of government employees and offices in conducting lotteries varied greatly. Most states operated their own lotteries, although some also licensed private companies to operate them. At one end were the north-eastern states of Mizoram, Nagaland, and Sikkim, which appeared to just authorize and sell the lottery concession to private corporations, which ran the entire business. The PSL officials I talked with about this joked that lottery divisions of these states have just one official who simply signs the contracts with the corporations, which then develop the lottery schemes and operate them. States such as Punjab developed their own schemes, got tickets printed, and conducted their own draws, leaving only sales operations for a network of companies. Many of the Hindi-belt states pressed their district management bureaucracies into service to the lottery, giving their district tax collectors supplementary appointments as "District Lottery Officers" with authority over "District Lottery Offices," which distributed tickets. Small vendors frequently complained that they were shut out of sales as large vendors converted bureaucratic control into market share through illegal payments. Kerala had long operated a lottery completely through government employees. Even the lowest level sellers who accosted drivers at traffic lights were Kerala state employees, who were part of a state-run social insurance arrangement.

By 1994, the tickets of some 150 lotteries from states throughout India could be bought every day in Delhi. The proliferation of lotteries generated serious concern about their effects on the urban poor. From the early 1990s, newspapers were filled with stories of lives ruined by the false promise of lottery riches as husbands hawked vehicles, sold their wives' wedding rings and earrings, and borrowed money to buy lottery tickets. Workers left their jobs to join ticket-buying frenzies, to scrutinize gazettes listing the winning numbers of past weeks, and await the next draw. Muslim clerics issued fatwas pronouncing them against the tenets of Islam (Sharma 1992a) and letters to the editors denounced lotteries as nothing more than "gambling." The rush of cash into government coffers generated vast opportunities for corruption.

Delhi took the lead in banning lotteries in 1995 and most of the Hindi-belt states closed them down within a few years. After closing their own lotteries, many states found that they were simply handing over revenues to other states whose lottery tickets flooded into their markets. The wrangling among states and the central government finally resulted in the Lotteries Regulation Act of 1998, which allowed states to ban the sales of tickets from other states. This act also specified that only state governments are authorized to operate lotteries, although just what arrangements satisfy the criteria of a state-operated lottery is still a matter of debate.

The PSL is run by a junior Indian Administrative Service (IAS) officer who heads the Directorate of the Punjab State Lottery, which has a staff of around fifty people. To date, the PSL is what is known as a "paper lottery," one that uses preprinted tickets with numbers on them, rather an "online lottery," which allows buyers to pick any number they would like by buying a ticket at a computer terminal in a lottery store. The selling of tickets is contracted through "selling agents," three different companies with a national footprint in the lottery business: New Delhi-based Sugal and Damani, which specializes in operating lotteries in India and Africa; Pan India Network Infravest, which sells under the Playwin brand, is a subsidiary of Essel group that includes Zee TV, among many other holdings; and Chennai-based Future Gaming Solutions owned by Santiago Martin, the self-made "Lottery King," who has been in and out of prison for lottery-related fraud. These firms are agents not only for the PSL, but for lotteries of all the other states being sold in Punjab. After being printed at a "security press," a high-security printing facility near Delhi (which also prints things such as stock certificates), PSL tickets are delivered to the offices of these three firms in Ludhiana, which has traditionally been the center of the lottery market in Punjab. The agents then sell them to around 60 "distributors" around the state, each of whom runs its own retail shops or sells the tickets to small retailers, which PSL staff estimated to be around 6000–7000. For the PSL weekly draw in 2015, agents bought the tickets from the state for Rs. 16.5, distributors for Rs. 17, sellers for Rs. 17.5, and the actual players for the retail price of Rs. 20.

As Stine Puri showed in her account of Delhi horserace bettors whose speculations are "oriented toward predicting people rather than horses" (Puri 2015: 466), the belief that outcomes are rigged can promote rather than undermine gambling. But transparency and trust have been part of the core pitch of the PSL from the start. The effort to cast PSL lotteries as a proper government operation and distinguish it from *matka* has generated intensive routines of credibility to show the lottery numbers are a matter of chance. Puri's analysis of betting on horse races in Delhi suggests that credibility is not important, but *matka* depended on the reputation of their operators for credibility, or on numbers generated by an event judged to be beyond the ability of operators to manipulate. Historically, most lotteries were likely kept small by the difficulty of extending reputation beyond a limited area, but there were exceptions. Ratan Khatri of Mumbai earned the trust of punters throughout India and abroad from the early 1960s by running his *matka* operation with renowned integrity, opening a new deck of cards every night in the presence of "patrons" (including Bollywood celebrities) to select the numbers determining the fates of hundreds of thousands of bettors. Long after his arrest in 1998 had driven him from the business, he told an interviewer: "People had great faith in my system. I would even ask them to open the three cards. I knew it was illegal but I ran it with complete honesty" (Awasthi 2007).

We have seen how the PSL struggles to capture the business of illegal lotteries. It is equally pitched against the power of personal reputation that made Khatri's *matka* such a success. The PSL website declares its first objective as "To prevent illegal activities like prize chits, *satta* and *matka* by providing a clean and transparent lottery environment to citizenry" (Punjab State Government 2012).

The heart of this effort is the method by which numbers are drawn. Every Wednesday an official from the lottery directorate in Chandigarh makes the two-hour trip to its office in Ludhiana, the largest market for the PSL, to oversee the weekly draws. These draws are a mixture of theater and bureaucratic procedure. Numbers are drawn using noisy electric "drawing machines" (Figure 11.2), which are kept locked whenever an officer from the Chandigarh office and a judge are not present. To ensure the machine is not tampered with, every articulation between external parts of the drawing machine is covered with seals, pieces of paper affixed to both parts with six daubs of wax and signed by two judges, two officers of the PSL, and representatives of the three agents (Figure 11.3).

The machines are operated by a PSL staff person (Figure 11.2 right), who presses a button for each machine to get its wheels spinning and then presses it again to let it wind down, which generates displays of numbers. One person reads off numbers (far left) as another PSL staff person types them into software written for the PSL and a sessions judge (center) writes them down on paper. This procedure is repeated until they have the 1,100 plus numbers needed for that week's draw. Sometimes representatives of the agents are invited for token runs of

Figure 11.2 Officials of the PSL and a sessions judge draw and authorize winning numbers

the machine as part of the exhibition that it makes no difference who operates it. No staff member is allowed near the machines when they are being run for the draws. (Use of an older machine with metal spinning parts was stopped when it was discovered that staff were manipulating the draw by standing near it with magnets.) Behind the room with the machines, separated by steel bars is a gallery for the public to attend to watch the draw. Aside from representatives of the three agents who come every week, weekly draws rarely attract any visitors. However, the high-prize bumper lottery draws often pack the gallery with hopefuls.

PSL staff persons are very proud of the "transparency" of the draw, achieved by its literal visibility and elaborate checking and counter-checking and signing of documents by PSL staff and the judge, who legally certifies the numbers. They contrast this method not only with the way *matka* numbers are drawn but also the computer draws of the northeastern states lotteries.

One lower-level assistant asked me skeptically, "how to make computer draw transparent?" referring to the invisibility of computer

Figure 11.3 Seals on articulations between parts of a drawing machine

processing. His superior insisted that only machines like they use can do it, a "computer can't qualify," that the 2010 rules require that the draw be as he put it, "visibly transparent, open to view." Indeed, the rules stipulate that the method of a draw must be "visibly transparent to the viewers" (2[d]).

From its start until the 1990s, PSL ran the same games or, in official parlance, "schemes": forty-eight single-digit lottery draws that paid nine times the ticket price, not coincidentally the same payout rates as *matka*. In 1995 it added double-digit draws that paid ninety times the ticket price. The state also ran what are called "bumper" lotteries for festivals such as Diwali, Raksha Bandhan, and the New Year, with first prizes in lakh, the bulk of the revenue came from single-double digit lotteries. In an attempt to depress lottery sales, 1998 Lotteries Regulation Act banned one-digit lotteries but Punjab lottery revenues from two- and three-digit draws remained strong. As you can see from Table 11.1, in 2009–2010, the gross revenues almost reached an astonishing Rs. 4,034 crore (around $860 million at 2010 exchange rates).

Table 11.1 *Annual revenue of the PSL (Rs. in crore [10 millions])*

Year	Gross receipts	Expenditure	Gross profit	Tax	Net profit
2002–03	2606.66	2547.10	59.56	22.08	37.48
2003–04	2441.91	2371.85	70.06	26.62	43.44
2004–05	2694.43	2597.17	97.26	32.08	65.18
2005–06	3218.68	3059.12	159.56	51.91	107.65
2006–07	2164.70	2008.35	156.35	48.79	107.56
2007–08	3557.24	3395.17	162.07	84.88	77.19
2008–09	3565.22	3396.25	168.97	139.00	29.97
2009–10	4033.96	3864.10	169.86	141.70	28.16
2010–11	3799.56	3793.88	5.68	9.71	–3.49
2011–12	63.11	41.33	21.78	8.25	13.53

Table 11.2 *Prizes and draws for June 6, 2017*

	Prize amount (in Rs.)	No. of draws	No. of digits	No. winning numbers
1st prize	5,00,000	1	7	1
2nd prize	1,00,000	2	7	2
3rd prize	50,000	20	7	2
4th prize	5,000	4	last 5	20
5th prize	2,000	1	last 4	20
6th prize	100	100	last 4	2,000
7th prize	40	810	last 4	20,000

However, a provision in the 2010 rules banning two- and three-digit lotteries produced a sharp decline in sales, which plunged to only Rs. 63.11 crore. PSL has attempted to attract lottery players who like odds of every kind by offering seven levels of prizes, by varying the number of draws and the digits (Table 11.2).

PSL tried to replace its two- and three-digit lotteries by increasing the number of draws for its sixth- and seventh-prize lotteries. Although it is still a four-digit draw, the 800–1,000 draws for the seventh-place prize of Rs. 40, effectively reduce the odds for that prize to the odds of a single-digit lottery. Nevertheless, since more digits are identified with higher odds, the four-digit draws obscure the actual odds of winning. Some people do not know about the extra draws for the seventh-place prize but none of the bettors I talked with had done the calculations required to know what the real odds of winning are. These factors and the entry of new competitors has kept the PSL from maintaining its market share.

Sharing

The collapse of PSL revenues after 2010 was not only due to the ban on two- and three-digit lotteries. Another provision of the 2010 rules revoked the ability of a state to close its market to the lottery tickets of other states unless it closed its own state lottery. States conducting their own lotteries were forced to share their lottery markets with lotteries of other states, except when they could be shown to violate central government rules. At the time, Goa, Kerala, Manipur, Meghalaya, Mizoram, Punjab, Maharashtra, Nagaland, Sikkim, and West Bengal had their own lotteries. With the active promotion of lottery agent firms, the lotteries of Mizoram, Nagaland, Sikkim gained a significant share of the lottery market in Punjab. From this point, three kinds of lottery accounted for most of the lottery revenue in Punjab: the PSL, the state lotteries of northeastern states (Mizoram, Nagaland, and Sikkim), and the illegal lotteries running on the northeastern lotteries. While each of these kinds of lottery competes with the others for business, they constitute a complex network of dependencies, each one needing at least one of their competitors in order to be a viable business.

Like the PSL, the Kerala state lottery struggled to recreate the odds of its own successful two-digit lottery by selling four-digit tickets with two fixed digits that were announced ahead of time. But the central government eventually enforced the rule of the Lotteries Act that banned the use of a "pre-announced number" (§4(¶a)). The lottery firm Sugal and Damani had a more creative solution for its northeastern states' clients. No doubt the framers of the 2010 rules requiring a minimum of four "digits" were thinking of digits as numbers 0–9, but there is no explicit statement regarding the numerical range of digits or even that the digits be numbers. Sugal and Damani invented an online game that replaced three of the four numbers with other characters: each ticket has a face card (jack, queen, king), a suit (diamond, heart, spade, clubs), a letter (A or B), and a number (1–5).

Known as the "card" game, with echoes of Bhagat's Mumbai card-based *matka*, it is very popular. As Geertz (1973) argued about cockfighting, favorable odds may not be what really draws players to a game, but the odds of the card games make them comparable to the long-running, attractive high-odds one- and two-digit games. The probability of winning (P_win), one in 120, approaches that of two-digit *matka*, one in 100:

$$\frac{1}{3}[face\ cards] \cdot \frac{1}{4}[suits] \cdot \frac{1}{2}[letters] \cdot \frac{1}{5}[numbers] = \frac{1}{120}$$

The card payoff is 100 times to *matka*'s 90 times; for example, the payoff for a Rs. 2 ticket is Rs. 200, which compensates somewhat for the lower odds of the card game. Combining odds and payoff, we can see what mathematicians call the "expected profit" (Packel 1981: 147–57) from playing a single Rs. 2 ticket paying a prize of Rs. 200.

$$Expected\ profit = P_\text{win}(payoff - ticket\ price) + P_\text{loss}(ticket\ price)$$

$$Expected\ profit = \frac{1}{120}(Rs.\ 200 - Rs.\ 2) + \frac{119}{120}(-Rs.\ 2)$$
$$= -Rs.\ 0.33$$

That is, a player would expect to lose, on average, Rs. 0.33 on every Rs. 2 ticket he purchases. We can compare this with the expected profit of a Rs. 2 ticket for a two-digit *matka*, which would pay Rs. 180:

$$Expected\ profit = \frac{1}{100}(Rs.\ 180 - Rs.\ 2) + \frac{99}{100}(-Rs.\ 2)$$
$$= -Rs.\ 0.2$$

That is, a player can expect to lose, on average, Rs. 0.2 on every Rs. 2 ticket he purchases. While the expected return is much higher in *matka*, the card game is not far off compared to odds for the seventh-place prize of the PSL, with its higher ticket price and lower payout.

Beyond the odds and the expected return, the northeastern states' card game has other attractions: the draws take place every fifteen minutes and the payouts are immediate; the frequency and number of draws allows players to search for patterns; and players can pick their own numbers, unlike the PSL, which distributes tickets with preprinted numbers on them. Results of each draw are written on boards displayed at the entrances to lottery shops. Punters scrutinize these numbers with extreme attention to find patterns that will point them to a winning play. When I first started going to these shops, I expected them to have the easy sociability of a teashop. To an extent that is true for those working there or simply hanging out. But many of those planning their next play are too absorbed with the results board to chat, often pausing only to turn to a fellow player to point to some pattern quizzically. They usually push their analyses to the last minute before the draw, when the seller frantically tries to enter the plays of a rush of his clients.

According to government reports from the mid-1990s as well as the PSL staff and managers at private corporation firms, high-odds quick-turnaround games are especially attractive to the poor industrial workers and service people who make up a large portion of the lottery market buyers. Sounding a bit like Oscar Lewis (1959) describing the short time horizon of the poor, the head of one agency told me: "They are poor and they have no patience, they want to spend their daily wages quickly." Middle-class buyers favor the less frequent bumper lotteries that have lower odds and higher payouts and require more paperwork to claim prizes.

Punjab has been protesting to the central government that these card games and other northeastern lottery practices violate central government rules, that they are really operated by corporations rather than the states themselves. If the central government accepted this claim, Punjab would be legally allowed to ban them. But so far, the center has refused to declare a violation. The agents, in contrast, have been aggressively fighting against efforts to ban this game, since it has allowed them to recover business that was lost when one-, two-, and three-digit lotteries were banned. Furthermore, the lottery contracts of the northeastern states are awarded on much more favorable terms than those of the PSL, therefore margins on them are much higher. PSL staff argue that these agents like dealing with the small, weak, and corrupt northeastern states that let them do whatever they want. One PSL staff person told me: "Punjab is a developed state. We have a reputation to preserve. But these little states, no one bothers with rules there." Another PSL staff person quipped: "They don't pay the state for their [lottery] contracts, they just give the money directly to the director of lotteries! The state governments get almost nothing."

It is unclear to me how much the three large corporate players of the Indian lottery business cooperate at the national level on legislative strategy. But they clearly coordinate relations among themselves and northeastern states to schedule the forty-two daily draws, one every fifteen minutes, from 10:45 am until 9 pm, so that draws from different lotteries do not take place simultaneously. The lotteries are also all the same, the card game invented by Sugal and Damani. Lottery websites for different northeastern states are also identical, suggesting they are all maintained by one site manager. The relationships of managers of the agent firms at their Punjab head offices in Ludhiana very cozy. They coordinate both day-to-day operations and their strategic engagement with the Punjab state government on issues of taxation and regulation.

Most striking is the retail-sales arrangement they have established. In local parlance, lotteries of the northeastern states are called "online lotteries," but they are not online in the sense that tickets can be bought over the Internet. Rather, tickets are bought and registered through network terminals in lottery shops, which also deliver draw results immediately after the draw. Each of the three firms provides its own terminal for the northeastern states online lotteries to each retail lottery seller. Each agent contracts for some or all of the draws of a particular state lottery.

Although these northeastern lotteries are all the same card game and government officials and business people usually talk about "draws," each one has its own name, for example Amoli and Makrand-Super Card. Naming each "draw" uniquely designates them legally as a separate "lottery," an arrangement that skirts the Lotteries Regulation Act's rule that no lottery may have more than one draw in a week (§4(¶h)).

All these arrangements raise the legal question of what it means for a state to run a lottery or even more generally, with so many government activities contracted to private firms, what does it mean for a state government to operate a lottery? The Lotteries Regulation Act of 1998 requires that "State Government itself shall conduct the draws of all the lotteries" (§4(¶e)). If a government contracts with a lottery corporation to handle the generation of random numbers, is it conducting the draw in the way that the PSL clearly does? For PSL staff, all these arrangements are evidence that these northeastern lotteries are actually private lotteries merely branded by the states, which are therefore violating the 1998 Act, which stipulates that only state governments can "organize, conduct and promote" lotteries (¶3). Setting aside the legal question, perhaps we might best understand these northeastern states lotteries as operated by an informal consortium of state governments and companies that have made two markets, a consumer market for legal lotteries and a market for the state authority to run them, and have built the technology infrastructure both markets require. Although it seems likely just as these corporations collude to shape the consumer market, they might also collude to fix the market for state authority to run lotteries.

The technologically advanced and lucrative arrangement of northeastern states lotteries frustrated the entrepreneurial spirit of the PSL staff, which felt hamstrung by the limitations of their paper lottery and adherence to legal propriety. In 2014, when I began this research, the PSL, with help from the consulting firm of Ernst & Young, was at work on a tender offer for its own online lottery. When I initially turned up at the Finance Ministry dressed in a black suit and tie to request access to the Directorate of Lotteries, I was enthusiastically received, not least perhaps because the IAS officer initially hoped I might be doing research for a foreign direct investor interested in making a bid on the imminent tender offer. The same suspicion generated what I can only characterize as undisguised hostility on the part of the managers of agencies in Ludhiana. Fearing I might make an offer that would upset the arrangement they were making to refuse to bid on the tender offer and hold out for more profitable terms, they grilled me with prosecutorial zeal about why I was looking into the lottery in Punjab.

The agents had no interest in supporting an online PSL because it would simply cannibalize their existing market and subject them to the unwanted regulation and less profitable terms required by the Punjab state. In fact, none of the agent corporations submitted a bid. (When I returned a year later to talk with the heads of these agents in Punjab, after the tender had failed to attract any bids from me or any other foreign direct investor, I was welcomed with great warmth.) Punjab lottery staff and Finance Ministry officials I talked with insisted that terms of the tender were generous and that only the collusive stranglehold of the agents had sunk it. Against this background, the Punjab state government decided to raise the taxes on the northeastern state lotteries, allowable under Home Ministry rules, to the point where an online PSL would be relatively profitable. Taxes for outside lotteries operating in Punjab are assessed on the basis of draws. Up to this point, Punjab had been taxing them at a rate of Rs. 55,000 per draw and the government raised the rate to Rs. 80,000 per draw. This generated a standoff between the Punjab state government and the agents, who closed their online lotteries and refused to sell PSL tickets for four months, from September to December of 2014. This deprived the state of both lottery and tax revenue, but the state refused to budge.

In January, the agencies reopened their northeastern state operations again, but they reduced their draws to twenty-seven a day.

If the agents and the PSL remain antagonistic, they have found common cause in opposition to the explosion of the illegal lotteries, which rushed to meet the demand while the legal lotteries were closed and managed to hold onto much of the market share they gained during this period.

In Punjab, illegal lotteries, sometimes called *dara* or, more often, *satta* (Hindi for speculation), operate using the legal operations of the north-eastern state lotteries. There is anecdotal evidence for this sort of relation between illegal and legal lottery markets all over India – that local operators sell their own tickets using the results of state lotteries, often offering better odds and payoffs than the official state lotteries. However, in Punjab, the infrastructure for generating regular, credible numbers established by northeastern state lotteries and their agents has generated an entirely new market of illegal lotteries. That is, although this new *satta* draws on longstanding preferences of lower-class bettors, it is a separate market from the *satta* that has been run out of Mumbai. If the PSL was established to appropriate lotteries for the legal market, the northeastern states lotteries have generated a whole new kind of illegal lottery, one that threatens to dominate the lottery market. One PSL official told me that the 2010 rules prohibiting one- and two-digit lotteries had "destroyed the market" for legal lotteries and are very much "favoring *dara/satta.*"

As one PSL staff person put it, *satta* and legal lotteries are "parallel." *Satta* is run out of the same shops, using the same results, and even the same paper as the northeastern states lotteries. It is a one-digit game with the same odds, 9:1, and payout as *matka*, nine times the wager. Numbers 1–10 are yielded by converting the last two digits of the card games, as we can see in Table 11.3.

Table 11.3 *Conversion of card game results to one-digit* matka

A1 = 1	B1 = 6
A2 = 2	B2 = 7
A3 = 3	B3 = 8
A4 = 4	B4 = 9
A5 = 5	B5 = 10

The licenses to sell legal lotteries allow sellers to run their *satta* business openly in markets, without the need to conceal the comings and goings of players, and the giving and taking of money. *Satta* players buy their chits from the same person who would sell them a legal lottery ticket. There is never any question of which lottery a customer wants to play. If he names four "digits" he wants to play, the seller enters it in the computer and prints out a ticket. If he asks for a single digit, the operator will snap up a losing computer-printed ticket from a previous draw lying on his counter or even the floor of the shop and write on the back the number, time, and amount of the bet. Some customers play both the card game and *satta* on different draws. If the *satta* player's number comes up, the seller reaches into the same till he pays card game winners from and pays the *satta* winner.

PSL officials resent the lotteries of the northeastern states, but true to the original purpose of the PSL, one official told me, "Our real competition is *satta*." In 2014, government and industry people estimated that 30–40 percent of the lottery market in Punjab measured by revenue was *satta*. The four-month closure of the northeastern lotteries allowed *satta* to capture a larger share of the market and by June of 2015 dispirited agents and PSL staff agreed that *satta* accounted for as much as 70–80 percent of the market. With the growth of *satta*, Mohali (adjacent to Chandigarh, the joint capital of the states of Punjab and Haryana) has become the largest market for legal lotteries, because a great proportion of customers are government employees with concerns about getting involved in illegal activities.

The head of one agent firm told me that such illegal single-digit lotteries are everywhere in India but that the "taste of the customers" for single-digit lotteries is much stronger in Punjab and nearby regions. One PSL official told me the illegal, low-odds gambling cannot be stopped and that when they banned it in Delhi in 1995, he heard stories of people betting on all kinds of things, such as whether the next car that goes by will be blue or not. He was often dispirited by the lack of regard for the law evidenced by *satta* players, who "don't care who is selling, only about the money"; "he is not caring whether it is legal or illegal, he just says 'Give me the ticket, the one that pays more.'" PSL staff are critical of the illegal lotteries not only because they compete with legal ones but because they tarnish all lotteries and the image of PSL staff themselves by associating them with their seediness in the mind of the public.

Agents are more concerned with the revenue they lose to *satta* even as they pay for the entire computer and network infrastructure that makes *satta* possible. Agents think of these illegal lotteries as parasites on the organization and infrastructure of the northeastern lotteries. But as Gustav Peebles suggests (personal communication), we might compare the northeastern states lotteries to central banks that establish currency systems that enable private banks to transact in what is, in fact, private money.[4] And, like central banks, agents function in practice as regulators of the "private" (*satta*) lotteries, through the technical infrastructure they supply and through their policing of sales. One agent makes all the sellers who use its terminals sign English-language legal statement pledging that they will not sell illegal lotteries. The manager of this agent firm told me that he carefully tracks the data on ticket sales levels on each of his terminals and compares it with terminals in comparable commercial locations to figure out which lottery sellers are using his terminals mostly to provide results to *satta* players, rather than to sell the northeastern states tickets. It is mainly a matter of trying to reduce rather than eliminate the practice. When an agent catches a seller excessively dealing in illegal lotteries, he threatens to block his terminal. He also asks the other two other agents about the seller. If all three are having a problem, the agents block their terminals for an agreed on period of time, halting the seller's business in both legal tickets and *satta*. But the manager told me that he tries to stay friendly because he usually cannot catch them outright and his business depends on their goodwill and their willingness to play by the rules to some extent: "We don't have any enemies or friends, we don't have any interest except money," he told me.

Lottery sellers I talked with said bettors are the ones choosing between legal lotteries and *satta*, but sellers make an effort to sell legal tickets. They do this not only to evade sanction from the agents but also because they have a clear interest in making sure that the legal northeastern lotteries are profitable, because both legal and illegal sales depend on the infrastructure the agents supply. Like all the other actors in this market, the illegal lotteries need the northeastern states lotteries to stay viable.

---

[4] We could also see *satta* as "riding the rails" of the northeastern lottery system, as proponents of new payments systems describe their relation to older payment infrastructures (Nelms et al. 2018).

Agents would like the police to curb *satta*, but some police make good money in bribes to allow the trade. One lottery agent claimed the new station house officer (SHO) of the area with the main market for lottery tickets in Ludhiana called all the lottery sellers and told them he expected Rs. 5,000 per month from each of them. The basic interest that some police have in the success of *satta* broke into the open in 1992 with newspaper reports that police in Madhya Pradesh were "harassing" the ticket dealers for the recently opened and very much legal state lottery (Sharma 1992b). The agent said he had tried to meet with the senior superintendent of police, the SHO's superior, but to no avail. He refuses to complain openly because he is afraid of both the police benefiting from the *satta* racket and the criminals who run the protection racket for *satta*: "We are not mafia, not *goonda*s [thugs]. We are business people. They have guns," he told me. A PSL staff officer confirmed that agents are afraid of "*satta* dons, they don't want to fight with them, they hide behind a curtain. The police require a written complaint, but they are too afraid. They talk to the Punjab State about it, but they will not even write one thing to the Punjab State, they never want to get involved in front." Punjab police have asked PSL staff and agents to go with them to point out who is running illegal operations so they could make arrests, but staff members always refuse, because, as one told me, "this is very dangerous."

The lower-level police I talked with in Ludhiana confirmed much of this. But they also countered that it is very difficult is to obtain actual evidence that a shop is running *satta*. Selling a *satta* chit looks just like selling a legal ticket and one has to be right on top of the buyer and seller to be able to know. The only way to catch a seller is to get him to sell you a *satta* chit, but police are recognized, so it is not easy. A senior officer told me that most police stations arrest two or three people a month for selling *satta*, just to show their superiors they are enforcing the law. But even if a seller is convicted, they pay a fine of just Rs. 500 and get back to work.

Mutual Dependence

One of the most striking features of lottery organization and practices in Punjab today is the degree to which each kind of lottery depends on the operations and legal status of the others. Most obviously, *satta* depends on the technological infrastructure, organization, legal cover, and even the paper provided by the corporate agents through the northeastern states lotteries. Dependent on illegal lotteries, the police are similarly beneficiaries of the laws that prohibit them and the organizations that adhere to those laws. The corporate agents, like the monopolies of the seventeenth-century regulated companies, would be clear losers if the lottery market were "freed" from the nominal authority of states and effective corporate control. Although the agents would prefer to expand their northeastern states lotteries at the expense of the PSL, they must ensure it earns enough to protect it from politicians who would rather see it closed, which would enable the state to ban all other lotteries. PSL officials see the northeastern lotteries as parasites on the open market that the state of Punjab establishes by having its own lottery; the agents of the northeastern states lotteries similarly see illegal lotteries as parasites on their arrangements. Characterizations of parasitism are always based on a view of what entity is functionally paramount. But if the northeastern states and *satta* lotteries are parasites, they are the kind of microbiota, in aggregate a large mass, that biologists increasingly recognize are required for the healthy functioning of the host body.

The PSL probably has the greatest potential for legal and economic autonomy from all the other actors in this field. But as long as the Punjab state government is unwilling to bring the sales and marketing in house and operate it with state employees as does Kerala, it needs not only lottery agents, but the northeastern states lotteries that keep these agents in business. Even illegal lotteries play a role in supporting the PSL, as the illegal trade keeps many more small-time sellers of their tickets in business, which strengthens the PSL distribution network.

The complex relations among different actors involved in the lottery business in Punjab shows how varied the role of law can be. Obviously enough, legal regulations defining the difference between legal and illegal activities format markets in illegal practices and set the terms of trade within them. Even as the tax requirements of regulations are evaded, virtually all of the other provisions of the regulations are extended through illegal activity. The success of the northeastern states lotteries vis-à-vis the PSL also shows how regulation generates practices that, while not illegal, depend on the fact that competitors are subject to the stronger legal enforcement or maintain a moral or bureaucratic commitment to legality. The commitments of the PSL to transparent financial practices and draws, accounting requirements, and profit for the public budget cost it market share, both because their games are less attractive and agents prefer to promote the northeastern states lotteries. In fact, the agents are very grateful for these commitments. We can compare the position of the agents on Punjab state good governance practices to those of Uber, which surreptitiously fights to maintain the strict regulations on licensed taxi companies that do not apply to Uber, allowing the company to undercut the taxi market.

Finally, we can note the varying regulatory role of the technical infrastructures of state lotteries. The securely printed PSL tickets, computer-generated tickets, and drawing machines can be seen to have pulled lotteries outside the relations of reputation and trust linked to the actions of individuals, that is, people like Khatri drawing his cards in Mumbai, drawing a stark divide between the illegal networks of *matka* and the legal organization of government staff. Ironically, the infrastructure of the northeastern states lotteries has similarly enabled illegal lotteries in Punjab to have the same qualities of regularity and transparency as state-run lotteries, independent from the reputation of individuals.

On the other hand, the computer network infrastructure built to handle the online lotteries of the northeastern states enabled the closest possible merger of mafia-managed illegal lotteries and legal lotteries, to the point where police investigations cannot capture evidence of it for prosecution. Infrastructure linking cities in Punjab with far-off states, designed to give large corporate operators access to local markets, provided the means for the local interpersonal relations of influence of the police and mafia groups to expand. The very technology that makes results credible by displacing them beyond the local social world at the same time strengthens the role of local social relations. This dynamic is beautifully captured in the losing online ticket that becomes a *satta* chit, two sides of the same paper.

References

Awasthi, S 2007, From Matka King to Anonymous Punter, Life's Come a Full Circle for Him (www.expressindia.com/latest-news/f rom-matka-king-to-anonymous-punter-lifes-come-a-full-circle-for-him. Accessed November 12, 2013).

Birla, R 2009, *Stages of Capital: Law, Culture, and Market Governance in Late Colonial India*, Duke University Press, Durham.

Casey, E 2003, "Gambling and Consumption: Working-Class Women and UK National Lottery Play," *Journal of Consumer Culture*, 3, 2: 245–63.

Davis, R 2006, "All or Nothing: Video Lottery Terminal Gambling and Economic Restructuring in Rural Newfoundland," *Identities: Global Studies in Culture and Power*, 13: 503–31.

Frith, WGC 1976, *The Royal Calcutta Turf Club. Some Notes on Its Foundation, History and Development*, The Royal Calcutta Turf Club, Calcutta.

Geertz, C 1973, "Notes on the Balinese Cockfight," in *The Interpretation of Cultures*, Basic Books, New York, pp. 412–53.

Guyer, J 1993, "'Toiling Ingenuity': Food Regulation in Britain and Nigeria," *American Ethnologist*, 20, 4: 797–817.

Hardgrove, A 2007, *Community and Public Culture: The Marwaris in Calcutta, 1897–1997*, Columbia University Press, New York.

Hart, K 2006, "Bureaucratic Form and the Informal Economy," in B Guha-Khasnobis, R Kanbur, & E Ostrom (eds.) *Linking the Formal and Informal Economy: Concepts and Policies*, Oxford University Press, Oxford, pp. 21–35.

Hart, K 2008, "Between Bureaucracy and the People: A Political History of Informality," Danish Institute for International Studies Working Paper no 2008/27.

Klima, A 2006, "Spirits of 'Dark Finance' in Thailand: A Local Hazard for the International Moral Fund," *Cultural Dynamics*, 18, 1: 33–60.

Krige, D 2011, "We Are Running for a Living: Work, Leisure and Speculative Accumulation in an Underground Numbers Lottery in Johannesburg," *African Studies*, 70, 1: 3–24.

Lewis, O 1959, *Five Families; Mexican Case Studies in the Culture of Poverty*, Basic Books, New York.

Majumder, R & Patel, B 2007, It's the Bhagats, You Bet (http://epaper.timesofindia.com. Accessed May 4, 2014).

Mosquera, A & Garcia de Molero, I 2004, "The Cosmological Ritual of Lottery: Venezuelan Study," *Acta Ethnographica Hungarica*, 49, 1–2: 125–39.

Nelms, TC, Maurer, B, Swartz, L, & Mainwaring, S 2018, "Social Payments: Innovation, Trust, Bitcoin, and the Sharing Economy," *Theory, Culture & Society*, 35, 3: 13–33.

Packel, EW 1981, *Mathematics of Games and Gambling*, Mathematical Association of America, Washington.

Peebles, G 2011, *The Euro and Its Rivals: Currency and the Construction of a Transnational City*, Indiana University Press, Bloomington.

Punjab State Government 2014, Concept Paper for Starting Punjab State Online Lottery – first draft.

Punjab State Government, 2013, About Us (http://punjabstatelotteries .gov.in/en/about_us.php. Accessed December 18, 2013).

Puri, SS 2014, *Speculation in Fixed Futures: An Ethnography of Betting in Between Legal and Illegal Economies at the Delhi Racecourse*, Københavns Universitet, Det Humanistiske Fakultet, Copenhagen.

Puri, SS 2015, "Betting on Performed Futures: Predictive Procedures at Delhi Racecourse," *Comparative Studies of South Asia, Africa and the Middle East*, 35, 3: 466–80.

Roitman, J 2004, *Fiscal Disobedience: An Anthropology of Economic Regulation in Central Africa*, Princeton University Press, Princeton.

Saini, DD & Sethi, G 1963, *Law Relating to Gambling, Betting, Lotteries and Clubs, etc.* Law Publishers, Allahabad.

Sami, SMA 1938, *Law and the Practice of Gambling in India*, Law Book Co., Allahabad.

Sanju, G, Velleman, R, & Nadkarni, A 2017, "Gambling in India: Past, Present and Future," *Asian Journal of Psychiatry*, 26: 39–43.

Selby, W 1996, "Social Evil or Social Good? Lotteries and State Regulation in Australia and the United States," in J McMillen (ed.) *Gambling Cultures*, Routledge, London, pp. 65–85.

Sharma, A 1992a, "Fatwa to Muslims against Lottery," *Times of India*, March 16, p. 8.

Sharma, A 1992b, "BJP Leaders Flay M.P. Govt.'s Move on Lottery," *Times of India*, March 4, p. 9.

Van-Wyk, I 2012, "Tata Ma Chance-On Contingency and the Lottery in Post-Apartheid South Africa," *Journal of the International African Institute*, 82, 1: 41–68.

Van-Wyk, I 2013, "Bad Luck, Slippery Soney and the South African Lottery," in R Cassidy, A Pisac, & C Loussouarn (eds.) *Qualitative Research in Gambling: Exploring the Production and Consumption of Risk*, Routledge, New York, pp. 156–70.

12 Liquid Assets: Transactional Grammars of Alcohol in Jharkhand

ROGER BEGRICH

It was a hot and dry day in April 2008. I was sitting in the shade with Sagar and his son Dhanit,[1] in front of their house in Diankel, Jharkhand, working on my field notes. Sagar is a Munda subsistence farmer, and I usually stay with his family when I am in Diankel. I had come to observe the annual *sarhul* festival – but due to complications of ritual nature, the sacrificial offerings with which the celebrations usually begin had been postponed, and I was trying to understand the logic behind that. Suddenly, Mangra, Sagar's neighbor, came running. He was gesticulating frantically, pointing eastwards, and spoke loud and fast – much too fast for my limited Mundari skills. Sagar jumped up and said "Come, we have work," and we all started to run in the direction Mangra had pointed, across the parched, harvested paddy fields. After a few minutes, we reached a pit, and I realized what the urgency was about: a calf had fallen into it while grazing and was unable to get out of it – it was a big pit, about two meters wide and two meters deep, which someone had probably dug with the intention of building a well. It took us about twenty minutes of strategizing, quite a bit of physical effort, and a long pole along which we finally pushed and lifted the terrified bovine out of the hole. A short while after we had returned to the village, we were called to Mangra's house. The owner of the rescued calf was sitting in the courtyard of his mud house, reaching with both hands into an aluminum pot to pick up handfuls of fermented rice, pressing each of them slowly and tightly to squeeze the *bodé* (Mundari for rice beer) out of it, letting the liquid drop back into the pot. We sat down, and after about twenty minutes, the rice solids were separated from the liquids, and the *bodé* was ready. Mangra's wife

---

[1] Names of individuals and villages have been changed – even though my interlocutors in Jharkhand would have preferred it otherwise – in order to comply with the requirements of Internal Review Boards and the National Science Foundation, which supported my fieldwork.

brought steel cups, a snack of roasted dal, some salt and green chillies, from the house. She laid out the snack, using *sal* leaves[2] as small plates, and began pouring the *bodé* into the cups. Then she ceremoniously handed each of us one of the cups, every time bowing down and putting together her flat hands in front of her face to say *joar*. We reciprocated this greeting and began drinking.

As far as I could tell, Mangra and his wife enjoyed serving us rice beer (and drinking with us), but they would have done so even if they did not enjoy it; because we had assisted in rescuing their calf, they were obligated to offer us *bodé*: if Mundas ask neighbors or even relatives (living in a different household) for help with a task, they will provide them with *bodé* after the work is completed (or in winter maybe with *arki*, the liquor distilled from *mahua* flowers).[3] This practice of distributing alcohol after benefiting from somebody's labor is something that many Adivasi in Jharkhand find very characteristic for their communities, and which they also take pride in. Several times, in the early phase of my research, when I was invited to join a drinking party after a particular task had been completed collectively, I was told: "This is how we Adivasi do it. We don't pay for work with money; we pay with rice beer." However, even though things were put in this manner, I later came to understand that the explanation offered was a somewhat hyperstylized interpretation of these transactions: occurring in a context where insisting on the essential alterity of adivasiness/indigeneity operates as a political survival strategy, a perceived cultural specificity (a feature distinguishing Adivasi from others, i.e., remuneration in the form of alcohol) was isolated from the larger context in which these transactions occurred for purposes of self-representation. But as I came to understand in the course of my research, the significance of such transactional relations is not primarily (or at least not exclusively) remuneration but rather the validation of the relation itself. Even though the exchange of liquor for labor does at the surface

---

[2] The *sal* tree (Shorea robusta) is a species native to northern South Asia, and it is very important for Adivasis in Jharkhand. Its wood is used for construction and its leaves are, among other things, used to make cups for rice beer – especially on ritual occasions or at large celebrations such as weddings. *Sal* is also of spiritual relevance for the Munda and other tribes in Jharkhand. One of the most important annual religious festivals, *sarhul*, during which village deities are worshipped, is celebrated (around April) with the *sal* tree flowers.

[3] Bassia longifolia L. is also known as Madhuca indica J. F. Gmel or Madhuca longfolia.

appear like an economic transaction, I would argue that it is much rather a moral transaction, and an obligation in Maussian terms (1990).

An observation may illustrate this claim: Contrary to what was repeatedly stated to me in the early phase of my research, alcohol is not the only thing that is offered in exchange for labor. I noted, especially in urban settings, that work, such as the fixing of a roof, for example, was paid for in cash, as well as concluded with rice beer or *mahua*. The tasks for which such transactions of alcohol took place were always the ones that required more hands or bodies than were available in a particular household – such as, transplanting rice seedlings, tying up bundles of paddy for storage, or, as just mentioned, the fixing of a roof. The exchange of liquor for labor was thus not primarily a form of remuneration, but rather a validation of the relationship between the involved parties.

Social transactions of alcohol among Mundas are not restricted to contexts of communal labor – rather, their social world is permeated by alcoholic obligations: important moments in the trajectory of a life, such as child births, weddings, and funerals involve transactions of rice beer or various forms of liquor, as do hospitality, conflict resolution, and the closing of contracts. However, the drinking occasion made possible by the rescued calf involved at least two further kinds of transaction. For one, there was an economic transaction, as there was no ready fermented rice for *bodé*[4] in Mangra's house – Mangra had to procure it from a neighbor. And then there were *spiritual* transactions: Sagar, his son, Mangra, and his wife all dipped three or four fingers of their right hand into their cups of *bodé* and then sprinkled a few drops in libation on the ground before taking the first sip; an offering to their ancestors and the spirits and deities that constitute the world and make life in it possible (or impossible).

This chapter describes different landscapes of alcohol production and consumption in Jharkhand and begins with a broader discussion of how various kinds of transaction involving alcohol are embedded in

---

[4] *Bodé* (also known as *illi*, or *haṛia* in Hindi) is prepared from half-boiled rice, which is mixed with a fermenting agent called *ranu* (which means medicine) and left to sit for several days, until the yeast in the *ranu* has transformed carbohydrates from the rice into alcohol. Depending on the season (or rather the temperature) this can take anywhere from three to seven days. When it is ready, it needs to be consumed before it becomes sour and rotten.

the moral and economic lives of Adivasis. The example above shows how transactions of alcohol are tied up with social as well as cosmological obligations and reciprocities for Mundas. In the second half of the chapter, I will describe how such transactions are subject to complex issues of regulation involving intersecting cosmologies and sovereignties. In the following, I will briefly discuss transactions of alcohol between Mundas and the realms of spirits, ancestors, and deities – collectively known as *bonga*s, and then add an account of various ways in which alcohol forms part of the economic life of Adivasi in two distinct landscapes of Jharkhand. My intention is not to isolate discrete transactional domains but to illustrate the multilayered relations between humans and alcohol.[5] Finally, I will turn to a discussion on how law and policing inflect transactional grammars of alcohol in Jharkhand, and in doing so, impinge on issues of livelihood – and existence itself – for many Adivasi families.

The landscape in which the Mundas live is constituted by various spirits or deities known as *bonga*s, and inhabited not just by the living, but also by their ancestors. To prevent misfortune, disease, and disaster, it is important to heed the rules, needs, and desires of the *bonga*s and the ancestors, and this entails propitiating them with alcohol (and occasional animal sacrifices). Offerings of a few drops in libation before taking the first sip of an alcoholic beverage are spiritual transactions, which are as common as they are fundamental for the relations between Mundas and spirit-beings. When asked about libations, Mundas would usually tell me that they make these offerings because their ancestors also like to drink. Sharing *bodé* with their ancestors and *bonga*s is a practice deeply woven into the texture of everyday life. It is not done in a ceremonial manner – these transactions frequently happens very casually, or instinctively, without the need to interrupt an ongoing conversation, for example.[6]

---

[5] While my focus in this chapter is on transactions of alcohol, I have elsewhere developed a more detailed argument, which approaches the role of alcohol in the lives of Adivasi in Jharkhand as a problem of moral governance and ethical practice, and builds on theories of obligation to offer a rejection of stereotypical descriptions of Adivasis as drunkards, as well as a critique of addiction concepts (Begrich 2013).

[6] Many Christian Adivasis (especially those who do not abstain from alcohol) also follow this practice of sharing drinks with *bonga*s and ancestors, indicating that the theological intervention which the advent of Christianity meant for the Mundas did not completely uproot the cosmological order of their world.

Understanding the significance of spiritual transactions of rice beer begins with the fact that *bodé* is a conditio sine qua non for all religious or ritual tasks. During my fieldwork, I was frequently told that "without *bodé*, no work is possible," meaning that no celebration, no worship, and no contract is complete without rice beer. The spiritual or cosmological significance of *bodé* is best illustrated with a myth of creation of the Munda tribe, which I was told many times in Jharkhand, and which (or variations thereof) is also frequently documented in ethnographic accounts (Hunter 1877: 41; Roy 1912: 328; van Exem 1982: 31). According to this myth, after *Singbonga* – the Supreme Being – had created the world, a giant bird laid an egg, out of which came a boy and a girl who were to grow up to become the progenitors of the Mundas. However, they remained childless for many years as they were completely unaware of the nature of sexuality. Only after *Singbonga* taught them how to prepare rice beer did they procreate. The importance of *bodé* for religious occasions such as the *sarhul* festival I had come to observe in Diankel, can thus be derived from the mythological truth that *Singbonga* himself had taught the Mundas how to prepare rice beer and encouraged intoxication as a creative force. *Bodé* is thus of vital significance for the Mundas, and the availability of rice beer a condition for the existence of their people. The gift of life came with the gift of rice beer, and the relationship between the Mundas and the Creator initiated by this gift, entails the obligation to worship *Singbonga*, and to return the gift of rice beer.

Two Landscapes of Liquor

It took no effort for Mangra to procure *bodé* that day, as many families had been preparing for the *sarhul* festival, during which copious amounts of rice beer are consumed. But because the opening sacrifices for the festival had had to be postponed, as already mentioned, the

---

However, this does not mean that Christianity has not substantially impacted the world of Adivasis. As a matter of fact, the importance of Christianity for Adivasi modernity cannot be underestimated. Since colonial days, churches have been the primary provider of education for Adivasis in many rural parts of Jharkhand. Furthermore, Christianity played an important role in configuring the political and ethnic identities of Adivasis in Jharkhand, and the beginnings of the movement for a separate state of Jharkhand lay with Christian Adivasis (Aaron 2007; Bara 2007).

celebrations (and the drinking) could not begin. However, the *bodé* was ready to be consumed and thus available for sale.

This is not always the case, as there is no regular market for rice beer in Diankel – and the same is true for *arki*, the liquor distilled from *mahua* flowers. People in the village prepare these beverages when they need them, for example, for a religious occasion, when they call on communal labor, when they expect guests or a baby, when they are invited to a wedding, etc. And sometimes they prepare them just because they like to have a drink at the end of an exhausting day of work in the fields or forest. Nevertheless, *bodé* and *arki* are occasional commodities in Diankel; some villagers brew *bodé* – or distill *arki* – every week to sell them on market days, and others prepare them occasionally, when they are in need for cash.

The landscape of liquor transactions is quite different in Koylatoli, a settlement of Munda migrant laborers in Hatia, an industrial township at the outskirts of the state's capital, Ranchi. In 1958, the government of India set up there the Heavy Engineering Corporation (HEC, http://www.hecltd.com), the largest integrated engineering industrial complex in India. HEC is a paradigmatic example for the vision of rapid modernization through massive industrialization of Jawaharlal Nehru. HEC was once glorified as the "giant behind industrial modernization," as a decrepit signboard (which was taken off in the course of my fieldwork) near its head office declared. While still operational, HEC is now an ailing enterprise and has become, at least for many middle-class Indians, a symbol for the inefficiency of public sector undertakings and a testimony to their inability to perform according to the needs of a booming, liberal economy.

While establishing HEC in the late 1950s, the government of India had acquired 7,500 acres of land, in the process of which thirty-two villages and several thousand residents (the vast majority of them Adivasi) were displaced. The premises of the company (and its auxiliary enterprises, employee quarters, etc.) however, although huge, cover only a fraction of the land it owns. Vast stretches of the HEC-owned land lie vacant, while settlements (*basti*s) have come up at many places; some of them are inhabited by the formerly landholding families or, mostly, by migrant laborers who have come to the city from rural areas in search of livelihood.

Koylatoli is one such *basti*. At the time of my fieldwork there, it consisted of fifty-six households. Except for two households, whose members are Oraon, all of Koylatoli's inhabitants were Mundas who had migrated there in search of work from rural parts of Jharkhand. A total of eight households in Koylatoli prepared rice beer on a daily basis and sold it in their courtyards, houses, alleyways, or along an abandoned railway track adjacent to the *basti*. When I first began my fieldwork, I knew only of two such houses where *bodé* was available for sale, but I later found out that there were in fact several more. They had arranged themselves in such a way that their hours of operation did not significantly overlap – while some started offering rice beer in the early morning, others would get their batch ready around midday, and yet others would follow in the afternoon. Two households also offered the liquor distilled from *mahua* flowers locally known as *arki* (or *daru*, which simply means liquor). For all these households, the sale of alcohol was indispensable, as they depended on the cash thus generated – either exclusively, or because their other sources of income were too scarce or irregular. With eight out of fifty-six households, every seventh household in the *basti* was thus making a living selling alcohol.[7]

Even though Koylatoli came into existence in the late 1950s as a settlement accommodating migrant laborers who built – and of whom some later worked for – HEC, when I conducted my fieldwork, not a single one of its inhabitants had a job there. At the time, only one person in all of Koylatoli had a permanent job – working at the state's traffic department, and thus with a guaranteed, albeit meager income. All the other people going for work, day by day, were hired temporarily by contractors as wage laborers on construction sites or in one of the factories in HEC's economic field of gravity. There are a number of so-called *ancillaries and auxiliary industries* that came up in the 1970s on the land acquired by the central government in the 1950s for (but not used by) HEC. These auxiliary plants were originally intended to produce items required by HEC, but, in the meantime, many operated in completely different domains (a testimony to the fact that probably HEC was not – and had never been – a thriving enterprise, and that it had been conceptualized at a capacity much larger than economically sensible). One such factory that was located in the "Ancillary Industries

---

[7] Unfortunately, I could not precisely assess where the customers came from. But based on my observations, between 50 and 70 percent of the alcohol sold in Koylatoli was consumed by inhabitants of the *basti* itself.

Area" of Hatia was a bottling plant operated by the local liquor syndicate, where several of Koylatoli's women worked. Thus, interestingly enough, even some of the women who did not prepare or sell rice beer in Koylatoli were dependent on alcohol as a source of livelihood.

The story of the villages around Hatia that were displaced in the 1950s to make space for the company is well-known throughout Jharkhand and serves as a deterrent for other Adivasi communities facing the prospect of giving up their land for industrial developments. The villagers who were displaced for HEC were made to believe at the time that they were not only contributing to the grand Nehruvian project of industrial development, but that they could participate in the progress that was to ensue. Families were offered jobs in exchange for the land they were giving up, and they were promised to be resettled. However, only one of the thirty-two displaced villages was ever relocated, and in this case, resettlement concerned only the houses of the displaced families – their agricultural land was not replaced. Proportional to their land holdings, families were given a certain number of jobs in the factory. However, while land could be handed down from generation to generation, the same would not apply in the case of jobs. More than fifty years later, many of the families who had been dislocated the late 1950s were without both land and a regular source of income. For many of the displaced families, the only livelihood available is the production and sale of alcohol. In conversations with middle-class Ranchiites, the image of an Adivasi woman sitting at the roadside or at the weekly bazaar in Hulhundu (near Hatia), selling rice beer or *mahua* liquor epitomizes the relationship between Adivasis and the promise of industrialization: while many (mostly Adivasis) find this image expressive of widespread disregard for Adivasis (as in: *disowned and neglected, tricked out of their property and their future, Adivasis are left with no option but making a living in illegality and inebriety*), others (many non-Adivasis) argue that the reliance of Adivasis on illegal alcohol as a livelihood is expressive of both their inherent laziness and their perpetual drunkenness. While the former blame *dikus* (outsiders) for this failure of the promise industrial development had offered, the latter hold Adivasi responsible – and the widespread notion that "[t]heir love of drink appears to [be] almost an inborn propensity with the tribe" (Roy 1912: 66).

The village of Diankel – where Mangra and Sagar live, with whom I began this chapter – is situated on the left bank of the Karo river, in a rural area which I refer to as the Koel-Karo region because of the significance that a planned dam project (across the rivers Koel and Karo) and the Adivasi-led resistance against this dam (the *Koel-Karo Jan Sangathan*) have had for the region. Since 2005, the village can be reached by road from Ranchi, which is approximately seventy kilometers to the northeast, via the market town of Tapkara. At the time of my fieldwork, electricity was not available in the area (but it is being established there now), and neither were telephone lines nor cell phone towers. The only form of state infrastructure established in the village were poorly operating primary schools (the needs in the region with regard to education are attended to primarily by Christian missionaries). In many ways, this is an impoverished, neglected, remote rural area, and must be described as – with a hat tip to Anna Tsing (1993) – an out-of-the-way place.

Diankel is inhabited primarily by members of the Munda tribe,[8] who live there as subsistence farmers. Owing to the lack of infrastructure for irrigation, only one harvest a year is possible, and for that people are dependent on the monsoon rains. While in most years, sufficient rice can be harvested to feed everybody, there is certainly no plenty here. The diet is almost exclusively carbohydrate based and mostly consists of rice, with potatoes (or jackfruits during the rainy season) – lentils, so common throughout India, are prepared only occasionally. Families depend on sending members away for wage labor – girls and young women would often get hired as domestic help in Delhi or Calcutta, and boys and young men work for contractors in agriculture, construction, or in brick kilns in Haryana, Punjab, and elsewhere.

The possibility of making a decent profit off their produce and to improve their economic condition is an important concern for the villagers of Diankel. At the time of my fieldwork, they sold their vegetables, fruits, and forest produce at the weekly market in Tapkara, when cash was needed. Here the prices are considerably lower than in the state capital, Ranchi. However, they could not reach the markets in Ranchi unless they sold to middlemen, whose prices are exploitative. I was told how, a few years earlier, the

---

[8] Apart from Mundas, there are also a few Chik Baraik families (another community classified in India's registers of governmentality as *Scheduled Tribes*, who used to live as weavers among other tribal communities in Chotanagpur) as well as descendants of former Rautia landlords, who are classified as OBC (*Other Backward Classes*).

villagers had collectively rented a truck and brought their combined tamarind harvest to Ranchi. There, however, they had to face the reality that the traders immediately recognized them as Adivasis and farmers, and collectively refused to buy at a higher price than what the middlemen in Tapkara would have offered. This illustrates that selling produce is not simply a question of supply and demand, but that access to a market requires certain networks, skills, and social capital. This is complicated, moreover, in a place like Jharkhand, by the question of caste, as the markets are controlled by certain trading communities (Sahus, Banyas), which is also why for Adivasis, alternatives to cultivation have thus far been limited to the government sector (including the army and the police), as well as to precarious forms of physical labor (as already mentioned: domestic help, construction, etc.).

While the sale of produce is important for the subsistence farmers of Diankel in order to endure in the contemporary market economy of Jharkhand, cash is not a requirement for the sheer physical survival of their families. This is therefore a distinct contrast to the context of Koylatoli, where a cash income is absolutely required as a source of livelihood. Consequently, the presence of alcohol – on which every seventh household in Koylatoli depended – is somewhat different in Diankel, as mentioned above. While *mahua* and rice beer are produced, and sold, here as well, they do not constitute the livelihood of any of the families in the village. As a consequence (and also because in such an economic environment, fewer people have disposable cash at hand), alcohol is not available for sale there on a daily basis. Places where alcohol is sold do exist – where people gather to drink, either in groups or alone, and buy small snacks to go along with their beverages – but they only emerge on certain days of the week. On Saturdays, for example, when the weekly market is held, *bodé* and *mahua* (especially in the cold season) are sold at various places along the road leading there. Some people prepare rice beer or *mahua* also on other days (and for reasons other than selling), and may then take the opportunity to make a few rupees if any other villager would suddenly face an obligation to offer alcohol to someone – this is what allowed Mangra to obtain rice beer after we had helped him rescue his calf. And because there is no regular market for alcohol, it can also happen that people would prepare *bodé* in anticipation of selling it, but then end up having to drink it before it went bad.

A second contrast with regard to the alcohol economy between the urban setting of Koylatoli and the rural context of the Koel-Karo region is the *mahua* trade. In Koylatoli, *mahua* liquor is only sold, there are no *mahua* trees growing in the area (and the liquor sold there comes from moonshiners like Gautam, whom I will discuss below). The flowers are collected in forested areas, such as the Koel-Karo region, when they fall off the trees around April. After that, they are dried and then sold to traders at a weekly *hat* bazaar, or to traders in a market town such as Tapkara. In April 2007, the rate at which dried *mahua* flowers could be sold was Rs. 15 a kilogram. Half a year later, around October, after the monsoon rains, when temperatures began to drop, the demand in *mahua* liquor began to rise. In order to distill – and sell – *mahua* liquor, Adivasis then purchased the flowers back from traders at the market in Tapkara, but now at a rate of Rs. 60 a kilogram. The substantial loss incurred, if these transactions are added up, is not something that the villagers from Jilingsereng with whom I discussed this matter were unaware of. They would also have had space to store the flowers during the intervening hot and rainy months, during which the demand for rice beer significantly outweighed the demand for *mahua* liquor. The villa-gers were nevertheless forced to sell the flowers at a low price, and later buy them back from the traders at four times the rate, because at both times they needed the cash (from selling the flowers in April and May, and from selling the liquor during the cold months) to cover immediate expenses (such as school fees, clothes, fuel for a motorbike, or talk time for a cellphone, but also things like soap, oil, salt, spices, etc.).

My account of transactions involving alcohol among Adivasi in Jharkhand has thus far largely neglected that these transactions occur in the context of a nation-state that claims sovereignty over the terri-tories (and the lives) of the Mundas (and other Scheduled Tribe com-munities). A considerable range of these transactions, however, is deemed illegal by the state. In the remainder of this chapter, I will, therefore, shift my focus toward the ways in which the state and its representatives, through liquor laws and their implementation, inflect transactional grammars of alcohol in Jharkhand.

Gautam is a young Adivasi father and moonshiner. He distills and sells approximately fifteen to twenty liters of *mahua* liquor every day. Even though this business is illegal, about thirty other families in Gautam's village Mahatoli depend on it for their livelihood. There are also three distilleries in the village that commercially produce *mahua* liquor in large quantities. Mahatoli is about twenty kilometers from Ranchi, the state capital, and can only be reached on shabby dirt roads. Neither electricity nor telephone lines reach there; communications in every sense of the word are everything but easy. It is this spatial situation – the remoteness in combination with the proximity to the city – that predestines Mahatoli for the illegal liquor business because even though there is great demand for *mahua* liquor in Ranchi, distilleries are not tolerated there.

Gautam studied up to 10th grade and is, because of his education, as he told me, not interested in tilling the land of his ancestors and leading the life of a cultivator. But because it is not possible for him to find a job (due to the nature and structure of the job markets) he makes a living distilling and selling *mahua*. I was first introduced to Gautam in early 2007, as I was tracing the circuits of both legal as well as illegal liquor markets around Jharkhand's capital, Ranchi. Conversations with Mohan, an acquaintance of mine who sells *mahua* near Koylatoli had led me to Mahatoli, and to Gautam and his improvised still.

When I asked Gautam during our first meeting since when he had been making his livelihood from *mahua*, he did not answer but instead began telling me about a raid the excise department had conducted in Mahatoli several years before. After the three large distilleries in the village had been busted and dismantled, Gautam managed to persuade the officer commanding the raid not to enter further into the village to search the smaller enterprises. He thereby succeeded to argue that the small businesses – in contrast to the large distilleries – do not yield profits but simply provide for livelihoods. This difference between the commercial producers and the subsistence distillers made sense to the commanding excise officer – an Adivasi himself, as Gautam explained – who was appreciative of the circumstances that would make a family man like Gautam earn his livelihood beyond the legal; he let the small distillers go scot-free. Contrary to my expectations, the agreement between Gautam and the excise officer was not facilitated by a transaction (i.e., a bribe) – the officer simply demanded purity, meaning, that the liquor was to remain unadulterated and that its production was not to be expedited with the help of chemicals.[9] Gautam

---

[9] It is a widespread fear in Jharkhand that alcohol might be adulterated. The concern is not methanol poisoning but rather the mixing in of pesticides or fertilizers.

and his fellow small-scale distillers could thus benefit from the fact that there are occasional discrepancies between laws and their implementation. Such gaps can be of advantage to the laws' subjects, or to their disadvantage. In this case, the moonshiners of Mahatoli – with the exception of the commercial producers – were lucky; the officer-in-charge decided to overlook the illegality of their livelihood, and to spare them.

The Logics of Liquor Laws

Excise laws regulate taxes, duties, and licensing fees for the production, trade and purchase of alcoholic beverages (among other things). The generation of state revenue from substances such as liquor and opium by means of excise duties had been introduced in India already in 1790 by the East India Company. By the end of the nineteenth century, the excise revenues generated by mood-altering substances amounted to almost 15 percent of the total revenues of the Government of India, and had thus become indispensable (Gilbert 2007; Saldanha 1995). However, taxes or duties levied on intoxicating substances are also supposed to be incentives for lowering the consumption of the respective substances, and are thus measures of regulation, not simply of the intoxicants but of behavior. Liquor laws are therefore simultaneously instruments of taxation and of public health and morality. As a 2006 report on the revision of Jharkhand's liquor policies – commissioned by the Government of Jharkhand with the aim of increasing tax revenue – states, "liquor traffic has always been looked upon as a source of pauperism and crime" (Srivastava & Prasad 2006: 53). The study makes explicit that the trade in alcoholic beverages is subject to state control because it is not a right, but a privilege, and that the "power of control rests upon the right of the State to care for the health, morals and welfare of the people" (Srivastava & Prasad 2006: 53).

In regulating for which beverages licenses can be issued, excise laws thus define which beverages are legal, and which ones fall within the domain of illegality. If one consults the excise law of Jharkhand, one notices that all forms of alcohol mentioned therein – with the exception of customary Adivasi beverages, such as *mahua* liquor and rice beer – can be variously licensed and thus legally produced, traded, and consumed. The exempted beverages *mahua* liquor and rice beer are widely used (and sold) in Jharkhand, as elaborated above – primarily but not exclusively by Adivasis. While rice beer can be legally prepared by members of Scheduled Tribes for what the law calls "bona fide personal consumption on festive and social occasions" its sale is prohibited. *Mahua* liquor, however, is completely illegal in Jharkhand. Since all other forms of alcohol mentioned in the excise law are available for licensing, it can thus be argued that the law contains a separate sphere of (il-)legality for customary Adivasi beverages.

The difference between legal and illegal forms of alcohol makes apparent that laws which regulate production, trade, and consumption of intoxicants operate according to an inherently contradictory logic: on one hand, taxes and duties are being levied while, on the other hand, prohibitions are put in place. The state is interested in generating revenue to satisfy its fiscal needs by enabling the sale of regulated substances – while simultaneously limiting the availability of such harmful substances in order to pursue its biopolitical responsibility to protect the population. In trying to understand why the sale of customary Adivasi beverages is prohibited in Jharkhand, one could assume that these forms of alcohol are considered to be particularly harmful, while beverages such as beer, whisky, gin, and rum, or even country liquor from authorized outlets do not pose similar threats. One might argue that different substances require differing regulations. But the fact that there is a distinct difference between the populations consuming the respective substances (which is the case in the situation at hand, since *mahua* liquor and rice beer are primarily consumed by Adivasis) indicates that there might be something different at stake here. However, the state uses economistic arguments to justify the different treatment of the various substances. In an interview with the deputy commissioner of excise, I learned that it is simply not worth the bureaucratic effort to license the production or trade of *mahua* liquor or rice beer, since these beverages are traded at very low prices, and consumed by the poorest demographic, and that therefore no significant taxes could be added to their market value. This line of argument is consistent with the emphasis of Indian excise laws on revenue generation, but it is contradicted, for example, by the fact that the neighboring state of Orissa allows for the licensing of *mahua* liquor.[10] Furthermore, the excise law of Jharkhand rules that even the trade in legally licensed liquor is banned in *panchayat*s with an Adivasi population of more

---

[10] *Mahua* liquor in Orissa is a market with an annual growth rate of 40 percent (private conversation with the license holders).

than 50 percent, and provisions of the Panchayats (Extension to Scheduled Areas) Act hold that "the Panchayats at the appropriate level and the Gram Sabha are endowed specifically with [...] the power to enforce prohibition or to regulate or restrict the sale and consumption of any intoxicant" (Government of India 1996). All this indicates that the state sees a need for specific measures to govern the alcohol consumption of its tribal populations. The deputy commissioner of excise explained this need for a population-specific ban on trade in alcohol to me: Adivasis are prone to drinking, and prone to ruining themselves financially by drinking. Special measures are thus required for the benefit of tribal subjects.

Custom, Not Commodity

The role rice beer plays in the Excise Laws of Jharkhand is of particular interest, as it is the only form of alcohol that is dealt with not only in terms of either prohibition, or licensing and taxation, but also in terms of permission. However, the permission to prepare and consume rice beer is limited to members of Scheduled Tribes, that is, to Adivasis. When I asked the Deputy Commissioner of Excise, however: "How could such a legal norm be implemented – would the excise police go around asking people for their caste certificates?" he responded, "that it is not enforced." There is thus a specific legal provision, applicable to a specific population, that exists the impossibility of its implementation notwithstanding. Rice beer furthermore represents an anomaly in the liquor laws of Jharkhand, as it is deemed unworthy of licensing and can consequently not be a commodity; it is therefore reduced to a ritual, or cultural good, representative of a population for which it is considered as typical as it is detrimental. It is part of an argument I am developing elsewhere that this paradox is an expression of the ways in which the governance of alcohol in Jharkhand reifies the inherent alterity of the tribal subject in India and marks Adivasi as a distinct, racialized population, and a population worthy of reform and paternalistic care.[11]

---

[11] Various social actors are involved in a range of moral interventions in Jharkhand – there is, for one, the missionary attempt (mirrored to a certain extent by Hindu and Sarna forces) of bringing about modernity through spiritual reform, the Maoist/Naxalist attempt to introduce justice through political and economic reform (i.e., revolution), or the efforts of various state and non-state actors to facilitate "development" by propagating a reform of

During an interview with the Deputy Excise Commissioner, I asked him why rice beer was permitted to a population the members of which – according to the logic of the law as well as his own reasoning – were unable to drink responsibly. He replied by elaborating on the political impossibility to prohibit rice beer in tribal areas. Adivasis were so fond of their *haṛia* (rice beer), he explained, that any candidate advocating a complete ban on rice beer would be committing political suicide. As I will discuss below, the success of Maoist bans on liquor seems to prove the excise officer wrong in his advocating of cultural recognition as a political necessity.

Even though their trade is prohibited, *mahua* liquor and especially rice beer are ubiquitously and openly offered for sale in most parts of Jharkhand. The excise department does not attempt to prosecute the sale of rice beer and leaves the enforcement of its prohibition to the occasional policeman who will express his authority by destroying a stock of fermenting rice, or, more likely, routinely ask for bribes to look the other way. The prohibition against the production of *mahua* liquor, by the same token, is occasionally enforced, as the story of Gautam illustrates, but the excise department does not have the means to conduct raids and relies on vehicles, intelligence, and man-power provided to them by the local liquor syndicate.[12] The presence of the law in the domain of customary Adivasi beverages is thus not permanent or ubiquitous, but it appears irregularly, with interruptions, quasi-accidentally (cf. Das 2004; Randeria 2003). Thus, Gautam the moonshiner was let off scot-free during a raid by the excise department, the doubtless illegality of his livelihood as a producer of *mahua* liquor notwithstanding. He thus profited from the fuzziness of the law, but he nevertheless cannot feel secure about his livelihood because he knows that he cannot count on law-enforcement officers to neglect their duty. One day there might be another raid, and there might be a different

economic survival strategies (e.g., with the formation of *Mahila Mandals* and *self-help groups* women are trained in skills for income generation and to run microfinance schemes).

[12] I learned about this public–private collaboration during conversations with two representatives of a family who has controlled the market of all licensed forms of alcohol in Ranchi district for three generations. The cooperation between the authorities and the liquor barons is not so much a case of outsourcing, as it is the manifestation of a well-established form of corruption, and is only one of many transactions between the excise department and the liquor syndicate occurring on a regular basis.

excise officer who might be less sympathetic to the predicament of people like him. Every time I come to Mahatoli, I inquire with Gautam, and thus far he would always respond with "so far he [the excise officer] hasn't come." But it is obvious that Gautam's livelihood makes him very vulnerable. The fuzziness of the law and its half-hearted implementation ultimately create a great deal of power in the hands of representatives of the state – which can be used, as just mentioned, to extract bribes. The existence of the law, which supposedly facilitates a predictable and rational administration, results in permanent insecurity and precariousness for Adivasis. It is as if the law is in force always only temporarily and as if by accident, only to be suspended again, or, as Walter Benjamin famously stated: "[T]he tradition of the oppressed teaches us that the 'state of emergency' in which we live is not the exception but the rule" (Benjamin 1961).[13]

Conclusion

I have described here transactions of alcohol occurring at various registers of Adivasi life in Jharkhand. I began with transactions between people that at the surface might appear as if they were concerned with remuneration and commensuration – rice beer in exchange for time and labor given to a neighbor who needed help in fixing a roof, for example. I argue, however, that such transactions are social or moral rather than economic, and that their importance lies in establishing or sustaining social ties, in validating relationships. I then discussed transactions of alcohol involving the worlds of spirits, deities, and ancestors: everyday libations and ritual offerings. These spiritual or cosmological transactions are necessitated by the dependence of the Mundas (and other humans) on maintaining proper relationships with nonhuman forces – as these forces set the conditions and limits for the world and life itself. I also described commercial transactions of

[13] Obviously, the lack of enforcement of the laws that ban the sale of customary Adivasi beverages can be to the advantage of Gautam and many Adivasi families (such as the ones in Koylatoli mentioned above) who have no other source of cash income – and, of course, to those who relish their daily supply of booze. But it is to the discontent of many Adivasis who worry about the harmful effects of alcohol on individuals, families, and communities, and who feel that the state's lack of attention is a form of betrayal resulting in the ongoing subjection of Adivasis to marginality – or even a conspiracy to finally annihilate them in order to claim their land.

alcohol by looking at two distinct ecologies of Munda life: a peri-urban context, in which displaced and/or landless Adivasis are producing and selling customary forms of alcohol because of a complete lack of alternatives for economic survival, and a rural setting in which subsistence farmers generate supplementary cash with occasional commercial transactions of alcohol.

The second part of the chapter is concerned with how excise laws and policing inflect these transactions of alcohol. I show that in Jharkhand, excise regulations isolate customary Adivasi beverages (such as rice beer or *mahua* liquor) from other alcoholic beverages and prohibit any commercial transactions of the former. Policy reports as well as excise officials I interviewed justified this prohibition of the sale of *bodé* and *arki*, on one hand, with fiscal arguments: taxing customary Adivasi beverages would not be worthwhile because these commodities are too low-priced. On the other hand, a curious conflation of moralistic as well as public health concerns is used to explain that Adivasis need to be protected from alcohol, which is why commercial transactions of *bodé* and *arki* are prohibited. However, interesting gaps become apparent between these liquor laws and their implementation if one pays attention to how excise regulations are translated into policing. The case of Gautam the moonshiner shows that officers of the state can use their discretion to not enforce prohibition in a particular instance. And the accounts of many Adivasi liquor sellers I interviewed indicate that the prospect of having to offer bribes – yet another level of transactions – to the police or representatives of the excise department to circumvent prosecution is a constant threat looming over their livelihood.

It might be tempting to consider these bribes given in exchange for the temporary suspension of the law as mere corruption. However, looking at these transactions alongside the social and spiritual transactions of alcohol, which I discussed in the first part of this chapter, allows for a different interpretation, in which two concurrent notions of sovereignty demand sacrifices: while the social and spiritual transactions of alcohol are offerings that occur under the eyes of the forces that created the world and that have the sovereign power to maintain human existence in it, the bribes can similarly be seen – rather than merely as transgressions of the legal order – as offerings, as sacrifices necessary to maintain the sovereignty of the state. There are thus intersecting cosmologies – the one formulated by the spirits, deities and ancestors that are collectively known as *bonga*s, and the one imposed by the modern state and its institutions.[14]

It is important to note that with regard to transactions of alcohol, the state's sovereign claim over the lives of Adivasis intersects but does compete with the cosmology of the *bonga*s: even though the law prohibits the sale of customary forms of alcohol, it permits customary social transactions or ritual offerings of rice beer. One might thus be led to believe that the state is mindful of Adivasi alterity. However, all the different registers of transactions involving alcohol that I discussed here are matters of survival for Adivasis: life is not possible without sustaining community ties or without maintaining relationships with the *bonga*s, neither is it possible without access to livelihood and/or cash. In limiting rice beer to the domain of the customary, and in preventing its becoming a legitimate commodity, the law criminalizes the only access many Adivasi families have to cash due to persistent exclusion from other markets, thus undermining their livelihood, and life itself.

Because significant gaps exist between laws and their enforcement, Adivasis are often able to sell their customary alcoholic beverages, interference from state authorities notwithstanding. Various interpretations of this are possible: the tolerance of law enforcement agents for illegal transactions of liquor by Adivasis can be understood as an expression of solidarity (that is, the law enforcement agents sympathize with the predicaments under which livelihood needs to be maintained beyond the bounds of legality), or it could be a sign of cultural recognition (what has been used since time immemorial is "traditional" and can therefore not be criminal). Or one recalls a point Jacques Derrida made during an interview on drugs and addiction, in which he declared sobriety a basic condition for the possibility of subjects becoming responsible citizens, that is, owners, or partners in a legal order, rather than simply being subjected to it (Derrida 1993). According to this line of reasoning, the letting off scot-free of law-breaking Adivasis would be a betrayal of the latter's entitlement to equal rights of citizenship, because it is not sobriety that is favored, but inebriety that is enabled. Whatever it may be, the toleration of illegal transactions of alcohol is always only temporary

[14] I thank Ajay Gandhi for his comments that made me think about these concurrent sovereignties.

and therefore does not suspend the principal, criminalized nature of the ways many Adivasi families maintain their livelihood. And because it is always only a phase that can end at any moment, the Adivasi subject permanently oscillates between experiences of illegality, stigmatization, solidarity, recognition, and betrayal.

References

Aaron, SJ 2007, "Contrarian Lives: Christians and Contemporary Protest in Jharkhand," Working Paper (18), Asia Research Centre, London School of Economics and Political Science.

Bara, J 2007, "Colonialism, Christianity and the Tribes of Chhotanagpur in East India, 1845–1890," *South Asia: Journal of South Asian Studies*, 30, 2: 195–222.

Begrich, R 2013, Inebriety and Indigeneity: The Moral Governance of Adivasis and Alcohol in Jharkhand, India, unpublished PhD dissertation, Johns Hopkins University.

Benjamin, W 1968, "Theses on the Philosophy of History," in H Arendt (ed.) *Illuminations*, trans. H Zohn, Schocken Books, New York, pp. 253–64.

Das, V 2004 "The Signature of the State: The Paradox of Illegibility," in *Anthropology in the Margins of the State*, School of American Research Advances Seminar Series, James Currey: Oxford, pp. 225–52.

Derrida, J 1993, "The Rhetoric of Drugs. An Interview," trans. Michael Israel, in *Differences: A Journal of Feminist Cultural Studies*, 5, 1: 1–25.

Gilbert, MJ 2007, "Empire and Excise: Drugs and Drink Revenue and the Fate of States in South Asia," in JH Mills and P Barton (eds.) *Drugs and Empires. Essays in Modern Imperialism and Intoxication, c. 1500–c. 1930*, Palgrave Macmillan, New York, pp. 116–41.

Government of India 1996, *The Provisions of the Panchayats (Extension to the Scheduled Areas) Act No. 40 of 1996*. PESA 1996.

Hunter, WW 1877, *A Statistical Account of Bengal*, vol. 17, Trübner & Co., London.

Mauss, M 1990 (1925), *Die Gabe: Form und Funktion des Austauschs in archaischen Gesellschaften*, trans. E Moldenhauer, Suhrkamp, Frankfurt am Main.

Randeria, S 2003, "Cunning States and Unaccountable International Institutions: Legal Plurality, Social Movements and Rights of Local Communities to Common Property Resources," *European Journal of Sociology*, 44, 1: 27–60.

Roy, SC 1912, *The Mundas and Their Country*, Jogendra Nath Sarkar, Calcutta.

Saldanha, IM 1995, "On Drinking and 'Drunkenness': History of Liquor in Colonial India," *Economic and Political Weekly*, 30, 37: 2323–31.

Srivastava, NP & Prasad, B 2006, *Impact of the New Excise Policy of the State and Ways and Means of Boosting Revenue in the Medium Term*, Government of Jharkhand, Fiscal Policy Analysis Cell (FPAC), Ranchi.

Tsing, AL 1993, *In the Realm of the Diamond Queen: Marginality in an Out-of-the-Way Place*, Princeton University Press, Princeton.

Van Exem, A 1982, *The Religious system of the Munda Tribe. An Essay in Religious Anthropology*, Haus Völker und Kulturen, St. Augustin.

13 | Building on Sand? Criminal Markets and Politics in Tamil Nadu

BARBARA HARRISS-WHITE
AND J. JEYARANJAN

Crime is the register through which societies think out loud.

(Comaroff 2018)

Introduction

For criminal anthropologists Jean and John Comaroff deploying evidence from South Africa, the USA, and Europe, criminality is the new normal, the "master signifier," fully neoliberally modern (Comaroff & Comaroff 2016: 52). Across the globe, the management of the consequences of crime has become an idiom for social life. This chapter seeks to use Indian fieldglasses to examine the scope of their intervention, to question whether criminality and criminal markets have Indian characteristics, and, if so, to pursue their implications for democratic politics.

When the commodification of public services allows market forces to enter and construe the state, the workforce providing such services is forced out to become profit-making employees or to be displaced by them, social needs become demand (in the UK, for instance, taxpayers are now addressed as "customers"), and services transform into supply. The state mostly bears the risks of this transformation, in the course of which collective values atrophy and regulative law drags behind the penetration of market values and behavior (Leys 2001). One of the outcomes is criminal activity. The Centre for Health and the Public Interest (CHPI 2017) gives a British example in the relatively poorly regulated private segment of the partially marketized national health system where a surgeon working for private profit performed unnecessary breast surgery on over 500 women. In times gone by, citizens and subjects had trust in the system, but now they have to be on their guard.

The Comaroffs (2016) have pushed our understanding of the privatization of the state into the sphere of law and order, finding not only crime but also commodified punishment and protection. In their bleak optic, the petty criminal has become a ubiquitous part of routine social life and its imagination. When market ideology, privatization, and the corporate capture of the state have contrived to cause the social experience and awareness of crime to increase, to be vernacularized, and to blur the boundary between the legal and the transgressive, sovereignty is then pluralized. The dual commodification and pluralization of the executive reduces states to franchising authorities, "protection rackets in need of legitimation," side by side with privatized, subcontracted – and increasingly criminalized – institutions of discipline and enforcement. When the public interest of commodified states is no more than the sum total of private interests, the state's failure to ensure the protection of private property raises insecurity and the specter of crime up the agenda of social preoccupations. With the guarantee of sovereignty threatened, facsimiles of the state and democracy develop. John Comaroff (2018) called them "lateralized sovereignties." They are similar to the "contested jurisdictions" of this book's introduction. The citizen/consumer is no longer formed within an ecosystem of institutions but is required to engage with these sovereignties as an unsupported individual. In conditions of partial or lateralized sovereignty, the guardians of law and order, the police, "break the law they make and make the law they break ... You cannot tell who is a cop. A fake cop. A bent cop. A secret cop. A private cop" (ibid.; cf. Comaroffs 2016: 101–24). As the ecology of citizenship changes form, revenue is redistributed via private hands and even "the business of welfare becomes the welfare of businesses" (of criminal businesses as the British example of medical business shows).

The Comaroffs' Scenario and Indian Conditions

The Comaroffs' general proposition is not built on Indian foundations. But how does India relate to it? The Indian field of criminal anthropology has not approached economic crime through the Comaroffs' critical lenses of statistical "quantifacts" and popular culture. But eleven case studies of criminal economy by a team of field economists and anthropologists between 2012 and 2016 can shed light on the extent to which their depiction is recognizable in Indian conditions (Harriss-White & Michelutti 2019a). Here we distinguish features that are in common with the Comaroffs' model from outliers that might be distinctively Indian. We then see how the case of riverbed sand can contribute to rethinking markets and politics.

Crime as Normal and Ubiquitous

While the case study is no match for the random sample generated from population data – or population data themselves – as bases for generalization (Flyvbjerg 2006) and while there is no body of systematic evidence from which we could extrapolate the degree to which crime is a routine part of everyday life in India, "how important" it is, the eleven case studies are indicative. Wherever supply chains for the four elements – earth (coal and sand), fire, water, and air – and for other parts of the economic base of urban societies – land, timber, fuel energy, construction, property, and municipal procurement – have been studied through ethnography, criminal activity is found to be pervasive, systemic, and durable. Yet it is also fluid, fragmented, and opportunist. Michelutti (2019) conjures the term "assemblage" to capture the combinations of contingency, instability, and hierarchy, of legality and illegality, market and non-market institutions through which the criminal economy is construed. It resembles the "ensemble" of the book's introduction. While individuals may fall or disappear, these assemblages appear to be remarkably persistent.

Petty and Grand Business

In a criminal assemblage, mighty portfolios coexist with a pediment of petty – even subsistence – activity. In Jharkhand, for example, *coal cycle wallah*s scavenge illegally from abandoned mines and tailings and use fortified bikes to distribute the raw material for heat. This petty trade forms part of a system at the apex of which are twenty-four coal mafia dynasties, able to openly command rakes[1] from Indian Railways, which invest in productive

---

[1] A rake is a length of coupled wagons.

and unproductive activity, legal and illegal. One such portfolio, revealed in a rare court case, included coal, iron, media, tourism, hotels, liquor, real estate, education, and fleets of lorries (Singh & Harriss-White 2019). Another criminal organization accumulated control over illegal arms, illegal timber, illegal alcohol, quarries, construction, and a network of petrol pumps (Picherit 2019). In these types of portfolio, illegal commodities (drugs, arms, types of liquor, ancient artworks, sports betting, trafficked women, children, and body parts) are traded alongside legal ones. Many other activities are also required to coordinate these economic and the political transactions: fixers, protectors, middlemen, contractors, and subcontractors, money managers, lawyers, forgers, and vigilantes. At all scales of business, the criminal assemblage requires armies of wage workers: more often than not found to be low caste or tribal, precarious, migrant, debt-bonded and unfree, ignorant of other stages of the system in which they toil, working in exacting conditions and controlled under intense physical discipline.

The case studies also reveal how normalized is the criminal seizing not so much of private property but of common property. The wage workforce and their families are deprived of access to resources like fuelwood, fodder, and water on which they have relied to reproduce their households (Jodha 1990), substitutes for which are, in turn, commodified and have to be purchased for cash.

Cultures of Crime

The case of Red Sanders timber, smuggled from Andhra Pradesh to the Middle East and China, shows how the criminal may be transformed into a polysemic figure in popular myth, in movies, and even in commodity brands. Veerappan, a sandalwood and ivory smuggler, killing elephants and operating out of South Indian forests, a serial killer himself killed by police in Operation Cocoon in 2004, is still regarded by local tribal people as a "social bandit," a Robin Hood figure. Subsequently, "his" forests have also been branded for the high skills in timber handling of labor originating there. By contrast, people's allegiance to the memory of Veerappan is deployed by police to legitimize their murder in encounters with suspected smugglers, often, in fact, migrant wage laborers (Picherit 2019).

Crime and the Pluralization of Sovereignty

There is quite a discursive Tower of Babel resulting from attempts by scholars of India to capture the prevalent coexistence of state-like authority alongside that of the state. Some have invented terms such as shadow state and parallel state. Others have pointed to the interpenetration of state and non-state authority, conjuring neologisms such as hybrid state, informal or vernacular governance, and *intreccio* (entanglement). It is another matter when criminal organizations have comprehensive countervailing power to the state and when concepts such as "Mafia Raj" and "Mastan Raj" are summoned into use (Harriss-White & Michelutti 2019b).

Most non-state forms of authority regulating criminal markets are grounded in preexisting customary and collective action. Patriarchy constrains the assets and occupational choices of (inferior) men as well as women; caste and ethnicity supply a corporatist ideology to market exchange, they structure access and define insiders and outsiders with whom the terms of transactions may vary; religious communities supply collective identity and institutions to regulate distributive activity as well as accumulation. Business associations consolidate socially corporatist economies (Basile & Harriss-White 2010). And while law-making institutions and the protection of property and people – even those uninvolved in criminal activity – are being privatized and sites of economic authority (and sovereignty) multiply, the case studies indicate that wherever they operate, the mafia has developed paramount regulatory authority. In an era of rampant nationalism, the unit of moral accountability of the criminal economy – clan, caste, dynasty – is far removed from the banner of the nation.

Not all law-breaking involves violence but in the eleven case studies the only one that did not feature episodes of physical violence was of spectrum for telecom at the apex of the national economy (Bhatia 2019). The "criminal life of legal commodities," epitomized by economic crime, is regarded as "soft" behavior when contrasted with violent predations on the state (Ruud 2019). Yet even the labor, commodity, and money markets comprising the soft criminal order are policed by threats, extortion, and intimidation and by violent abusive enforcement frequently involving private armies, militias, and goons. Over half the eleven case studies reported murder as a weapon of regulation. Evidently, as Marx once wrote, force itself "is an economic power" (Marx 1887: chapter 31).

Criminal violence takes other forms. The seizure of private property by armed robbery is one. Vandalism of, and theft from, state/public property – infrastructure such as pipelines – is another. Trafficking in endangered species, the destruction of water-courses and water-tables, of soils and slopes, and wanton air pollution are crimes against society perpetrated through nature. When property is held in common pool, as open access or in public hands, it is far less easy to protect physically than when property is held privately (Gadgil 2011).

Meanwhile the justice system is implicated in the criminal economy in context-specific ways. For every instance of the courts' marshalling expert evidence, nailing crime, and meting out enforceable punishment, there is other evidence of the courts being avoided entirely (so quasi-legal settlements are made elsewhere or illegal ones are forced) – or judgements ignored. Irregular investments are made to delay or suspend hearings, to determine judgements, and their outcomes. Yet the power of money may yield to that of organized interests. Party political pressure can also force legally unjustified interpretations of procedure and evidence, the nonappearance of witnesses, threats to witnesses in court, etc. (Harriss-White 2019).

Law breaking is not confined to criminal organizations with the complicity of the police, judiciary, and politicians. Many state agencies are found to be extensively involved in law-breaking activity: failing to raise revenue, diverting state resources to private uses, and failing to regulate the economy. Bribery and corruption, extensively invoked in economic models of state failure (Bardhan & Mookherjee 2007), are very crude proxies for the diversity of practices involved.

The Indian cases reveal systematic institutional preconditions for criminal activity. Prime among these is the regulative law. Every sector in the case studied is found festooned in a complexity of law likely to have been publicly debated only at its inception, if then. Criminal assemblages cut through great swathes of law that lawyers themselves strain to master. At the same time, law can clash with custom. Customary norms and law regulate the joint family – the real building block of the Indian economy. The increasingly frequent violation of customary norms of violation (which govern socially irregular access to much common property) may go unpunished because of lack of institutional precedent and practice. Lack of punishment may then be routinized as a norm. Fear which generates self-censorship and silent complicity also regulates criminal economic activity.

Certain kinds of modern regulative law are even revealed as crime-friendly: first, deliberately or through incompetence drafted with loopholes and incentives for crime; second, law for which punishment is so disproportionate that it incentivizes criminal evasion; third, law where evidence is stipulated in forms so difficult to provide that evasion is easier: riskier but cheaper. Manifestly socially unjust law is also asking to be broken. And law whose amendments shift faster than arrangements for its enforcement will also facilitate its social disregard.[2] Pervasive cultures of noncompliance then mean that, as the Tamil proverb has it: "[A]n honest man is he who does not know how to live." The socially deviant is actually the legally compliant.

From case studies that have amassed evidence different in kind from that used by the Comaroffs, we see that many features they outline are present in the Indian context. Even the substitution in the Indian cases of caste, ethnicity, religion, and gender for the Comaroffs' characterization of modern crime as racialized is a minor mutation in the genetic sequencing of crime.

The Indian cases, however, are distinctive insofar as it is not possible to avoid the distinctive fusing of the criminal economy with democratic politics.

Criminal Economy and Democratic Politics

India's recent history has been used to generate a model comparable in sweep to that of the Comaroffs' while not claiming the same global relevance. Instead of exploring the role played by crime in the social imagination, PS Jha's account mobilizes evidence to address processes criminalizing politics and politicizing crime, following their joint impact on the economy (2013). Using Occam's Razor, Jha's argument

---

[2] Examples are respectively: environmental law for dam sites; the Antiquities and Treasures Act; compensation valuations; negligent Rehabilitation & Resettlement from threats from subterranean fires; and the Essential Commodities Act.

starts from the huge size of India's constituencies, in terms of both territory and population. These are costly to contest through electoral democracy. Election costs and between-election fixed costs of party's political maintenance have always exceeded the Election Commission's ceilings for allowances; hence, they have to be untraceable. With the possible exception of AAP and of rare wealthy individuals, the subsequent voracious appetite for funds has had major impacts on the internal democratic politics of all parties. When, in the late 1960s, Indira Gandhi, the then Prime Minister, banned company donations so as to hobble competition from right-wing parties, fundraising for these costly political spasms had to slip below the radar, to spill out into India's states, and to involve ever expanding operational scales and fractions of capital. Black fundraising bureaucracies developed to channel elastic exchanges of money for illegal favors, protection, and exemptions; and illegal physical security forces developed to secure the safety of the untraceable party funds that reflected these political-financial markets, those handling them and those representing their interests (see also Vaishnav 2017).

Parties based on identity/aspiration/region emerged not only as a result of national parties' neglecting the factors used for mobilizing newer parties (such as caste, ethnicity, regional neglect, and underdevelopment) but also as a reaction to the political spaces created by criminalization. Jha argues, however, that the newer parties must suffer similar pressures and negotiate – and embody – political forces contradictory to their social aspirations. The exclusive nature of information and contacts, safes, and allocative practices through which such financial–political assemblages have been maintained, have encouraged path-dependent relations of clientelism. These eventually solidified into dynasties because these financial-political transactions could be reproduced most efficiently and securely through political families. However, when political protection was experienced as incomplete, old-style criminal political clients and new-style members and leaders of criminal organizations started to enter party politics directly.

Once installed, the abuse of discretionary budgets for legislators supplemented quid pro quo financial exchanges between funders and politicians with the latter benefiting from immunity. India's vast informal economy – agriculture plus nonagricultural production, trade and services in tiny firms below the deliberately imposed size thresholds for regulation[3] – has become seamlessly interwoven with the black economy, a component of which funds democratic party politics and navigates changes in ruling parties in the center and states.[4]

The stream of corporate tribute has major implications for capitalism with Indian characteristics. Reciprocal political–economic exchanges privilege crony capitalism. Where competence yields to political connections, inefficiencies are hard-wired into the "formal" economy. Jha provides evidence for the inflation of capital costs, inflated-cost benchmarks for future projects, the "gold-plating" of future investments with necessary subsidies to enable them to compete, the institutionalizing of extremely costly delays and forfeited benefits, the chopping up of projects into components in the name of competition so as to multiply kickbacks, shoddy work, and irrationalities that result from the politically driven shattering of megaprojects. The state is put up for sale through informal and criminal bureaucratic practices which complicate Leys' model of market-driven politics. According to Jha (2013), *Outlook* reported in 2009 that, between 1990 and 2008, thirty-three scams cost the public exchequer $100 billion per year. In consequence, the neglect of redistributivist development makes a mockery of much progressive development discourse.

During the reform period, company donations to parties have been rehabilitated but such donations are unable to meet more than 10 percent of election costs, so it is rational to finance individual powerful candidates. The mature clientelist state, Jha concludes, is one where power is exercised by a congeries of relations among business, career politicians, gangland mafiosi, and the police. India has succeeded not only in criminalizing politics but also in politicizing crime.

Jha's conclusion disturbs political science interpretations of the character of state politics. When the roles of the coal-fire mafia are stirred into Jharkhand's politics of tribal neglect and of homeland aspiration, when private hydrocriminal plunder is added to Arunachal Pradesh's politics of tribal competition, of center–state dependence and of Himalayan frontier militarization, politics in both states is seen as consistent with domination by predatory criminal interests (Gupta 2019; Mishra 2019). In the rest of this chapter, we turn to a case in

---

[3] See Dietrich Wielenga (2019) for the roles of state and business in the early postwar creation of the informal economy.
[4] See Kar (2010) for evidence for its role in capital flight.

Tamil Nadu using field material from its interlocked markets for riverbed sand and democratic politics.

Although ignored in mainstream economics, the print media's business pages routinely celebrate the fact that every commodity has quiddity. The concept of quiddity combines the essential physical attributes and cultural meanings of a given commodity; together they are able to shape the structure and functioning of their markets. Tomatoes, for instance, are a pretty indispensable food item, a fruit known as a vegetable, red and juicy, but bulky and highly perishable. Before cold stores and refrigerated transport, markets for tomatoes had to use cash and spot contracts (Harriss-White 2003). What is the quiddity of sand? A nonperishable granular silica, sand is the easily processed, but not easily substituted, invisible mineral component of cement and concrete, through which the entire physical fabric of urban and rural India, real estate, and infrastructure, is constructed. Sand is also a common property resource, the geological product of deposition over millennia, on a continuum between silt and gravel. Riverbed sand is also one among many natural resources (including granite and beach sand), and manufactured commodities (including liquor and real estate) developed to be structured as markets to supply political funds in a state whose Dravidian politics is widely understood as populist.

Be it "protection populism," "empowerment populism," "assertive populism," "paternalist," "technocratic," "people-centered," or "crony-populism," people's welfare is put at its political core (Jeyaranjan 2019). However, while the widely assumed link between welfarist interventions[5] and party political outcomes is hard to substantiate factually, the one between targeted cash handouts (piloted through the "Thirumangalam formula" by 2009 and estimated as needing some Rs. 5 crores[6] per constituency in 2011) and election success is increasingly strong. While both populist and pork barrel politics require considerable public finance, that of the pork barrel must be prepared through the appropriation and intertwining of both public and illicit private funds. What role do sand markets perform?

---

[5] Subsidized rice, noon meals for school children, loan waivers, television sets, LPG stoves, health insurance, and social security for the rural poor, housing programs, and so on.

[6] Note on currency and exchange. A crore is 10 million; a lakh is 100,000. In 2016, when this narrative ends, the exchange rate was Rs. 91 per £, Rs. 67 per $, and Rs. 74.4 per €.

To answer this question, we must trace the history of development of markets for sand from the 1980s onward. This will be done through a series of interviews carried out between 2014 and 2016 with politicians, bureaucrats, contractors, journalists, law officers, and middlemen who shared evidence on condition of anonymity. Except for court cases, the evidence in this chapter is not attributed and has to be taken on trust. While mainstream economic analyses of markets focus on the firms constituting market structure and behavior (their sizes, costs, returns, and price fluctuations), the analysis of this criminal market has to place relations of regulation center stage.

The Commodification and Politicization of Sand in Tamil Nadu

When Tamil Nadu's urban and infrastructural boom was in its infancy, in the 1970s and 80s, sand was a free good filling the wide, mostly dry beds of the great river courses that traverse the state. It was appropriated by the low-caste owners of otherwise idle bullocks and carts on payment of a paltry fee to the littoral *panchayat*. Even when small, "half-body" lorries and manual labor were hired by builders to collect sand nearby Tamil Nadu's cities, profits covered costs and little else. From oral accounts, sand was distributed through locally territorialized competitive markets. The supplementary markets of part-time and petty open-cast sand-miners originated unregulated by the state. Remaining below political and administrative radar screens until in the mid–late 1980s, petty-scale supplies proved unable to match demand. At this point, sand started to acquire value as a commodity. And sand mining turned fulltime and regular. Mining demanded the skills and energy of fit youngsters. Dedicated fleets emerged along with labor gangs to mine and transport sand. Round-the-clock operations became the new normal. The price of sand then had to cover the costs of labor, transport, agents' commissions, fees to the local *panchayat*, bribes to the police and revenue administrators, plus profit for the operator. Prices and net margins rose because of increased demand. Rough competition then became visible to local politicians who, busy accumulating portfolios in *arrack* shops, bars, and local real estate, began investing in the extraction of sand. Higher level politician–traders then coopted smaller, local ones in partnerships to mine and trade sand. From being completely unregulated, scaled-up sand transactions evaded both the village administrative officials, custodians of local revenue and responsible for regulations, and the police, law enforcers acting in part on complaints from the revenue administration. Sensing its profitability, both local wings of state authority started testing its resilience through demands for bribes.

Enter a third branch of the state in the form of the Public Works Department (PWD) tasked with the unhindered flow of water in riverbeds. Since natural sand deposits could and did obstruct flows, the PWD set up regulations for mining them. These were observed in the breach.[7] Vigilance was undeveloped. Strips were not marked out; maximum depths were not observed and overladen lorries carved deep ruts in the beds, ruts that could be deepened by monsoon water erosion. The silent routinization of such practices heralded an era of terrible environmental damage.

Meanwhile, bipartisan cartels formed from politician–miners in both the DMK and the AIADMK parties. This structure of cartels contrived to capture the bidding process for sand contracts in each river valley and to share profits both individually, through the two parties at the district level and between local politician–miners and political patrons higher up the parties. In these cartels, competition took place in order to prevent competition. If competition for PWD contracts ever broke out, it would be regulated through shows of threat and/or physical violence from the two parties. Petty-scale business was eased out and mechanization enabled the scale of individual sand quarries to increase vastly.

Enter individual agency and a moment of concatenation in the social relations regulating sand. During the first tenure of Jayalalithaa as AIADMK party supremo and Chief Minister, in 1991–2003, a *Dalit* fleet owner, X, supplier of sand to Chennai and part of a cartel paying the district administration regularly for Palar river sand negotiated a deal mediated through the district collector that ensured X's monopoly control of a major stretch of the river basin's sand in return for Rs. 1 crore per week tribute to be paid in cash to the CM's confidante. Cover was provided by the Tamil Nadu Minor Mineral Concession Rules (39), which had been enacted to conserve mineral wealth in the

---

[7] Indeed, one understanding of the purpose of these regulations is that they could be brandished in court as a defense against litigants' accusations of gross negligence on the part of the state and of state failure to protect against environmental devastation.

public interest and provided for the state to exercise rights over deposits, waive auctions, and lease plots. The supply chain that developed was not complicated. People needing sand contacted fleet owners or their commission agents.[8] Meanwhile X brazenly collected a fixed fee for each load of riverbed sand excavated, transported, and retailed by "his" subcontractors. Accumulating at an unprecedented pace, X achieved notoriety by rapidly buying a symbol of feudal wealth in the form of a local landlord's much filmed opulent bungalow. Given the evident mutual benefit of this contract, the same model was rapidly diffused to other river basins, deals for which were captured by criminal trader Y.

Control of, and returns to, sand mining was shifting to the CM's office in Fort St. George. The state government machinery experienced a translation of roles, from being an employer resourced from legal revenue to being a set of employees paid from illegal tribute to regulate and secure the vast stream of politically legitimized criminal money against capture or sabotage by others. The government's principal duty was thus to check "illicit" sand mining while protecting their contractor Y's "legal" mining.

In the 1996 elections, the AIADMK government fell to the DMK. Control over sand crossed parties, initiating a phase of musical chairs in politics and market structure. A DMK cartel seized the Northern Palar contract and worked it using Y, who was in turn outsmarted in his original Kaveri river basin quarries by a new criminal Z, who seized control in the south of the country. In violation of all rules, sand mining expanded in scale; sand started to be traded throughout the southern states and massive revenue streams were privatized and politicized. With the firm hold of the top political boss of the day, a single-window system for cash flows increased the efficiency with which money was extracted from sand contractors.

These arrangements were challenged between 1997 and 2001 by a leading lawyer and social activist who filed a writ petition in the Madras High Court. Records were summoned to court, on the basis of which the government's behavior was condemned as "whimsical." After a list of violations emerged, and when income from a single quarry, estimated at Rs. 1 crore per week, was set against its rental payments or "consideration" to the state of Rs. 1 lakh per year, the

[8] These agents were also arranging bricks from the kilns for a commission.

scale of the plunder at last became public knowledge. Quashing a total of thirty-six leases and grants made under Rule 39, the judge concluded "that the exercise of power is not *bona fide* but it had been ... born out of corrupt motive, and (that) corrupt obligation had advanced the cause of individual to the detriment of the state exchequer."[9]

In the wake of a second High Court condemnation of political corruption, the absence of enforcement and well-entrenched collusion between the civil administration and illicit sand extraction in the Kosathali riverbed north of Chennai city, an expert committee of scientists was appointed in 2002 at the court's behest to evaluate the environmental impacts of the criminal markets in sand. A year later, this committee reported serious damage to river ecology, geomorphology, and hydrology. In response, the state, now governed by the AIADMK, issued an order containing the strict regulations for sand mining suggested by the expert committee. It cancelled leases, and amended the law to confer a state monopoly over sand and its revenue – in perpetuity.[10] In effect, the government regularized huge cash flows to the state that were hitherto the domain of the party and private coffers and selected the PWD to manage sand.[11] This lasted three months during which sand supplies declined by 90 percent and prices rocketed from Rs. 1,000 per lorry to Rs. 3,000–4,000 per lorry.[12] Whether the root cause was bureaucratic incompetence or sabotage by ousted smugglers was debated – until the contractors were restored through a new system of "second sales." A process of tendering with *benami*[13] contracts rapidly fell into the hands of "lifting contractor"/trader Y, who became de facto owner of the entire state's sand, its related market logistics, and riverbed infrastructure, paying the salaries of PWD officials directly and now supplying Rs. 25 crores of cash tribute per month

[9] W.P. No.16010/97 and 6712, 6713 of 1998 p. 50 of the Judgment dated April 30, 2004 in the High Court Judicature at Madras.

[10] G.O. M.S. No. 95 dated October 1, 2003; Tamil Nadu Minor Mineral Concession Rules 1959, new clause, 38A, 2003.

[11] These cash flows were not spent entirely on elections. Massive properties were acquired over time and because of such accumulation both CM Jayalalithaa and her confidante Sasikala were sentenced to four years' imprisonment by the Supreme Court of India. At the time of writing, 2019, Sasikala is serving her prison sentence, while Jayalalithaa died in 2016. See Subbramanian (2017) for an attempt to unravel the wealth accumulated by Jayalalithaa and Sasikala.

[12] See www.thehindu.com/news/national/tamil-nadu/sand-at-affordable-price-remains-a-mirage/article3851386.ece.

[13] A contract in the name of a third party.

to the CM. Careful estimates for 2015–2016 indicate an annual turn-over of Rs. 19,163 crores.[14] Annual proceeds from sand sales remitted to the state's treasury account were recorded as Rs. 200 crores (Ilangovan 2015). The residue, some Rs. 19,000 crores gross, was shared between Y, his contractors, politicians, the bureaucracy, police, and derived markets of fixers. By 2018, while three major lifting con-tractors were jostling for the state's market shares in sand, one in an open business partnership with a minister, the tribute was reported to involve them in paying the CM Rs. 10 crores in cash daily.

And this was only at the apex. In the political territories of sand mines, village councilors are reported to receive Rs. 10,000 monthly, *panchayat* presidents Rs. 1,00,000, and MLAs Rs. 5,00,000. Meanwhile the lifting contractors pay representatives who pay retai-ners to *panchayat* union secretaries at the base of the ruling party hierarchy. The subdistrict level, union secretaries of the main Dravidian opposition party, other useful politicians, and strategically useful members of the state's civil administration, police are also paid – as well as local media executives to silence the information industry. So institutions of state and market have been systemically intertwined in order to maximize the supply of one of the principal raw materials for civilized social life.

Sand is regulated to saturation point through constraints on plot sizes, on the planning of extraction, its depth, its work shifts, and duration, on the building of temporary roads in riverbeds, the scale of mechanized mining, the loads carried by lorries, the recording of quan-tities of sand mined and market transactions. This fine-grained specifi-cation is unenforced. Existing infrastructure, such as protective bunds, is vandalized. Wage-labor works illegally long and strenuous shifts for reputedly high returns. Local labor is assigned the lightest work to cement loyalty and silence.[15] Externalities are unconceived, uncosted, and ignored. These include erratic lowering of water tables, affecting drinking water, the destruction of pathways, roads and ways across

---

[14] This estimate, detailed in Jeyaranjan (2019), is extrapolated from interviews in 2015–2016 with former sand yard managers and employees in Tiruchirappalli district. It is consistent with that made by MK Stalin, grounded in his experience as Deputy Chief Minister from 2006 to 2011, when the same arrangement was functioning during DMK rule, *Dinakaran, Tamil*, September 3, 2015 Trichy edition p. 5. For an all-India estimate, see Rege (2016).

[15] Violations of rules published in various Advocate Commissioners' court reports.

riverbeds, the accidents that result, especially at night. The flouting of laws protecting the environment fetch local protests, petitions, even hunger strikes.

In response, the lifting contractor has the power to organize a vast repertoire of market-protecting tactics, which also both parody and distort the manifold objectives of the state administration: to mobilize private armies to terrorize and injure – even to murder – resisters, to force the police to fabricate cases against them, to initiate protracted litigation, and to purchase lawyers, to whip up caste hatreds to divide opposition, to offer work, lend money, prioritize local vehicles for sand transport, allocate the regulation of lorry parks to local leaders, fund temples, and village festivals, give educational scholarships to promis- ing children and organize medical camps. On the very rare occasions when court cases have ruled against the sand mafia, judgments have been enforced only temporarily or not at all. Instead of scrutinizing the failure of the state machinery and the plethora of affidavits revealed as bogus by court committees, courts keep suggesting ever more regula- tion. They therefore assign more and more responsibilities to the very departments that are the principal violators of the law. No court in Tamil Nadu has ever demanded evidence of – or from – the benefici- aries of the commodification of sand. And this is how sand markets work to this day.

Conclusions and Reflections

In this book's introduction, models of markets from orthodox econom- ics are criticized for their Eurocentrism and their fantastic oversimpli- fication of actually existing markets. But we started with an example from private health showing how even actually existing European markets deviate from neoclassical models. And scenarios generated by Western dissent and critique such as the Comaroffs' are found here to be as useful as is the Indian account of PS Jha in providing the yardsticks for what Fernand Braudel called good or bad models "against which events can be interpreted" (1974: xi). Indeed, when we set aside the tyrannical purity of neoclassical economic modeling of markets, we cannot avoid the explosion of heterodox paradigms, sub- fields, and discourses, sometimes individualized in the search for ori- ginality. Our field moves analogically from Mondrian's stylized polders to the buffeted corn evoked by late van Gogh just as it might to Krishen Khanna's Tara Devi fields or the sprinkled poppies of impressionists such as Monet. Even the act of simplifying terms of art, as we have tried to do here, does little to alleviate the problems of translation into the reader's more familiar scholarly languages and comfort zones.

Our chapter has provided support for the concept of "contested jurisdictions," even if, in the case of sand, the contest resulted in a private monopoly of regulative force. As for the Comaroffs' "lateralized sovereignty," the politically corrupt, mafianized sand market (and remember that in Tamil Nadu alone similar arrangements are widely alleged for beach sand, granite, liquor, and construction (Jeyaranjan 2019)) coexists with fiscally distributive arrangements reputed to be so relatively well-run that the state remains widely characterized as developed. While India's vast informal economy is regulated through forms of social authority outside the state's, it would not be entirely correct to cast the criminal economy of sand as "socially embedded," as if social institutions form a bed. The case of sand markets exemplifies the Italian concept of *intreccio* (Michelutti 2019): an entanglement of entities conventionally regarded as separate – legislature, executive, judiciary, capital, labor, and civil society. And while the fusion In Tamil Nadu of populist politics with that of the predatory pork barrel fully supports Jha's argument about the politicization of crime and the criminalization of politics, its economic outcomes are not inevitably inefficient in the way Jha predicts. Rapid technological change, increases in scale and in size, a transformation in structure from petty production and trade to spatially defined monopolies and vast accumulative power have not been hindered by the feedback relation between crime and politics.

The case of sand has further ideas to contribute to the understanding of actually existing markets. We see not only that a common property resource, poorly regulated as common property, is remarkably easy to commodify, but also that a regime of regulation has developed to control commodified sand while a vast number of markets have to proliferate to form the preconditions for sand to be commodified in defiance of this regulatory regime. While the book's introduction invokes the concept of "elasticity," it is important to theories of commodification to recognize the "derived" nature of these markets. For sand creates livelihoods, even as capital-biased technological change in sand extraction will destroy them. After sand is mined, even after sand is retailed, productive activity such as the provision of fuel/energy, transport, bulking, and breaking of bulk creates labor market segments – as do services including repair, maintenance, and the organization of cash. In sand, a further range of markets, structured through political parties, bring criminal order to the encounter with the state; for instance, through fixing contracts and bribes, the provision of cash flows, the maintenance of public silence and the organization of private protection and regulative force.

The case of sand contributes to understanding institutional change, in particular how a given institution that persists – the cash transaction is an example – may contain contradictory social forces working for and against its change. Through the decades, the need for untraceability persists in balancing the costly bulkiness of cash as a mode of exchange. Sand has also revealed the rapidity of institutional change – from local to regional and national market scope, from petty production and trade to spatial monopoly and collusive oligopoly structures, from unregulated to criminally regulated markets. It has revealed many nonprice causes of institutional change. It has also revealed new processes at work in established institutions. From the outset, the sand market was captured by the state through party political control rather than the classical process in which independent regulators are captured by the state and then the state is captured by politicians. Last but not least, the case of sand shows how complex processes of institutional change coexist in which new institutions are created (the assemblage of sand; private police forces) while other institutions die (petty trade); but at the same time some institutions persist in form and function (the use of violence) while others persist in form but are reworked to serve the interests of accumulation (the political party and the assemblage).

One further reflection concerns the Indianness of criminal markets as revealed through sand. For the Comaroffs, the phenomenon of criminality is global, while for Jha, it is rooted in the particularities of Indian democratic election finance. While Jha's argument is undeniable, what else is Indian about the Indian case in general and the case of sand in particular? Some of the distinctive features of India's non-state regulated economy are missing from this account – the roles of authority grounded in caste, ethnicity religion, locality, and gender are major omissions here in spite of their likely shaping of local sand-market histories. But crime needs law to break and we have seen here how

Indian law is, by accident or design, permeated with crime-friendliness. It is also so deeply complex that in local society procedural literacy (how to work the police and justice system) exceeds legal literacy. The case of sand reveals an electoral democracy in which future returns from the politicized control of markets are such as to transcend party competition and to incentivize party collusion. It is only through party collusion that the criminal market structure can change political hands in periods when election outcomes, energized by pork barrel fraud, shift the ruling party. Sand also reveals a market structure of systemically interlocked political and economic contracts in which sales returns are dispersed in widely ramified ways: in the forms of retainers or rents, as profit to hierarchies of subcontractors in sand and its logistical and political derivatives, in wages to labor, in vast streams of political tribute in return for laissez-aller and in vast and concentrated profits to the lifting contractor(s).

In ceding permission to non-state power to prevail, the state's capacities morph as a result. The state loses definition as well as legitimacy. Given that such vast resources are appropriated by parties and individuals its capacity to regulate in any kind of public interest or to redistribute are compromised. Its capacity to resist the brake failure of criminal commodification is as compromised as is its capacity to act as an environmental steward. Nature is far from being an active Latourian agent; it is a vulnerable victim of rape with the state as prurient abettor.

Finally, the concept of the criminal market attracts the concept of primitive accumulation. In its classical formulation, the German concept can also be translated as primary and as original. The twenty-first century is far from the original cradle of capitalism so it is primary accumulation that may be of analytical relevance to India. Primary accumulation has two roles: the amassing of capital prior to its productive investment, while at the same time ensuring the material preconditions for labor to have nothing to sell but itself (Perelman 2001, after Marx). On this count, the labor force has already long been liberated for wage work, while the returns to sand are both productively invested in expanding sand mining and in supplying political conditions for social reproduction. Rather than exemplifying primitive accumulation, criminal sand markets represent capitalist accumulation with Indian characteristics.

Slippery grains of sand are used in the making of rock-hard cement. As a metaphor, sand has potential. Unless and until the institutions of capital require viable state apparatuses and publicly funded political parties to control accumulation through criminal rents and to regulate the economy, and unless and until laboring people organize countervailing power, criminal markets will prevail as does cement – rock hard. Meanwhile, it is for scholars to develop research into the roles of criminal markets and to mainstream their many and serious implications for the economy, politics and policy processes, in teaching and in public deliberation.

References

Bardhan, P & Mookherjee, D 2007, "Decentralisation, Corruption and Government Accountability," in S Rose-Ackerman (ed.) *International Handbook on the Economics of Corruption*, Edward Elgar, Cheltenham, pp. 161–88.

Basile, E & Harriss-White B 2010, "India's Informal Capitalism and Its Regulation," *International Review of Sociology* (Special Issue), 20, 3: 457–71.

Bhatia, J 2019, "Crime in the Air: Spectrum Markets and the Telecommunications Sector in India," in B Harriss-White & L Michelutti (eds.) *The Wild East? Criminal Political Economies across South Asia*, UCL Press, London, pp. 140–67.

Braudel, F 1974, *Capitalism and Material Life, 1400–1800*, Harper & Row, London.

CHPI 2017, No Safety Without Liability: Reforming Private Hospitals in England after the Ian Paterson Scandal (https://chpi.org.uk/papers/rep orts/no-safety-without-liability-reforming-private-hospitals-england-ia n-paterson-scandal/. Accessed September 22, 2019).

Comaroff, J & Comaroff, JL 2016, *The Truth about Crime: Sovereignty, Knowledge, Social Order*, University of Chicago Press, Chicago.

Comaroff, J & Comaroff, JL 2018, "Crime, Sovereignty and the State, Lecture," May 31, 2018, St. Antony's College, Oxford.

Flyvbjerg, B 2006, "Five Misunderstandings about Case-Study Research," *Qualitative Inquiry*, 12, 2: 219 45.

Gadgil, M (Chair) 2011, "Report of the Western Ghats Ecology Expert Panel," Ministry of Environment and Forests, New Delhi, GoI (www .moef.nic.in/downloads/public-information/wg-23052012.pdf).

Gupta, S 2019, "Jharia's Century-Old Fire Kept Ablaze by Crime and Politics," in B Harriss-White & L Michelutti (eds.) *The Wild East?*

Criminal Political Economies across South Asia, UCL Press, London, pp. 8–91.

Harriss-White, B 2003, *India Working: Essays in Economy and Society*, Cambridge University Press, Cambridge.

Harriss-White, B 2019, "Epilogue," in B Harriss-White & L Michelutti (eds.) *The Wild East? Criminal Political Economies across South Asia*, UCL Press, London, pp. 322–51.

Harriss-White, B & Michelutti, L (eds.) 2019a, *The Wild East? Criminal Political Economies across South Asia*, UCL Press, London.

Harriss-White, B & Michelutti, L 2019b, "Introduction," in B Harriss-White & L Michelutti (eds.) *The Wild East? Criminal Political Economies across South Asia*, UCL Press, London, pp. 1–34.

Ilangovan, R 2015, "The Mother of all Loot," *Frontline*, 32, 14.

Jeyaranjan, J 2019, "Sand and the Politics of Plunder in Tamil Nadu, India," in B Harriss-White & L Michelutti (eds.) *The Wild East? Criminal Political Economies across South Asia*, UCL Press, London, pp. 92–114.

Jha, PS 2013, How Did India Become a Predatory State? Unpublished.

Jodha, NS 1990, "Rural Common Property Resources, Contributions and Crisis," *Economic and Political Weekly, Review of Agriculture*, June: A65–A78.

Kar, D 2010, *The Drivers and Dynamics of Illicit Financial Flows from India 1948–2008*, Global Financial Integrity, Washington.

Leys, C 2001, *Market-Driven Politics: Neoliberal Democracy and the Public Interest*, Verso, London.

Marx, K 1887, "Capital, a Critique of Political Economy," *The Process of Production of Capital*, 1, chapter 31 (www.marxists.org/archive/marx/works/download/pdf/Capital-Volume-I.pdf. Accessed May 28, 2012).

Michelutti, L 2019, "The Inter-State Criminal Life of Sand and Oil in North India, Western Uttar Pradesh," in B Harriss-White & L Michelutti (eds.) *The Wild East? Criminal Political Economies across South Asia*, UCL Press, London, chapter 6.

Mishra, D 2019, "Himalayan 'Hydro-criminality': Dams, Development and Politics in Arunachal Pradesh, India," in B Harriss-White & L Michelutti (eds.) *The Wild East? Criminal Political Economies across South Asia*, UCL Press, London, pp. 115–39.

Perelman, M 2001, *The Invention of Capitalism: Classical Political Economy and the Secret History of Primitive Accumulation*, Duke University Press, Durham.

Picherit, D 2019, "Red Sanders Mafia in South India: Violence, Electoral Democracy and Labour," in B Harriss-White & L Michelutti (eds.) *The*

Wild East? Criminal Political Economies across South Asia, UCL Press, London, pp. 194–214.

Rege, A 2016, "Not Biting the Dust: Using a Tripartite Model of Organized Crime to Examine India's Sand Mafia," *International Journal of Comparative and Applied Criminal Justice*, 40, 2: 101–21.

Ruud, A 2019, "The Politics of Contracting in Provincial Bangladesh," in B Harriss-White & L Michelutti (eds.) *The Wild East? Criminal Political Economies across South Asia*, UCL Press, London, pp. 262–87.

Singh, N & Harriss-White, B 2019, "The Criminal Economics and Politics of Black Coal in Jharkhand, 2014," in B Harriss-White & L Michelutti (eds.) *The Wild East? Criminal Political Economies across South Asia*, UCL Press, London, pp. 35–67.

Subbramanian, L 2017, "The Hunt for Amma's Assets," *The Week*, June 4.

Vaishnav, M 2017, *When Crime Pays: Money and Muscle in Indian Politics*, HarperCollins, New Delhi.

Wielenga, Dietrich K 2019, "The Emergence of the Informal Sector: Labour, Legislation and Politics in South India, 1940–1960," *Modern Asian Studies*, published online by Cambridge University Press September 11, 2019, pp. 1–36.

Index